Lecture Notes in Artificial Intelligence 3187

Edited by J. G. Carbonell and J. Siekmann

Subseries of Lecture Notes in Computer Science

Gabriela Lindemann   Jörg Denzinger
Ingo J. Timm   Rainer Unland (Eds.)

Multiagent
System Technologies

Second German Conference, MATES 2004
Erfurt, Germany, September 29-30, 2004
Proceedings

 Springer

Series Editors

Jaime G. Carbonell, Carnegie Mellon University, Pittsburgh, PA, USA
Jörg Siekmann, University of Saarland, Saarbrücken, Germany

Volume Editors

Gabriela Lindemann
Humboldt-University Berlin
Institute for Computer Science, Division Artificial Intelligence
Rudower Chaussee 25, 10099 Berlin, Germany
E-mail: lindeman@informatik.hu-berlin.de

Jörg Denzinger
University of Calgary
Department of Computer Science
2500 University Drive NW, Calgary, Alberta T2N 1N4, Canada
E-mail: denzinge@cpsc.ucalgary.ca

Ingo J. Timm
University of Bremen
Center for Computing Technologies (TZI), Intelligent Systems
Postfach 33 04 40, 28334 Bremen, Germany
E-mail: itimm@acm.org

Rainer Unland
University of Duisburg-Essen
Institute for Computer Science and Business Information Systems
Schützenbahn 70, 45117 Essen, Germany
E-mail: UnlandR@informatik.uni-essen.de

Library of Congress Control Number: 1004112164

CR Subject Classification (1998): I.2.11, I.2, C.2.4, D.2.12, D.1.3, J.1

ISSN 0302-9743
ISBN 3-540-23222-2 Springer Berlin Heidelberg New York

Springer is a part of Springer Science+Business Media

springeronline.com

© Springer-Verlag Berlin Heidelberg 2004
Printed in Germany

Typesetting: Camera-ready by author, data conversion by Olgun Computergrafik
Printed on acid-free paper   SPIN: 11326557   06/3142   5 4 3 2 1 0

Preface

After the huge success of the first German Conference on Multiagent System Technologies (MATES) last year in Erfurt the German Special Interest Group on Distributed Artificial Intelligence together with the steering committee of MATES proudly organized and conducted this international conference for the second time.

The goal of the MATES conference is to constitute a high-quality platform for the presentation and discussion of new research results and system developments. It provides an interdisciplinary forum for researchers, users, and developers, to present and discuss the latest advances in research work, as well as prototyped or fielded systems of intelligent agents. The conference covers the complete range from theory to application of agent and multiagent technologies.

MATES 2004 was conducted

- as an integral part of the 5th International Conference Net.Object Days 2004 along with the
- 8th International Workshop on Cooperative Information Agents (CIA) 2004
- Autumn meeting of FIPA (Foundation for Intelligent Physical Agents)
- Prototype and Product Exhibition of Agent Related Platforms, Frameworks, Systems, Applications, and Tools

As such all these events together may have formed the biggest agent-related event of this year in Europe and one of the biggest worldwide.

The call-for-papers attracted about 60 submissions from all over the world. After a careful reviewing process, the international program committee accepted 22 high-quality papers of particular relevance and quality. The selected contributions cover a wide range of exciting topics, in particular agent analysis and security, agent negotiation and control, agents and software engineering, simulation and agents, and agent policies and testing. Exciting highlights of the conference were the invited talks, by Jim Odell on *Agent UML 2.0: Too Radical or Not Radical Enough?*, and Cristiano Castelfranchi on *Emergence and Cognition: Towards a Synthetic Paradigm in AI and Cognitive Science*. Moreover, several agent-related tutorials were conducted.

As editors of this volume, we would like to thank all the authors for their contributions and, especially, the program committee members and the external reviewers who sacrificed their valuable time to review the papers. Their careful, critical, and thoughtful reviews helped not only the authors but also us in putting together a truly convincing program.

There were also some sponsors that helped to conduct this conference in these difficult times. Our highest gratitude goes to the Ministry for Business, Work, and Infrastructure of the state Thuringia (Thüringer Ministerium für Wirtschaft, Arbeit und Infrastruktur), which provided all the support needed to conduct such a big and successful event. A big supporter of MATES was also the Foundation for Intelligent Physical Agents (FIPA), which not only sponsored this event but also conducted its 2004 autumn meeting in Erfurt at the same time as MATES and Net.ObjectDays.

We would also like to thank Alfred Hofmann from Springer for his support and cooperation in putting this volume together.

Calgary, Berlin, Bremen, Essen   Jörg Denzinger
July 2004   (Program Committee Co-chair)
                                                          Gabriela Lindemann
                                                    (Program Committee Co-chair)
                                                                  Ingo J. Timm
                                                    (Program Committee Co-chair)
                                                                Rainer Unland
                                                    (Program Committee Co-chair)

Members of the International Program Committee

Marian Nodine (Telcordia, USA)
James J. Odell (Agentis Software, USA)
Gregory O'Hare (University College Dublin, Ireland)
Lin Padgham (RMIT, Australia)
Michal Pechoucek (Czech Technical University, Prague, Czech Republic)
Anna Perini (Istituto Trentino di Cultura, Italy)
Paolo Petta (Vienna University of Technology, Austria)
Stefan Poslad (Queen Mary University, UK)
Frank Puppe (University of Würzburg, Germany)
Alois Reitbauer (PROFACTOR, Austria)
Michael M. Richter (University of Kaiserslautern, Germany)
Giovanni Rimassa (FRAMeTech s.r.l., Italy)
Michael Schillo (DFKI, Germany)
Christoph Schlieder (Bamberg University, Germany)
John Shepherdson (British Telecom, UK)
Christina Stoica (University of Duisburg-Essen, Germany)
Frieder Stolzenburg (Hochschule Harz, Germany)
Huaglory Tianfield (Glasgow Caledonian University, UK)
Robert Tolksdorf (Technische Universität Berlin, Germany)
Thomas Uthmann (University of Mainz, Germany)
Georg Weichhart (PROFACTOR, Austria)
Gerhard Weiss (Technische Universität München, Germany)
Danny Weyns (Katholieke Universiteit Leuven, Belgium)
Mike Wooldridge (University of Liverpool, UK)
Lotfi A. Zadeh (University of Berkeley, USA)

External Reviewers

Ralf Berger
Tibor Bosse
Lars Brauchbach
William Gardner
Andreas Gerber
Jan Hoffmann
Sven Jakobi
Matthias Jüngel
Helmut Myritz
Nicoleta Neagu

Ralf Neubert
Alexander Pokahr
Viara Popova
Thorsten Scholz
Amandeep S. Sidhu
Angelo Susi
Jim Juan Tan
Ingo Zinnikus
Ahmed K. Zohdy

MATES Steering Committee

Hans-Dieter Burkhard (HU Berlin, Germany)
Stefan Kirn (TU Ilmenau, Germany)
Matthias Klusch (DFKI, Germany)
Jörg Müller (Siemens AG, Germany)
Rainer Unland (Universität Duisburg-Essen, Germany)
Gerhard Weiss (TU München, Germany)

Table of Contents

Agents and Software Engineering

Simulation and Agents I

Simulation and Agents II

Policies and Testing

Agent UML 2.0: Too Radical or Not Radical Enough?

James Odell

Agentis Software

Abstract. The theory and application of agents and multi-agent systems is now experiencing a new surge in interest in the international commercial sector. As a result, a cacophony of modeling notations is beginning to emerge. This presentation discusses the issues involved in extending the OMG's UML 2.0 as a possible starting point. This approach is under debate from both the object and agent groups. Some believe that agents are just objects with a few more feature, and some believe that agents share absolutely nothing in common with objects. This talk presents examples from work already underway and discusses the work that still needs to be addressed.

G. Lindemann et al. (Eds.): MATES 2004, LNAI 3187, p. 1, 2004.
© Springer-Verlag Berlin Heidelberg 2004

Emergence and Cognition: Towards a Synthetic Paradigm in AI and Cognitive Science*

(Extended Abstract)

Cristiano Castelfranchi

National Research Council - Institute of Psychology
Division of "Artificial Intelligence, Cognitive and Interaction Modelling"
`cris@pscs2.irmkant.rm.cnr.it`

Abstract. In this (very) extended abstract I will make explicit the general ideological perspective and theoretical claims of the talk (like in a *manifesto*). As for the exemplification of these claims within the AI domain - in particular within the Agent and Multi-Agent Systems area - I will provide the overall blueprint but I will develop here only some part and give only some examples. I will illustrate how a synthetic paradigm can be built through the notion of different levels of reality description and of scientific theory, and through their interconnections thanks to *bridge-theories*, *cross-layered theories*, and *layered ontologies*. I will provide several examples of bridge-theories and layered ontologies with special attention to agents and multi-agent systems. In particular I will sketch the problem of emotions in agents with reference to agent/mind re-embodiment (the theory of needs and the relation between 'believing' and 'feeling'); I will examine the theory of the mental counterparts of social objects illustrating the mental facet of norms and of commitment; the grounding of social power in the personal power; the cognitive bases of organisations; the layered notions of conflict, cooperation, communication, goal, agent, delegation, as applied to different levels of agenthood.
I will examine the problem of emergence among intelligent agents by exploring the problem of unplanned cooperation and social functions. I will conclude with the importance of the new "social" computational paradigm in this perspective, and the emergent character of computation in Agent Based Computing.

1 Premise. At the Frontier of a Millennium: The Challenge

Will the "representational paradigm" - that characterised Artificial Intelligence (AI) and Cognitive Science (CS) from their very birth - be eliminated in the 21th century? Will this paradigm be replaced by the new one based on dynamic systems, connectionism, situatedness, embodiedness, etc.? Will this be the end of the AI ambitious project? I do not think so. Challenges and attacks to AI and CS have been hard and radical in the last 15 years, however I believe that the next century will start with a renewed rush of AI and we will not assist to a paradigmatic revolutio, with connectionism replacing cognitivism and symbolic models; emergentist, dynamic and evolutionary models eliminating reasoning on explicit representations and planning; neuro-

---

* Published in H. Coelho (Ed.) *Progress in AI - IBERAMIA '98* Springer, LNAI 1484. 13-26.

G. Lindemann et al. (Eds.): MATES 2004, LNAI 3187, pp. 2–28, 2004.
© Springer-Verlag Berlin Heidelberg 2004

science (plus phenomenology) eliminating cognitive processing; situatedness, reactivity, cultural constructivism eliminating general concepts, context independent abstractions, ideal-typical models.

I claim that the major scientific challenge of the first part of the century will precisely be the construction of a new "synthetic" paradigm: a paradigm that puts together, in a principled and non-eclectic way, cognition and emergence, information processing and self-organisation, reactivity and intentionality, situatedness and planning, etc. [Cas98a] [Tag96].

AI is going out of a crisis: crisis of grants, of prestige, and of identity. This crisis was not only due - on my view- to exaggerated expectations and overselling of specific technologies (like expert systems) tout court identified with AI. It was due to the restriction of cultural interests and influence of the discipline, and of its ambitions; to the dominance either of the logicist approach (identifying logics and theory, logics and foundations) or of a mere technological/applicative view of AI (see the debate about the 'pure reason' [McD87] and 'rigor mortis'). New domains were growing as external and antagonistic to AI: neural nets, reactive systems, evolutionary computing, CSCW, cognitive modelling, etc. Hard attacks were made to the "classical" AI approach: situatedness [Suc87], anti-symbolism, reactivity [Bro89] [Agr89], dynamic systems, bounded and limited resources, uncertainty, and so on (on the challenges to AI and CS see also [Tha96]).

However, by relaxing previous frameworks; by some contagion and hybridisation, by incorporating some of those criticisms; by re-absorbing as its own descendants neural nets, reactive systems, evolutionary computing, etc.; by developing important internal domains like machine learning and DAI-MAS; by important developments in logics and in languages; and finally with the new successful Agents framework, AI is now in a revival phase. It is trying to recover all the original challenges of the discipline, its strong scientific identity, its cultural role and influence.

We may in fact say that there is already a neo-cognitivism and a new AI.

In this new AI of the '90s systems and models are conceived for reasoning and acting in open unpredictable worlds, with limited and uncertain knowledge, in real time, with bounded (both cognitive and material) resources, interfering – either cooperatively or competitively – with other systems. The new password is *interaction* [Bob91]: interaction with an evolving environment; among several, distributed and heterogeneous artificial systems in a network; with human users; among humans through computers.

The new AI and CS are – to me – only the beginning of a highly transformative and adaptive reaction to all those radical and fruitful challenges. They are paving the way for the needed synthesis and are starting the job.

1.1 The Synthesis

Synthetic theories should explain the dynamic and emergent aspects of cognition and symbolic computation; how cognitive processing and individual intelligence emerge from sub-symbolic or sub-cognitive distributed computation, and causally feedbacks into it; how collective phenomena emerge from individual action and intelligence and causally shape back the individual mind. We need a principled theory which is able to reconcile cognition with emergence and with reactivity:

Reconciling "Reactivity" and "Cognition"

We shouldn't consider reactivity as alternative to reasoning or to mental states [Cas95] [Tag96]. A reactive agent is not necessarily an agent without mental states and reasoning. Reactivity is not equal to reflexes. Also cognitive and planning agents are and must be reactive (like in several BDI models). They are reactive not only in the sense that they can have some hybrid and compound architecture that includes both deliberated actions and reflexes or other forms of low level reactions (for example, [Kur97]), but because there is some form of high level *cognitive reactivity*: the agent reacts by changing its mind: plans, goals, intentions.

Also Suchman's provocative claims against planning are clearly too extreme and false.

In general we have to bring all the anti-cognitivist claims, applied to sub-symbolic or insect-like systems, at the level of cognitive system[1].

Reconciling "Emergence" and "Cognition"

Emergence and cognition are not incompatible: they are not two alternative approaches to intelligence and cooperation, two competing paradigms. They must be reconciled:

− first, considering **cognition itself as a level of emergence**: both as an emergence *from sub-symbolic to symbolic* (symbol grounding, emergent symbolic computation), and as a transition *from objective to subjective* representation (awareness) (see later for example on dependence and on conflicts) and from *implicit to explicit knowledge*;

− second, recognising the necessity for going **beyond cognition**, modelling emergent unaware, functional social phenomena (ex. unaware cooperation, non-orchestrated problem solving, and swarm intelligence) also *among cognitive and planning agents*. In fact, for a theory of cooperation and society among intelligent agents *mind is not enough* [Con96]. We have to explain how collective phenomena emerge from individual action and intelligence, and how a collaborative plan can be only partially represented in the minds of the participants, and some part represented in no mind at all [Hay67].

Emergent intelligence and cooperation do not pertain only to reactive agents. Mind cannot understand, predict, and dominate all the global and compound effects of actions at the collective level. Some of these effects are self-reinforcing and self-organising. There are forms of cooperation which are not based on knowledge, mutual beliefs, reasoning and constructed social structure and agreements.

---

[1] Cognitive agents are agents whose actions are internally regulated by goals (goal-directed) and whose goals, decisions, and plans are based on beliefs. Both goals and beliefs are cognitive representations that can be internally generated, manipulated, and subject to inferences and reasoning. Since a cognitive agent may have more than one goal active in the same situation, it must have some form of choice/decision, based on some "reason" i.e. on some belief and evaluation.

Notice that I use "goal" as the general family term for all motivational representations: from desires to intentions, from objectives to motives, from needs to ambitions, etc. By "sub-cognitive" agents I mean agents whose behaviour is not regulated by an internal explicit representation of its purposes and by explicit beliefs. Sub-cognitive agents are for example simple neural-net agents, or mere reactive agents.

But what kind/notion of emergence do we need to model these forms of social behaviour? The notion of emergence simply relative to an observer (which sees something interesting or some beautiful effect looking at the screen of a computer running some simulation) or a merely *accidental* cooperation, are not enough for social theory and for artificial social systems. We need an emerging structure *playing some causal role in the system* evolution/dynamics; not merely an epiphenomenon. This is for example the case of the emergent dependence structure (see 3.1). Possibly we need even more than this: really *self-organizing emergent structures*. Emergent organisations and phenomena should reproduce, maintain, stabilize themselves through some feedback: either through evolutionary/selective mechanisms or through some form of learning. Otherwise we do not have a real emergence of some causal property (a new complexity level of organisation of the domain); but simply some subjective and unreliable global interpretation.

This is true also among cognitive/deliberative agents: the emergent phenomena should feedback on them and reproduce themselves without being understood and deliberated [Cas97b]. This is the most challenging problem of reconciliation between cognition and emergence: unaware *social functions* impinging on intentional actions. AI can significantly contribute to solve the main theoretical problem of all the social sciences [Hay67]: the problem of the micro-macro link, the problem of theoretically reconciling individual decisions and utility with the global, collective phenomena and interests. AI will contribute uniquely to solve this crucial problem, because it is able to formally model and to simulate at the same time the individual minds and behaviors, the emerging collective action, structure or effect, and their feedback to shape minds and reproduce themselves.

Thus in the (formal and experimental) elaboration of this *synthetic paradigm* a major role will be played by AI, in particular by its agent-based and socially oriented approach to intelligence.

2 Neo-reductionism and the Micro-macro Integration of Scientific Theories

The real problem is the "integration" between different levels of description and/or explanation of reality; between different levels of granularity and complexity of systems. I claim that simple "compatibility" (non obvious contradiction) between principles and laws of one level and principles and laws of another level is only a minimal requirement. Much more is needed. We should systematically orchestrate one scientific layer (macro) with the other scientific layer, and one kind/level of explanation with a deeper level of explanation.

I adopt a "neo-reductionist" perspective (as Miguel Virasoro defines it [Vir97]). *Neo-reductionism* postulates that from the number and the interactions of the elements of a complex system some behaviours will emerge whose laws *can and must* be described at such superior layer. *Old reductionist* position claims that the emerging level has no autonomy of description, that you cannot formulate specific concepts and laws; you have just to explain it in terms of the underlying level: the only valid scientific position is to study the micro-units.

By contrast, an *anti-reductionist* position will claim that the laws of the higher level of description (organisation) have nothing to do with the laws at the underlying level, and that there is no reason for searching a strong link between the two levels.

The neo-reductionist position considers both approaches as necessary, by describing the laws typical of each level and investigating how from the basic level a complex behaviour can emerge and organise at the macro-level, and how it can possibly feedback into the micro-level (Virasoro does not take into account the feedback from macro to micro: he only considers the process of emergence -as typical of physics- while ignoring the process of "immergence" so relevant at the psychological and sociological levels).

I claim that the integration between different description layers requires at least three devices.

A) **Cross-Layer Theories.** By 'Cross-layer Theories' I mean general models and laws valid at any or at least at several levels. The evolutionary framework for example can be successfully applied from molecules to species, cultures, organisations, ideas. Analogously, the system dynamics approach can be applied to weather, to atoms, to neurons, to animal populations, to market [Weis97].

B) **Bridge-Theories.** By 'Bridge-Theories' I mean theories that explicitly connect two levels of explanation, i.e. theories able to explain how a high level complex system works through (is implemented in) the micro-activities of its components; how complex phenomena emerge from simple behaviours; how the emerging global structure and behaviour feed-backs into and shapes the behaviours of its units.

C) **Layered Ontologies and Concepts.** General broad notions are needed -applicable at different levels - but also level-specific definitions of the same notion are needed. For example we cannot have two independent notions of action, or of communication, one for simple reactive agents (for ex. for insects), the other for intentional agents (for ex. for human kind). We have to characterise the general features of 'action' or of 'communication' and at the same time to have more specific notions for sub-cognitive and for cognitive agents.

I will give some examples of all these different integrating devices in modelling agents and MAS .

3   Cross-Layer Theories

Also in AI some principles are valid at different levels of granularity and complexity, both at the micro and at the to macro level. For example general principles of coordination, or general principles of search, and so on. I will shortly illustrate only one very important structure emerging at any Multi-Agent level independently of the granularity and cognitive complexity of the agents: the interdependence objective structure.

3.1   An Emergent Social Structure: The Dependence Network

There is "interference" (either positive or negative) between two agents if the actions of the former can affect through their effects the goals/outcomes of the other. A strong case of interference is "dependence" when an agent needs an action or a resource of the other agent to fulfil one of its goals. The structure of interference and interdependence within a population of agents is an *emergent* and *objective* one, *independent of the agents' awareness and decisions*, but it constrains the agents' actions by determining their success and efficacy.

Given a bunch of agents in a common world, and given their goals and their *different* and *limited* abilities and resources, they *are* in fact dependent on each other: a dependence structure emerges. In fact, given the agent A with its goal Ga, and its plan Pa for Ga, and given the fact that this plan requires actions a1 and a2 and resource r1, if the agent A is able to do a1 and a2 and possesses resource r1, we can say that it is self-sufficient relative to Ga and Pa; when on the contrary A is either unable to perform for ex. a1, or cannot access r1 (so does not have the *power of* achieving Ga by itself) while there is another agent B which is able to do a1 or disposes of r1, A *depends on* B as for a1 or r1 for the goal Ga and the plan Pa. A is *objectively* depending on B (even if it ignores or does not want this): actually it cannot achieve Ga if B does not perform a1 or does not make r1 accessible [Cas92] [Con95] [Sic97].

There are several typical dependence patterns. In [Con95] the *OR-Dependence*, a disjunctive composition of dependence relations, and the *AND-dependence*, a conjunction of dependence relations, were distinguished. To give a flavour of those distinctions let me just detail the case of a two-way dependence between agents (*bilateral dependence*). There are two possible kinds of bilateral dependence:

Mutual dependence, which occurs when A and B depend on each other for realising a common goal p, which can be achieved by means of a plan including at least two different acts such that A depends on B's doing a1 and B depends on A's doing a2. Cooperation, in the strict sense, is a function of mutual dependence: in cooperation agents depend on one another to achieve one and the same goal; they are co-interested in the convergent result of the common activity.

Reciprocal dependence, which occurs when A and B depend on each other for realising different goals, that is, when A depends on B for realising A's goal that p, while B depends on A for realising B's goal that q, with p - q. Reciprocal dependence is to *social exchange* what mutual dependence is to cooperation.

The Dependence network *determines* and *predicts* partnerships and coalitions formation, competition, cooperation, exchange, functional structure in organisations, rational and effective communication, and negotiation power. Notice that this emerging structure is very dynamic: simply introducing a new agent or eliminating some agent, or simply changing some goal or some plan or ability of one agent, the entire network could change.

Clearly this is a quite abstract structure: it simply presupposes agents endowed with their goals/tasks, their abilities and resources, their autonomy (non pre-established cooperation), and interfering with each other, i.e. the usual notion of "agent". This notion applies to sub-cognitive agents (since beliefs, awareness, reasoning, intentions, are not necessary), to cognitive agents, and to complex agents like groups, organizations, states. Also organizations compete or cooperate in a common world on the basis of their interference and dependence relationships.

As I said by 'Cross-layer Theories' I mean general models and laws valid at any or at least at several levels. The dependence theory (and the related power theory - see 4.2) is a Cross-layer theory: it usefully applies to different level of agenthood and contributes to theoretically unify these levels.

However, the "unification" wee look for is different from uniformity, from a unique law, or from a unique vocabulary. A unique vocabulary can be too poor and vague about specific domains or phenomena (take the example of the general system theory). Specific and different vocabularies and specific theories and laws are needed at different description levels. Thus, to unify them, cross-layer theories are not enough and also bridge-theories are needed.

4   Bridge-Theories: The *Micro-implementation* and *Counterparts* of Macro-behaviours and Entities

Macro-level social phenomena are implemented through the (social) actions of the individual agents. In the case of cognitive agents, without an explicit theory of the agents' minds that founds agents' actions we cannot understand and explain several macro-level social phenomena (like team work, organizations), and in particular how they work.

Let's consider the individual counterparts of social norms, social power, organisational commitment and team-work.

4.1   The Mental Counterpart and Cognitive Implementation of Social Norms

Social norms are a multi-agent and multi-facets social object: in fact in order to work they should be represented in the minds of the involved agents, but these representations are not always the same: the agents play different *normative roles* and have different mental representations of the norms. Consider the *addressee* of the norm: it has to understand (believe) that there is a given expectation and prescription regarding its behaviour, and that it has to adopt this goal; but it has also to understand that this is not a personal or arbitrary request, but a 'group will', issued by some authority and in principle not aimed at personal interests. The addressee has also to believe that it is concerned by the norm and that a given act is an instance of the class of prescribed behaviours. The attitude and the normative mind of a "policeman", i.e. of an agent entitled to control norm obedience, is different. And also different is the mind of a neutral observer or of the "legislator" issuing the norm [Con95].

In other words, a norm N emerges *as a norm* only when it emerges as a norm *into the mind* of the involved agents; not only *through* their minds (like in approaches based on imitation or behavioural conformity, ex. [Bic90]). In other words, it works as a N only when the agents *recognise* it as a N, use it as a N, "conceive" it as a N [Con95] [Cas98b]. Norm emergence and formation implies "cognitive emergence" (hence cognitive agents): *a social N is really a N after its Cognitive Emergence (CE)*[2]. As long as the agents interpret the normative behaviour of the group merely as a statistical "norm", and comply by imitation, the real normative character of N re-

---

[2]   When the micro-units of emerging dynamic processes are cognitive agents, a very important and unique phenomenon arises: the Cognitive Emergence (CE) [Con95] [Cas98b]. There is "cognitive emergence" *when agents become aware, through a given "conceptualisation", of a certain "objective" pre-cognitive (unknown and non deliberated) phenomenon* that is influencing their results and outcomes, and then, indirectly, their actions. CE is a feedback effect of the emergent phenomenon on its ground elements (the agents): the emergent phenomenon changes their representations in a special way: it is (partially) represented into their minds. The "cognitive emergence" (through experience and learning, or through communication) of such "objective" relations, strongly changes social situation: from known interference, relations of competition/aggression or exploitation can rise; from acknowledged dependence, relations of power, goals of influencing and asking, possible exchanges or cooperation, will rise.

mains unacknowledged, and the efficacy of such "misunderstood N" is quite limited. Only when the normative (which implies "prescriptive") character of N becomes acknowledged by the agent the N starts to operate efficaciously as a N through the true normative behaviour of that agent. Thus *the effective "cognitive emergence" of N in the agent's mind is a precondition for its social emergence in the group, for its efficacy and complete functioning as a N.*

Notice that this CE is partial: for their working it is not necessary that social Ns as a macro-phenomenon be completely understood and transparent to the agents. What is necessary (and sufficient) is that the agents recognise the prescriptive and anonymous character of the N; the entitled authority, and the implicit *pretence* of N to protect or enforce some group-interest (which may be against particular interests). It is not necessary for example that the involved agents (for ex. the addressee or the controller) understood or agree about the specific function or purpose of that N. They should respect it because it is a N (or, sub-ideally, because of surveillance and sanctions), but in any case because they understand that it is a N, and do not mix it up with a diffused habit or a personal order or expectation. Norms, to work as norms, cannot remain unconscious to the addressee, but, the agent can remain absolutely ignorant of the emerging effects and of the *functions* of the prescribed behaviour in many kinds of Norm-adoption [Con95] [Cas97b].

4.2 How to (Partially) Reduce Social Power to Individual Power

Social power has several facets: status comparison and value hierarchies; power of controlling the others' rewards; power of influencing the others (command power); institutional power due to an institutional position or delegation. I will not consider here the most complex facet (the institutional one, see [Jon96]), and I will focus on the most classical notion in the social sciences (very relevant also in artificial systems): *the ability of deliberately inducing other agents to do or not to do as you want.* This social power is mainly based on other forms of power at the interpersonal and then at the personal level.

Let's take the simplest case and say that A has the goal that p but it is not able to achieve it while B is able to bring about that p: she has the "power of" (ability and opportunity for) p [Cas92]. Given this power of B and A's dependence on B, B gets a "power over" A (as for p): she has an *incentive* or *reward power* over A, because she is able to prevent B from or to allow him to achieve p. So the social dependence relation produces a social interpersonal power from a personal one.

Moreover, B can use her *incentive power* or *"power over"* A to acquire a *command or influencing power* on A. In fact she can use her power over A relative to p in order to induce A to do or not do some action (a) she likes. For example, she can promise A to (let him to) realise p, or she can threaten A relative to p: "if you do a, you will have p", or "if you don't do a you cannot have p". If A can do a and the value of p is grater than the cost of doing a (and there are no better alternatives) A will adopt B's goal and will do as expected: B succeeds in influencing A. She exercises her "power of influencing" through her "power over" which in turn is based on her personal "power of" p.

Of course, the influencing power is not only based on the manipulation of incentives, but this is a major basement; and of course not all social power is based on personal powers, since on the contrary several personal powers are derived from the institutional ones.

4.3   Grounding Joint Action in Group-Commitment, Social Commitment, and Personal Commitment

Many of the theories about joint or group action try to build it up on the basis of individual action: by directly reducing, for example, joint intention to individual intentions, joint plan to individual plans, group commitment (to a given joint intention and plan) to individual commitments to individual tasks. In [Cas97a] I claim that in this attempt the intermediate level between individual and collective action is bypassed; the real basis of all sociality (cooperation, competition, groups, organization, etc.) is missed: i.e. *the individual social action and mind. One cannot reduce or connect action at the collective level to action at the individual level without passing through the social character of the individual action.*

It is right that we cannot understand and explain collaboration [Gro95], cooperation [Tuo93] [Tuo88] [Con95], teamwork [Lev90] without explicitly modelling - among cognitive agents - the beliefs, the intentions, plans, commitments of the involved agents. However the attempt to connect collective intentions and plans to individual intentions has been too direct and simplistic, in that some mediating level and object has been ignored: in particular social intentions and social commitments.

How to Reduce Collective Goals to Individual Goals
In my view the most important point is that in joint activity (be it cooperation or exchange):

- the agents do not have only *beliefs* about the intentions of the other agents, but they have *positive expectations* about the actions (and then the *goals*) of their partners. Expectations imply beliefs + goals about the actions (the goals) of the other: each agent *delegates* the partner to do part of the joint plan.

So the *social goal* that the other intends to do a given action and does it, is the first basic ingredient of collaboration.

On the other side:

- each partner or member has to *adopt* (agree about) this delegation (task assignment), then she has the goal of doing her share not only because she shares a common goal and/or a common plan, but also because she *adopts* the expectations of the other members and of the group (as a whole, as a collective-agent). She *adheres* to the explicit or implicit request of the group or of the partners.

There is also the reciprocal adoption of several other goals/expectations: that of not to be cheated, that of be informed about the course of the joint activity [Jen93], etc...

In several approaches basically derived from Tuomela and Miller's theory of we-intentions [Tuo88] the crucial conditions are the following ones: "A member A_i of a collective G we-intends to do X (the joint activity) if and only if:

(i) A_i intends to do his part of X (as his part of X);

(ii) A_i has a belief to the effect that the joint action opportunities for an intentional performance of X will obtain;

(iii) A_i believes that there is a mutual belief among the participating members of G to the effect that the joint action opportunities for an intentional performance of X will obtain." [Tuo93].

In this kind of definition both the delegation goals, the expectations (not just beliefs) about the others' intentions, and the G-adoption among the members are at least not very explicit. In Levesque and Cohen' formal analysis of team work [Lev90] they are clearly missed.

As claimed by [Con95], *if a collective goal is derived from an individual goal* (i.e., it is not a primitive goal, in Searle's sense), *it necessarily implies some goal- or interest-adoption*. Therefore, a collective goal can be reduced, and unless it is a primitive, *must* be reduced to individual goals by means of complementary *social goals* of delegation and of adoption. Collective goals cannot be *directly* and simply reduced to individual intentions plus mutual beliefs; they can be reduced to complementary individual social goals, that will imply also individual intentions to do the individual actions.

As social goals and actions can be formed out of the agent's self-interest, and M-A plans can be derived from individual plans by means of goal-delegation and goal-adoption, so collective goals are not needed to be built into the agents.

Social Commitment
Social Commitment is exactly such a relation of complementary individual social goals that results from the merging of a strong delegation and the corresponding strong adoption: *reciprocal Social Commitments constitute the real structure of group and organizations*.

Also here, we need a notion of Commitment as a mediation between the individual and the collective one.

There is a pre-social level of commitment: the **Internal Commitment** (I-Commitment) that corresponds to that defined by Cohen and Levesque (on the basis of Bratman's analysis) [Coh90]. It refers to *a relation between an agent and an action*. The agent has decided to do something, the agent is determined to execute a certain action (at the scheduled time), the goal (intention) is a persistent one. For example, the way to ctch such a persistence is to establish that the intention will be abandoned only if and when the agent believes that the goal has been reached, or that it is impossible to achieve, or that it is no longer motivated. The term "Internal" is to be preferred to "Individual" because one may attribute I-Commitments also to a group. Thus, an "individual Commitment" is just the I-Commitment of an individual agent.

A "social commitment" is not an individual Commitment shared by several agents. **Social Commitment** (S-Commitment) is a relational concept: *the Commitment of one agent to another* [Sin92] [Cas96]. It expresses a relation between at least two agents. More precisely, S-Commitment is a 4-argument relation: (S-COMM x y a z); where x is the committed agent; a is the action x is committed to do; y is the other agent whom x is committed to; z is a third agent before whom x is committed. Let us neglect the third agent (z), i. e. *the witness*. Here, I will focus on the relation between x and y.

We should also distinguish S-Commitment from **Collective Commitment** (C-Commitment) or Group Commitment. The latter is just *an Internal Commitment of a Collective agent* or Group to a collective action. In other terms, a set of agents is Internally Committed to a certain intention and (usually) there is mutual knowledge about that. It remains to be clarified which are the relationships between S-Commitment and C-Commitment (later).

Let's now better analyse S-Commitment, in terms of our basic social ingredients (plus other special "normative" ingredients introduced elsewhere [Cas96].

a) *S-Commitment is a form of G-Adoption*. In other terms: x is committed to y to do a, if y is interested in a. The result of a is a goal of y. More than this: y has the goal that x does a.

b) *S-Commitment is a form of Goal Delegation*: y relies on x's promised action, decides of not doing it by herself; and x knows and agrees about this delegation.

c) Thus, combining acceptance-based Delegation and acceptance-based Adoption, *S-Commitment is G-Adhesion*: we should include in a formal definition of S-Commitment the fact that *(S-COMM x y a z)* requires the mutual belief that *(GOAL y (DOES x a))*.

d) Finally, *when x is S-Committed to y, then y can (is entitled to)*:
   - *control* if x does what he "promised";
   - *exact/require* that he does it;
   - *complain/protest* with x if he doesn't do a;
   - (in some cases) *make good his losses* (pledges, compensations, retaliations)

Thus in S-Commitment, x and y mutually know that x intends to do a and that this is y 's goal, and that as for a y has specific *rights on x (y* is entitled by x to a). One should introduce a relation of "entitlement" between x and y meaning that y *has the rights* of controlling a, of exacting a, of protesting (and punishing), in other words, x *is S-Committed to y to acknowledge these rights* of y.

These aspects deserve to be better examined and others deserve to be mentioned:

i) If x has just the I-Commitment to favour one of y 's goals, this is not sufficient for a S-Commitment (even if there is common awareness): y should "accept" this. In other words, y is I-Committed to achieve her goal by means of x's action. This acceptance is known by x, there is an agreement. Then, *the S-Commitment of x to y implies a S-Commitment of y to x to delegate and to accept x's action (y* can not refuse, or protest, can not say "who told you!", ...). Without such (often implicit) agreement (which is a reciprocal S-Commitment) no true S-Commitment of x to y has been established.

ii) As we saw, *the very act of committing oneself to someone else is a "rights-producing" act*: before the S-Commitment, before the "promise", y has no rights over x, y is not entitled (by x) to exact this action. After the S-Commitment it exists such a new and crucial social relation: y has some rights on x, he is entitled by the very act of Commitment on x's part. So, the notion of S-Commitment is well defined only if it implies these other relations:
   - y is entitled (to control, to exact/require, to complain/protest);
   - x is in debt to y ;
   - x acknowledges to be in debt to y and y 's rights.

In other terms, x cannot protest (or better *he is committed to not protesting*) if y protests (exacts, etc.).

iii) What I said just now implies also that *if x is S-Committed to y, he has a duty, an obligation*, he ought to do what he is Committed to.

So, when x is committed, a is more than an Intention of x, it is a special more cogent kind of goal. For a complete theory of S-Commitment, of its representation and of its social effects, we also need a theory of the mental representation of obligations, and of the different sources and kinds of goals that cannot be considered "desires" or "wishes" (like duties)!

iv) The more cogent and normative nature of S-Commitment explains why abandoning a Joint Intention or plan, a coalition or a team is not so simple as dropping a private Intention (I-Commitment). This is not because the dropping agent must inform her partners [Lev90] [Jen93] - behaviour that sometimes is even irrational, but precisely because Joint Intentions, team work, coalitions (and what I call C-Commitments) imply S-Commitments among the members and between the member and her group. In fact, one cannot drop a S-Commitment in the same way one can drop an I-Commitment. The consequences (and thus utilities taken into account in the decision) are quite different because in droping S-Commitments one violates obligations, frustrates expectations and rights she created. We could not trust others in teams and coalitions and cooperate with them if the stability of reciprocal and collective Commitments were just like the stability of I-Commitments.

v) If the agent x is "honest", x's S-Commitment to y to do a also implies an I-Commitment to do a. But, if x is "dishonest", if the act of socially-committing himself is "insincere", in this case he is not I-Committed to do a, while *he is still S-Committed to do so*, and he actually got an Obligation to do a. So:

x's I-Commitment on a is neither a necessary nor a sufficient condition for his S-Commitment on a. Just y's belief that x is I-Committed to a, is a necessary condition of x's S-Commitment.

Anyway, postulating that our agents are always "honest" like in other models of Commitment, we may remark that *the S-Commitment of x to y to a implies an I-Commitment of x to a.*

In our approach, it is possible to state such a precise relation between the two notions, because also the S-Commitment is analysed in terms of the mental states of the partners. It is not a primitive notion (like in [Sin92]).

Relationships Between Social and Collective Commitment

Is a true CollectiveCommitment of a group of agents just the sum of the I-Commitments of the members to their tasks, or does it require S-Commitments among those members?

In strictly "cooperative" groups (which in our sense are based on a Common Goal and Mutual Dependence), in team work, a S-Commitment of everybody to everybody arises: each one not only intends but *has to* do his own job. Given that the members form the group, we may say that *each member is S-Committed to the group* to do his share [Sin92].

So, the C-Commitment (defined as the I-Commitment of a collective agent) will imply (at least in the case of a fully cooperative group):

− the S-Commitment of each member to the group: x is S-Committed not simply to another member y, *but* to the all set/group X he belongs to;

− the S-Commitment of each member to each other; then also many Reciprocal Commitments;

− the I-Commitment of each member to do his action.

Joint Intentions, team work, coalitions (and what I call C-Commitments) imply S-Commitments among the members and between the member and her group, and S-Commitment (usually) implies I-Commitment. This is the bridge-theory connecting joint activity and individual mind. Although, the S-Commitment is not completely "reducible" to the I-Commitment, because it is an intrinsically relational /social notion (among agents), and contains much more than the I-Commitment of the involved agents, the social level construct is clearly linked to the individual level construct. Notice also that the I-Commitment is a cross-layer notion.

5 Layered Ontologies and Concepts

Clearly we need the notions of communication, coordination, cooperation, social action, of conflict, deception, agenthood, etc. both for cognitive, intentional agents and for sub-cognitive, merely reactive agents. Analogously, in natural sciences the same notions are needed for very simple animals and for human beings. These notions cannot be the same at the two levels but they can neither be unrelated one with the other. The ideal result would be to have a coherent ontological system where general notions that are valid at any level are specified in more specialised notions at different levels. This is what I call 'Layered Ontologies and Concepts' as a powerful tool for a neo-reductionist synthetic theory. Let us examine some of these notions from an AI and MAS perspective.

5.1 Agent

The proliferating notion of "agent" - so crucial that it is transforming the whole AI and the notion of computing itself - waits for some "systematisation". However, my claim is that what is needed is *not* a unique definition, which will be either to generic or too specific to computer science and technical. I think that what is needed is a system and, more precisely, a hierarchy of well-orchestrated definitions.

The notion of agent (both the one we need, and the natural concept) is a layered one: there are broader notions (ex. any causal factor) and narrow notions (ex. intentional actors), but these notions are in a definable conceptual relation that can/should be made explicit. The problem is that there is not just one simple conceptual hierarchy. This is a heterarchical notion: a hierarchy with several independent roots. For ex. the dimension "delegated"/"non delegated" is very important for the notion of "agent" in economics and in some AI domain. Another very important hierarchy to be clarified is that relative to "software" agents: a piece of software; an 'object'; an agent: what the relationships? Also other notions from system and control theory are important on my view.

I believe that we need a hierarchical definition conceptual structure of different levels and kinds of agenthood/agency. Unfortunately computer science and AI seem not so interested in their conceptual foundations (while they are more interested in their logical foundations, which is not the same thing). The growing domain of Ontology (although mainly focused on the conceptualisation of the application domains of knowledge based systems) gives now some more room to analytical conceptual work.

Here I will just give some necessary ingredients of one of these conceptual hierarchies in which the AI notion of agent should be situated.

What is an Agent? Elements for a Definition

In spite of Wittgenstein's view, I believe that the main readings of "agent" as defined -for example- in the dictionaries of modern languages are hierarchically organised and share some basic semantic nucleus.

The weakest and more basic notion of "agent" is that of a causal entity able to produce some change, some effect on a world, in an environment. This is the very poor meaning of physical forces as agents, or of "atmospheric agents" and so on. This *capability to cause effects* holds (as a component of the notion of "action") in each of the more specific notions of agent. An agent can cause, can do something. More than this, when we conceive some causal force as "agent" we do not focus on the previous possible causal chain; we focus on this cause as an initial *causa prima*, as independent if not autonomous. This notion of agent (relevant for example in semantics) is not sufficient either in AI or in Psychology. The notion starts to be interesting for Cognitive Science when the effects are no longer accidental or simply "efficient": when the causal behaviour is finalistic (teleonomic) and becomes a true "action". This is the case of Teleonomic or Goal-oriented agents

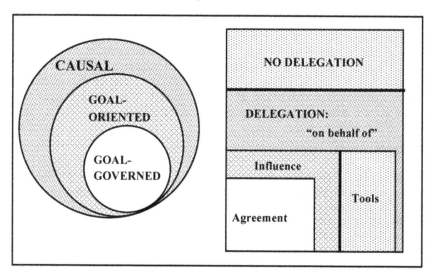

Mere Goal-Oriented vs Goal-Governed Systems

There are two basic types of system with finalistic (teleonomic) behaviour: intentional (more generally: goal-governed) and functional (mere goal-oriented).

Goal oriented systems [McF83] are systems whose behaviour is finalistic, aimed at realising a given result which is not necessarily understood or explicitly represented (as an anticipatory representation) within the system itself. A typical sub-type of these systems are in fact *Mere-Goal-oriented systems* which are rule-based (production rules or classifiers) or reflex-, or releaser-, or association-based: they react to a given circumstance with a given behaviour (and they can possibly learn and adapt).

Goal-governed systems are anticipatory systems. I call goal-governed a system or behaviour that is controlled and regulated purposively by an internally represented goal, a "set-point" or "goal-state" (cf. [Ros68]). The simplest example is a boiler-thermostat system. A "goal-governed" system responds to external functions through its internal goals.

This is the basic notion of Agent of interest to AI: exploitable *goal-oriented processes*. This substantially converges with Franklin & Graesser' definition [Fra95]. It is crucial to stress that mere goal-oriented systems and goal-governed systems are mutually exclusive classes, but that goal-governed systems can be also goal-oriented. Goal-government can be incomplete. It implements and improves goal-orientation, but it does not (completely) replace the latter: it does not make the latter redundant (contrary to Elster's claim [Els82] that intentional behaviour excludes functional behaviour - see later).

So we have causal entities, teleonomic causal entities, and, among the latter, mere goal-oriented and goal-governed agents including also intentional agents. However, this is only one hierarchy. Another very important one is that based on delegation: AI agents in fact frequently need to work autonomously but 'on behalf of' the user or of some other agent. So one should distinguish between non-delegated and delegated agents, and between different kind of delegation (see later) and different kinds of autonomy.

I propose to call *Agenthood* the capability to act; and to call *Agency* the capability to act under "delegation" of another agent. In this definition Agency presupposes Agenthood: only an agent in the full sense (goal-oriented) can be an agency, and necessarily it is delegated by (acts on behalf of) another agent.

As we will see "delegation" (in its weaker forms) does not require agents in the full sense: the weakest notion of causal entity is enough. However, a delegating and delegated agent is what is needed in agent-based computing.

5.2 Delegation

There are at least three necessary notions of Delegation: weak delegation, strong delegation, and institutional delegation (delegating organizational responsibilities or powers). Let us consider only the more basic ones.

In **Delegation** in general *x needs (or likes) an action of y and includes it in her own plan: she relies on y. If x is a cognitive agent, she plans to achieve p through the activity of y. So, she is constructing a MA plan and y has a share in this plan; y's delegated task is either a state-goal or an action-goal* [Cast97c].

Weak Delegation

In Weak Delegation there is neither bilateral awareness of the delegation, nor agreement: *y* is not aware of the fact that *x* is exploiting his action. One can even "delegate" some task to an object or tool, relying on it for some support and result [Luc95] [Con95, ch. 8]. In the weakest and passive form of delegation, *x* is just exploiting the autonomous behavior of *y*; she does not cause or elicit it. In a stronger form (delegation by induction) *x* is herself eliciting or inducing *y's* behavior in order to exploit it. Depending on the reactive or deliberative character of *y*, the induction is either based on some stimulus or on beliefs and complex types of influence.

Weak delegation applies to any level of agents and agency as for the delegated agent, but a broader notion of delegation would be needed for delegating sub-cognitive agents.

Strong Delegation (Delegation by Acceptance)
This Delegation is based on y's awareness of x's intention to exploit his action; normally it is based on y's adopting x's goal (Social Goal-Adoption), possibly after some negotiation (request, offer, etc.) concluded by some agreement and social commitment. Thus this important and more social form of Delegation holds among cognitive agents.

5.3 Social Action

A SA is *an action that deals with another entity __as an agent__, i.e. as an active, autonomous, goal-oriented entity*.

For *cognitive agents*, a SA is *an action that deals with another cognitive agent considered as a cognitive agent, whose behavior is regulated by beliefs and goals*. [Cas97a]. In SA the agent takes an Intentional Stance towards the other agents: i.e. a representation of the other agent's mind in intentional terms [Den81].

Consider a person (or a robot) running in a corridor and suddenly changing direction or stopping because of a moving obstacle which crosses its path. Such a moving obstacle might be either a door (opened by the wind) or another person (or robot). The agent's action doesn't change its nature depending on the objective nature of the obstacle. If x acts towards another agent as if it were just a physical object, her action *is not a SA*. Whether it is a social action or not depends -in cognitive agents- on how x *subjectively* considers the other entity in her plan. Consider the same situation but with some more pro-active than reactive attitude by x: x foresees that y will cross her way on the basis of her beliefs about y's goals, as it happens in traffic, when we slow down or change our way because we understand the intention of the other driver just on the basis of his behavior (without any special signal). This action of x starts to be "social", since it is based on x's belief about y's mind and action (not just behaviour).

So, *an action related to another agent is not necessarily social*. Also the opposite is true. A merely practical action, not directly involving other agents, may be or become social. The practical action of closing a door is social when we close the door to avoid that some agent enters or looks inside our room; the *same* action performed to block the wind (or rain or noise) is not social. *Not behavioral differences but goals distinguish social action from non social action*.

We may call "weak SA" the one based just on *social beliefs*: beliefs about other agents' minds or actions; and "strong SA" that which is also directed by *social goals*.

It is common agreement in AI that "social agents" are equivalent to "communicating agents". According to many students communication is a necessary feature of agenthood (in the AI sense) [Woo95] [Gen94] [Rus95]. Moreover, the advantages of communication are systematically mixed up with the advantages of coordination or of cooperation.

Communication is an instrument for SA (of any kind: either cooperative or aggressive). Communication is also a kind of SA aimed at giving beliefs to the addressee. This is a true and typical Social Goal, since the intended result concerns a mental state of another agent.

However, *communication is not a necessary component of social action and interaction*. To kill somebody is for sure a SA (although not very sociable!) but it neither is nor requires communication. Also pro-social actions do not necessarily require communication. In sum, neither agency nor sociality are grounded on communication, although, of course, communication is very important for social interaction.

Strong social action is characterised by social goals. A social goal is defined as a goal that is *directed toward* another agent, i.e. whose intended results include another agent as a cognitive agent: *a social goal is a goal about other agents' minds or actions* . Examples of typical social goals (strong SAs) are: changing the other's mind, communication, hostility (blocking the other's goal), strong delegation, adoption (favouring the other's goal). In this case, we not only have *Beliefs* about others' Beliefs or Goals (weak social action) but also *Goals* about the mind of the other: A wants that B believes something; A wants that B wants something. We cannot understand social interaction or collaboration or organisations without these *social goals*. Personal intentions of doing one's own tasks, plus beliefs (although mutual) about others' intentions (as used in the great majority of current AI models of collaboration) are not enough.

Action and social action are possible, of course, also at the reactive level, among sub-cognitive agents (like bees). A definition of SA, communication, adoption, aggression, etc. is possible also for non-cognitive agents. However, also at this level those notions must be goal-based. Thus, a theory of merely goal-oriented (not "goal-directed") systems and of *implicit goals* is needed[3]. However, there are levels of sociality that cannot be attained reactively.

Also at a sub-cognitive level, a SA is an action that deals with another entity *as an agent,* i.e. as an active, autonomous, goal-oriented entity. However the problem here is that there is not an agent's mind for considering the other agent 'as an agent'. Subjectively the first agent acts as towards a physical entity: it just reacts to stimuli or conditions. So, in which sense its action is social? in which sense it treats the other entity 'as an agent'? We cannot consider social any behaviour that simply *accidentally* affects another agent; teleonomy is needed: either the behaviour is intended (and this is not the case) or it is goal-oriented, functional to affecting another agent. This *function* is either due to evolution, selection and learning, or is due to design. Simple animals' (for ex. insects') behaviour is social because it has been selected by its effects on the behaviour and interests of the other agents. Analogously in very simple agents we can design social behaviours that are social because of their function not because of of their mind (beliefs or intentions).

5.4 Communication

The same reasoning applies to communication (which in fact is a social action). As I said a definition of communication is possible also for non-cognitive agents. However, also at this level, that notion must be goal-based: either intentional or functional. We cannot consider as communication any information/sign arriving from A to B, unless it is aimed at informing B. For example, B can observe A -A not being aware of this- and can understand a lot of things about A, but A is not communicating with B or informing B about all those things. I reject Watzlawich's thesis [Wat67] that any behaviour in a social context is communication ("It is impossible to not communicate"). This claim, which is now again very trendy – also in MAS – is too strong.

---

[3] For an attempt to theoretically unify mental and non-mental notions of goal, action, sociality, etc. see [Con95, Ch. 8; 5.3].

Here there is a very dangerous confusion between signs (signification) and communication: that something is a 'sign', has a meaning for the receiver, and gives it some information is a necessary but not a sufficient condition for communication [Eco75]. A source is necessary which sends 'on purpose' such a 'message' to the receiver. A teleological 'sending' action by the source is needed. In other terms, the source has to perform a given behaviour *in order* to make the other agent interpret it in a given way, receive the message and its meaning.

Analogously, I cannot accept the current attitude in ALife studies to consider communication any element produced by an agent and taken into account by the reaction of another agent: what they call indirect communication via changing the environment. Such a notion of communication, covering everything, would be useless.

Consider for example animal communication. One cannot consider as "communication" any meaningful signal arriving to an agent, for example the light of a fire-fly intercepted by a predator. For sure neither the prey is sending this message to the predator, nor the fire-fly's message has been selected by evolution for informing the predator about the position of the prey. The "function" of that signal -what it is for- is to inform the male fire-fly about the position of the female. So, first, there may be "meaning" and "sign" without communication; second, there is communication when the signal is purposively or at least finalistically sent to the addressee. In this case the "goal" is the biological "function" of the behavior.

This restriction of the notion of communication is also one of the reasons why *coordination is not necessarily based on communication* [Fran98] [Cas98]. It can be based on mere reactions or - among cognitive agents- on the "interpretation" of the other's behavior. Strictly speaking, the other's behavior becomes a "sign" of the other's mind. This *understanding*, is the true basis of reciprocal coordination and collaboration [Ric97]. Also behavioural *implicit communication* (when A knows and exploits the fact that B is observing it) is very important before explicit communication (special message sending). In contrast to current machines, human beings do not coordinate with each other by continuously sending special messages (like in the first CSCW systems): we monitor the other's behavior or its results, and let the other do the same.

5.5 Conflict

Agents in a "common world" – i.e. interfering with each other – may be *in conflict*: *their goals can be incompatible*. However, it is necessary to distinguish between the mere objective incompatibility between the goals of two agents, and a full social conflict between them. I call "competition" or "objective conflict" the situation of mere external conflict between their goals. The agents might also be unaware of this situation. A full "social conflict" should be seen as the subjective awareness of this competitive situation.

Thus, there is "competition" (or objective conflict) between two agents when their goals are in conflict (incompatible). There is a full *social conflict* when there is the subjective awareness of this competitive situation. By having the notion conflict both at the objective and at the subjective level we can characterise conflicts among sub-cognitive as well as among cognitive agents. However the introduction of subjectivity in terms of awareness has complex consequences on conflict taxonomy. Not only we can have objective conflicts and aware social conflicts - which imply the former - but merely subjective conflicts[4]: conflicts that are only in the agents' minds; they believe to be in conflict while they aren't (and this notion does not implies the other).

Awareness of course may be unilateral, bilateral, and mutual.

Bilateral, for example, is like:

$$(\text{Bel } x \text{ (Competition } x \text{ y p q))} \; 3 \; (\text{Bel } y \text{ (Competition } x \text{ y p q))}$$

where (Competition x y p q) is defined as: (Goal x p) 3 (Goal y q) 3 (p ∨ q).

Both aware conflicts and merely subjective ones leads to *Hostility* or *Aggression*, then to a higher level of conflict: fight. This is a typical case of *Cognitive Emergence* and of its feedback into the agents' minds.

Hostility is just a consequence of competition and conflict. It is the exact opposite of Adoption (help): in Adoption an agent adopts the goal of another agent, because she believes that it is his goal, and in order to make the other agent fulfil it [Con95]. In *Hostility* an agent has the goal that the other agent does not fulfil or achieve some of his goals. Generalised hostility is the opposite of "benevolence". Hostility is a quite unavoidable consequence of social conflict: if agent x believes that there is a conflict with the goal of agent y, she will have the goal that y does not fulfil his goal. In this case Hostility is not generalised to any goal of y, but just to y's goals in conflict with x's goals. Thus, each hostile agent has the goal that the other does not achieve his goal. When each of them actively pursues this goal, trying to prevent the other from achieving his goal, or to damage the other (*aggressive actions*, [Con95]), there is a new level of conflict: *fighting*: y has the goal to prevent or obstacle the aggressive action/goal of x: she has the goal that the aggressive goal of x fails <*defensive move*>; and so on.

6 Towards a Bridge Between Cognition and Emergence, Intention and Function, Autonomous Goal-Governed Agents and Goal-Oriented Social Systems

To claim that social action and functioning at the macro-level is implemented in and works through the individual minds of the agents (since it works through their individual actions which are controlled by their minds) *is not the same* as claiming that this macro-social functioning is reflected in the minds of the agents, is represented in it, known, and deliberately or contractually constructed. A large part of the macro-social phenomena works thanks to the agents' mental representations but without being mentally represented. How is this possible?

I call [Con95] *hyper-cognitive view* and subjectivism the reduction of social structures, of social roles and organisation, of social cooperation, to the beliefs, the intentions, the shared and mutual knowledge and the commitments of the agents. Agents are modelled as having in their minds the representations of their social links. These links seem to hold precisely in virtue of the fact that they are known or intended (subjectivism): *any social phenomenon* (be it global cooperation, the group, or an organization) is represented in the agents' minds and *consists in such representations* (ex. [Bon89]). This is an easy way-out from the micro-macro problem: global social phenomena are but *idols* produced by the individual minds to facilitate social interaction.

---

[4] And also objective unaware conflicts among cognitive agents.

6.1 Emergent Forms of Cooperation Among Cognitive Agents

Although the cognitive analysis of cooperation and teamwork (4.3) is very important (without representing agents' social intentions and beliefs we cannot explain this level of cooperation), it cannot be exclusive or generalised: social cooperation does not always need agents' understanding, agreement, rational and joint planning.

On the one hand, ignoring the material agents' interdependences and constraints we cannot evaluate the "adaptivity" of individual decisions and group behaviour.

On the other hand, contrary for ex. to what claimed by Bond [Bon89] social relations and organisations are not held or created by commitments (mutual or social) of the individuals. Most of the social relations and of the social structures pre-exist to the interactions and commitments of the individuals. Agents find themselves in a network of relations (dependence, competition, power, interests, etc.) that are independent of their awareness and choice.

Social cooperation does not necessarily need agents' understanding, agreement, contracts, rational planning, collective decisions [Mac98]. There are forms of cooperation that are deliberated and contractual (like a company, a team, an organised strike), and other forms of cooperation that are emergent: non contractual and even unaware. Modelling those forms is very important. Our claim [Cas97b] [Cas92] is that it is important to model them not just among sub-cognitive (using learning or selection of simple rules) [Ste80] [Mat92], but also among cognitive and planning agents whose behaviour is regulated by anticipatory representations. In fact, also *these agents cannot understand, predict, and dominate all the global and compound effects of their actions at the collective level.* Some of these effects are self-reinforcing and self-organising.

Thus, there are important forms of cooperation which do not require joint intention, shared plans, mutual awareness among the co-operating agents. The cooperative plan, where the sub-plans represented into the mind of each participants and their actions are "complementary", is not represented in their mind.

- For instance in the case of *hetero-directed or orchestrated cooperation*, only a boss' mind conceives and knows the plan, while the involved agents may even ignore the existence of a global plan and of the other participants.
- This is also the case of *functional self-organising forms of social cooperation* (like the technical division of labour) where no mind at all conceives or know the emerging plan and organisation. Each agent is simply interested in its own local goal, interest and plan; nobody directly takes care of the task distribution, of the global plan and equilibrium.

6.2 Social Functions and Cognition

As I said, the real challenge is how to reconcile cognition with emergence, intention and deliberation with unaware or unplanned social functions and "social order". Both objective structures and unplanned self-organising complex forms of social order and social functions emerge from the interactions of agents in a common world and from their individual mental states; both these structures and self-organising systems feedback into the agents behaviours through the agents' individual minds either by the agent's understanding the collective situation (cognitive emergence) or by constraining and conditioning agent goals and decisions. This feedback (from macro-emergent structures/systems) either reinforces or changes the individual social behaviour producing either the dynamics or the self-reproduction of the macro-system.

The aim of this section is to analyse the crucial relationship between social "functions" and cognition: cognitive agents' mental representations.

This relationship is so crucial for at least two reasons:

a) on the one side, *no theory of social functions is possible* and tenable without clearly solving this problem ;

b) on the other side, *without a theory of emerging functions among cognitive agents, social behavior cannot be fully explained* .

In my view, current approaches to cognitive agent architectures (in terms of Beliefs and Goals) allow for a solution of this problem; though perhaps we need some more treatment of emotions. One can explain quite precisely this relation between cognition and the emergence and reproduction of social functions. In particular, functions install and maintain themselves parasitarely to cognition:

- *functions install and maintain themselves thanks to and through the agents' mental representations but not as mental representations: i.e. without being known or at least intended.*

For a Social Norm to work as a social norm and be fully effective, agents should understand it as a social norm. However the effectiveness of a social function is independent of the agents' understanding of this function of their behavior. In fact:

a) the function can rise and maintain itself without the awareness of the agents;

b) if the agents intend the results of their behavior, these would no longer be "social functions" of their behavior but just "intentions" [Els82].

I accept Elster's crucial objection to classical functional notions, but I think that it is possible to reconcile intentional and functional behavior. With an evolutionary view of "functions" it is possible to argue that *intentional actions can acquire unintended functional effects*. Let us rephrase Elster's problem as follows.

- Since functions should not be *what the observer likes or notices*, but should be indeed observer-independent, and be based on self-organising and self-reproducing phenomena, "positivity" can just consists in this. Thus, we cannot exclude phenomena that could be bad, i.e. negative from the observer's point of view, from the involved agents' point of view, or for the OverSystem's point of view. We cannot exclude "negative functions" (Merton) (kakofunctions) from the theory: perhaps the same mechanisms are responsible for both positive and negative functions.

- How is it possible that a system which acts intentionally and on the basis of the evaluation of the effects relative to its internal goals reproduces bad habits *thanks to* their bad effects? And, more crucial, if a behavior is reproduced *thanks to* its good effects, that are good relatively to the goals of the agent (individual or collective) who reproduces them by acting intentionally, there is no room for "functions". If the agent appreciates the goodness of these effects and the action is replied in order to reproduce these effects, they are simply "intended". *The notion of intention is sufficient and invalids the notion of function.*

I argue that it is not sufficient to put deliberation and intentional action (with intended effects) together with some reactive or rule-based or associative layer/ behaviour and let emerge from this layer some social unintended function, and let operate on this layer the feedback of the unintended reinforcing effects [van82]. The real issue is precisely the fact that *the intentional actions of the agents* give rise to functional, unaware collective phenomena (ex. the division of labour), not (only) their unintentional behaviours. How to build unaware functions and cooperation on top of intentional actions and intended effects? How is it possible that positive results - thanks to their advantages- reinforce and reproduce the actions of intentional agents, and self-organise and reproduce themselves, without becoming simple intentions? [Els82]. This is the real theoretical challenge for reconciling emergence and cognition, intentional behavior and social functions, planning agents and unaware cooperation.

We need more complex forms of reinforcement learning, not just based on classifiers, rules, associations, etc. but *operating on the cognitive representations governing the action, i.e. on beliefs and goals.*

In this view "the consequences of the action, which may or may not have been consciously anticipated, then modify the probability that the action will be repeated next time the input conditions are met" [Mac98]. More precisely:

Functions are just effects of the behavior of the agents, that go beyond the intended effects and succeed in reproducing themselves because they reinforce the beliefs and the goals of the agents that caused that behavior. Then:

- First, behavior is goal-directed and reasons-based; i.e. is intentional action. The agent bases its goal-adoption, its preferences and decisions, and its actions on its Beliefs (this is the definition of "cognitive agents").
- Second, there is some effect of those actions that is unknown or at least unintended by the agent.
- Third, there is circular causality: a feedback loop from those unintended effects to increment, reinforce the Beliefs or the Goals that generated those actions.
- Fourth, this "reinforcement" increases the probability that in similar circumstances (activating the same Beliefs and Goals) the agent will produce the same behavior, then "reproducing" those effects.
- Fifth, at this point such effects are no longer "accidental" or unimportant: although remaining unintended they are teleonomically produced [Con95, ch.8]: *that behavior exists (also) thanks to its unintended effects; it was selected by these effects, and it is functional to them.* Even if these effects could be negative for the goals or the interest of (some of) the involved agents, their behavior is "goal-oriented" to these effects.

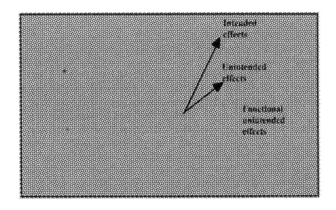

Notice that the agents do not necessarily intend or suspect to reinforce their Beliefs or their Goals, and then their own behaviour and the behaviour of the other[5].

7 Cognition and Body. To 'Believe' vs to 'Feel': The Case for 'Needs' and Emotions

In the perspective of a synthetic paradigm in AI and in the Cognitive Science (CS) a very crucial role is played by the problem of the "(re)embodiment" of mind. There are several important aspects of this problem. One is the relation between symbols and brain: for example how to let emerge or implement symbols, rules, etc. in a neural structure (ex. [Sun 97]). Another is the "symbol grounding problem" and how to go beyond the mere syntactic treatment of symbols to give them a full semantics which seems necessarily related to perception, action, sensory-motor intelligence (ex. [Cot90]).

One aspect of this relation between mind and body is particularly important to me, and I would like to shortly analyse it just because this is one pillar of a synthetic paradigm in CS while I mainly treated the individual-social relation. I do believe that cognitive models (in cognitive psychology, in AI, and in general in CS) put aside for too long time the problem of subjective experience, of "feeling something". My view on this issue is quite trivial: to "feel" something is necessarily "somatic": it presupposes to have a body, and to receive some perceptual signal from it. You cannot experience or feel anything without a body. Also in AI, if we have to take emotions seriously we have to re-embody our artificial minds and to model the difference between believing and 'feeling'. Can Agents have a 'subjective experience'?

As in the other cases, current approaches claiming the role of the body, and of feelings, emotions, drives, (and several biological mechanisms) tend to put this as a radical alternative to cognition, as incompatible with the traditional apparatus of CS (beliefs, intentions, plans, decision, and so on).

I believe that to characterise several important mental states (kinds of beliefs or kinds of goals, like *needs*) modelling the bodily information is necessary; but on the other side I argue that also traditional mental representations are necessary.

In the talk I will analyse objective and subjective needs [Cas98b]. I will argue for a very strong tenant and for a very restrictive and precise notion of "feeling a need"(more precisely "feeling the need for"), claiming that to feel needs not only a body is necessary but also a cognitive agent with its beliefs and goals.

---

[5] There is another plausible mechanism for accounting for this reinforcement of expectation-driven (intentional) behaviour: *the learned emotional reactions to anticipatory representations* (like possible goals). I believe that these mechanisms are both real and complementary. There is something in our body that unconsciously and automatically orients our decisions and actions, attracting or repulsing us; giving us an unreasoned **appraisal** of possible scenarios [Mic in press]. These unreasoned "preferences" and choices can be accounted for by Damasio's "somatic markers" [Dama94] that produce an immediate screening of the alternatives we - as proactive, anticipatory animals - are prospecting. They are generated by the experienced emotions in previous situations, and are *associated* (by learning) to the prospect of future possible scenarios (and notice, not simply to the behavioural response). So there is some sort of pre-decision, some *pre-selection* of possible goals, which is based on emotion and learning (positive and negative reinforcement).

Modelling subjective "experience", is obviously fundamental also for modelling emotions; and modelling emotions is crucial for several reasons:

- integrating high level reactivity also in cognitive agents;
- understanding the relationship between cognition and rationality (which are not the same) on one side and emotions on the other side, as part of the new integrated paradigm in CS (see note 5);
- understanding the whole range of motivations in an autonomous agent (and give it a 'character')
- accounting for fundamental aspects of social behaviour, group belonging, social influence and power, organisation, and learning (see note 5).

I believe that in the very important cognitive approach to emotions that has been developed in the last 20 years (see for example the *Cognition and Emotion* journal), the phenomenological components of the emotion, its "feeling" part has been ignored for too much time. **XXXexpand**

Analogously I claim that the weakest point in artificial models of emotion (which, of course are quite interesting, ex. [Bot97] [Bot98] [Can97] [Loy96]) is the following. Everybody stresses how emotion is important for reacting adaptively and just in time to the 'relevant' environment changes. The emotions give us an immediate appraisal of events that are relevant for our concerns/goals, or orient our attention towards the novelty, and provide us an unreasoned behavioural orientation: ether a high priority goal or a pre-assembled behavioural sequence. Now, precisely this characterisation of emotions and the existence of various types of reactive mechanisms in autonomous agents create the theoretical problem. If emotion is simply a mechanism for eliciting a reaction, why is not enough a reactive mechanism?! why do we have to feel something? what is the specificity of the emotional reaction? what is the function of feeling something, for ex. of a "fear state"?! And why should artificial creatures "feel pain" or fear or other emotional states if what really matters is the fact that they reactively withdraw? The claim that they have emotions seems quite an ad hoc and superfluous postulation.

In my view both the AI and ALife approaches to emotion till now miss the real argument for emotions functionality: *the function of feeling*.

8 Towards Social Computing

I will conclude with the importance in this perspective of the new "social" computational paradigm [Gas98], and the emergent character of computation in Agent Based Computing.

9 Conclusions

To arrive to a new synthetic paradigm does not mean simply to be tolerant or to let different candidate-paradigms compete. Nor it is sufficient to propose hybrid models and architectures in which reaction and deliberation, neural nets and symbolic manipulation, reasoning and selection, emotions and rationality, coexist as competing and cooperating layers. This is just one (a preliminary) solution. Synthetic theories should explain the dynamic and emergent aspects of cognition and symbolic computation; how cognitive processing and individual intelligence emerge from sub-symbolic or sub-cognitive distributed computation, and causally feedbacks into it; how collective phenomena emerge from individual action and intelligence and causally shape back the individual mind.

We need a principled theory which is able to reconcile cognition with emergence and with reactivity, and AI can play a major role in this challenge, in particular by its agent-based and socially oriented approach to intelligence.

References

[Agr89] Agre, P.E. 1989. *The dynamic structure of everyday life*. Phd Thesis, Depertment of Electrical Engineering and Computer Science, Boston: MIT.

[Bic90] Bicchieri, C. 1990. Norms of cooperation. *Ethics*, 100, 838-861.

[Bob91] D. Bobrow. "Dimensions of Interaction", *AI Magazine*, 12, 3,64-80,1991.

[Bon89] A. H. Bond, Commitments, Some DAI insigths from Symbolic Interactionist Sociology. *AAAI Workshop on DAI*. 239-261. Menlo Park, Calif.: AAAI, Inc. 1989.

[Bot98] Botelho, L.M. and Coelho H. Artificial Autonomous Agents with Artificial Emotions. Autonomous Agents'98, Mineapolis, ACM Press.

[Bro89] Brooks, R.A. 1989. *A robot that walks. Emergent behaviours from a carefully evolved network*. Tech. Rep. Artificial Intelligence Laboratory. Cambridge, Mass.: MIT.

[Can97] Canamero, D. Modeling Motivations and Emotions as a Basis for Intelligent Behavior. *Autonomous Agents'98*, ACM Press, 148-55, 1997.

[Cas91] C. Castelfranchi. Social Power: a missed point in DAI, MA and HCI. In Y. Demazeau & J.P.Mueller (eds), *Decentralized AI*. 49-62. Amsterdam: Elsevier, 1991.

[Cas92a] C. Castelfranchi and R. Conte. Emergent functionalitiy among intelligent systems: Cooperation within and without minds. *AI & Society, 6*, 78-93, 1992.

[Cas92b] C. Castelfranchi., M. Miceli, A. Cesta. Dependence Relations among Autonomous Agents, in Y.Demazeau, E.Werner (Eds), *Decentralized A.I. - 3*, Elsevier (North Holland), 1992.

[Cas95] C, Castelfranchi, Guaranties for Autonomy in Cognitive Agent Architecture. In [Woo95]

[Cas96] Castelfranchi, C., Commitment: from intentions to groups and organizations. In *Proceedings of ICMAS'96*, S.Francisco, June 1996, AAAI-MIT Press.

[Cas97a] C. Castelfranchi. Individual Social Action. In G. Holmstrom-Hintikka and R. Tuomela (eds.) *Contemporary Theory of action*. vol. II, 163-92. Dordrecht, Kluwer, 1997.

[Cas97b] Castelfranchi, C. Challenges for agent-based social simulation. The theory of social functions. IP-CNR, TR. Sett.97; invited talk at *SimSoc'97*, Cortona, Italy

[Cas97c] C Castelfranchi and R Falcone. Delegation Conflicts. In M. Boman and W. van De Welde (Eds.)*Proceedings of MAAMAW '97*, Springer-Verlag, 1997.

[Cas98a] Castelfranchi, C., Modelling Social Action for AI Agents. *Artificial Intelligence*, (forthcoming).

[Cas98b] Castelfranchi, C., To *believe* and to *feel*: To embody cognition and to cognitize body The case for "needs". In 1998 AAAI Fall Symposium "Emotional and Intelligent: The Tangled Knot of Cognition."

[Coh90] P. R. Cohen and H. J. Levesque. Rational interaction as the basis for communication. in P R Cohen, J Morgan and M E Pollack (Eds): *Intentions in Communication*. The MIT Press, 1990.

[Con95] Conte,R. and Castelfranchi, C. *Cognitive and Social Action*, UCL Press, London, 1995.

[Con96] R. Conte and C. Castelfranchi. Mind is not enough. Precognitive bases of social inter-action. In N. Gilbert (Ed.) *Proceedings of the 1992 Symposium on Simulating Societies*. London, University College of London Press, 1996.

[Cot90] Cottrell, G.W., Bartell, B., and Haupt, C.1990. Grounding meaning in perception. In H. Marburger (ed.) 14th German Workshop on AI. Berlin, Springer, 307-21.

[Dam94] Damasio, A.R. *Descartes' Error*. N.Y., Putnam's Sons, 1994

[Den81] Dennet, Daniel.C. *Brainstorms*. Harvest Press, N.Y 1981.

[Eco75] Eco, U. 1975. *Trattato di Semiotica generale*. Bompiani, Milano.

[Els82] J. Elster. Marxism, functionalism and game-theory: the case for methodological indi-vidualism. *Theory and Society* 11, 453-81.

[Gas91] L. Gasser. Social conceptions of knowledge and action: DAI foundations and open systems semantics. *Artificial Intelligence* 47: 107-138.

[Gas98] L. Gasser. Invited talk at *Autonomous Agents'98*, Minneapoli May 1998.

[Gen94] M.R. Genesereth and S.P. Ketchpel, S.P. 1994. *Software Agents*. TR, CSD, Stanford University.

[Gro95] B. Grosz, Collaborative Systems. AI Magazine, summer 1996, 67-85.

[Hay67] F.A. Hayek, The result of human action but not of human design. In *Studies in Phi-losophy, Politics and Economics*, Routledge & Kegan, London, 1967.

[Jen93] N. R. Jennings. Commitments and conventions: The foundation of coordination in multi-agent systems. *The Knowledge Engineering Review* 3, 1993: 223-50.

[Jon96] Jones, A.J.I. & Sergot, M. 1996. A Formal Characterisation of Institutionalised Power. Journal of the Interest Group in Pure and Applied Logics, 4(3): 427-45.

[Kur97] S. Kurihara, S. Aoyagi, R. Onai. Adaptive Selection or Reactive/Deliberate Planning for the Dynamic Environment. In M. Boman and W. Van de Welde (Eds.) *Multi-Agent Ra-tionality - Proceedings of MAAMAW'97* , Berlin, Springer, LNAI 1237,1997, p.112-27

[Lev90] Levesque H.J., P.R. Cohen, Nunes J.H.T. On acting together. In Proceedings of the 8th National Conference on Artificial Intelligence, 94-100. Kaufmann. 1990

[Loy97] Loyall, A.B. Believable Agents: Building Interactive Personalities. PhD Thesis. CMU, Pittsburg, May 1997

[Luc95] M. Luck and M. d'Inverno, "A formal freamwork for agency and autonomy". In pro-ceedings of the First International Conference on Multi-Agent Systems, 254-260. AAAI Press/MIT Press, 1995.

[Mac98] Macy, R. , In *JASSS*, I, 1, 1998.

[Mat92] M. Mataric. Designing Emergent Behaviors: From Local Interactions to Collective Intelligence. In *Simulation of Adaptive Behavior 2*. MIT Press. Cambridge, 1992.

[McD87] McDermott D. 1987. A critique of pure reason. In Computational Intelligence, 3, 151-60.

[McF83] McFarland, D. 1983. Intentions as goals, open commentary to Dennet, D.C. Inten-tional systems in cognitive ethology: the "Panglossian paradigm" defended. *The Behav-ioural and Brain Sciences*, 6, 343-90.

[Mic in press] Miceli, M. and Castelfranchi, C. The role of evaluation in cognition and social interaction. In K. Dautenhahn (Ed.), "Human Cognition and Social Agent Technology". John Benjamins, in press.

[Ric97] Ch. Rich and C L Sidner. COLLAGEN: When Agents Collaborate with People. In Proceedings of *Autonomous Agents 97*, Marina Del Rey, Cal., pp. 284-91

[Ros68] Rosenblueth, A. & N. Wiener 1968. Purposeful and Non-Purposeful Behavior. In *Modern systems research for the behavioral scientist,* Buckley, W. (ed.). Chicago: Aldine.

[Rus95] S.J. Russell and P. Norvig *Artificial Intelligence: A Modern Approach*. Prentice Hall, 1995.

[Sic95] J Sichman, Du Raisonnement Social Chez les Agents. PhD Thesis, Polytechnique - LAFORIA, Grenoble

[Sin91] M.P. Singh, Social and Psychological Commitments in Multiagent Systems. In Prepro-ceedings of "Knowledge and Action at Social & Organizational Levels", Fall Symposium Series, 1991. Menlo Park, Calif.: AAAI, Inc.

[Ste90] L. Steels. Cooperation between distributed agents through self-organization. In Y. Demazeau & J.P. Mueller (eds.) *Decentralized AI* North-Holland, Elsevier, 1990.

[Suc87] Suchman, L.A. 1987. Plans and situated actions: The problem of human-machine communication. Cambridge: Cambridge University Press.

[Sun97] Sun, R. and Alexandre F. (eds.) 1997 Connectionist Symbolic Integration, Lawrence Erlbaum, Hillsdale, NJ.

[Tha96] Thagard, P. 1996 *Mind. Introduction to Cognitive Science.* MIT Press.

[Tuo93] Tuomela, R. What is Cooperation. *Erkenntnis*, 38, 1993, 87-101

[Tuo88] R. Tuomela and K. Miller. "We-Intentions", *Philosophical Studies*, 53, 1988, 115-37.

[van82] van Parijs, P. 1982. Functionalist marxism rehabilited. A comment to Elster. *Theory and Society*, 11, 497-511.

[Vir96] Virasoro, M.A. *Intervista* a cura di Franco Foresta Martin, SISSA, Trieste, 1996

[Wat67] Watzlawick, P., Beavin, J.H. and Jeckson D.D. 1967. Pragmatics of Human Communication.. N.Y., Norton.

[Wei97] Weisbuch G. 1997 Societies, cultures and fisheries from a modeling perspective. *SimSoc'97*, Cortona, Italy

[Woo95a] M. Wooldridge and N. Jennings. Intelligent agents: Theory and practice. *The Knowledge Engineering Review*, 10(2): 115-52. 1995.

[Woo95b] Wooldridge M.J. and Jennings N.R. (Eds.) 1995 *Intelligent Agents: Theories, Architectures, and Languages.* LNAI 890, Springer-Verlag, Heidelberg, Germany.

The Emergence of Social Order in a Robotic Society

Jürgen Klüver[1], Maarten Sierhuis[2], and Christina Stoica[1]

[1] University of Duisburg-Essen, Information Technologies and Educational Processes
45117 Essen, Germany
{juergen.kluever,christina.stoica}@uni-essen.de
http://www.cobasc.de
[2] USRA/RIACS, NASA Ames Research Center, M/S B269-1
Moffett Field, CA 94035-1000
msierhuis@mail.arc.nasa.gov
http://home.comcast.net/~msierhuis

Abstract. The article presents a general model of the emergence of social order in multi-agent-systems (MAS). The agents consist of two types of neural networks that have the task to generate social actions as their output and to adjust these actions to the actions of other agents. The result is a form of social order, i.e., a set of rules of interaction. The agents can generalize these rules by applying them on new but similar agents. An example is given how this model could be applied to the interaction of humans and roboters for some tasks of NASA.

Keywords: emergence of order, neural nets, robotics, multi-agent-systems, emergent programming

1 Introduction

Multi agent systems (MAS) are a powerful technique for very different modeling purposes and have demonstrated their possibilities in many domains of application [14]. Yet despite the advantages MAS offer for modeling and simulation purposes most MAS have a characteristic shortcoming that restrict their applicability: It is practically always necessary to implement the rules that determine the interactions between the different agents before the start of the specific system. That is, e.g., the case with such well-known MAS-shells, like SWARM , MASON [3] and BRAHMS [1] .

In a lot of practical applications this shortcoming is no problem if the rules of interaction are well known. But in cases where such rules are not known and in particular if one does not know what kind of different agents may occur in the system then the specific MAS should have the capability of self-organizing its own order. In other words, a MAS should consist of agents that are able to generate suited rules of interaction when meeting other unknown agents. Such capabilities are needed, for example, in the case of agents that operate in the Internet and have to interact with agents they do not know before. Another example, which is described in the fourth section, is the case of robots that fulfill certain tasks in a strange territory and have to adjust their behavior with respect to other robots and humans. A third, more theoretical example is the simulation of a social community where only a part of the rules of interaction is known and where the agents have to "complete" the implementation of the specific rules via the interactions with other agents.

G. Lindemann et al. (Eds.): MATES 2004, LNAI 3187, pp. 29–46, 2004.

MAS that contain agents with such capabilities of "social learning" would literally be programs that are incomplete at their beginning or at the phase of their implementation but they would have the ability to complete themselves. There is a strong parallel to the paradigm of evolutionary programming that via the use of evolutionary algorithms allows to construct programs with the capability of self-organized adaptation and to define certain rules by their adaptive processes [11],[10]. Because essential parts of the structure of the program would emerge by the self-organization of the whole system this new paradigm could be called "emergent programming". It could enable programmers to implement just MAS-shells, to define the tasks the programs should fulfill and to let the agents find their specific rules of interaction by themselves. These in turn enable the agents to cooperate, to organize division of labor and so on. By referring to some results from the social sciences with respect to the emergence of social order we argue that it is possible to design such programs.

In the following sections we refer to suited approaches from the social sciences, namely Rational Choice (RC) and the approach of social typifying. Then we describe a first model of a MAS in which the agents are able to generate specific rules of interaction by mutually adjusting their behavior. In that way the agents are creating a simple form of social order. In particular, the agents are able to remember the rules they generated with respect to other agents, to recognize other agents they have met before and to react with the specific behavior they have learned some time ago. In addition, the agents can form "types", i.e., when they meet new agents they did not meet before the agents "typify" the newcomers: they are perceived as being from the same "type" as agents which were met before and with which already certain rules of interaction were established. In the final section we give some examples how this model of self-organized social order can be applied to specific problems of robotics, i.e. problems that arise when applying robots for specifics tasks of NASA.

2   Social Sciences Approaches

Most prominent in the social sciences with respect to the problem of the emergence of social order is the Rational Choice approach (RC). It is based, roughly speaking, on the assumption that social "behavior is a function of its payoffs" and that it is basically an "exchange process" [8], [7]. The anthropological basis of this definition is the conception of man as an egoistical being that rationally searches in each action situation for the best strategy and tries this way to maximize its own profit. The outcomes of the actions are measured as "payoffs", that is in certain rewards or punishments. According to the sociologist Dahrendorf this anthropological conception is also called *homo oeconomicus*.

RC approaches have the advantage that they can be rather naturally expressed in mathematical models and analyzed via computer simulations. Rather famous in this context is the treatment of the so-called "Prisoner's Dilemma" (PD): Imagine two prisoners who are suspected having done a common crime. Both are separately interrogated and the police is suggesting a deal: If just one of the prisoners confesses, he is released and the other gets a severe sentence. If neither of them confesses they both get a minor sentence because of a little crime; if both confess then they both get a severe sentence but not so severe as in the case of only one confession.

The case is clear if the situation occurs only once: From a rational point of view both should confess in order not to risk the most severe sentence if only the other confesses. The dilemma arises if the situation is repeated, i.e., if there is an "Iterated PD". In a game theoretical formulation we have a two person's non-zero-sum strategy game that can be formalized as follows (A and B are the two prisoners):

$$
\begin{array}{c|cc}
A/B & C & D \\
\hline
C & 3 & 0 \\
D & 5 & 1 \\
\end{array}
$$

This is a payoff-matrix of the iterated PD that has to be understood the following way: C means "cooperative" behavior of one prisoner with respect to the other – not with respect to the police! Cooperative means that he does not confess, i.e. he does not betray his comrade. D means "defective behavior", i.e. one of them betrays the other. The numbers mean that A gets a payoff of 3, if he acts cooperatively with respect to B and B gets the same for acting the same way. A gets 0 points when acting coopera-tively but is betrayed by B. In this case B gets 5 points. If both are acting in a defec-tive manner both are getting 1 point.

In a famous computer simulation using genetic algorithms Axelrod [2] could show that with the assumption of RC and using the iterated PD cooperative behavior emerged as a necessary consequence, although only in the long run. To be more ex-act: Axelrod demonstrated that certain strategies evolved from the type of "tit for tat" (TFT): If A cooperates, B will obtain the best results if he also cooperates; if A de-fects, B should do the same. Although his results are not as simple as they were often quoted it is at least possible to assume the emergence of social order by only presum-ing the interest of social actors of maximizing their own welfare.

The shortcoming of RC approaches is that they demonstrate the possibility of emergent cooperative behavior but not of a social order, i.e., of established social rules of interactions. RC approaches, so to speak, give a basis for dealing with the problem of social order, but they do not give a solution. This is given by another theo-retical approach, namely that of Berger and Luckmann in their classical study "The Social Construction of Reality" [3]:

Imagine the first meeting of two persons A and B who have the problem to develop some kind of social order that is specific rules of interaction. The first meeting of Robinson and Friday is such a case because both did not know each other and both were forced to establish a particular social order as they could not leave the island. A and B are both estimating the other and try to develop an action strategy that suits the specific actor and that is accepted by the other. In other words, both try to act accord-ing to their own interests but both have to take into regard the reactions of the other. In the end of such a process of mutual adjusting and adaptation A and B establish some form of interaction, that is they establish a simple form of social order by hav-ing developed certain rules of interaction. According to Berger and Luckmann, social order like institutions must be understood as the result of such processes of "ex-change", i.e., as the result of the mutual adjustment of the respective behavior.

Berger and Luckmann did not transform this basic idea into precise models and did not develop it in detail. Yet in our opinion this approach is very well suited to over-come the shortcoming of RC approaches without leaving their simple anthropological assumptions. The mutual adjustment is, of course, driven by the wish to get along with the other in a way most satisfying for oneself. In this sense RC is still valid because the adjustment processes follow a rational strategy. But the outcome is not just cooperative behavior but certain *rules of interaction* that remain valid even after a period of separation. In particular, the combination of certain rules to social institutions allows the distinction between an individual person and the social role this person occupies. But this goes beyond the goal of this article.

3 The Model

When transforming the basic ideas of RC and Berger/Luckmann into a computational model we made the following assumptions:

A certain social actor or an agent respectively has a specific "personality", i.e., he has some personal characteristics that allow to identify him and to recognize him again when meeting him after a time. These personal characteristics are in the case of human persons features like size, sex, age, intelligence (as far as this can be perceived), certain personal manners like a specific way to speak and so on. In the case of robots such characteristics can also be physical attributes like size or form; the characteristics may in addition be certain competences like physical strength, abilities to move in a certain landscape and so on. Internet agents, to give another illustration, may be identified by features like a specific knowledge base, certain computing capabilities, a particular degree of autonomy and so on. The actions of the respective agents are dependent on the personal characteristics, although not in a fixed way.

The agents have a general learning capability: They are able to recognize their own mistakes and to correct their behavior accordingly. These learning processes are performed by varying an "internal structure" of the agents that transforms the personal characteristics into particular actions. In the case of human beings one can describe this internal structure as a kind of self-image. It is a truism that human social actions are a result both from a certain personality and the image a person has of himself. Social learning in the sense that one has to adjust one's own behavior according to the other actors or agents one meets is the changing of the self-image in order to generate adequate forms of social action.

The most fundamental assumption is that at the first meeting of two agents the mutual learning process must take into account

a) the two personalities of the agents,
b) the own actions and the actions of the other as a reaction to one's own actions and
c) the necessity that both agents must be content with the result of the mutual adjustment. In this sense is the establishing of certain social rules of interactions always a compromise between the different personalities and the according interests.

The general model of artificial agents with the capability is this: each agent consists of two different artificial neural nets (NN), the action net (AN) and the perception net (PN). The combination of two networks enables the agents to perform two different tasks, namely the generation of suited rules of interaction on the one hand and the recognizing of "acquainted" agents after a time on the other hand. In addition, the perception network also performs the process of "typifying".

3.1 The Action Network

The action net whose task is the generation of adequate rules of action is a feed forward network: the activation flow between the artificial neurons as units of the net is only directed from the input layer via the connecting layer(s) to the output layer. Mathematically that means that only the upper half of the weight matrix is of importance; the second half can be fixed to zero. The most important rule is the linear activation rule

$$A(j) = \Sigma_i \, w_{ij} \, A(i) \tag{1}$$

if $A(j)$ is the activation value of the receiving neuron j, $A(i)$ the activation values of the sending neurons i and w_{ij} are the weight values between the sending neurons i and the receiving neuron j. At the present we are experimenting with actions nets of different architecture, i.e. different numbers of layers. We shall show below the architecture and results from a network with three layers, i.e. an input layer, an output layer and a hidden layer. According to our experiments using networks with only two layers can obtain similar results, i.e., without a hidden layer.

The input layer of the action network represents the personality of the particular agent, written as a vector $X = (x_1,...,x_5)$; the five dimensions are – at present – arbitrarily chosen. During the training processes of the AN the X-vector of each agent remains constant, that is, the network always gets the same input.

The output layer $Y = (y_1,...,y_5)$ represents components of action like the selection of certain words, miming, gestures, keeping a certain distance, being respectful and so on in the case of human actors. In the case of robots, for example, the Y-vector, that is the action vector, would contain components like coming near, asking for something, obeying an order – or disobeying – and the like.

The weight matrix of the AN represents the internal structure of the agents or the *self-image* respectively. In our experiments we usually restrict the connections in that way that only the weight values between the components x_i and y_i are

$$\begin{aligned} w_{ii} &\neq 0 \text{ and} \\ w_{ij} &= 0 \text{ else.} \end{aligned} \tag{2}$$

A two-layered action net can be visualized as

Agent A
AN:

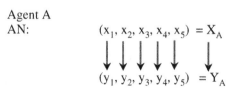

Fig. 1. Graph of an action network.

The simulations start with five agents A, B, C, D, and E, each of them containing an action network of the described feed-forward type and a perception network (see below).

When A for the first time meets B, both have to evaluate the other, that is they have mutually to find a behavior Y that is suitable for oneself and for the other. Both A and B start with random weight matrices with the described restrictions.

A starts – with its AN - with a vector Y_A and B with Y_B. "Starting" means that the ANs get the respective X-vectors as input and generate via the linear activation rule an according Y-vector as their actions.

Both actions are then evaluated by the formula

$$\delta = 1 - \frac{|(X_A - X_B)|}{|(Y_A - Y_B)|} \qquad (3)$$

The basic idea of this formula is that when establishing rules of behavior between two persons both the personalities and the respective actions must be mutually taken into account. A orientates himself to B and vice versa. The mutual task of A and B is to minimize δ, i.e., to approximate the quotient to 1.

A behavior that is satisfying for both is reached when the relation between the personalities is nearly the same as the relation between the actions. The reason for this interpretation is that a person tends to act rather "strongly" in those characteristics where he is good or even superior in relation to others; in turn, other agents accept this type of action if they perceive that the first agent is indeed superior in the respective aspect. To be sure, an agent may be in error whether he is indeed good in certain aspects. Then the mutual adjusting process forces the agent to correct his internal structure at least in this aspect.

When this is the case, i.e. if the first actions are not satisfactory, the well-known delta-rule is used for the changing of the internal structure of both agents:

$$w_{ij}(t+1) = w_{ij}(t) + \eta * \delta * o. \qquad (4)$$

if $w_{ij}(t)$ is the weight value between the units i and j at time t and accordingly $w_{ij}(t+1)$ the new value at time t +1, η is a so called learning rate, i.e. a measure for the changing of the weight value, o is the output of the unit j at time t and finally δ is the size of the "error", i.e. the difference between a target value and the factual value of the respective unit. The delta-rule is applied in the case of supervised learning, i.e. the network computes its error by "knowing" the right solution.

Obviously the learning situation for A and B is one of a *moving target*, i.e. the adjusting processes of A depend on the adjusting processes of B and vice versa. This is not the usual learning process of supervised learning because normally the target vector is constant. Therefore, it was not obvious when starting the experiments with the networks that they would be able to converge. Yet in most cases they do. The experiments of Axelrod that were mentioned above, by the way, analyze a similar situation of moving targets. Our results confirm that not only genetic algorithms but also rather simple neural feed forward networks are able to master such a situation.

In the end, that is defined by a minimized δ, A and B have developed vectors Y_{AB} and Y_{BY}, i.e. action vectors with respect to one another. These vectors are social rules in the sense "**if** A meets B, **then** A acts with the vector Y_{AB}" and vice versa.

Now this process of establishing rules of interactions is repeated with the other agents. As a final result we have a social group where each agent is connected with each other agent by a specific Y-vector Y_{NM} for two persons N and M.

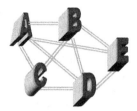

Fig. 2. Social order as the result of adaptive interactions.

The set of all Y-vectors, i.e. the 20 respective rules of behavior is the social order of this group, generated by the perception and evaluation of the other agents. Note that these rules are still just valid with respect to one pair of agents. The rules are not general in the sense that they are valid for different persons or pairs of persons respectively. This needs another process, namely the recognition and typifying of known and new agents by the perception network.

3.2 Mathematical Elaborations

The crucial point of this model is the evaluation formula (3), i.e. the equation by which the network computes the size of its error. Apparently the equation does not determine one unique solution but many – usually the different X-vectors are coded with $0 \leq x_i \leq 1$ and accordingly with the Y-components. Despite of this problem the networks usually "force" the convergence process to results that are quite sensible with respect to the criteria defined above. But the evaluation formula (3) is still too rough to allow always for satisfying results: The most important changing factor δ is the same for all connections of the network, in contrast to the possibilities of the delta- rule that allows different values of δ for each connection. In order to obtain a more differentiated adjustment process equation (3) is elaborated to

$$\delta_i = \frac{(X_{Ai} - X_{Bi})}{(Y_{Ai} - Y_{Bi})} \tag{5}$$

if x_{Ai} is the i-th component of the X-vector of A and accordingly x_{Bi} the i-th component of the X-vector of B; the same definition is valid for the y-components. δ_i then is the specific changing value, i.e. the specific size of the error with respect to a particular pair of components.

For the initial training processes the networks just contained connections between pairs of x- and y-components, as was mentioned above. This is not always enough, in particular if the X- and Y-vectors become much larger than three or five dimensions. If additional connections with weights $w_{ij} \neq 0$ are needed, the evaluation is computed according to

$$\delta_{ij} = \frac{(X_{Ai} - X_{Bj})}{(Y_{Ai} - Y_{Bj})} \tag{6}$$

for the new connections.

The equation (3), (5) and (6) both presume a symmetric adjustment process, that is, both agents change their internal structure the same way according to the size of the error. That is not very realistic, in particular with respect to "real" social situations. Stronger personalities tend to change their internal structure not as much as weaker ones. To take this into account and make the adjustment processes more realistic, a factor must be introduced that takes into regard the difference of the personalities. "Stronger" and "weaker" is defined by the respective size of the components of the X-vectors.

If x_{Ai} und x_{Bi} are again the i-th components of the X-vectors of A and B and accordingly in the case of the Y-vectors and if $x_{Ai} = q * x_{Bi}$ with $q > 1$, then

$$\delta_{Ai} = \frac{1}{q * \delta_{Bi}} \tag{7}$$

that is the error of the i-th component with respect to the difference in personalities.

In other words, A changes its internal structure less than B by the factor in which the X-components of A are greater than those of B.

Another evaluation possibility is obtained by a geometrical representation of the X- and Y-vectors in the two-dimensional plane. The general evalutation formula that does not take into account the specific components can also be computed via the angles of the two pairs of vectors:

$$\frac{\left((X_1 * X_2) / |X_1| * |X_2| \right)}{\left((Y_1 * Y_2) / |Y_1| * |Y_2| \right)} = \frac{\cos (X_1, X_2)}{\cos (Y_1, Y_2)} \tag{8}$$

and

$$\delta = 1 - \frac{\cos(X_1, X_2)}{\cos(Y_1, Y_2)} \tag{9}$$

An evaluation that takes again into account the difference between the personalities is then – computed for the vectors, not the particular components – if $|X1| = q * |X2|$ – as

$$\delta = 1 - \frac{\left(\dfrac{1}{q * \cos(X_1, X_2)} \right)}{\cos(Y_1, Y_2)} \tag{10}$$

Experiments done with that formula obtained similar results as with the other equations; this is a strong indicator for the fact that our results are not artifacts due to the particular forms of evaluation.

3.3 An Example

For illustrating purposes we show one of our prototypes, implemented by Ulf Ackermann and Moritz Balz. It is a three-layered feed-forward network with only three X- and Y-components. After one typical training process we obtain the following results:

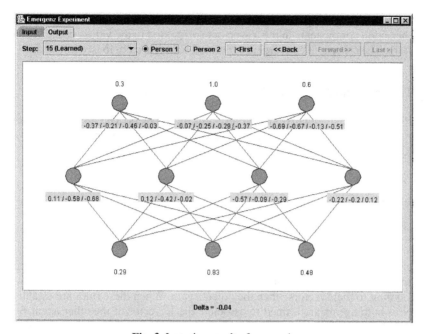

Fig. 3. Learning result of person 1.

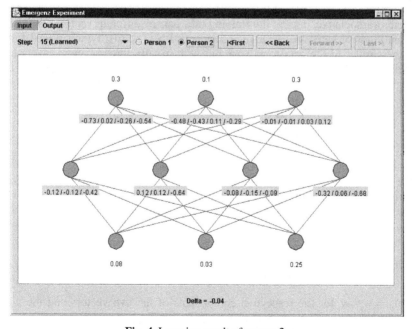

Fig. 4. Learning result of person 2.

By comparing the respective X- and Y-values of agents A and B one sees that indeed the action components in the Y-vectors correspond to the values of the according X-vectors. The criteria of convergence, defined above, are obviously fulfilled.

3.4 The Perception Network PN

The PN is a hetero-associative net with two or more layers. The input layer is the X-vector of a person B, which the person A meets. The output layer is the Y-vector according to the person B.

PN X_B

$$\downarrow$$

Y_{AB}

Y_{AB} is the action vector of A with respect to person B.

A and B mutually generate action vectors Y with respect to one another, as was described above. These vectors are rules of interaction insofar as A and B always both act according to their vectors when they meet again. When these rules are established, the PN of both agents are trained to associate the X-vector of the other agent B with the own vector Y_{AB} (in the case of A). The same is the case after A has established a mutual rule with C, D and E. A then has 4 rules at its disposal that are "stored" in its PN via the training processes of associating a certain X-vector with the corresponding action vector.

"Hetero-associative" means the training of a pair of different vectors. We use two different kinds of hetero-associative networks as PN. The first type is a feed-forward network, similar to the action network but with usually three or more layers (again depending on the size of the vectors). The training is done by using the back-propagation rule, one of the most powerful learning rules in neural networks:

$$\delta_j = \left\{ \begin{array}{l} f_j'(net_j)(t_j - o_j) \text{ if j is an output unit} \\ f_j'(net_j)\sum_k (\delta_k w_{ik}) \text{ if j is a hidden unit} \end{array} \right\} \qquad (11)$$

The back propagation rule is basically just a generalized delta-rule.

The second type of PNs is a so-called bi-directional-associative network (BAM). Its training is done in a quite different way, i.e. by using a certain form of matrix- and vector multiplication. Two vectors V and W are associated by multiplying X with a matrix M, obtaining

$$V * M = W \qquad (12)$$

Conversely, we obtain

$$V * W = M \qquad (13)$$

with $m_{ij} = v_{ij} * w_j$ for the respective components of the two vectors and the matrix. Technical details can be looked up in any textbook on neural networks.

When after the establishing of this order A meets B again (or C or D), then the PN of A is able to recognize B by taking his X-vector as input and by generating the according action vector Y_{AB} as output. A thus remembers B and is able to act according to the established rule.

When A meets a new person F, there are two possibilities:

a) F is not similar to any member of the group. In this case the PN of A will not recognize F; A and F will have to establish specific rules of behavior according to the procedure described above.

b) F is similar to a member of the group, say D.

Then the PN of A will generate the vector Y_{AD} when receiving the X-vector of F. In this case F will be perceived by A *as the same type as D*, although F is not identical with D (F is another person or agent respectively).

When A acts with Y_{AD}, F has to adjust his own Y-vector with respect to A; the adjusting process is not mutual but only the task of the newcomer F. The reason for this is the consideration that members of an already established group only typify a newcomer, whereas the newcomer has to adjust his behavior with respect to all members of the group.

Now the rules of interaction become *general* rules in the sense that they are valid not only for a particular agent B but also with respect to all other agents that belong to the same type as B. In terms of sociology, the rules are valid for all agents that belong to the same social type, i.e., that occupy the same social role. But that is just one possibility of interpretation. In any case, the agents now are able to typify, i.e. to abstract from individual peculiarities of other agents and to perceive them as representatives of a certain type.

By applying concepts of the theory of complex systems to our model we obtain some new definitions and theoretical results:

First result:

A type is an attractor of a PN; the agents that belong to this type are the members of the basin of attraction of this attractor.

An attractor is a steady state of the PN that is generated after the input of the X-vector of the specific agent. The basin of attraction of a particular attractor is the set of all initial states of the complex systems that "lead" into the attractor. In that sense all agents whose X-vectors generate the same Y-vector of a certain agent belong to the same basin of attraction, i. e. they belong to the same type.

Second result:

The size of this basin of attraction, i.e., the capability of the PN to distinguish between different persons, is a parameter for the generation of certain types of social order. The smaller the basin, the more differentiated are the typifying processes and vice versa.

It is well known from complex systems theory that these systems in particular differ with respect to their sensitivity with regard to initial states. Large basins of attraction mean that the system abstracts from individual differences between initial states; in our model that means that small individual differences of the respective X-vectors – the initial states – will not be taken into account and all agents whose personality is rather similar will be perceived as members of the same type. This insight obtains a

Theoretical consequence:

Differentiated processes of typifying are only possible with PNs that belong to Wolfram class 4, i.e. that are really complex systems.

Complex systems can be classified according to a schema of Wolfram [15]. Wolfram classes 1 and 2 contain systems with rather large basins of attraction, in extreme cases only one basin with one attractor. Such systems can only roughly typify, i.e. they put agents in the same type that are not very similar. That is, e.g., the case with children who classify adults only according to "own parents" and "others". Differentiated classifying needs systems of complexity class 4, that is systems with both large and small basins of attraction.

By using so called ordering parameters, i.e. numerical characteristics of the rule sets of complex systems it is possible at least in principle to describe what features systems of Wolfram class 4 – or 1 and 2 - must possess [9],[10]. Therefore, when constructing a MAS via the procedure of emergent programming it is just necessary to implement the necessary type of agent, i.e., to determine how differentiated its capability of typifying should be, implement the AN and in particular the PN of the agent as a complex system of the desired Wolfram class, define the respective evaluation formula for the adjustment process and let the whole system do the rest: The interactional structure of the MAS will then emerge as the result of the adaptive interactions of the agents themselves.

4 Typifying Social Order in Human-Robot Teams

The following example does not describe a factual application of the model to problems of NASA. It serves as an illustration how the model *could be* applied to specific problems that demand the interaction of certain agents, in this case human astronauts and robots.

In this section we describe an application of our model in the domain of human-robot teams. In recent announcements the NASA administration has decided that they will work towards human missions to the Moon and Mars in the next 20 years. To achieve this it is obvious that humans and robots will have to work together to first build structures to go to and then live on these planetary surfaces, while humans and robots will also work together to explore the planets. Current robot technology has to advance to incorporate models of teamwork and social order. We are not claiming that robots can become social creatures in a similar way as humans. This, we feel, is neither possible nor desirable. However, we are claiming that for humans and robots to effectively work together the robots need to share understanding of the social order and structure within the team.

An example from our experience with human-robot teamwork in the NASA Mobile Agents project, in which we test our human-robot teams every year in a two-week field test in a Mars-like environment in the Utah desert, shows that when robots lack social knowledge the teamwork with people suffers [5],[6],[13]. During an extravehicular activity (EVA) to a deep canyon, five kilometers from the Mars Desert Research Station habitat, two astronauts and their robot enter the canyon for science exploration (MDRS 2004). While in the canyon the robot plays many different roles. It is a mule for the astronauts, carrying their tools and samples. It is a videographer for EVA support back in the habitat, as well as recording the EVA for remote scientists back on Earth. It is an in-situ science laboratory, allowing the astronauts to use its science instruments, such as panoramic cameras and spectrometers. It is a geologist's field helper, handing the astronauts the right tools, taking pictures of geologic features asked by the astronaut. At the same time it is also a mobile network relay antenna, making sure the astronauts are in constant communication with each other, the robot, and the habitat communicator (HabCom) back in the habitat. During such an EVA the robot plays all these roles at the same time, supporting not only the EVA astronauts, but also HabCom and even, while in delayed communication, remote scientists back on Earth. How is the robot able to play these multiple roles effectively? Who should it serve when? How should it serve the different groups of people? What should it decide to do if HabCom asks it to perform a task, while one of the two astronauts needs its help? Without a model of social order and an ability to typify the dynamic relationship between everyone involved, the robot has a hard time making good decisions in serving its teammates. Next, we show in a simple example how our model would help the robot in making good teamwork decisions, based on its ability to typify each team interaction within the model of social order.

We create a model of an institution, as defined by Berger and Luckmann, for an EVA Team [3]. The institution is subdivided into social subgroups representing the different participants in an EVA. Figure 5 shows the institution model in a UML representation. We implemented this model in the Brahms multi-agent language. The subgroups of the institution displayed in Figure 5 maps easily onto the *group* concept in the Brahms language. We use Brahms to implement and execute our model. The Brahms language is used in NASA's Mobile Agents project to implement the Mobile Agents Architecture, allowing humans and software agents to interact, and has been proven as a multi-agent language for developing human-robot teams.

The X-vector attributes for the institutional team members are defined within the model (5). The X-vector attributes for each agent are defined in the different groups, depending on the group inheritance rules. The attributes relevant for all members of

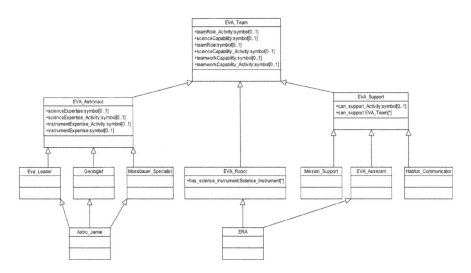

Fig. 5. Institution model for EVA Teams.

the institution are defined at the top-level in the EVA_Team group. This means that any member of the EVA_Team institution inherits these attributes. More subgroup-specific attributes are defined at the subgroup-level, which means that only member-agents of that subgroup have these X-vector attributes defined. In this way every member of the institution has a set of X-vector attributes that can be used to describe the X-vector for a particular agent in the model. For example, the ERA robot agent is a member of the EVA_Robot group and thus inherits all the X-vector attributes in its inheritance path:

> *ERA* memberof *EVA_Robot*
>   *X-Vector attributes:*
>   EVA_Team::*teamRole*
>   EVA_Team::*teamworkCapability*
>   EVA_Team::*scienceCapability*
>   EVA_Support::EVA_Team *can_support*
>   EVA_Robot::Science_Instrument *has_science_instrument*

In the above example, the attribute *teamRole* defines the role of the agent in the EVA team. For example, the ERA robot can play the role of the EVA assistant for the astronauts. The attribute *teamworkCapability* defines what the ERA robot can do during a particular EVA. For example, although the actual capability of the ERA includes much more, in a particular EVA the ERA teamwork capability could be restricted to following astronauts and being a network repeater. Similarly, the attribute *scienceCapability* can be restricted to only enable the ERA to take panorama images. The attribute *can_support* defines which team-member the ERA can actually support during the EVA. For example, we can constrain the ERA to only support a particular EVA astronaut. Finally, with the *has_science_instrument* attribute we can define what science instruments are available to the ERA on the EVA. This attribute is related to the *scienceCapability* attribute. Thus, in our example here, the *has_science_instrument* attribute defines the panorama camera with which the ERA is able to take panorama images. Thus, in summary, the X-vector for the ERA agent (X_{ERA}) in the above example would be:

> *(ERA.teamRole = EVA_Assistant);*
> *(ERA.teamworkCapability = Mobile_Relay_Antenna);*
> *(ERA.scienceCapability = panoramas);*
> *(ERA.can_support = Astro_Jamie);*
> *(ERA.has_science_instrument = PanCam1);*

In a similar manner, for example Astro_Jamie is an astronaut agent and is a member of the EVA_Astronaut group, therefore inheriting the following X-Vector attributes:

> *Astro_Jamie* memberof *EVA_Astronaut*
>   *X-Vector attributes:*
>   EVA_Team::*teamRole*
>   EVA_Team::*teamworkCapability*
>   EVA_Team::*scienceCapability*
>   EVA_Astronaut::*scienceExpertise*
>   EVA_Astronaut::*instrumentExpertise*

Astro_Jamie agent inherits the same EVA_Team X-vector attributes, but instead of inheriting the EVA_Support and EVA_robot attributes the agent now has two EVA_Astronaut attributes. The attribute *scienceExpertise* specifies the main expertise of the astronaut, such as being a geologist or biologist, whereas the attribute *instrumentExpertise* specifies the astronaut's expertise regarding the use of a particular science instrument. It is not uncommon that planetary scientists specialize in a particular science instrument and are thus seen as the expert for that instrument. For example, astronaut Jamie can be a specialist in the Mössbauer spectrometer. The X-vector for the Astro_Jamie agent (X_{Astro_Jamie}) might thus be defines as:

> *(Astro_Jamie.teamRole = Eva_Astronaut);*
> *(Astro_Jamie.teamworkCapability = Eva_Leader);*
> *(Astro_Jamie.scienceCapability = spectral_imaging);*
> *(Astro_Jamie.scienceExpertise = Geologist);*
> *(Astro_Jamie.instrumentExpertise = Mössbauer_Spectrometer);*

These X-vectors of the ERA and Astro_Jamie agents can now be defined by providing them as initial beliefs to the individual agents when loading the model.

The Y-vector for the agents are generated using the previously discussed action network (AN) with the agent's X-vector defined above as input. Each agent A has an AN Y-vector (Y_{AB}) for each agent B in the EVA Team group. These Y-vectors are generated by the AN network algorithm before hand and are provided to all agents at model initialization as initial beliefs for the agents. Each agent needs an initial Y-vector describing the agent's self image knowledge as far as the teamwork typification of the agent in relation to its social activities during an EVA.

An EVA_Astronaut has the following Y-vector attributes inherited from the groups in Figure 5:

> *Astro_Jamie* memberof *EVA_Astronaut*
> > *Y-Vector attributes:*
> > > EVA_Team::*teamRole_Activity*
> > > EVA_Team::*teamworkCapability_Activity*
> > > EVA_Team::*scienceCapability_Activity*
> > > EVA_Astronaut::*scienceExpertise_Activity*
> > > EVA_Astronaut::*instrumentExpertise_Activity*

For example, agent Astro_Jamie has the initial vector Y_{astro_Jamie}:

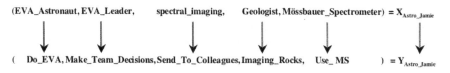

Fig. 6. Y_{Astro_Jamie} Vector.

The Y-vector in Figure 6 states that astronaut Jamie as an EVA_Astronaut can participate in the *Do_EVA* activity and because she is an EVA_Leader she makes the team decisions (*Make_Decision*). Her science capability is spectral imaging and she will send all images taken to her colleagues on Earth (*Send_To_Earth*). Because she is a Geologist she will use spectral imaging techniques to image rocks (*Imaging_Rocks*) and because she is carrying a *Mössbauer_Spectrometer* she will use it in taking spectral images (*Use_MS*).

Just as the X-vector, agent Astro_Jamie receives its Y-vector as initial believes:

> *(Astro_Jamie.teamRole_Activity = Do_EVA);*
> *(Astro_Jamie.teamworkCapability_Activity = Make_Decision);*
> *(Astro_Jamie.scienceCapability_Activity = Send_Data_To_Earth);*
> *(Astro_Jamie.scienceExpertise_Activity = Imaging_Rocks);*
> *(Astro_Jamie.instrumentExpertise_Activity = Use_MS);*

The ERA robot agent has a different Y-vector that is also based on its X-vector and the Y-vector attributes inherited from Figure 5:

ERA memberof *EVA_Robot*
Y-Vector attributes:
> EVA_Team::*teamRole_Activity*
> EVA_Team::*teamworkCapability_Activity*
> EVA_Team::*scienceCapability_Activity*
> EVA_Support::EVA_Team *can_support_Activity*
> EVA_Robot::Science_Instrument *has_science_instrument_Activity*

For example, the robot agent ERA has the initial vector Y_{ERA} shown in Figure 7:

Fig. 7. Y_{ERA} Vector.

The Y-vector in Figure 7 states that the ERA agent will participate as an EVA_Assistant in the *Do_EVA* activity. Because the ERA's teamwork capability for the EVA is that of a mobile relay antenna, it has to follow the astronaut during the EVA (*Follow_Astronaut*). The task of the ERA is to keep astronaut Jamie connected to the wireless EVA network at all times. This is why following the astronaut is an important social activity for the robot. The science capability of the ERA is taking panorama images. When the ERA has taken a panorama image it will send the image to the crewmembers in the habitat. Besides being a mobile antenna, the ERA can support astronaut Jamie in performing her science work during the EVA by taking panorama images (*Taking_Panorama_Using_GPS*). Last, the Y-vector of the ERA states that it uses its PanCam camera science instrument to take panorama images (*Use_PanCam*).

> *(ERA.teamRole_Activity = Do_EVA);*
> *(ERA.teamworkCapability_Activity = Follow_Astronaut);*
> *(ERA.scienceCapability_Activity = Send_To_Hab);*
> *(ERA.can_support_Activity = Taking_Panorama_Using_GPS);*
> *(ERA.has_science_instrument_Activity = Use_PanCam);*

Here we briefly describe the use of the PN and the Y-vector in a meeting between the two agents.

While on an EVA the astronaut and robot perform their individual activities as defined by their roles. The EVA astronaut Jamie could be walking in a canyon doing geological exploration taking spectral images of rocks in the canyon, while the ERA robot is following Jamie to keep her network connection back to the habitat in tact. Let's now take the scenario a step further, and explain what would happen when the EVA astronaut comes to an area where she wants to have a panorama image taken. She is not able to perform that task herself, and thus asks the ERA robot to perform that task for her. How does the Astro_Jamie agent know what and how to ask the ERA agent?

The $Y_{Astro\_JamieERA}$ vector tells Astro_Jamie agent how to ask the question (in the form of a speech act) to the ERA agent. Astro_Jamie would ask the same question differently when it would ask it of another astronaut instead of the ERA. To ask the ERA agent to take a panorama image the ERA needs to know the GPS location where it has to go to take the image. This is where different Y-vectors for different agents would make Astro_Jamie agent ask the question differently, depending on whom it is asking. For instance, in case Astro_Jamie would ask another astronaut agent it does not give the GPS location because that would be not very helpful to the astronaut, instead it has to show the astronaut agent where to go. It might also have to say to the astronaut what to do with the image because the astronaut does not know this, while the ERA agent knows to send each panorama image back to the habitat (see its Y-vector definition above).

As we said at the beginning of this section, this is just a would-be application. Neither the model nor the possibilities of NASA are advanced enough to try the model on Mars or another planet. But although this article is no contribution to science fiction, perhaps one day some variants of this model are indeed applied on some extra terrestrial landscape.

References

1. AiS (2000): Brahms Website: http://www.agentisolutions.com, Ron van Hoof. 2004.
2. Axelrod, R.: The Evolution of Strategies in the Iterated Prisoner's Dilemma. In: Davis, L. (ed.): Genetic Algorithms and Simulated Annealing. Los Altos (CA): Morgan Kauffman (1987)
3. Berger, P. and Luckmann, T.: The Social Construction of Reality. New York: Doubleday (1966)
4. Cioffi-Revilla, C., Gotts, N.: Comparative Analysis of Agent-based Social Simulations: GeoSim and FEARLUS models. In: JASSS – Journal for Artificial Societies and Social Simulation (2003), Volume 6, Issue 4 http://jasss.soc.surrey.ac.uk/6/4
5. Clancey, W. J., M. Sierhuis, et al.: Brahms Mobile Agents: Architecture and Field Tests. AAAI 2002 Fall Symposium on Human-Robot Interaction, North Fallmouth, MA, The AAAI Press (2002)
6. Clancey, W. J., M. Sierhuis, et al.: The Mobile Agents Integrated Field Test: Mars Dessert Research Station 2003. FLAIRS 2004, Miami Beach, Florida (2004)
7. Fararo, T. J.: Social Action Systems. Foundations and Synthesis in Sociological Theory. Westport (CO): Praeger (2000)
8. Homans, G. C.: Social Behavior: Its Elementary Forms. New York: Harcourt, Brace, Jovanovitch (1974)

9. Kauffman, S.: The Origins of Order. Oxford: Oxford University Press (1993)
10. Klüver, J.: The Dynamics and Evolution of Social Systems. Dordrecht (NL): Kluwer Academic Publishers (2000)
11. Koza, J.R.: Artificial Life: Spontaneous Emergence of Self-Replicating and Evolutionary Self-Improving Computer Programs. In: Langton, C. (ed.): Artificial Life III. Reading (MA): Addison Wesley (1994)
12. MDRS (2004). MDRS Crew 29:2004 Mobile Agents Field Test at the Mars Desert Research Station, http://www.marssociety.org/MDRS/fs03/crew29/, Mars Society (2004)
13. Sierhuis, M., J. M. Bradshaw, et al.: Human-Agent Teamwork and Adjustable Autonomy in Practice. The 7th International Symposium on Artificial Intelligence, Robotics and Automation in Space (i-SAIRAS), Nara, Japan (2003)
14. Weiss, G., Sen, S.: Adaptation and Learning in Multi-Agent Systems. Heidelberg – New York: Springer (1996)
15. Wolfram, S.: A New Kind of Science. Champaign (IL): Wolfram Media (2002)

Evolution of Agent Coordination in an Asynchronous Version of the Predator-Prey Pursuit Game

Stefan Mandl and Herbert Stoyan

Department of Computer Science 8 (AI)
University of Erlangen-Nuremberg, Germany
{mandl,hstoyan}@informatik.uni-erlangen.de
http://www8.informatik.uni-erlangen.de

Abstract. In this paper, we introduce an asynchronous version of the well-known pursuit game. The validity of past results on the synchronous version of the pursuit game is verified in this new setting by considering five kinds of prey: Still prey, randomly moving prey, avoiding prey, linear prey, and linear prey with switching behavior. Genetic programming is used to evolve teams of predators whose capture rates are compared to that of a greedy strategy. Task assignment is used as an explicit means of coordination in the evolved teams of predators. We conclude that evolved teams with explicit coordination outperform greedy non-cooperative strategies when more competent prey is faced.

1 Introduction

The pursuit game of "predators and prey" (PNP) is a widely used testbed in distributed AI. It has been used to study different kinds of problems like case based online learning (see [3]), competetive coevolution (see [6]), multi-agent communication (see [9]), multi-agent strategies (see [8]), and certainly some more.

Its appeal to researchers is due to the fact that it is on the one hand easy to describe and apparently an abstraction of real-world behavior of animals, or military operations. On the other hand, despite its simple description, it turns out, that without certain restricting assumptions, it is very hard to solve. One such assumptions is that the agents are synchronous by either moving simultaneously or taking turns. This means that the time needed to compute the next move is not taken into account.

The intention of our work is twofold: Firstly, we introduce asynchronous PNP as we think it is closer to the real world, and because the trade-off between fast acting and lengthy computations contributes to the fairness of the game. Secondly, we test whether or not more explicit communication between the predators helps in catching special kinds of prey that have been reported to be very hard to catch. This work could also be considered a case-study showing that agent interaction has to become more explicit with increasing problem difficulty.

Instead of handcrafting the cooperating agents, we facilitate genetic programming techniques in order to evolve teams of predators. The evolved teams are then compared to a team of greedy predators.

G. Lindemann et al. (Eds.): MATES 2004, LNAI 3187, pp. 47–57, 2004.

2 Problem Description

The domain of PNP considered here consists of a rectangular grid of size 30×30. It contains one prey agent and four predator agents, each of which occupies exactly one grid cell at a time. Any two agents must not occupy the same grid cell. The agents can move one cell a time, either horizontally or vertically, or not move at all. Diagonal movement is not allowed. The world is torodial, which causes an agent which moves past the grid boundaries on one side to re-appear at the opposite side. The goal of the predator agents is to capture the prey. In order to do so, they have to surround the prey, whereby they effectively block any further prey movement (see figure 1).

Korf calls the variant described here the "orthogonal game" ([10]). He additionally examines the "diagonal game", where diagonal movements are allowed and eight predators are needed in oder to surround the prey. He also examines the "hexagonal game" where each grid cell has six neighbor cells. We restrict ourself to the orthogonal game, as according to Korf, it is the hardest to solve.

The environment contains exactly the number of predators required for capturing the prey, thus it is necessary that the predators are coordinated.

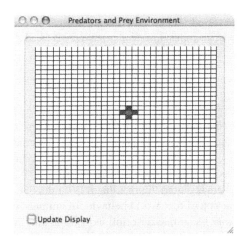

Fig. 1. Four predators capturing the prey

In previous work, there have been two different kinds of synchronization: The prey and the predators would move alternately by taking turns. This kind of behavior is advantageous for the predators. Alternatively, there would be fully synchronized behavior: All agents move at the same time. New positions can only be observed after each agent has decided on its move. Both of the strategies have the consequence, that the computer time consumed by an agent in order to reach the decision for the next move is not taken into account. Contrary, we decided not to use any synchronization at all. We think this is more realistic, as the time a predator needs to decide on where to move could be used by the prey to escape to a new position. Consequently, we cannot count the number of turns in order to decide when to stop the game. It is therefore necessary to use a time limit, after which to stop the game. So an asynchronous approach made it necessary to use real time.

Throughout the rest of this paper, we usually use the *manhattan distance*, which is the (minimal) sum of the vertical and the horizontal distance between two grid cells, as distance metric.

3   Related Work

The pursuit game was introduced by Benda [2]. In [10], Korf showed that a simple greedy strategy is sufficient to solve the initial problem. Haynes et. al. showed in [7], [8], [4] that the problem can be addressed with evolutionary programming techniques based on strongly typed genetic programming. Jim and Giles ([9]) evolved a communication language showing the resulting behavior of the system equivalent to Mealy finite state machine. In [13], Brooks and Maes evolved conditions for behavior activation in order to make a six feet robot walk forward.

Another classic testbed for agent coordination strategies is the *iterated prisoner's dilemma* (IPD) [1]. It is different in nature from PNP, as it features a trade-off between acting cooperatively in the long run and actin selfishly in the short run, which makes the problem interesting. The PNP scenario is interesting, because the problem is difficult.

4   Experiment Description

We use an *explicit* environment model as proposed in [14]. This means that relevant properties of the environment are query-able at runtime, thus the functionality available to the agents need not be specified beforehand.

Figure 2 lists the actions agents may take in the PNP environment. Actions are only executed if possible, i.e. when they don't conflict with the requirement that each grid cell may be occupied by one agent at most. Actions don't take parameters.

Action	Description
up	Move the agent up, when free
down	Move the agent down, when free
left	Move the agent left, when free
right	Move the agent right, when free

Fig. 2. PNP actions

Figure 3 lists the predicates an agent may test. The argument taken by some predicates is an integer number denoting the index of a predator.

Figure 4 shows the list of basic functions available.

4.1   Prey Behavior

For the experiments, we use five different kinds of prey behavior, which are gathered from the literature:

Predicate	#Args	Description
true	0	Always true
hSameAsPrey	0	True iff in the same grid column as the prey
vSameAsPrey	0	True iff in the same grid row as the prey
nextTo	1	True iff manhattan distance to the predator equals 1
hOppositeToPredator	1	True iff on different sides relative to prey (horizontally)
vOppositeToPredator	1	True iff on different sides relative to prey (vertically)
hSameAsPredator	1	True iff on the same side relative to prey (horizontally)
vSameAsPredator	1	True iff on the same side relative to prey (vertically)

Fig. 3. PNP predicates

Function	#Args	Description
distanceToPrey	0	Manhattan distance to the prey
closerToPreyBy	0	Direction code decreasing distance to the prey
distanceTo	1	Manhattan distance to predator with given index
closerBy	1	Direction code decreasing distance to given predator

Fig. 4. PNP functions

- Still prey: The prey stays at its initial position.
- Random prey: The prey moves by randomly selecting one of the available actions.
- Avoiding prey: The prey computes, which of the predators is closest and then chooses its move in such a way as to maximize the distance to the closest predator.
- Linear prey: The prey chooses a direction to move and does not change it anymore.
- Linear switching prey: They prey chooses a direction to go. Only when a collision occurs, the prey selects a new random direction and proceeds.

For each of the prey behaviors (except for the still prey) we run the experiments in two modes: Slow and fast. In fast mode, the prey agent operates as fast as possible. In slow mode, the prey has a delay of 20ms after each move. The 20ms are in fact chosen quite arbitrarily. The idea is to make the predator agents faster than the prey agent as this provision was taken in most of the previous work.

4.2   Predator Behavior

Predators act in two phases: task serving and rule processing. In task serving phase, the predator tries to serve any task that was assigned to it. When no more tasks are present, the predator switches to rule processing mode. Task assignment is the only form of explicit coordination in our setting. In rule processing mode, rules of the form

$$C_1 \wedge \ldots \wedge C_n \Rightarrow \{A, T\}$$

are interpreted. C_i denotes a conditional expression; A and T denote action statement and task publication statement, respectively. A condition is either a predicate test, the comparison of a function value with an provided integer value, or the comparison of a function value with another function's value. The rule interpreter checks the left-hand-side of each rule. When the condition is true, the right-hand-side part is executed. If the right-hand-side is an action statement, the accordant action is performed, if the right-hand-side is a task publication statement, the described task is assigned to the agent specified in the task description. Task descriptions consist of a task name and the index of the predator to whom the task should be assigned to. Figure 5 lists the available task names. When all rules have been tried, the predator switches back to task serving mode. Unlike the actions, functions and predicates, the tasks are not part of the PNP environment, instead they are a convention among the predator agents. The methods

Task name	Description
`closerToMe`	Decrease the manhattan distance to the client
`awayFromMe`	Increase the manhattan distance to the client
`closerToPrey`	Decrease the manhattan distance to the prey
`awayFromPrey`	Increase the manhattan distance to the prey
`up,down,left,right,stay`	"Remote control" facility

Fig. 5. Predator tasks

to handle tasks are predefined and fixed for every agent. Therefore, the behavior of a predator is completely specified by the rule set. In order to generate random predators for the genetic programming runs, we need to generate random rule sets. We chose to have up to 20 rules per rule set. The right-hand-side of the rules is a task publication statement with probability $\frac{1}{3}$ and an action statement otherwise. The left-hand-side of the rules will contains three conditions on average. The condition tests are predicate tests or function tests with equal probability.

4.3 Evolution Parameters

We give a short outline of the major parameters of the genetic programming runs.

Individuals of the Population: We follow Haynes et. al. [5] and define an individual of the population to comprise a complete set of predators, effectively circumventing the credit assignment problem.

Population Size: After various experiments, it turned out that a population of size 150 worked well.

Selection: We chose tournament selection as in [11] with tournament size 2. The winners of two subsequent tournaments are considered for reproduction, the two losers are removed from the population and replaced with the offspring of the two winners.

Fitness Function: The fitness function is a critical parameter of genetic programming. It is highly depending on the problem at hand. In our case, it seems reasonable to consider such individuals fitter than others, that – as a team – get closer to the prey. So we introduce a distance feature:

$$C = \sum_{1 \leq i \leq 4} \Delta_i^p \tag{1}$$

where Δ_i^p is the manhattan distance between the prey and predator with index i, One problem with the greedy approach is that predators tend to block each other and to build clusters on one side of the prey. We therefore introduce an additional feature:

$$N = \sum_{1 \leq i < j \leq 4} \Delta_{ij}' \tag{2}$$

where Δ_{ij}' is defined to be 1, if the manhattan distance between predator i and predator j is 1 (they are next to each other) and 0 otherwise. This feature measures how many pairs of predators are next to each other. The performance of an individual after a test run is defined to be:

$$P = \frac{1}{C - 4 + e^{4N}} \tag{3}$$

Performance ranges from 0 to 1 (where 1 is best). One problem with PNP is that the performance of teams is highly dependent on the initial placement of the predators on the grid. In [8], Haynes reports that the average of several runs on a number of training cases is used as fitness value. Our approach is slightly different. We use accumulated fitness. The rationale is that the performance of former runs should not be lost. The accumulated fitness F_n after n runs is defined like this:

$$F_n = P_n + \gamma P_{n-1} + \gamma^2 P_{n-2} + \ldots + \gamma^n P_0 = \sum_{i=0}^{n} \gamma^i P_{n-i} \tag{4}$$

where P_n denotes the performance in the n-th run of an individual (team). Equation 4 can be computed more efficiently by using the equivalent definition:

$$F_n = P_n + \gamma F_{n-1} \tag{5}$$

Please note that for $\gamma = \frac{1}{2}$, the condition $0 \leq F_n \leq 2$ holds for all $n \geq 1$, which can be seen by considering that the two summands are less or equal to 1 in equation 5.

The fitness diagrams in section 5 actually show the accumulated fitness and the selection of individuals for reproduction relies on accumulated fitness only.

With our definition, the fitness function (F_n) should be *maximized* by the evolutionary process.

Reproduction. When two individuals (sets of four predators) are selected to reproduce, a crossover-like operation is applied. As individuals comprise four predator agents, there are several possibilities to do crossover. In [12], Luke and Spector point out that restricted crossover performs better than free crossover. In restricted crossover, the four predators in a individual are considered separately. Each predator in the first individual is crossed only with the corresponding predator in the second individual. This effectively leads to separate breeding pools with the possibility that specialized behavior evolves. For two individuals (teams) $A = \langle a_1, a_2, a_3, a_4 \rangle$ and $B = \langle b_1, b_2, b_3, b_4 \rangle$, crossover is performed by performing crossover on the team members such that c_1, d_1

Experiment	Greedy Captures	Moves Ratio	Evolved Captures	Moves Ratio
Still Prey	99.3%	∞	99%	∞
Slow Random Prey	95.4%	4.32	100%	4.53
Fast Random Prey	74.5%	0.56	95.5%	0.58
Slow Avoiding Prey	96.2%	8.57	96.7%	5.09
Fast Avoiding Prey	84.7%	3.69	96.07%	3.94
Slow Linear Prey	58.1%	1.92	92.3%	2.7
Fast Linear Prey	94.07%	0.68	97.02%	0.46
Slow Linear Switching Prey	26.5%	1.93	96.05%	2.72
Fast Linear Switching Prey	5.41%	0.210	2.63%	0.14

Fig. 6. Performance table

$= cross(a_1, b_1)$, $c_2, d_2 = cross(a_2, b_2)$, $c_3, d_3 = cross(a_3, b_3)$, and $c_4, d_4 = cross(a_4, b_4)$. The teams $C = \langle c_1, c_2, c_3, c_4 \rangle$ and $D = \langle d_1, d_2, d_3, d_4 \rangle$ are the offspring of A and B.

Crossover on team members ($cross(\cdot, \cdot)$) is performed by randomly choosing a crossover point in the list of rules for each of the two predators. The first offspring is generated by using the rules up to the crossover point from the first predator and using the rules after the crossover point from the second predator. The second offspring is generated accordingly.

Mutation. Mutation rate is set to 30%. Mutation is performed by replacing a single predator of a team by a new randomly generated predator.

5 Discussion of the Experimental Results

The experimental results are shown in figure 6. The first column contains the kind of prey used. The second column shows the percentage of captures by a team of four greedy predators. The third column displays the average number of moves of the greedy predators divided by the number of moves of the prey. The fourth column displays the percentage of captures by the best evolved team. The last column displays the average number of moves of the evolved predators divided by the number of prey moves. The percentage of captures was obtained by running the very team many hundred times.

Previous work on synchronous PNP considered only such prey that was slower than or at most equally fast as the predators. We found that in some cases, much faster prey is actually easier to catch.

The evolution diagrams that are presented in this section show the best and the average fitness (ranging from 0 to 2) in the population on the vertical axis and the number of combinations (reproductions) on the horizontal axis. For each combination, four runs of the pursuit game are necessary in order to select the parents (see above).

5.1 Still Prey

The still prey is easy to catch for the greedy team, which selects the move that leads to the smallest distance to the prey among all the possible moves and only such moves

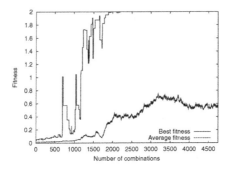

Fig. 7. Evolution diagram for the still prey

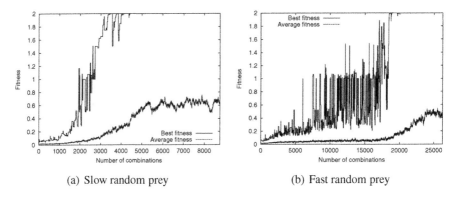

(a) Slow random prey   (b) Fast random prey

Fig. 8. Evolution diagrams for the random prey

are considered that don't lead to an already occupied location. Without the latter condition, the predators would simply block themselves in most cases. The evolved team of predators also has got a nearly perfect capture rate. The evolution diagram in figure 7 shows that already after 2500 combinations a good solution has evolved. Interestingly the performance table in figure 6 shows no 100% capture rate. This fact may be due to too little time for the predators for both, the greedy and the evolved team).

5.2   Slow Random Prey

The slow random moving prey is expected to be easy to catch, as it reveals a high degree of locality which prevents the predators from blocking each other. Accordingly, figure 6 shows a very good capture performance for the greedy predators and an excellent performance for the evolved predators. The evolution diagram in figure 8 shows very fast convergence of the genetic programming run.

5.3   Fast Random Prey

The fast random moving prey is interesting, as the prey is actually moving much faster than the predators, which can be observed from the move ratios in figure 6. Still, the high degree of locality allows the greedy predators to achieve an acceptable capture rate. The capture rate of the evolved predators is very good. The evolution diagram in figure 8 shows that convergence is much slower than for the slow random moving prey. It exhibits a large amount of variability before actual convergence.

5.4 Slow Avoiding Prey

For the slow avoiding prey both, the greedy and the evolved team have nearly similar (very good) performance. It stands out that the prey moves very slowly compared to the predators, which may explain the high capture rate. This result shows that in asynchronous PNP the trade off between complex computations and fast actions is relevant. Even though the avoiding prey may eventually choose a good direction, the world has completely changed when it reaches such a conclusion. As figure 9 shows, convergence was very fast.

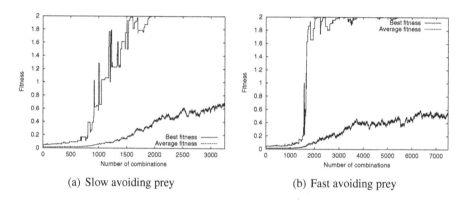

(a) Slow avoiding prey   (b) Fast avoiding prey

Fig. 9. Evolution diagrams for the avoiding prey

5.5 Fast Avoiding Prey

The fast avoiding prey is considerably harder to catch for the greedy team, while the evolved team performs very good. The move ratios show that the prey is still much slower than the predators due to the costly computations it performs. Figure 9 shows, that convergence is quite fast for the fast avoiding prey.

5.6 Slow Linear Prey

As reported by Haynes in [6], the slow linear prey is hard to catch with a greedy strategy, as the predators tend to group behind the prey due to the lack of locality of movement. For the evolved team, capture performance is very good. Figure 10 shows fast convergence.

5.7 Fast Linear Prey

Surprisingly, the fast linear prey is very easy to catch for both the greedy and the evolved team. The reason is that the prey is much faster than the predators, effectively scanning

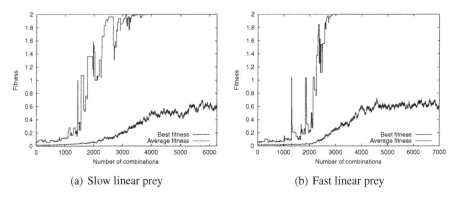

(a) Slow linear prey   (b) Fast linear prey

Fig. 10. Evolution diagrams for the linear prey

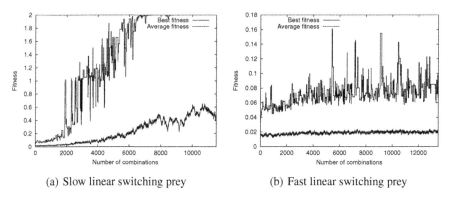

(a) Slow linear switching prey   (b) Fast linear switching prey

Fig. 11. Evolution diagrams for the linear switching prey

a single row or a single column of the grid with high speed. When a predator enters this row or column, there is a large probability that the prey blocks, due to its high frequency, effectively degenerating to a still prey.

5.8 Slow Linear Switching Prey

The slow linear switching prey was designed to be more difficult to catch than the linear prey. Instead of blocking, it will randomly change its direction when blocked by a predator, otherwise behaving like a linear prey. Figure 6 shows very good performance for the evolved team, but unsatisfying performance for the greedy team. Figure 11 shows that the problem is considerably harder than the linear prey as convergence is slower.

5.9 Fast Linear Switching Prey

Given the results on the slow linear switching prey, we expect it to be nearly impossible to catch the fast linear switching prey. This expectation is backed up by the results in figure 6.

6 Conclusion

We introduced an asynchronous version of PNP. Former results from the synchronous PNP seem to be valid in the asynchronous version when considered with some care. The random and the still prey are easy to catch, while the linear prey is harder for the greedy predators. Large speed differences between predators and prey and especially much faster prey have not been considered before. One result is that high speed is not always advantageous as it turnes out in the case of the fast linear prey. Explicitly coordinating agents can excel at problems where greedy strategies fail, as exemplified by the cases of the slow linear prey and the slow linear switching prey. Genetic programming turned out to successfully evolve a team of predators that is able to catch the prey at a quite satisfying rate at all cases, besides the fast linear switching prey. One problem with genetic programming is that there are many parameters that could be used to tune it for the specific problem at hand: the tournament size, the number of rules per predator, or the set of basic functions, to name few. The kinds of tasks, agents could assign to each other are predefined in an ad-hoc manner. In the future, we would like to see how the task language could also be evolved alongside the task handling inside of the agents. Furthermore, we would like to analyze the evolved rules more closely.

References

1. R. Axelrod. *The Evolution of Strategies in the Iterated Prisoner's Dilemma.* in Lawrence Davis (ed.), Genetic Algorithms and Simulated Annealing, Morgan Kaufman, 1987
2. M. Benda, V. Jagannathan, R. Dodhiawalla. *On optimal cooperation of knowledge sources.* Technical Report BCS-G2010-28, Boeing AI Center, Boeing Computer Services, Bellevue, WA, August 1985
3. T. Haynes, S.Sen. *Learning Cases to Resolve Conflicts and Improve Group Behavior.* Working Notes of the AAAI-96 Workshop on Agent Modeling, 1996
4. T. Haynes, S. Sen. *Evolving Behavioral Strategies in Predators and Prey.* IJCAI-95 Workshop on Adaptation and Learning in Multiagent Systems, 1996
5. T. Haynes, S. Sen. *Cooperation of the Fittest.* Late Breaking Papers at the Genetic Programming 1996 Conference, Stanford University July 28-31, 1996
6. T.Haynes, S. Sen. *The Evolution of Multiagent Coordination Strategies.* Adaptive Behavior, 1997
7. T. Haynes, R. Wainwright, S. Sen, D. Schoenefeld. *Strongly Typed Genetic Programming in Evolving Cooperation Strategies.* Genetic Algorithms: Proceedings of the Sixth International Conference (ICGA95), 1995
8. T. Haynes, R. Wainwright, S. Sen. *Evolving Cooperation Strategies.* Proceedings of the First International Conference on Multi–Agent Systems, MIT Press, San Francisco, CA, 1995
9. K. Jim, C. L. Giles. *Talking Helps: Evolving Communicating Agents for the Predator-Prey Pursuit Problem.* Artificial Life, 6(3), pp. 237-254, 2000
10. R. Korf. *A Simple Solution to Pursuit Games.* Proceedings of the 2nd International Workshop on Distributed Artificial Intelligence, Glen Arbor, Mich., Feb. 1992
11. J. R. Koza. *Genetic Programming: On the Programming of Computers by Natural Selection.* MIT Press, Cambridge, MA, 1992
12. S. Luke, L. Spector. *Evolving Teamwork and Coordination with Genetic Programming.* Genetic Programming 1996: Proceedings of the First Annual Conference, MIT Press, Stanford University, CA, USA, 1996, pages 150–156
13. P. Maes, R. Brooks. *Learning to Coordinate Behaviors.* National Conference on Artificial Intelligence, 1990
14. S. Mandl, R. Bimazubute, H. Stoyan. *Mobile Intelligent Agents in Erlang.* Fourth International ICSC Symposium on Engineering of Intelligent Systems (EIS), 2004

Towards Models of Incomplete and Uncertain Knowledge of Collaborators' Internal Resources

Christian Guttmann and Ingrid Zukerman

School of Computer Science and Software Engineering
Monash University
VICTORIA, 3800, Australia
{xtg,ingrid}@csse.monash.edu.au

Abstract. Collaboration plays a critical role when a group is striving for goals which are difficult or impossible to achieve by an individual. Knowledge about collaborators' contributions to a task is an important factor when establishing collaboration, in particular when a decision determines the assignment of activities to members of the group. Although there are several systems that implement collaboration, one important problem has not yet received much attention – determining the effect of incomplete and uncertain knowledge of collaborators' internal resources (i.e. capabilities and knowledge) on the outcomes of the collaboration. We approach this problem by building models of internal resources of individuals and groups of collaborators. These models enable a system to estimate collaborators' contributions to the task. We then assess the effect of model accuracy on task performance. An empirical evaluation is performed in order to validate this approach.

1 Introduction

Humans tend to form collaborative groups to achieve goals that are difficult or impossible to attain by individuals. Most people are naturally endowed with capabilities in order to approach the solution of a problem collectively. However, the incorporation of collaboration into complex computational systems (hereafter called agents) is a challenging problem (corroborated by Cohen & Levesque [1991], Kinny *et al.* [1992], Grosz & Kraus [1996], Panzarasa *et al.* [2002]). The interest in the solution of this problem has increased due to technologies such as peer-to-peer and wireless mobile computing (e.g. Ad-Hoc networking, Digital Home, computational grid) and large-scale traffic simulations (e.g. car, train and air traffic).

One important aspect of collaboration in networks of agents or Multi-Agent Systems (MAS) is knowledge about collaborators when activities are planned or performed together. For example, different features of collaborators are modelled in order to achieve flexible team behaviour in military domains [Tambe 1997], establish domain-dependent conventions among agents [Alterman & Garland 2001], determine behaviour based on collaborators' utility-functions [Gmytrasiewicz & Durfee 2001], or predict behaviour of "soccer-agents" under commonly-known domain dynamics [Stone *et al.* 2000] or commonly-known action policies [Kok & Vlassis 2001]. Denzinger &

G. Lindemann et al. (Eds.): MATES 2004, LNAI 3187, pp. 58–72, 2004.

Kordt [2000] describe how modelled strategies of agents facilitate on-line learning processes.

An implicit assumption made by these systems is that each agent possesses (or can easily derive) complete and accurate models of its collaborators' capabilities, thus simplifying collaboration scenarios. However, this assumption does not always hold, e.g. when agents in established groups are coping with idiosyncratic capabilities of new agents. In this paper, we consider how the relaxation of this assumption affects task performance. To this effect we build models of collaborators' capabilities (employed by each agent) and perform empirical studies that assess the impact of model accuracy. Our approach is particularly applicable for agents which have to use these models in a decentralized fashion, viz. when there is no overarching central administration that can supervise the overall collaboration due to technical or computational restrictions.

The central issue addressed in this paper is how the accuracy of these models influences the task performance of decentralized agents (where the evaluation of the task performance is based on the extent of the goal achievement, Section 2.1.2). A major consideration in our approach is the reduction of overhead costs (i.e. transaction and resource costs) resulting from the introduction of these models. For our empirical study, we focus on operating parameters such as the memory boundedness of individual agents and the model-updating and group-decision-making processes.

To illustrate the motivation of this approach let us consider an example where several parties have decided to collaborate and merge their system resources in order to achieve a joint goal, e.g. when several distinct groups of mobile devices (i.e. the devices in each group are made by the same company and the devices in different groups are made by different companies) intend to establish a decentralized telecommunication infrastructure. Assume that all agents have a common language, common interaction protocols, a joint intention and a shared ontology of the activities in this domain, but that the capabilities of each mobile device in each group differ significantly and are not known to the other groups of mobile devices prior to the collaboration. Thus, an agent that collaborates well with mobile devices of its own kind may encounter problems when collaborating with agents in other groups. In order to support this collaboration, a structure is needed which enables the distinct groups of agents from different companies to collaborate with each other. Hence, we propose to build models of internal resources of other devices, and integrate these models into each agent in a team.

The remainder of this paper is structured as follows. In Section 2, we present our notation for collaborative scenarios, which includes the tasks, agents and algorithms, and in particular the agents' internal resources and the models of collaborators' resources. Additionally, we define the overhead costs for these scenarios. In Section 3, we describe our empirical evaluation, including the description of a Surf Rescue (SR) scenario, the procedure for simulating agent collaboration, the definition of various simulation parameters, and the results and analysis of several simulations. In Section 4, we present our conclusions and outline future work.

2   Notation

We first describe terms and specifications which provide the basis for an implementation and formal analysis of collaborative agents which perform tasks together. Second, we provide the definitions for the overhead costs that can arise in collaboration scenarios due to the use of models of collaborators.

Groups of agents are referred to in uppercase letters (e.g. A), individual agents are referred to in uppercase letters with an index (e.g. A_i), and subgroups of agents in uppercase letters with tilde and an index (e.g. $\tilde{A}_j$). Activities are referred to in lowercase letters with an index (e.g. a_i) and parameters of activities are referred to in Greek letters with an index (e.g. α_i). Cardinalities of sets are referred to in lowercase letters (e.g. m, n, q, r, s).

2.1 Collaborative Scenario S

Definition 1. *A collaborative scenario S is denoted by a tuple with four elements, $S = < E, T_E, A, P_A >$, where E corresponds to an environmental state space under which a task specification T_E is defined, A denotes a group of agents that is assigned to a task T_E, and P_A is a policy which assists the agents in A to make decisions together.*

A collaborative scenario assumes that agents share a joint intention, use the same language and ontology to communicate, and are selfless[1]. We define the elements of a collaborative scenario S throughout the remainder of this section.

2.1.1 Environmental State Space E

Definition 2. *An environment E is a state space described by first-order logic facts and predicates (i.e. properties of facts and relations among them). A state $e \in E$ describes the current status of these facts and predicates at a particular step in the collaboration.*

For example, E consists of a set of locations $L = \{loc_1, ..., loc_k\}$ and a set of objects $O = \{obj_1, ..., obj_l\}$. Each location is described by static coordinates, e.g. $loc_i = (x_i, y_i, z_i)$. Each object is described by features such as location $(loc(obj_i) = loc_i)$, weight $(weight(obj_i))$ and size $(size(obj_i))$. Consider a "table environment" which consists of two locations: $house_a$ and $house_b$ and two objects: a *car* and a *table*. An example for a state e is $e = (at(car, house_a) \land in(table, car))$, viz. the *car* is located at $house_a$ and the *table* is located in the *car*.

2.1.2 Task T_E

Definition 3. *A task T_E is a tuple with two elements $T_E = < EC_T, MS_T >$, where*
1. *EC_T denotes a set of Evaluation Criteria of a Task $EC_T = \{ec_1, ..., ec_n\}$, where $n = |EC_T|$. Each element in EC_T is a function $ec_i : e \mapsto [0..1]$ which maps an environmental state e to a real number between 0 and 1, where 0 corresponds to the worst possible performance and 1 corresponds to the optimal performance.*
2. *MS_T denotes a set of MileStones of a Task $MS_T = \{ms_0, ..., ms_m\}$, where $m = |MS_T|$, ms_0 represents the initial state (and is satisfied by default) and ms_m represents the goal state of the task. Each milestone has to hold once in order to reach the goal state and thus accomplish the task. The elements in MS_T are partially ordered.*

---

[1] Selflessness is understood as an antonym for selfishness, viz. an agent that is selfless prioritizes the utility of the group rather than its own utility.

For instance, in the "table scenario" the task is to move the *table* from $house_a$ to $house_b$ by using the *car*. To evaluate how well the task is performed we denote two evaluation criteria. First, the goal of this task should be achieved quickly, i.e. the time to the completion of the milestones (including the initial and goal state) ought to be minimal (expressed by a function min_{time}). Second, the *table* should not be damaged during the performance of the task, i.e. the quality of the completed milestones and the completed goal of the task ought to be maximal (expressed by a function max_{qual}). These two elements are represented as follows:

$$EC_T = \{ec_1, ec_2\} = \{min_{time}, max_{qual}\}$$

The elements of EC_T provide the units which may be needed in further calculations, e.g. min_{time} includes the unit *seconds*.

A plan to achieve milestones is generated by a planner. The table scenario has four milestones, which are described as follows:

$$MS_T = \{ms_0, ms_1, ms_2, ms_3\}, \text{ where}$$

- $ms_0 = (in(table, house_a) \wedge at(car, house_a))$,
- $ms_1 = (in(table, car) \wedge at(car, house_a))$,
- $ms_2 = (in(table, car) \wedge at(car, house_b))$,
- $ms_3 = (in(table, house_b))$.

The task specification T_E (EC_T and MS_T respectively) is known and accessible to all agents in the group during the collaboration.

2.1.3   Agents and Groups of Agents A

Definition 4. *A selfless group (or team) of agents A is denoted by a set $A = \{A_1, ..., A_q\}$ with $q = |A|$, where $A_i \in A : i \in \{1, ..., q\}$ is an individual agent and $\widetilde{A}_j \subseteq A : j \in \{1, ..., r\}$ denotes a subset of A (with $r = |\wp(A)|$ being the cardinality of the powerset of A).*

A group of agents A is assigned to a task T_E, if each agent in the group acts in order to optimize functions $ec_i \in EC_T$, and if the agents perform activities in order to achieve $ms_j \in MS_T$.

We consider two main factors that determine the performance of an activity: Internal Resources (IR) of agents and the Context Parameter (CP). CP depends on the activity. In the table scenario, CP is determined by features of the objects that are manipulated (e.g. the weight and size of the *table*) and other contextual features (e.g. the *table* is lifted for a certain distance). IR are not known to other agents in many collaboration scenarios and thus can be estimated by Models (M).

Definition 5. *Let A_i be an agent in set A, so that $A_i = <IR_{A_i}, M_{A_i}, RA_{A_i}>$, where*

1. *IR_{A_i} denotes a measure of the influence of agent A_i's Internal Resources (e.g. capabilities, such as skills or knowledge) on the performance of activities. Formally, we say that*
   - *$IR_{A_i} : A_i \rightarrow \{act_k : k \in \{1, ..., s\}\}$ is a set of activity tuples act_k, where s denotes the number of activities that agents can perform.*
   - *$act_k = (a_k, \alpha_1(a_k), ..., \alpha_n(a_k))$ is a tuple with $n + 1$ elements for each activity a_k, where each α_j is based on $ec_j \in EC_T$ for $j = \{1, ..., n\}$ (with $n = |EC_T|$).*

- $\alpha_l(a_k) : (l, a_k) \to [0..1]$ represents a "real" internal factor which influences the performance of an activity a_k performed by A_i, where 0 represents the lowest possible performance and 1 represents the highest possible performance.

2. M_{A_i} denotes agent A_i's Models measuring the influence of subgroups $\widetilde{A}_j$ on the performance of activities. Formally, we say that

  - M_{A_i} is a family of models $\{M_{A_i}(\widetilde{A}_j) : j = \{1, ..., r\}\}$ [2].
  - Each model $M_{A_i}(\widetilde{A}_j) : \{A_i, \widetilde{A}_j\} \to \{\widehat{act}_k : k \in \{1, ..., s\}\}$ is a set of activity tuples $\widehat{act}_k$, where s denotes the number of activities that agents can perform.
  - $\widehat{act}_k = (a_k, \widehat{\alpha_1}(a_k), ..., \widehat{\alpha_n}(a_k))$ is a tuple with $n + 1$ elements for each activity a_j, where each $\widehat{\alpha}_j$ is based on $ec_j \in EC_T$ for $j=\{1,...,n\}$ (with $n = |EC_T|$).
  - $\widehat{\alpha_l}(a_k) : (l, a_k) \to [0..1]$ represents an "estimated" internal factor, which agent A_i believes influences the performance of activity a_k performed by the subgroup $\widetilde{A}_j$, where 0 represents the lowest possible performance and 1 represents the highest possible performance.
  - If a model of $\widetilde{A}_j$ is not known to A_i then $M_{A_i}(\widetilde{A}_j) = \emptyset$.

3. RA_{A_i} is the Reasoning Apparatus of A_i which consists of a set of algorithms that enable an agent to act in an environment and to interact with collaborators. The main algorithm is illustrated in Figure 1. Its inputs are: an environment E, a task T, models M_{A_i}, and a policy P_A. The output is a set of updated models UM in the same form as M_{A_i}. The side effects of this algorithm are the actual actions performed by the agents chosen to perform a task.

We first illustrate internal resources IR_{A_i} and models of internal resources M_{A_i}, and towards the end of this section we explain the algorithms in RA_{A_i}.

Let us return to the table scenario, where time and quality are defined as the evaluation criteria. According to Definition 5, IR_{A_i} and M_{A_i} are based on these criteria ($n = 2$). Assume that two agents A_1 and A_2 perform the "table task" and both agents are able to perform two activities: lift (which moves a "liftable" object from one location to another location) and drive (which moves a "driveable" object from one location to another location). The internal resources for A_1 are as follows:

$IR_{A_1} = \{(a_1, \alpha_{time}(a_1), \alpha_{qual}(a_1)), (a_2, \alpha_{time}(a_2), \alpha_{qual}(a_2))\}$, where

- $a_1 = lift$, $\alpha_{time}(a_1) = 0.5, \alpha_{qual}(a_1) = 0.5$,
- $a_2 = drive, \alpha_{time}(a_2) = 0.4, \alpha_{qual}(a_2) = 0.7$.

and for A_2:

$IR_{A_2} = \{(a_1, \alpha_{time}(a_1), \alpha_{qual}(a_1)), (a_2, \alpha_{time}(a_2), \alpha_{qual}(a_2))\}$, where

- $a_1 = lift$, $\alpha_{time}(a_1) = 0.3, \alpha_{qual}(a_1) = 0.4$,
- $a_2 = drive, \alpha_{time}(a_2) = 0.6, \alpha_{qual}(a_2) = 0.5$.

For instance, the activity tuple act_1 of agent A_1 has two real internal factors which influence the performance of the activity lift, i.e. 0.5 is the internal factor for the performance in relation to time, and 0.4 is the internal factor for the performance in relation to quality. According to IR_{A_1} and IR_{A_2}, A_2 lifts an obj_i faster than A_1 (i.e. $0.5 > 0.3$), and the

---

[2] If agents have unlimited memory, they could maintain $2^q - 1$ models (excluding a model about "no agent"), where q is the number of agents. However, in most collaboration scenarios, agents have limited memory and collaborate without maintaining an exhaustive number of models.

outcome of A_1's lift is of better quality than that of A_2's lift (i.e. $0.5 > 0.4$), while CP stays constant.

However, IR_{A_1} and IR_{A_2} are not known or accessible to A_1 and A_2. Therefore, the internal resources of A_1 and A_2 are estimated through models M. Set M_{A_1} for A_1 is as follows:

$M_{A_1} = \{M_{A_1}(\widetilde{A_1} = A_1), M_{A_1}(\widetilde{A_2} = A_2), M_{A_1}(\widetilde{A_3} = (A_1, A_2))\}$, where
  · $M_{A_1}(A_1) = \{(lift, 0.3, 0.2), (drive, 0.3, 0.5)\}$,
  · $M_{A_1}(A_2) = \{(lift, 0.5, 0.7), (drive, 0.6, 0.1)\}$,
  · $M_{A_1}((A_1, A_2)) = \{(lift, 0.8, 0.9), (drive, \lambda, \lambda)\}$.

and the model set M_{A_2} for A_2 is as follows:

$M_{A_2} = \{M_{A_2}(\widetilde{A_1} = A_1), M_{A_2}(\widetilde{A_2} = A_2), M_{A_2}(\widetilde{A_3} = (A_1, A_2))\}$, where
  · $M_{A_2}(A_2) = \{(lift, 0.2, 0.4), (drive, 0.1, 0.1)\}$,
  · $M_{A_2}(A_1) = \{(lift, 0.3, 0.2), (drive, 0.3, 0.4)\}$,
  · $M_{A_2}((A_1, A_2)) = \{(lift, 0.5, 0.6), (drive, \lambda, \lambda)\}$.

λ corresponds to a parameter of an activity which cannot be performed by two agents. Activity parameters for models with $|\widetilde{A_j}| > 1$ are determined by combining models of individual agents by using specific functions for different activities, e.g. $M_{A_2}(A_1, A_2)$ is a model where the parameters of the *lift* activity of A_1 and A_2 respectively are added.

An agent can only access its own models (it can not access the models maintained by other agents), e.g. M_{A_1} is accessible only by A_1. These models allow each agent to estimate the potential contribution of individuals or subgroups of the team. The estimated time and quality for each activity is calculated by using the parameters $\widehat{\alpha}$ and the Context Parameter (CP). For instance, A_1 calculates the time that it would take A_2 to *lift* the *table* based on $\widehat{\alpha}_{time}(lift) \in M_{A_1}(A_2)$ and the weight and size of the *table*. In this example, we multiply these factors: $time(lift, \widehat{\alpha}_{time}, table) = \widehat{\alpha}_{time}(lift) * CP = 0.5 seconds * 500 = 250 seconds$.

Let us continue with the illustration of the algorithms in RA_{A_i} as described in Definition 5. The main algorithm (Figure 1) uses the following variables:

 – PROPOSAL is a tuple that specifies an action a_i that shall be carried out by agent(s) $\widetilde{A_j}$ to reach ms_i according to EC_T. In the table scenario, EC_T comprises time and quality, and proposals have the form (milestone ms_i, action a_i, agent(s) $\widetilde{A_j}$, time, quality),
 – PROPOSAL_LIST is a list of proposals communicated by agents,
 – UM is an updated model of the same form as a model in $M_{A_i}(\widetilde{A_j})$.

In line 5 of Figure 1, the subroutine *generate_best_proposal(m_i, M_{A_i})* provides a proposal which matches one or more agents with an activity, e.g. $(A_1, lift(table))$. A_i first calculates the time and quality of the performance for each activity by using the estimated internal parameters $\widehat{\alpha} \in M_{A_i}$ and CP. A_i orders possible proposals according to the functions $ec_i \in EC_T$ and then selects the best proposal.

Once an individual agent has calculated a proposal, it is communicated to other agents (line 6 in Figure 1). This is done by broadcasting it to every collaborator. The proposal from collaborators ($\forall A_j : j \neq i$) and the proposal made by A_i are stored in the PROPOSAL_LIST.

A joint decision is reached by choosing one of the proposals made by the agents. This is done by means of an election mechanism or policy P_A (line 8 in Figure 1). Agents commit to a joint policy before they join a collaboration with other agents (similar to voters in a democracy). The concept of a policy P_A is discussed below.

Other routines not fully described in this paper deal with the task performance and the model updating process (which is also understood as a learning process). Briefly, the performance of the activities are in accordance with the entries in PROPOSAL_LIST. For instance, if A_i is in the PROPOSAL_LIST, it may be chosen to reach ms_i. The calculation of the time and quality of the real performance uses IR of collaborators (instead of using the models M for the proposals). The real performance is then compared to the proposed performance and is used as a basis for updating the existing models. Currently, we employ a simple updating process, but we are considering other learning algorithms for the future [Garrido *et al.* 1998].

2.1.4   Policy P_A

Each member of the group A can have a different proposal, because each agent has different models. However, agents should follow only one proposal at a time in order to reach coordinated behaviour. Hence, agents have to collectively decide on one proposal. A sensible way to solve this problem is to introduce a joint policy P_A (or election mechanism) which is provided to each agent that joins a collaborative scenario S. Formally, a joint policy P_A is denoted as:

Definition 6. *A joint policy P_A describes an election mechanism which incorporates the proposals made by several agents in a democratic fashion (by incorporating the opinion of each individual). The outcome of an election is a collective choice for one proposal.*

Like a human voter in a democratic election, an agent is expected to accept and commit to the outcome of this policy, which implies that an agent may relinquish the exertion of its own proposal in order to follow the proposal resulting from such an election.

In this paper, we consider an *optimistic policy* to determine a collectively agreed proposal, i.e. agents choose the most optimistic proposal promising the best time and

---

1. INPUT: environment E, task T_E, models M_{A_i}, policy P_A
2. OUTPUT: updated models UM
3. PROPOSAL, PROPOSAL_LIST, UM ← ∅
4. **for** each $m_i \in MS$ **do**
5.   PROPOSAL ← *generate_best_proposal* (m_i, M_{A_i})
6.   *communicate_proposal* (PROPOSAL)
7.   PROPOSAL_LIST ← COMMUNICATED_PROPOSALS
8.   BEST_PROPOSAL ← *choose_best_proposal* (PROPOSAL_LIST,P_A)
9. **end for**
10. UM ← *observe_real_performance*(PROPOSAL_LIST)
11. return UM

Fig. 1. Pseudocode of find_best_proposal algorithm.

best quality of performance. For example, if agent A_1 proposes that the time to lift the *table* from *house_a* to the *car* takes A_2 100 seconds, and agent A_2 proposes that the time to perform this activity takes A_1 80 seconds, then the optimistic policy determines that A_2 should perform the activity. Due to the prior agreement to comply with the most optimistic proposal, agent A_2 will lift the the *table*, and A_1 will stay idle. A contravention of this policy would result in uncoordinated collective behaviour.

In the future, we propose to investigate other forms of joint policies. For instance, policies based on *hierarchy* (i.e. each proposal is weighed according to a dominance structure), *candidate voting* (i.e. agents choose the agent that is preferred by most agents), or *experience* (i.e. each proposal is weighed according to the experience level of each agent). These mechanisms enable agents to determine an appropriate agent(s)-action match based on proposals of members of the group, and facilitates the coordination of agents while incurring limited overhead costs. However, it has yet to be shown which mechanisms are the most effective.

It is worth mentioning that an aggregation policy may be less important if agents negotiate with each other. Such a negotiation among agents may reveal a better agent for an activity. However, it generates additional communication among agents (increasing overhead costs). In addition, agents must possess capabilities to negotiate, which is a research field in its own right [Chu-Carroll & Carberry 2000, Li *et al.* 2003, Rahwan *et al.* to appear].

2.2 Overhead Costs

We consider two types of overhead costs: resource and transaction. *Resource costs* are the costs in regards to the available memory for each agent. *Transaction costs* are incurred by agents when communicating to arrive at a joint proposal. We consider the following transaction costs:

- inference costs are the costs for the agents to generate a proposal.
- communication costs are the costs for the agents to communicate proposals.
- aggregation costs correspond to the effort to form a consensus.
- update costs are the costs of updating models about each other.

One could interpret those costs in terms of computational resources (for inference, aggregation and update costs), storage resources (for memory costs), and network infrastructure and traffic (for communication costs).

In the empirical study performed in the next section, the cost of communicating is the only factor that contributes to the transaction (and overhead) costs.

3 Empirical Study

In order to evaluate agent collaboration, we implement a Surf Rescue (SR) scenario where agents are selfless, have a joint intention, and share resources to perform a rescue task together. We run several simulations with varying parameters where agents rescue a person in distress and assign a lifesaver based on models of the capabilities of lifesavers.

3.1 Surf Rescue Scenario

Imagine an SR environment where lifesavers rescue a person in distress. All lifesavers (agents $A = \{A_1, A_2, A_3, A_4, A_5\}$) are located on the shore (*shore*) and the Distressed

Person (DP) is located in the ocean (*ocean*). The task is to rescue the person in the shortest time possible. The problem is to assign the best lifesaver to perform this task based on models that each lifesaver has about the other lifesavers. The SR scenario is shown in Figure 2.

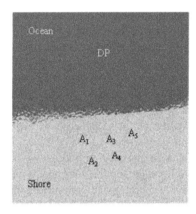

Fig. 2. A typical Surf Rescue scenario.

Each agent generates a proposal which specifies the agent that should swim and rescue the *DP*. The group decision procedure is based on an optimistic policy, which means that the proposed lifesaver with the most promising performance will be chosen.

EC_T consists of criteria for measuring the task performance of agents. In this scenario, EC_T consists only of minimizing the time required to complete a task (i.e. min_{time}). EC_T is given by

$$EC_T = \{min_{time}\}$$

The start state and goal state in this scenario is given by

$MS_T = \{ms_0, ms_1\}$, where
- $ms_0 = (at(loc(A), beach)) \wedge (at(loc(DP), ocean)))$,
- $ms_1 = (at(loc(DP), beach)) \wedge (at(loc(A), beach))$.

In other words, ms_0 represents the initial state, where the group of agents is located on the beach and the distressed person is in the ocean, and ms_1 represents the goal state, where the *DP* is brought back to the beach.

EC_T and MS_T are accessible to the agents which perform the task. Although all members in *A* independently possess the capabilities to perform an activity that will lead from ms_0 to ms_1, the purpose of this collaboration is to find the best agent(s)-activity match based on each agent's models of other agents.

3.2   Methodology

The parameters α (of the internal resources IR) and $\widehat{\alpha}$ (of the model sets M) are initialized with random real numbers between 0 and 1 for each lifesaver (IR is initialized once for the whole series of simulations, and M is initialized for each simulation). The activity that is considered in the rescue scenario is to *swim and rescue*. Models are about individual lifesavers (i.e. $|\widetilde{A}_j| = 1$) rather than several lifesavers together. We investigate several conditions of the collaboration scenario, which are described by the following parameters (expressed in percentages):

- Memory Boundedness (MB) determines the memory that is available to all agents, where 0% corresponds to no memory, and 100% to unlimited memory to accommodate all the models for the agents. For example, MB =80% means that on average 20% of the models are randomly discarded by each agent.
- Update Discrimination (UD) determines the number of agents that update (or learn) their models about other agents, where 0% corresponds to no agents updating their models, and 100% corresponds to all agents updating their models.
- Decision Discrimination (DD) determines the number of agents that make a proposal, where 0% indicates that no agents make a proposal, and 100% indicates that all agents make a proposal.
- M-IR Relationship (MIRR) determines the degree to which agents' real capabilities are underestimated at the initialization of M, where 0% corresponds to a full underestimation of agents' capabilities, and 100% corresponds to an estimation of agents' capabilities which matches real capabilities[3]. MIRR provides an upper bound for model initialization, e.g. if MIRR is 50% the models are randomized between 0% and 50% at the real capabilities.

The agents which are affected by changing these parameters are chosen randomly.

Restrictions of an agent's decision-making apparatus have been considered by Walker [1996] in collaborative task scenarios where the communicative choice of agents is influenced by inferential or attentional resource limitations. Rubinstein [1998] has investigated such restrictions on decision-making in a game-theoretic context. For example, he argues that agents have limited computational and memory resources, and therefore are not able to reason about all the alternatives in a decision problem.

We construct several collaboration scenarios from different settings of these parameters. We first define two benchmark scenarios:

- a "Lower Bound (LB)" scenario defines agents which do not maintain a model of their collaborators' resources, and thus do not communicate proposals and do not update models.
- an "Upper Bound (UB)" scenario consists of agents which have an accurate model of each lifesavers' capabilities in relation to EC_T, i.e. $IR_{A_i} = M_{A_i}(A_i)$, and an accurate $M_{A_i}(\widetilde{A}_j)$.

In an LB scenario, the rescue is conducted by an agent which has been chosen randomly from the group. The UB scenario is consistent with the traditional assumption of MAS where agents have accurate knowledge about the internal resources of other agents prior to the collaboration, which results in an optimal assignment of agents to an activity. In the UB scenario, agents do not update their models or communicate proposals, because the same models are provided to all agents.

In a "Default" scenario, all parameters are set to 100%, i.e. all agents have enough memory to maintain all models (MB =100%), communicate proposals (DD =100%),

---

[3] In the future, we will also consider overestimation of agents' capabilities.

update their models (UD =100%), and initialize models according to the real capabilities (MIRR =100%). The main difference between the default scenario and the UB scenario is that models are initialized with random values as opposed to values that reflect accurate and complete knowledge of collaborators. Additionally, we define the scenarios *Scen(SimParam)*, where *SimParam* $\in \{MB, UD, DD, MIRR\}$ and it varies from 0% to 100%, while the other parameters stay at a constant 100%.

In order to investigate how the combination of simulation parameters affects task performance, we construct two additional scenarios from two pairs of simulation parameters: MB and DD, and UD and DD. For the pair MB and DD we consider the scenario *Scen(MB,DD)* where the MB parameter varies from 0% to 100%, while the DD parameter varies from 0%,25%,50%,75% and 100%, and the scenario *Scen(DD,MB)* where this relationship is reversed. The same scenario definition applies for the pair UD and DD resulting in two scenarios: *Scen(UD,DD)* and *Scen(DD,UD)*.

To illustrate the effect of model accuracy on task performance, we average the result of a series of simulations for a particular *SimParam* with different models, which are depicted in the figures below. We obtained the most representative results by running 1000 simulations for each value of *SimParam*[4].

A better performance corresponds to a faster rescue, i.e. the measure of performance (depicted in the figures below) is an inverted function of time for a rescue. The transaction cost is measured by the total number of communicated proposals until convergence is reached. Initially, different lifesavers may be chosen for a rescue task due to the discrepancy between the models maintained by the agents and the internal resources. After each rescue, the agents update their models. The same rescue task is repeated until the agents choose the same lifesaver twice consecutively. The number of rescue tasks that is required to converge to one lifesaver determines the number of proposals that are communicated.

3.3   Results

Figure 3 plots task performance as a function of the different parameters in the scenarios, and Figure 4 plots the transaction costs against these parameters. Overall, the task performance is worse in simulations where agents have no models of agents in the group compared to simulations where agents maintain such models. The influence of model accuracy on the task performance differs in relation to each simulation parameter.

As expected, the results of the LB and UB scenarios correspond to the worst and best performance respectively, which are used as a benchmark for comparison with other scenarios. For instance, the agents in the Default scenario exhibit a constant task performance which is close to the performance of the UB scenario. We found that the task performance of agents appears to increase logarithmically as the available memory increases for each agent (MB scenario). In the UD scenario, the performance appears to increase polynomially as the agents' ability to update models increases. There is a quasi-linear increase in performance when more agents make proposals (DD scenario),

---

[4] We varied the number of simulations until the data about performance and transaction costs showed stable and continuous patterns (Section 3.3).

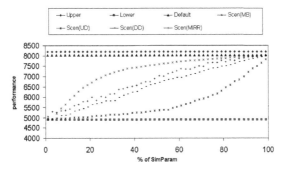

Fig. 3. Average task performance for 1000 simulations plotted against the simulation parameters from several scenarios.

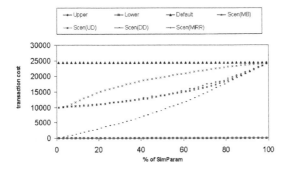

Fig. 4. Average transaction cost for 1000 simulations plotted against the simulation parameters from several scenarios.

which is similar to the results obtained when agents' estimation of other agents become more accurate (MIRR scenario).

As indicated above, we consider only communication cost as the transaction cost for different scenarios (depicted in Figure 4). The transaction costs are the highest for the Default scenario. In the DD and the MIRR scenarios, the transaction costs increase proportionally to the increase of the simulation parameters. The transaction cost in the UD scenario increases slowly compared to the transaction costs in scenario MB. There is no transaction cost in the benchmark scenarios LB and UB, because no models are communicated (the chart lines of the LB and UB scenario overlap in Figure 4).

Figures 5 and 6 demonstrate the impact of the varying DD parameter on five different UD parameters and vice versa for *Scen(UD,DD)*. Figure 5 shows that restricting the updating of models to 0% and 25% cancels the effect of the increasing percentage of agents that make proposals. In the reverse scenario (Figure 6), the four values of the DD parameter between 25% and 100% have little impact on the performance until approximately 75% of agents are able to update their models.

Figures 7 and 8 demonstrate the impact of the varying DD parameter on five different MB parameters and vice versa for *Scen(MB,DD)*. Figure 7 shows that varying the memory of agents between 50%, 75% and 100% has little impact as the percent-

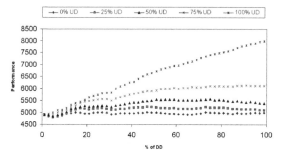

Fig. 5. The impact on the performance of the interaction between the increasing DD parameter and the five sets of UD parameters.

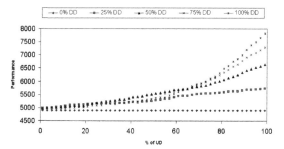

Fig. 6. The impact on the performance of the interaction between the increasing UD parameter and the five sets of DD parameters.

age of agents that are making proposals increases. In the reverse scenario (Figure 8), the performance for each value of DD increases proportionally to the percentage of the memory being used to store models.

4   Conclusion and Future Work

We have offered a notation for collaborative scenarios, which includes models of inaccurate and incomplete capabilities of collaborators (for each agent). This notation provided the basis for an empirical study. We demonstrated the effect of model accuracy on task performance of agents with varying operating parameters in regards to memory and decision-making processes. The findings of the empirical study support our thesis that agents improve their overall performance when employing these models, even under constrained scenario settings (e.g. limited memory and restricted decision-making). The evaluation of our study also included the cost of communication (in terms of the communicated proposals) resulting from the introduction of these models. Such costs may be considered in large-scale MAS, for example, when trying to avoid network congestion.

While our current framework offers a method to improve task performance, we are planning to extend this framework as follows. We propose to consider additional overhead costs in our empirical studies, such as memory costs, and inference and updating

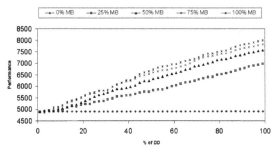

Fig. 7. The impact on the performance of the interaction between the increasing DD parameter and the five sets of MB parameters.

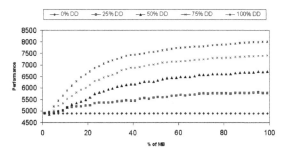

Fig. 8. The impact on the performance of the interaction between the increasing MB parameter and the five sets of DD parameters.

costs, in order to obtain more meaningful results. We also intend to consider different mechanisms for updating models from observed performance, and to evaluate the various aggregation policies mentioned in Section 2.1.4. Additionally, while we have assumed a domain with few uncertainties, more realistic scenarios exhibit probabilistic features, e.g. distorted observation of the real performance of other agents, unreliability of communication channels, or non-determinism of the outcome of activities. Probabilistic domain features may require an extension of the current framework.

Acknowledgements

This research was supported in part by Linkage Grant LP0347470 from the Australian Research Council, and by an endowment from Hewlett Packard. The authors would like to thank Michael Georgeff, Ian Peake, Yuval Marom, Bernard Burg, Iyad Rahwan, and Heinz Schmidt for helpful discussions. Additionally, we would like to thank the reviewers for valuable feedback.

References

ALTERMAN, RICHARD, & GARLAND, ANDREW. 2001. Convention in Joint Activity. *Cognitive Science*, **25**(4), 611–657.

CHU-CARROLL, JENNIFER, & CARBERRY, SANDRA. 2000. Conflict Resolution in Collaborative Planning Dialogues. *International Journal of Human Computer Studies*, **53**(6), 969–1015.

COHEN, P. R., & LEVESQUE, H. J. 1991. *Teamwork*. Tech. rept. 504. Stanford University, Menlo Park, CA.

DENZINGER, JOERG, & KORDT, MICHAEL. 2000. Evolutionary On-line Learning of Cooperative Behavior with Situation-Action-Pairs. *In: Proceedings of the International Conference of Multi-Agent Systems.*

GARRIDO, LEONARDO, BRENA, R., & SYCARA, KATIA. 1998 (December). Towards Modeling Other Agents: A Simulation-Based Study. *In: Multi-Agent Systems and Agent-Based Simulation, LNAI Series*, vol. 1534.

GMYTRASIEWICZ, PIOTR J., & DURFEE, EDMUND H. 2001. Rational Communication in Multi-Agent Environments. *Autonomous Agents and Multi-Agent Systems*, **4**(3), A233–272.

GROSZ, BARBARA J., & KRAUS, SARIT. 1996. Collaborative Plans for Complex Group Action. *Artificial Intelligence*, **86**(2), 269–357.

KINNY, D., LJUNGBERG, M., RAO, A. S., SONENBERG, E., TIDHAR, G., & WERNER, E. 1992. Planned Team Activity. *Pages 226–256 of:* C. CASTELFRANCHI AND E. WERNER (ed), *Artificial Social Systems — Selected Papers from the Fourth European Workshop on Modelling Autonomous Agents in a Multi-Agent World, MAAMAW-92 (LNAI Volume 830).* Springer-Verlag: Heidelberg, Germany.

KOK, JELLE R., & VLASSIS, NIKOS. 2001 (August). *Mutual Modeling of Teammate Behavior.* Tech. rept. UVA-02-04. Computer Science Institute, University of Amsterdam, The Netherlands.

LI, CUIHONG, GIAMPAPA, JOSEPH ANDREW, & SYCARA, KATIA. 2003 (November). *A Review of Research Literature on Bilateral Negotiations.* Tech. rept. CMU-RI-TR-03-41. Robotics Institute, Carnegie Mellon University, Pittsburgh, PA.

PANZARASA, P., JENNINGS, N., & NORMAN, T. 2002. Formalizing Collaborative Decision-Making and Practical Reasoning in Multi-Agent Systems. *Journal of Logic and Computation*, **12**(1), 55–117.

RAHWAN, I., RAMCHURN, S. D., JENNINGS, N. R., McBURNEY, P., PARSONS, S., & SONENBERG, L. to appear. Argumentation-Based Negotiation. *The Knowledge Engineering Review*.

RUBINSTEIN, ARIEL. 1998. *Modeling bounded rationality*. Zeuthen lecture book series. Cambridge, Mass.: MIT Press.

STONE, PETER, RILEY, PATRICK, & VELOSO, MANUELA M. 2000. Defining and Using Ideal Teammate and Opponent Agent Models. *Pages 1040–1045 of: In Proceedings of the Twelfth Annual Conference on Innovative Applications of Artificial Intelligence.*

TAMBE, MILIND. 1997. Towards Flexible Teamwork. *Journal of Artificial Intelligence Research*, **7**, 83–124.

WALKER, MARILYN A. 1996. The Effect of Resource Limits and Task Complexity on Collaborative Planning in Dialogue. *Artificial Intelligence Journal*, **1-2**(85), 181–243.

Agent-Based Communication Security

João Paulo Pimentão[1], Pedro A.C. Sousa[1],
Pedro Amaral[2], and Adolfo Steiger-Garção[1]

[1] Universidade Nova de Lisboa Faculdade de Ciências e Tecnologia
Campus da FCT/UNL, 2829-516 Caparica, Portugal
{pim,pas,asg}@fct.unl.pt
[2] UNINOVA - Instituto de Desenvolvimento de Novas Tecnologias
Campus da FCT/UNL, 2829-516 Caparica, Portugal
pmr@uninova.pt

Abstract. This paper presents an application of agent technology to the field of communication security. The proposed method, Split and Merge, is presented. The generic approach is on the denying of access to the message, instead of ciphering the message at the source and then sending it over a communication channel. This is achieved by splitting the message in parts and sending them to the destination through different routes, in an *ad-hoc* network of cooperating agents. The implementation of the method using multi-agent systems is detailed. The solutions found to deal with error detection and correction (loss of message fragments, message integrity and node misbehavior) are then discussed. An emphasis is put on the use reputation and trust mechanisms, with a fuzzy approach, to detect and cope with nodes with different levels of reliability.

1 Introduction

The focus of this paper is on providing communication security using agent-based systems; in particular it presents a new way to preserve the secrecy of the content of the messages being transmitted between two parties.

Traditionally, this kind of security relies strongly on cryptography. Most of the usual approaches to cryptography are based on two principles: the secrecy of the ciphering/deciphering key and the robustness of the ciphering functions.

Regarding key secrecy, methods have been designed ranging from the Diffie Hellman key agreement protocol [1] to the public key cryptography of Rivest, Shamir and Adleman [2].

For the second principle, the focus has been put in the infeasibility of determining, in a reasonable time, the solutions for some mathematical functions without the possession of the key (such as the case of the RSA ciphering method). Alas, the development of computational power as shown that what is "impossible" today may become common practice tomorrow. The increase of CPU speed is directly related to the increase of component density that has been following "Moore's Law" (stating that component density in integrated circuits would double each year), and which most experts believe will hold up to 2020 [3-5] although, in recent years, a slight decline has been noticed on the increase of the density of the circuits, mainly due to physical limitations.

G. Lindemann et al. (Eds.): MATES 2004, LNAI 3187, pp. 73–84, 2004.

It is obvious that the increase of computational power will also give rise to new cipher algorithms and methods that will try to maintain the competitive advantage over the potential threats.

Instead of relying on the lack of computational power for protecting the message communication, the proposed method (Split and Merge) further enhances the protection by providing inability to get hold of the message.

Other efforts have been made in approaches that may seem related to this, but they have different principles and objectives.

Some of such works include the long known principle of steganography, whose purpose is to hide the existence of communication [6, 7].

Other works try to hide the source of the communication in the World Wide Web, such as the work by Reiter and Rubin in Crowds [8] or the one by Goldschlag, Reed and Syverson in the Onion Routing Protocol [9, 10].

In Section 2 an overview of the Split and Merge method is presented.

Section 3 focuses on the attacks and countermeasures considered, where Fuzzy Logics are considered to deal with trust and reputation of the participating nodes.

In Section 4 the current implementation using Software Agents is described.

Finally, Section 5 presents the conclusions.

2 Split and Merge, the Secure Communication Method in Brief

In the Split and Merge method, the security of the message does not rely exclusively on the ability to decipher the message, but also on the ability to get the message itself. It does not deal with ciphering the contents of the message, but in splitting the message into fragments (as many and as small as whished) so that the possession of a fragment does not provide information about the contents of the message.

The next key concept is that the routing towards the destination node, of each fragment of the message, is done through different paths. This is done randomly, so that the paths (the list of nodes between the source and the destination) followed by each fragment are different. Its purpose is to decrease the possibility, which an attacker has, of intersecting all the message's fragments, by breaking one node's security.

The underlying principle of the method is depicted in Fig. 1 below. The message is produced at the start node A with Q as the destination. The message is split into fragments and spread all over the set of nodes in order to avoid interception.

At the start node the message is assigned with a "Number of Hops to Go" - NHG - (the numbers on the arrows) and then split into a random number of fragments of random sizes. The NHG parameter states the number of nodes that each fragment will have to go through before reaching the destination.

Each fragment is then sent to a randomly selected node (e.g. from A to B).

Upon arrival of the fragment, its NHG is tested and if it is different from 0 the fragment is re-split and the new fragments (of smaller dimension and with NHG decreased by one) are then transmitted. If the NHG reaches 0, the fragment is sent directly to the destination. If a fragment reaches the destination before NHG reaches 0, then instead of splitting it and resending it, the fragment is considered received.

When the fragments arrive at the destination they are sorted and the message is reassembled.

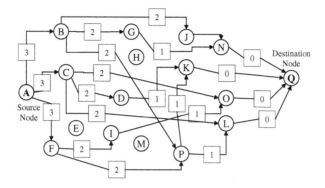

Fig. 1. An example of the split and merge method's operation.

The basis for the security of the method lays on the reduced probability an attacker has of breaking into a sufficient number of nodes to guarantee the collection of enough parts of the message to enable its understanding.

Whenever the message is split, the number of message fragments increases, each of which with a smaller dimension. Every time the splitting operation is done, the amount of original message in each resulting fragment is reduced and the number of fragments flowing in the network increases.

Trying to picture it, it is similar to what happens when looking at a television image. At a distance, you "get the whole image". Approaching the screen you will find a multitude of colorful pixels but, even if you see a few of them, you will not be able to understand of the whole image.

The main differences reside in the fact that in the Split and Merge, the "pixels" are of different dimensions and they are not "nice and ordered"; meaning that if you are able to perceive consecutive fragments of the message, it is likely that in the message they will be far apart.

Fig. 1 depicts the path from A to Q as straightforward; however, this was only done to facilitate the understanding of the method. In practice, given the randomness of the method, it is possible for fragments to travel backwards according to the selection done at each node.

It should be noted that the Split and Merge method deals very well with the scalability of the system by the increase of the number of participating nodes. In fact, Split and Merge will improve its efficiency regarding the security provided when the number of nodes increases since the probability of being able to capture fragments of a given message decreases with the increase of the number of nodes.

3 The Nodes, Message Forwarding, Attacks and Countermeasures

This section presents the basis for the construction of the Split and Merge network of participating nodes, then it details the process of message forwarding. It finally presents a set of possible attacks on the proposed method and the solutions devised to deal with them.

3.1 Using a Web of Trusted Nodes

In order to be able to forward the message fragments, each node needs to know a set of other nodes participating in the system.

Instead of relying on a central repository of addresses of participating nodes (more vulnerable to attacks), Split and Merge maintains distributed knowledge of system participants. Each of the nodes participating in such a system defines and maintains, in a local list, the set of nodes in which it trusts as forwarders of message fragments, thus creating a "web" of trust.

In this system trust is not necessarily bi-lateral and each node does not know which nodes trust on it, until a message fragment is sent to it. Even then, given the random nature of the system, the fact that a node has received a fragment of the message does not guarantee that it will ever receive another fragment of the same message, of a message from the same source or even of any other message.

3.2 Security Neighborhood

Although in most of the path between the source and the destination, different fragments of the message may flow through different routes, the start and end nodes are usually the single nodes through which the whole message will pass.

The Split and Merge method assumes that security of the start and end nodes themselves, and of their connection to the corporate intranet is not an issue.

To increase the difficulty on gathering all the fragments of the message at the start point of the communication channel, the concept of security neighborhood is introduced. The security neighborhood is represented by the set of nodes, inside a security border (e.g. the sender's intranet) that is used at the first stage of the message transmitting process. It is assumed that the nodes inside the security neighborhood are friendly (and bound by the organization's rules and security policies) and that no special provision should be made to protect against attacks from these nodes.

Considering the security neighborhoods, means that the source node, instead of randomly choosing a trusted node to receive the fragments that result from the first split process, it will randomly choose trusted nodes inside its security neighborhood.

With the concept of security neighborhood, any message leaving a site will be seen (by someone looking at the communication traffic) a set of messages coming from a random set of sources (inside the sources' security border) to a random set of destinations.

Furthermore, instead of considering a single access channel to/from a site, multiple channels can be used. Further enhancement of the security is achieved since it would imply that a hacker would have to secure access and to monitor simultaneously all the available connections. It is quite easy nowadays - and is becoming less expensive – to have multiple communication channels (e.g. leased lines, ISDN, Cable, ADSL, GPRS).

It should be noted that this approach can introduce some overhead in the message transfer process and can result in variable costs for sending the same message, depending upon how it is split and routed over the different access technologies.

3.3 Dealing with Fragment Loss

On normal operation end-to-end acknowledgement (Ack) is used; i.e., whenever the message is fully delivered to the destination, an acknowledgement is sent back to the source. If a timeout is reached and no acknowledgement is received, the source will resend the message.

Considering the fact that the message may not be considered delivered because only a small portion of the message is missing (e.g. a node fails to forward a message fragment), led us to consider an approach where Split and Merge produces its best effort to guarantee that if a fragment is delivered at the destination, so must the whole message be delivered. The solution lays on end-to-end partial acknowledgment.

A receiver's timeout monitor starts on the reception of first fragment. If the timeout is reached and the message is still incomplete, an e2ePAck (end-to-end partial acknowledgment) is sent back to the source containing a list of missing parts.

If the timeout was reached due to communication congestion, late fragments may arrive. In this case Split and Merge will use these fragments in order to speed up the message delivery process. The late fragments will be overlapped by fragments of different size related to the answer to the e2ePAck. Redundant information fully contained within the currently stored message fragments is discarded; fragments partially overlapping existing fragments will be adjusted to retrieve maximal information; i.e. non-overlapping portions are retrieved and added to already stored fragments.

Receiver timeout is restarted upon reception of the first fragment of the answer to the e2ePAck and the process is repeated as for the original message.

Upon message completion a list of fully received messages is kept to discard unneeded fragments.

At the sender side, a timeout is set as the message is sent out and if the timeout is reached without receiving either an acknowledgement or an e2ePAck, the message is assumed lost.

3.4 Detecting Message Tampering

The traditional method used to certify message integrity is the computation of a "Message Integrity Code" (or "Message Authentication Code" or "Message Digest"), which is usually done by computing a hash function over the message's text. There have been several proposals of hash functions over the years whose production's driving force has been the determination of possible attacks on some hash function's properties.

The usual scenario of application of message digest algorithms assumes that hackers may have access to the full message, thus allowing them to replace the whole message for another that may produce the same hash result.

The purpose of the use of hash functions within Split and Merge is specifically limited to the purpose of verifying the message's integrity at the destination. Here we assume that perpetrators may replace only a portion of the message; therefore, most hash functions will allow detection of the message tampering.

Nevertheless although the possibility of successfully tampering the message is quite reduced, there is no point in using hash functions for which attacks are already known. The selection, according to the matching between the studies conducted by Bosselaers [11] and by Barreto [12], should fall in the RIPE-MD 128 function, which is presently the algorithm with the highest performance, for which no successful method of attack has yet been known.

3.5 Dealing with Misbehaving Nodes

Assume that each node maintains a log of which message fragment was sent to each neighbor with the format depicted in Fig. 4.

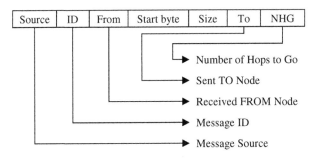

| Source | ID | From | Start byte | Size | To | NHG |

→ Number of Hops to Go

→ Sent TO Node

→ Received FROM Node

→ Message ID

→ Message Source

Fig. 2. Message fragment forwarding log.

When the destination reaches the timeout, an e2ePAck is sent back to the source, stating the list of fragments that are still missing. Based on this information and on the forwarding log, the source can inform the nodes that had the responsibility of forwarding the missing fragments, that it is initiating a trust revision on their performance based on the loss of the particular set of fragments. Each node will then repeat the process of trust evaluation for the nodes they consider responsible for the fragments loss.

This process is repeated until one of the nodes assumes 100% of guilt, or 100% of guilt is assumed for the next node (in case of a communication timeout occurs or there is no possibility that the node can blame another node because the NHG parameter has reached its limit).

The selection of nodes to forward message fragments is performed considering the trust factor.

The following details the definition and the computation of trust performed at each node.

The most cited definition of trust is given by Gambetta [13]:

"...trust (or, symmetrically, distrust) is a particular level of the subjective probability with which an agent assesses that another agent or group of agents will perform a particular action, both before he can monitor such action (or independently of his capacity ever to be able to monitor it) and in a context in which it affects his own action".

In the PhD thesis of Lik Mui [14], we find another definition of trust:

"Trust: a subjective expectation an agent has about another's future behaviour. Trust is a subjective quantity calculated based on the two agents concerned in a present or future dyadic encounter".

In the same work, reputation is defined as: *"the perception that an agent has of another's intentions and norms"*, where norms are *"... heuristics that individuals adopt from a moral perspective, in that these are the kinds of actions they wish to follow in living their life."* by the definition of Elinor Ostrom [15].

Reputation is a social quantity calculated based on actions by a given agent a_i and observations made by others in an "embedded social network" in which a_i resides (Granovetter [16]). A_i's reputation clearly affects the amount of trust that others have toward it.

Given the specific nature of Split and Merge, we need to adapt and refine these concepts.

In our view, trust reflects the subjective value that a node maintains regarding each of its neighbors, based on the historical analysis of their behavior.

Let N be the set of all nodes and n_i a node $\forall i : i \in |N|$. Trust is a function between two nodes such that:

$$t : N \times N \rightarrow [0,1]. \tag{1}$$

At the start we assume, by default, that for every node n_i :

$$t(n_i, n_j) = 1, \forall_j : n_j \in \{trusted\_neighbors(n_i)\}. \tag{2}$$

where trusted_neighbors(n_i) is the set of all nodes in the secure neighborhood of n_i. This is justifiable since it is assumed that, at start, the node's neighborhood is composed by a set of trusted nodes.

As the interactions progress, the trust value is updated by observing the node's performance, which is built both by direct observation of actions and by indirect information provided by trustworthy neighbors (reputation).

Direct trust is built based on the observation of the performance of the node in services directly rendered, which, in our case means the rate of successful deliveries, over the total number of deliveries requested; i.e.,

$$t(n_i, n_j) = \frac{\sum_{k=1}^{z} success\_delivery\_request(n_i, n_j, k)}{z}. \tag{3}$$

In equation 3, z stands for the total number of deliveries requested by node n_i from node n_j, $success\_delivery\_request : NxNxK \rightarrow \{0,1\}$ is the status of the k-th request for delivery of a fragment performed by node n_i to node n_j.

This approach for $t(n_i, n_j)$ is too drastic in penalizing the nodes if they fail some of their first delivery attempts. Under these circumstances, after the first failure, the node would be deemed unreliable and could never be used again. The solution is the inclusion of a value ($r(n_j)$) to help smooth the penalty for failure:

$$t(n_i, n_j) = \frac{\sum_{k=1}^{z} success(delivery\_request(n_i, n_j, k)) + r(n_j)}{z + r(n_j)}. \tag{4}$$

The value $r(n_j)$ is in fact our approach to deal with the reputation of the node.

In the absence of further reputation information, we start with a fixed value (e.g. 10). When a delivery failure occurs for a fragment that was forwarded by a given node A, we allow the faulty nodes (in A's perspective) to provide incrimination messages (guilt messages) that allows them to shift the blame to one or several of their neighbors.

The reputation values at the node A are then updated (decreased) considering the information provided in the "guilt" messages and A's trust on the nodes that produced the guilt messages. Reputation is only updated for nodes that are trusted neighbors of A and guilt messages reporting on other nodes or coming from other nodes (other than those neighbors that A assumes are guilty of loosing some message fragment), are discarded.

For every trusted neighbor n_j the value of his reputation is determined by:

$$r(n_j) = r(n_j) - \sum_{\forall n_g \in GN} \frac{guilt\_justification(n_g, n_j) \times t(A, n_g)}{|GN|}. \qquad (5)$$

where GN stands for subset of trusted neighbors of A that are considered to be guilty, from A's perspective. The $guilt\_justification(n_g, n_j)$ is a value that represents the amount of guilt on fragment loss attributed to node n_j by node n_g; $guilt\_justification : N \times N \rightarrow [0,1]$.

The value of the reputation can only decrease over time; however, this is not a problem since:

1. Reputation is only updated if something goes wrong and as a result of a forwarding request.
2. In good behaving nodes, it is expected that the direct trust will increase more rapidly than the reputation decreases.

The value of trust is used in the process of selection of nodes to forward the message fragments. This process is a mix between the random selection of neighbors and the fuzzy selection of neighbors; i.e. a random function is used to determine the number of fragments to be produced and then a fuzzy function is used to select the best-fitted neighbors to forward the fragments.

To this purpose we consider the following Fuzzy membership functions.

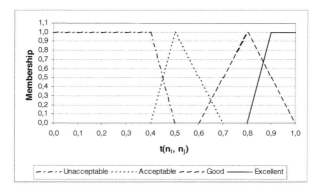

Fig. 3. Fuzzy membership functions for the selection of nodes.

The membership functions for each of the four categories are defined as:

$$Unacceptable(x) = \begin{cases} 1 & \text{for } x \le 0,4 \\ \dfrac{0,5-x}{0,1} & \text{for } 0,4 < x \le 0,5 \\ 0 & \text{for } x > 0,5 \end{cases} \qquad Acceptable(x) = \begin{cases} 0 & \text{for } x \le 0,4 \\ \dfrac{x-0,4}{0,1} & \text{for } 0,4 < x \le 0,5 \\ \dfrac{0,7-x}{0,2} & \text{for } 0,5 < x \le 0,7 \\ 0 & \text{for } x > 0,7 \end{cases} \tag{6}$$

$$Good(x) = \begin{cases} 0 & x \le 0,6 \\ \dfrac{x-0,6}{0,2} & 0,6 < x \le 0,8 \\ \dfrac{1-x}{0,2} & x > 0,8 \end{cases} \qquad Excellent(x) = \begin{cases} 0 & \text{for } x \le 0,8 \\ \dfrac{x-0,8}{0,1} & \text{for } 0,8 < x \le 0,9 \\ 1 & \text{for } x > 0,9 \end{cases}$$

The rating of each node is then determined by a set of *if-then* rules (see equation 7). The resulting rating is a pair consisting of the category attributed to the node (Excellent, Good, Acceptable or Unacceptable) and of the degree of membership for the selected category.

Based the ratings determined, the nodes are selected, considering first the ones with performance rate of Excellent, than the ones with Good and finally the ones with Acceptable. The nodes with Unacceptable performances are not selected.

$$
\begin{aligned}
&rating\,(n_i, n_j) = \text{case } t(n_i, n_j) \text{ in:} \\
&[0 \text{ to } 0,4[\quad (unacceptable, unacceptable(t(n_i, n_j))) \\
&[0,4 \text{ to } 0,5[\quad \text{if } unacceptable(t(n_i, n_j)) > acceptable(t(n_i, n_j)) \text{ then} \\
&\qquad\qquad\quad (unacceptable, unacceptable(t(n_i, n_j))) \text{ else} \\
&\qquad\qquad\quad (acceptable, acceptable(t(n_i, n_j))) \\
&[0,5 \text{ to } 0,8[\quad \text{if } acceptable(t(n_i, n_j)) > good(t(n_i, n_j)) \text{ then} \\
&\qquad\qquad\quad (acceptable, acceptable(t(n_i, n_j))) \text{ else} \\
&\qquad\qquad\quad (good, good(t(n_i, n_j))) \\
&[0,8 \text{ to } 1] \quad \text{if } good(t(n_i, n_j)) > excellent(t(n_i, n_j)) \text{ then} \\
&\qquad\qquad\quad (good, good(t(n_i, n_j))) \text{ else} \\
&\qquad\qquad\quad (ecxellent, excellent(t(n_i, n_j)))
\end{aligned}
\tag{7}
$$

4   Using Agents to Implement the Split and Merge

A first prototype of the system has been developed in Delphi, which was used as a test lab for the concepts being developed.

One of the major questions hindering the deployment of the first prototype at a wide scale was the need to secure access to a number of sites that would allow the deployment of an application. Nowadays, with the ever-growing number of virus and "Trojan horses", to secure such permission would be nearly impossible. It was then that our attention was drawn to the Agentcities/openNet forum network.

The Agentcities was an European IST project sponsoring a worldwide initiative designed to help realize the commercial and research potential of agent based applications by constructing a worldwide, open network of platforms hosting diverse agent based services. This project gave rise to an initiative "the openNet forum" designed to further expand and promote the efforts started in the Agentcities project.

The Agentcities/openNet forum network currently consists of 179 platforms [17] deployed in universities, RTD institutes as well as in companies.

These platforms act as a decentralized worldwide test-bed for the test of the system.

A second prototype of the system is being tested using software agents deployed in JADE [18] platforms, communicating using FIPA compliant messages [19]. The "Content" field of the ACL messages is used to transmit the message fragment and additional user-defined elements are used to transmit the Split and Merge's specific message parameters.

These prototypes have been developed considering both the possibility of sending simple text messages and files.

The agents used are purely reactive. They react to the reception of messages by means of "received message behaviors" witch are performed in order to fulfill the various facets of the nodes.

The current implementation of the system considers the following types of agents: the Split and Merge Agent, the Control Agent and a Logger Agent.

The **Split and Merge Agent** represents a node of the system. It agent reacts to incoming messages using reception behaviors. They react both to messages from other Split and Merge Agents and from the Control Agents.

Messages from other Split and Merge Agents (containing Message Fragments) are evaluated; if the Message Fragment is destined to a locally registered application, the agent assembles the incoming fragment into messages to be delivered to the applications. Possible fragment loss is detected and interaction with the source is performed in order to guarantee full message delivery, the trust revision process is updated maintaining the internal notion of reliability of the nodes that comprise its neighborhood. Upon full message delivery the agent informs the Control Agent.

Message Fragments destined to other nodes are split into additional fragments and sent to the Agent's trusted neighbors.

When the Split and Merge Agent receives a message from the control Agent it reacts by forming the requested message that is then split into fragments and sent to the trusted neighbors.

The **Control Agents** are user interface agents that react to user commands, which permit the use of the System. Control Agents can send messages to any Split and Merge Agent (local or remote) within the network giving them commands to form and send the requested messages.

The **Logger Agent** provides an interface with a mySQL database and with the Split and Merge Agents, where fragment forwarding is logged for future analysis of system behavior.

5 Conclusions and Future Work

This paper presents a method for the improvement of secure transmission of messages between computers on the Web, using agents.

The chosen strategy is based on denying the access of the perpetrators to the message, in contrast with the traditional approaches of ciphering the message. In this way,

Split and Merge presents a paradigm shift from the traditional approaches to communication security.

The Fuzzy Logic approach to deal with trust and reputation was introduced as a method to identify problematic nodes in the network.

For additional security the Split and Merge method can be complemented with traditional ciphering methods, such as end-to-end message ciphering and/or node to node header ciphering, at the cost of additional processing time.

The number of messages flowing in the day-by-day traffic further enhances the principle behind the Split and Merge method that relies on a "swarm" of message fragments, therefore compromising the ability of selecting the correct fragments of a given message.

A previous prototype has been produced as a proof of concept and a second prototype is being tested based on Agents to facilitate the deployment.

The use of behaviors on the agents to implement the different facets of the node has proven quite valid during the implementation contributing to expedite the development process.

The next steps will be a thorough assessment of the overhead introduced, under controlled conditions and, in parallel, the deployment of the service in the Agentcities/openNet forum network.

References

1. Diffie, W. and M.E. Hellman, *New Directions in Cryptography.* IEEE Transactions on Information Theory, 1976. **IT-22**(6): p. 644--654.
2. R.L. Rivest, A.S. and L.M. Adleman, *A method for obtaining digital signatures and public-key cryptosystems.* Communications of the ACM, 1978. **2**(21): p. 120-126.
3. Webopedia, *Moore's law.* 1998,
   http://www.webopedia.com/TERM/M/Moores_Law.html.
4. Mann, C.C., *The End of Moore's Law?* 2000, Technology Review,
   http://www.technologyreview.com/articles/mann0500.asp.
5. Rónai, C., *O Globo 08/2000.* 2000,
   http://www.almaden.ibm.com/projects/oglobo.htm.
6. NCIX, *Counterintelligence News & Developments, Volume 2, June 1998 - "Hidden in Plain Sight-Steganography".* 1998, Office of the National Counterintelligence Executive.
7. Judge, J.C., *Steganography: Past, Present, Future.* 2001, SANS - SysAdmin, Audit, Network, Security - http://www.sans.org/rr/steg/steganography4.php.
8. Reiter, M.K. and A.D. Rubin, *Crowds: Anonymity for Web Transactions.* 1997, DIMACS: New Jersey, USA. p. 21.
9. Goldschlag, D.M., M.G. Reed, and P.F. Syverson. *Hiding Routing Information.* in *Workshop on Information Hiding, LLNCS 1174.* 1996. Cambridge, UK: Springer-Verlag.
10. Goldschlag, D., M. Reed, and P. Syverson, *Onion Routing for Anonymous and Private Internet Connections.* Communications of the ACM, 1999. **42**(2).
11. Bosselaers, A., *Comparative performance of hash functions,*
    http://www.esat.kuleuven.ac.be/~bosselae/fast.html.
12. Barreto, P., *The Hashing Function Lounge.* 2000,
    http://planeta.terra.com.br/informatica/paulobarreto/hflounge.html.
13. Gambetta, D., *Can We Trust Trust?,* in *Trust: Making and Breaking Cooperative Relations, electronic edition,* D. Gambetta, Editor. 2000, Department of Sociology, University of Oxford, <http://www.sociology.ox.ac.uk/papers/gambetta213-237.pdf>. Oxford. p. 213-237.

14. Mui, L., *Computational Models of Trust and Reputation: Agents, Evolutionary Games, and Social Networks*, in *Department of Electrical Engineering and Computer Science*. 2002, Massachusetts Institute of Technology: Massachusetts. p. 139.

15. Ostrom, E., *A Behavioral Approach to the Rational-Choice Theory of Collective Action*. American Political Science Review, 1998. **92**(1): p. 1-22.

16. Granovetter, M., *Economic Action and Social Structure: The Problem of Embeddedness*. American Journal of Sociology, 1985. **91**(November): p. 481-510.

17. Willmott, S., et al., *Agentcities Network Architecture Recommendation*. 2002, Agentcities Task Force.

18. Bellifemine, F., A. Poggi, and G. Rimassa. *JADE - A FIPA-compliant agent framework*. in *4th International Conference and Exhibition on the Practical Application of Intelligent Agents and Multi-Agents*. 1999. London, UK.

19. FIPA00061, *FIPA ACL Message Structure Specification.*, in *Foundation for Intelligent Physical Agents*. 2000.

Modelling and Analysis of Agent Protocols with Petri Nets

Kolja Lehmann and Daniel Moldt

University of Hamburg, Faculty of Informatics
Vogt-Kölln-Str. 30, D-22527 Hamburg
{8lehmann,moldt}@informatik.uni-hamburg.de

Abstract. The behaviour of interacting agents in a Multi-agent System can be modelled effectively using Petri Nets. The interaction of several agents forms a distributed workflow, which can be analyzed in different ways using well-known Petri Net methods.
Therefore this paper proposes an approach to modelling and analysing agent interaction protocols using Petri Net analysis.

Keywords: Agent, analysis, modelling, MULAN, nets within nets, Petri nets, RENEW, verification, workflow

1 Introduction

In agent-oriented software engineering (AOSE) the communication of agents is of special interest. Due to the concurrent and distributed nature of agents their interactions have received a lot of attention. In the Agent Unified Modelling Language (AUML) community informal specification techniques have been established to describe the interactions.

What is missing is a formal foundation of these techniques. In this paper we describe how a partial formal analysis can be performed, without loosing the informal modelling.

Concepts from the area of workflows can be applied, due to the process character of interaction. Here Petri nets have a strong position in terms of expressability, efficient, direct, graphical, formal and intuitive modelling and analysis at the same time.

Based on our multi-agent system (MAS) framework MULAN we demonstrate how traditional (see [24, 22]) and a special kind of very high-level Petri nets, reference nets (see [17]), can be used in this context.

To illustrate our agent- and Petri net-based approach, the modelling and analysis of agent protocols will be described here. Section 2 will cover the basic concepts of modelling, (A)UML, Petri nets, workflows and agents needed in the course of this paper.

Section 3 describes the Petri net model used in section 4 for the analysis. In section 5 a small case study demonstrates the methods used for the analysis and the potential of this approach. The article closes with a discussion of the results and a conclusion.

G. Lindemann et al. (Eds.): MATES 2004, LNAI 3187, pp. 85–98, 2004.

2   Basic Concepts

This section will cover the basic concepts needed in the course of this paper. The context in which to place it will be made clear by explaining the terms "Agent", "Multi-agent System" and "Protocol". Also the technical basics for modelling and analysis of protocols will be laid.

Especially Petri nets and Petri net-based methods of analysis will be covered, as these will be used to analyse protocols. The modelling of agent interaction with Petri nets will be discussed with the example of the Petri net-based multi agent framework MULAN[23], which allows the modelling and execution of agent protocols with reference nets.

2.1   Agents and Multi-agent Systems

Although the term agent is central for an agent oriented approach to software engineering there are different notions on what comprises an agent. According to Wooldridge [29, p. 28ff] autonomy is the key feature of an agent.

Additional characteristics an agent can have are the possibilities to learn, to perceive its environment and to interact with other agents in its environment. Actions of the agent can be reactions to a perceived state in the environment or be undertaken proactively by the agent himself to reach its objectives.

Wooldridge und Jennings [28] differentiate between a strong and a weak notion of agenthood. The weak notion attributes an agent with the characteristics of autonomy, the option to interact in social contexts, react to its environment and to undertake actions proactively.

The strong notion adds features such as mobility, truthfulness, goodwill and rationality. This work will only rely on the characteristics of the weak notion.

A Multi-agent System (MAS) is a system in which multiple agents can interact with each other. They can be located on different interconnected platforms. An example architecture of an MAS will be given in section 2.4. An MAS provides the infrastructure necessary for communication and interaction between agents [13]. The agents within an MAS can either cooperate to solve a common problem or compete to reach their own personal goals, for example by trading on a virtual marketplace.

Key elements of an MAS are, according to Jennings [15]:

- every agent has got only limited information
- control is distributed
- data is distributed
- computation is asynchronous

The communication between agents can be structured by the use of protocols, structured descriptions of possible interactions between two or more agents. These interaction protocols will be analysed in this paper.

2.2   Protocols

Protocols are a formalization of processes, which allow the organization of recurring tasks. In the context of agents interaction and behaviour protocols can be distinguished.

A behaviour protocol describes the behaviour of an agent in a given state, characterizing specific situations. Only the actions and decisions of this agent are looked at, interaction with other agents is only locally seen as the events of incoming messages and the actions of sending outgoing messages. Other agents are only the environment as a whole for the agent, not necessarily as individual entities. The multi-agent framework MULAN, that is used here and will be described in section 2.4 uses the term "Protocol" in the sense of behaviour protocols.

An interaction protocol describes the interaction of several agents from a global point of view. The possible sequences of messages between agents can be described using for example interaction diagrams or Petri nets[21].

2.3 Petri Nets

Petri nets are a well known modelling technique for which a large set of verification and validation methods exist (see [22] or [11] for some details). Especially in the area of workflows efficient results can be reached (see [24], [2]). Most efficient result lay in the area of the traditional Petri net formalism of the place/transition nets (see [22]). However, nowadays high-level Petri nets are used for modelling. In our case these are the reference nets, developed by Olaf Kummer (see [17]). They provide some object-based modelling features (like net instances), extension with respect to arc types, the concept of synchronous channels, a smooth integration of and in Java and an modelling and execution environment called RENEW (Reference net workshop).

In [23], [16] and [7] an extension and integration of Petri nets and agents in the directions of MAS has been shown. We provide a conceptual framework for MAS and a practical framework with this work. It can be characterised as being FIPA conform, covering concurrent modelling and being fully integrated into Java to allow for a direct practical embedding.

A central aspect of an agent are its protocols which determine, beside its knowledge base, its behaviour. This behaviour can be described in term of simple or complex process descriptions. In the context of AUML and the agent interaction diagrams (AIPs) simple structures like workflows can be used to describe the agent protocols. Especially in [19] the expressive power of our Petri net formalism, the reference nets, has been shown in the context of workflows. Altogether we can claim that we can model any known pattern in the area of workflows in an intuitive and short way. When restriction ourselves to AIPs this gets even simpler since we can go back to the traditional place/transition nets.

For the analysis of these powerful tools exist in general (see the tool INAwin ([14])) and especially when looking at workflows (see the tool Woflan ([27])).

2.4 Mulan

MULAN is an MAS framework built entirely in reference nets [23], [16]. With its extension CAPA (See [6]) it forms a FIPA[1]-compliant multi agent system.

---

[1] See [9].

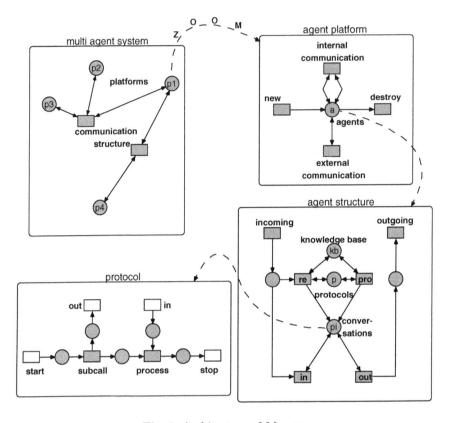

Fig. 1. Architecture of MULAN

The basic architecture is shown in figure 1. However, in this paper abstractions will be made from the more technical aspects, for example FIPA-compliance, to focus on the interaction of agents and agent protocols.

Each of the levels in this (simplified) architecture is a reference net. The topmost level is the multi-agent system, consisting of multiple interconnected platforms. Within the platforms multiple agents exist as tokens in a special place of the platform net. Each agent can have a number of protocols lying in a place within the agent net. These protocol nets are what describes the behaviour of the agents.

2.5   Workflow

One application of Petri nets is the analysis of workflows in organizations. A workflow consists of all activities needed to fulfil a certain piece of work and the interdependencies between those activities.

V.d. Aalst [3] uses a certain kind of Petri nets for the analysis of workflows, which build the basis for the protocol nets used in this article for analysis of agent interaction. This model and its extension will be described in the next section. The verification of these nets is shown in [1].

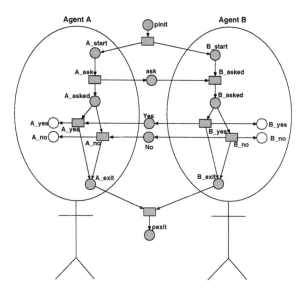

Fig. 2. Protocol net for a simple example protocol; information places (white) have been added for analysis reasons (see 4.2)

3   Modelling of Agent Protocols

To facilitate further analysis, agent protocols will be modelled using a specific class of P/T-nets, that will be called protocol nets. First the general model will be presented, then parallels to other methods of modelling agent interaction will be drawn.

3.1   Protocol Nets

Protocol nets are a modification of workflow nets, as proposed by v.d. Aalst [3]. A workflow Petri net is an S/T-net that has exactly one place that is a source and one that is a sink. All other net elements are located on paths between those two.

Additionally in a protocol net distinct connected regions within the net are laid out. Each agent participating in the interaction is associated with one such region, which forms a workflow net itself. Some places within these agent-subnets are marked as interface places. Those only have incoming arcs from other agent-subnets and outgoing arcs to transition within the agent-subnet to which they belong. Each transition within an agent-subnet must have at least one place as predecessor that is within its own agent-subnet and is not an interface place.

Message-passing within the protocol is modelled by placing tokens into these interface places. Each possible type of message from one agent to another must be modelled explicitly by one place. The complete formal model can be found in [18].

Figure 2 shows an example of a protocol net. The agent subnets are indicated to show the workflow nets of each agent. The whole net forms a workflow net, too. The message passing between the agents that usually happens through some kind of message transport is simplified to facilitate the analysis.

3.2 Modelling with AUML-Interaction-Diagrams

A current way to model agent interactions is to use AUML-Interaction-Diagrams (see [4]. These are an extension of the UML-Interaction-Diagrams. The features provided allow for a more compact modelling of sets of interactions. UML 2.0 will incorporate some of these. Due to the widespread usage of interaction diagrams in general a tool has been developed that allows for the modelling of them within our approach. In [10] a generation of reference nets has been provided. This allows to directly apply the AUML-Interaction-Diagrams within our MAS-framework. The agent protocols can therefore be generated automatically for the execution environment CAPA. This allows for the direct execution of the interaction models in form of reference nets which are the respective agent protocols. In [18] the transformation for the formal verification is shown. Verification of such interaction models is made possible due to the usage of Petri nets[2].

3.3 Conversion of Mulan Protocols

In MULAN the interaction between multiple agents is disperses among multiple separate nets, at least one for each agent involved. To get a global view of the interaction, these protocols have to be integrated into one single net.

The process to use here is outlined in [18]. Basically the protocol nets are placed next to each other and interface places are added. The transitions for sending and receiving messages are then connected with these interface places. Also a common start- and end-place are added to give the net the correct form of a protocol net.

4   Analysis

This section shows how different analysis methods can be applied to protocol nets to ensure certain properties of an agent interaction protocol.

4.1   Soundness

V.d. Aalst [1] formulates soundness as a minimum requirement to a workflow net. First the definition of soundness for workflow nets will be given, then modifications for protocol nets will be discussed and shown how to check for these properties.

---

[2] The mapping of the generated nets and the analysed nets is not done formal, however, the mapping is straight forward for humans.

Workflow Soundness. For a workflow to be sound, three criteria must be met [25]:

1. *option to complete* - From every state of the system it must be possible to terminate.
2. *proper completion* - Once a terminal state has been reached, no further computation may take place.
3. *no dead tasks* - For every task there is at least one sequence in which it is executed.

More formally it is required that from each reachable marking of the net a marking is reachable in which the end place is marked. However, to ensure the *proper completion* criterion, if the end place is marked, it must be the only place marked. Also, no transition may be initially dead.

To check these conditions, a shortcut net is constructed by connecting the end place with the start place by means of a shortcut transition. The original workflow net is sound iff the shortcut net is life and bounded [25].

This property can be checked with the coverability graph. The tool Woflan (see [27] and [25]) uses a more differentiated approach to allow more detailed analysis of weaknesses in the workflow design and to avoid, if possible, the rather expensive construction of the coverability graph.

Soundness of Protocol Nets. Soundness for protocol nets requires the same criteria as for workflow nets, due to the more specific nature of protocol nets the formal requirements can be changed slightly:

1. From every reachable marking a terminal marking can be reached in which the end places of all agent-subnets are marked. By firing the end transition the end place of the protocol can be marked, too.
2. Once the end place of an agent-subnet is marked, no transition within the agent can fire any more.
3. No transition is initially dead.

The first condition requires every agent-subnet excluding interface places to be a sound workflow net. So if the end place of an agent is marked, within this subnet no further tokens exist except maybe for interface places.

So once all subnets have reached a final state, no more transitions can be activated except for the final transition. If interface places are taken into consideration again, outgoing messages can be ignored, as these will only affect other agents. Incoming messages will not change the "proper completion" either, since every transition must have a place other than an interface place as predecessor. So once the "option to complete" is given, termination will be "proper".

This is a difference to workflow nets, where proper termination requires all places except for the end place to be empty upon completion. Due to the special form of protocol nets this restriction can be relaxed.

Analysis. The first step for determining the protocol soundness of a net consists in checking the workflow soundness of the agent-subnets. This step can for example be done with the Woflan-tool (see [27] and [25]). If this check succeeds, "proper completion" can be guaranteed.

After that, the whole net is checked for Soundness using Woflan. If workflow soundness is given for the net as a whole, protocol soundness follows. If not, protocol soundness might still be established.

If analysis with Woflan had as a result that the shortcut net is not bounded but only interface places are unbounded, analysis can go on. If other places in the shortcut net are unbounded or it is not life, the net is unsound. If the shortcut net is unbounded and not life analysis must go on, because deadlocks might be caused by tokens left over from an earlier protocol run and cannot happen in normal protocol execution.

The check for the "option to complete" is more difficult. It is not sufficient to check the shortcut net for lifeness, because the shortcut-transition does not reset the net completely. Therefore tokens from an earlier protocol run could cause a deadlock.

Instead of the shortcut-transition, the net can be augmented with an additional transition at the end place. This new transition takes one token from the end place and puts it back. If that transition is life in the start marking, then the "option to complete" is given.

Unfortunately the test for lifeness of a transition in unbounded nets is equivalent to the reachability problem (see [12]), therefore overexponential in complexity. Yet for small nets it might still be a viable solution.

Petri net analysis tools such as INAwin (See [14]) can be used to construct the reachability graph up to a certain depth. If it is finite, a definite decision can be made. Otherwise the construction must be stopped at some point either if a deadlock is found or with the assumption that there is none.

4.2   Correctness

After each agent has terminated the execution of the protocol, all involved parties must agree on the result. For example it cannot be that one agent thinks a contract has been made, while the other party thinks that the negotiation was aborted without result.

For every possible protocol result there must be a transition within the protocol net, that fires when the agent reaches the conclusion the associated result had been reached. Normally these transitions will be the last transition before termination.

For the analysis each of these transitions can put a token into a place added to the net for this result. Then, all legal and illegal combinations must be sorted out. For example it is not necessary that an agent who did not win an auction knows whether another agent has won or the auction was aborted, because the reservation prize was not reached. However, he may not think he won the auction while the auctioneer thinks differently.

The inconsistent combinations form a submarking of the net. Each of this can be checked against the coverability graph that might already have been constructed during the soundness-check. A marking is coverable iff there is a node in the coverability-graph that covers the marking (see [24]). If any one of the inconsistent markings is coverable, then the protocol is not correct.

4.3 Stability

In distributed systems all kinds of unforeseen events can happen in the course of an interaction. Messages between contracting parties might get delayed or lost or even the whole communication might break down. Robustness against such events is called stability.

Interactions can also be disturbed by malevolent agents, trying to disrupt the protocol by sending misleading messages. This kind of disturbance will not be subject here, agents are expected to follow the protocols.

In this article only problems arising from late and lost messages will be dealt with. To test the results of such an event, it needs to be modelled into the protocol. Then the results can be studied with the protocol net.

To simulate the potential loss of a message, a new transition can be added that takes a token out of an interface place instead of the intended addressee. Normally the probability of such an event happening will be very small, nevertheless if it can occur it needs to be modelled to check whether or not the protocol can still terminate correctly, even with a suboptimal result.

The delay of a message could be ignored in the model, if it is certain that a message will always eventually arrive. But if the protocol contains timeouts, either as part of the protocol or as a reaction to the possible loss of messages, caution has to be taken. A delayed message could be treated by the addressee as lost or not sent at all, although the sender thinks it has been sent alright. So not the delay of the message is modelled, but the reaction of the agent to a possible delay.

Once all possible losses of messages and reactions to delays have been modelled into the protocol net, the normal tests of soundness and correctness can be applied again. In case of message loss special care has to be taken that final confirmation messages have arrived properly before terminating the protocol. Otherwise one agent might terminate after sending confirmation for a positive protocol result, while the other one, not having received the confirmation, concludes that it has not been sent and the interaction has failed. However this would be an incorrect result and marked as such by the correctness test.

In this section methods have been presented to analyse protocol nets. Soundness and correctness of a net are prerequisites for further analysis, an explicit check for stability can be omitted if the platform used makes sure, no messages can get lost. In the next section some of the analysis methods will be demonstrated with the Contract Net protocol.

5   Case Study

In this section the described modelling and analysis techniques will be demonstrated at the example of the contract net protocol. The protocol was first proposed by Davis and Smith [5] for the coordination of cooperative agents in distributed problem solving.

A first version of the contract net protocol in AUML can be found in [20]. The FIPA has standardized the protocol as standard SC00029H [8]. Figure 3 shows the two versions next to each other.

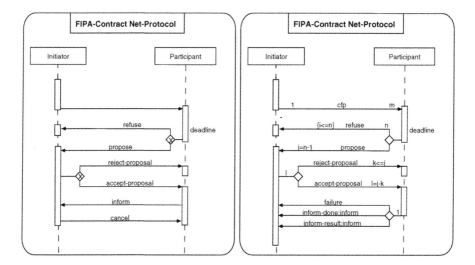

Fig. 3. Contract Net Protocol, on the left the version of Odell [20], on the right the FIPA standard [8], images have been redrawn by the authors

The difference between these two versions lies in the last message of the protocol. While the first version allowed a cancellation from the initiator after the final acceptance, the later version only knows a failure notice from the participant at this stage.

5.1   Modelling

Figures 4 and 5 show the protocol nets for the two versions of the contract net protocol. The difference between "inform-done" and "inform-result" is not important here, so there is only one message for a success. The places in the middle are the interface places for the communication between the agents, the agent subnets are in the left and the right column. The white places are information places for the correctness analysis later on.

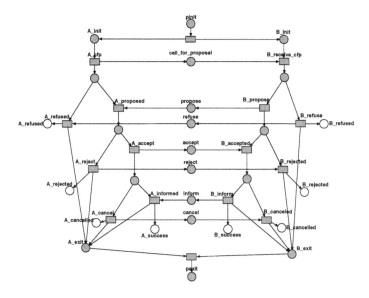

Fig. 4. Protocol net for the Contract Net Protocol: the Version of Odell [20] (taken from [18])

5.2 Analysis

Now the two versions of the protocol will be analysed, using the methods described earlier on to find out the difference between the two versions.

Soundness. To test the soundness of the protocol nets, first the workflow soundness of the agent-subnets must be established. Therefore the columns from A_init to A_exit and from B_init to B_exit are separated and opened in Woflan [27]. Note that these two are exactly the same in both versions of the protocol. The analysis returns that both agent-subnets are workflow sound.

Now the protocol nets in their entirety are analysed in Woflan. For the second version (the FIPA version) workflow soundness can be established, therefore protocol soundness is given here, too. For the Odell-version in [20], however, there are unbounded places, namely the places "inform" and "cancel". Woflan allows the calculation of "improper scenarios", i.e. scenarios that will inevitably lead to a situation where the workflow soundness is violated.

The scenario given here is that after accepting an offer, the initiator sends a "cancel" while the participant sends an "inform". Still both agents can terminate their protocols.

Analysis of the coverability graph shows that the net is still protocol sound. According to the simpler definition for workflow nets this protocol would already have been dismissed. Still the other version seems better, since it follows even the more restrictive workflow soundness condition.

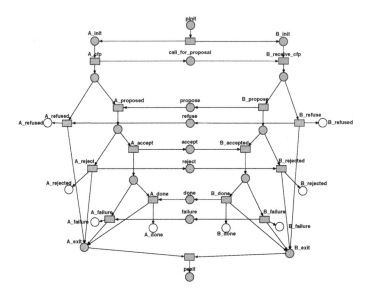

Fig. 5. Protocol net for the Contract Net Protocol: the FIPA standard [8] (taken from [18])

Correctness. Now that both protocols are sound, the next step is testing the correctness. Therefore the white places have been added to the protocol nets, showing the possible results of the protocol.

The first version knows the results "refused", "rejected" and "cancelled" for both agents, the FIPA-version has got "failure" instead of "cancelled". Every result must be seen as incorrect, in which not both agents share the same opinion about the outcome of the protocol.

For the analysis of coverability of incorrect submarkings, the INAwin tool [14] can be used. Result of the analysis is that in the Odell-version the marking A_cancelled/B_success is coverable. INAwin allows a backtracking of the path that led to this marking, it is the same that Woflan had output as an improper scenario.

Although both versions of the protocol can be considered sound, the older version of Odell in [20] was proved to be incorrect.

The test for stability will be omitted here, since the protocol has no timeouts. This example has shown the potential to discover flaws in protocol design that might otherwise lead to deadlocks or incorrect results.

6   Results and Conclusion

This article has shown methods for the analysis of agent protocols. A Petri net model based on workflow nets was proposed. The basic workflow nets were augmented with a concept of individual agents and messages between these agents. This form of protocol nets can be generated from other descriptions of agent interaction like MULAN-protocols and AUML-interaction diagrams.

Based on these protocol nets analysis methods were presented to test the soundness, correctness and stability of protocols. A case study showed how the proposed method can be used to find flaws in protocol design.

An automated analysis of agent interaction protocols could be used to facilitate the design of agent-based systems and to reduce errors in the definition of interaction. This is one way the quality of agent-oriented software engineering can be improved by usage of formal verification.

An interesting topic of further research is the application of our results in combination with some results from game theory, as has been done in [18] to some extend.

References

1. Wil van der Aalst. Verification of workflow nets. In Pierre Azéma and Gianfranco Balbo, editors, *Application and Theory of Petri Nets*, number 1248 in Lecture Notes in Computer Science, pages 407–426, Berlin Heidelberg New York, 1997. Springer Verlag.
2. Wil van der Aalst. WOFLAN: A Petri-net-based workflow analyser. In *International Conference on Application and Theory of Petri Nets in Lisbon*, number 1420 in Lecture Notes in Computer Science, Berlin Heidelberg New York, 1998. Springer Verlag.
3. W.M.P. van der Aalst. A class of Petri nets for modeling and analyzing business processes. Technical report, Department of Mathematics and Computing Science, Eindhoven University of Technology, P.O. Box 513, NL-5600 MB, Eindhoven, 1995.
4. The FIPA Agent UML web site. URL http://www.auml.org/, 2004.
5. R. Davis and R. Smith. Negotiation as a metaphor for distributed problem solving. *Artificial Intelligence*, 20(1):63–109, 1983.
6. Michael Duvigneau. Bereitstellung einer Agentenplattform für Petrinetzbasierte Agenten. Diplomarbeit, University of Hamburg, Department for Computer Science, Vogt-Kölln Str. 30, 22527 Hamburg, Germany, December 2002.
7. Michael Duvigneau, Daniel Moldt, and Heiko Rölke. Concurrent architecture for a multi-agent platform. In Fausto Giunchiglia, James Odell, and Gerhard Weiß, editors, *Third International Workshop, AOSE 2002, Bologna, Italy, July 15, 2002, Revised Papers and Invited Contributions*, volume 2585 of *LNCS*, Berlin Heidelberg New York, 2003. Springer.
8. Fipa contract net interaction protocol specification, December 2002. URL http://fipa.org/specs/fipa00029/SC00029H.pdf.
9. Foundation for intelligent physical agents. URL http://www.fipa.org/, 2004.
10. Olga Gertchikova. Transforming agent interaction-diagrams into executable petri nets based on FIPA conform protocols. B.Sc. Thesis, Universität Hamburg, Fachbereich Informatik, Vogt-Kölln Str. 30, 22527 Hamburg, 2004.
11. C. Girault and R. Valk. *Petri Nets for Systems Engineering - A Guide to Modeling, Verification, and Applications*. Springer-Verlag, 2003.
12. M. H. T. Hack. Decision problems for petri nets and vector addition systems. Project mac tr-59, MIT, Cambridge, 1975.
13. Michael N. Huhns and Larry M. Stephens. Multiagent systems and societies of agents. In Weiss [26], chapter 2, pages 79–120.

14. Integrated net analyzer - ina. URL
    http://www.informatik.hu-berlin.de/lehrstuehle/automaten/ina/, 2004. Informationen zum Petrinetzanalysator INA.
15. N. R. Jennings, K. Sycara, and M. Wooldridge. A roadmap of agent research and development. In *Autonomous Agents and Multi-Agent Systems* [26], pages 7–38.
16. Michael Köhler, Daniel Moldt, and Heiko Rölke. Modelling the structure and behaviour of Petri net agents. In J.M. Colom and M. Koutny, editors, *Proceedings of the 22nd Conference on Application and Theory of Petri Nets*, volume 2075 of *Lecture Notes in Computer Science*, pages 224–241. Springer-Verlag, 2001.
17. Olaf Kummer. *Referenznetze*. Dissertation, University of Hamburg, Department for Computer Science, Vogt-Kölln Str. 30, 22527 Hamburg, Germany, 2002.
18. Kolja Lehmann. Analyse und Bewertung von Agentenprotokollen mit Hilfe von Petrinetzen. Diplomarbeit, Universität Hamburg, Fachbereich Informatik, Vogt-Kölln Str. 30, 22527 Hamburg, 2003.
19. Daniel Moldt and Heiko Rölke. Pattern based workflow design using reference nets. In Wil van der Aalst, Arthur ter Hofstede, and Mathias Weske, editors, *Proc. of International Conference on BUSINESS PROCESS MANAGEMENT, Eindhoven, NL*, volume 2678, pages 246 – 260, Berlin Heidelberg New York, 2003. Springer-Verlag.
20. J. Odell, H. Parunak, and B. Bauer. Extending UML for agents, 2000.
21. S. Paurobally, J. Cunningham, and N. Jennings. Developing agent interaction protocols using graphical and logical methodologies, 2003. URL
    http://www.cs.uu.nl/ProMAS/papers/paper6.pdf.
22. Wolfgang Reisig. *Petrinetze; Eine Einführung*. Springer-Verlag, Berlin, Heidelberg, New York, 2. edition, 1986.
23. Heiko Rölke. Modellierung und Implementation eines Multi-Agenten-Systems auf der Basis von Referenznetzen. Diplomarbeit, Universität Hamburg, 1999.
24. Peter H. Starke. *Analyse von Petri-Netz-Modellen*. B.G. Teubner, Stuttgart, 1990.
25. H. M. W. Verbeek, T. Basten, and W. M. P. van der Aalst. Diagnosing workflow processes using Woflan. *The Computer Journal*, 44(4):246–279, 2001.
26. Gerhard Weiss, editor. *Multiagent Systems*. The MIT Press, Cambridge, Massachusetts London, England, second edition, 2000.
27. Woflan homepage. URL http://www.tm.tue.nl/it/woflan, 2004.
28. M. J. Wooldridge and N. R. Jennings. Intelligent agents: Theory and practice. *The Knowledge Engineering Review*, 2(10):115–152, 1995.
29. Michael Wooldridge. Intelligent agents. In Weiss [26], chapter 1, pages 27–77.

Paraconsistent Assertions*

Jørgen Villadsen

Computer Science, Roskilde University
Building 42.1, DK-4000 Roskilde, Denmark
jv@ruc.dk

Abstract. Classical logic predicts that everything (thus nothing useful at all) follows from inconsistency. A paraconsistent logic is a logic where inconsistency does not lead to such an explosion.

We argue that paraconsistent logics are especially advantageous in order to deal with assertions made by intelligent agents. Other propositional attitudes like knowledge and beliefs can in principle be treated along the same lines. We propose a many-valued paraconsistent logic based on a simple notion of indeterminacy. The proposed paraconsistent logic has a semantics that extends the one of classical logic and it is described using key equalities for the logical operators. A case study is included.

We briefly compare with logics based on bilattices. We finally investigate how to translate the paraconsistent logic into classical predicate logic thereby allowing us to make use of automated deduction of classical logic in the future. We base our initial translation on recent work by Muskens. Our final translation is polynomial in the size of the translated formula and follows the semantics for the paraconsistent logic directly.

The major motivation behind paraconsistent logic has always been the thought that in certain circumstances we may be in a situation where our information or theory is inconsistent, and yet where we are required to draw inferences in a sensible fashion...

Numerous examples of inconsistent information/theories from which one might want to draw inferences in a controlled way have been offered by paraconsistent logicians. For example:

1. *information in a computer data base;*
2. *various scientific theories;*
3. *constitutions and other legal documents;*
4. *descriptions of fictional (and other non-existent) objects;*
5. *descriptions of counterfactual situations.*

The first of these is fairly obvious...

Graham Priest: Paraconsistent Logic – Definition & Motivation
Handbook of Philosophical Logic, Second Edition, 2002

---

* This research was partly sponsored by the IT University of Copenhagen.

G. Lindemann et al. (Eds.): MATES 2004, LNAI 3187, pp. 99–113, 2004.

1   Introduction

Classical logic predicts that everything (thus nothing useful at all) follows from inconsistency. In paraconsistent logics the meanings of some or even all of the logical operators differ from classical logic in order to block the explosion of consequences from inconsistency. Since there are many ways to change the meanings of these operators there are many different paraconsistent logics [10, 8].

In the last decades paraconsistent logics have found various applications in artificial intelligence, cf. [1] for an overview. In particular paraconsistent logics have been explored in advanced data bases and/or knowledge bases [11, 5, 6, 13]. In the present paper we consider the possible use of paraconsistent logics in multiagent systems.

Let us recall the Belief-Desire-Intension (BDI) agent architecture [29, 9] with the following basic control loop:

Loop:

Observe the world.

Update internal world model.

Deliberate about what intention to achieve next.

Use means-ends reasoning to get a plan for the intention.

Execute the plan.

If classical logic is used in connection with the internal world model then the update algorithm (also known as the belief revision function) must ensure the consistency of the world model. But belief revision is often a very difficult task. The alternative is to use a paraconsistent, i.e. inconsistency-tolerent, logic instead of classical logic. However, the use of a paraconsistent logic is not without serious drawbacks – in order to block the explosion of consequences from inconsistency the logic might block so many essential logical inferences that the resulting system become virtually useless. Similar reservations must be made for several other types of intelligent agents, e.g. deductive or deliberate agents [14, 29, 17].

Hence these drawbacks can explain why paraconsistent logics are rarely used in the core of multiagent systems. But there is another potential use of paraconsistent logics that can be put forward, namely the treatment of assertions (assertions are here taken to be declarative sentences in some given natural or formal language). Communication between agents is vital, but assertions have some important characteristics:

- Assertions cannot be assumed consistent.
- Assertions can involve simple facts as well as rules (say, conditionals).

The reasons for lack of consistency in assertions are several: communication errors, inconsistent beliefs of other agents, or even dishonesty. Hence in many cases the inconsistency is not due to limited resources for reasoning – no matter how elaborate a belief revision function you apply, if the utterer of an assertion has inconsistent beliefs then you cannot just remove the inconsistency.

We consider a case study to illustrate these problems. The scenario is as follows: Assume that agent X thinks that his supervisor hides a secret that the public ought to know about. Agent X makes a number of assertions reflecting his analysis of the dilemma and these assertions are available to an observing agent:

#123   If I leak the secret then I keep my integrity.

#456   If I do not leak the secret then I keep my job.

#789   If I do not keep my job then I do not keep my integrity.

#1000   I do not keep my job.

The numbers indicate that the assertions are distibuted over some time interval and with other assertions interleaved. For simplicity present tense is used and taken to refer to a certain implicit time period of the immediate future.

Classically the assertions are inconsistent when taken together. This is not entirely obvious. As always we must keep in mind that both agent X and the observing agent are operating under time constraints. The assertions involve both simple facts (#1000) as well as rules (#123, #456, #789). A straightforward formalization is as follows:

$$L \rightarrow I \qquad \theta_1$$
$$\neg L \rightarrow J \qquad \theta_2$$
$$\neg J \rightarrow \neg I \qquad \theta_3$$
$$\neg J \qquad \theta_0$$

Here the propositional symbol L means that X leaks the secret, I that X keeps his integrity, and J that X keeps his job. As usual $\rightarrow$ is implication, $\wedge$ is conjunction, and $\neg$ is negation.

If the observing agent uses classical logic on the formulas $\theta_0, \theta_1, \theta_2, \theta_3$ she can conclude L, $\neg L$, I, $\neg I$, J, $\neg J$, and whatever other fact or rule considered. Of course it makes no sense to change the formulas $\theta_0, \theta_1, \theta_2, \theta_3$ because the assertions have been made as such.

One extreme approach would be just to leave the formulas $\theta_0, \theta_1, \theta_2, \theta_3$ as syntactic structures, hence not allowing them to participate in logical inferences at all. But that would severely restrict the use of assertions since not even, say, the usual commutative, associative, and distributive laws for conjunction $\wedge$ and disjunction $\vee$ could be used on the formulas.

In the present paper we propose to use a specific paraconsistent logic ∇ such that the agent can conclude only $\neg J$ or θ_0, which is reasonable (cf. section 2 for the discussion of monotonicity and reflexivity).

The paraconsistent logic ∇ is an extension of classical logic in the sense that classical reasoning is easily possible, just add the special formulas ΔL, ΔI, and ΔJ to the formulas $\theta_0, \theta_1, \theta_2, \theta_3$ and L, I, and J behave classically.

We now turn to the motivation behind the paraconsistent logic ∇ and provide an overview of the rest of the present paper. We return to the case study in section 5.

2   Motivation and Overview

As the above case study indicates, it is not really always possible to resolve the inconsistency and a paraconsistent logic seems worth investigating.

In the present paper we propose a paraconsistent logic ∇ based on a simple notion of indeterminacy. We are inspired by the use of the symbols Δ and ∇ in philosophical logic for determinacy and indeterminacy, respectively, cf. Evans [15] as the standard reference.

The paraconsistent logic ∇ grew out of recent work on the treatment of propositional attitudes like knowledge and belief in natural language [25, 27, 28]. It is a many-valued logic [19] and as such it differs from classical logic by the fundamental fact that it does not restrict the number of truth values to only two (to restrict the set of truth values of classical logic is meaningless, since at least two truth values are needed to distinguish truth from falsehood). It can be seen as a generalization of Łukasiewicz's three-valued logic (originally proposed 1920–30), with the intermediate value duplicated and ordered such that none of the copies of this value imply other ones, but it differs from Łukasiewicz's many-valued logics [19].

We allow equality $=$ between formulas. In classical logic equality $=$ corresponds to biimplication $\leftrightarrow$, but in the paraconsistent logic ∇ equality and biimplication differ as we shall see. We use the following binding priorities of the logical operators: equality $=$ (highest), conjunction $\wedge$, disjunction $\vee$, implication $\rightarrow$ and biimplication $\leftrightarrow$ (lowest). Parentheses are sometimes added for clarity. We use the symbol $\top$ for the designated truth value $\bullet$ (truth) and the symbol $\bot$ for the non-designated truth value $\circ$ (falsehood).

The paraconsistent logic ∇ has a quite simple semantics that extends the one of classical logic. In particular we describe the semantics of the logic using key equalities for the logical operators and we also argue in section 3 that three truth values ($\bullet$, $\circ$, and $\shortmid$) are not enough, but a four-valued logic is appropriate.

In the paraconsistent logic ∇ we have the usual inference rule *modus ponens* as in classical logic:

$$\frac{\varphi \quad \varphi \rightarrow \psi}{\psi}$$

But when formulated as a formula it does not hold:

$$(\varphi \wedge (\varphi \rightarrow \psi)) \rightarrow \psi$$

A counter-example would be when φ is $\shortmid$ and ψ is $\circ$, cf. section 3. However, the usual commutative, associative and distributive laws hold for $\wedge$ and $\vee$. Also the following De Morgan laws and the double negation law hold as in classical logic.

$$\neg(\varphi \wedge \psi) \ = \ (\neg\varphi \vee \neg\psi) \qquad \neg(\varphi \vee \psi) \ = \ (\neg\varphi \wedge \neg\psi) \qquad \neg\neg\varphi \ = \ \varphi$$

It is also important to note that the paraconsistent logic ∇ is a monotonic logic; further assumptions can safely be added:

$$\frac{(\varphi_1 \wedge \ldots \wedge \varphi_n) \rightarrow \psi}{(\varphi_1 \wedge \ldots \wedge \varphi_n \wedge \theta) \rightarrow \psi}$$

Let us discuss the paraconsistent logic ∇ with the first theorems considered by Church for classical logic as a starting point [12, pp. 81–84] (we use a modern notation where φ and ψ range over arbitrary formulas). The very first theorem is simply:

$$\varphi \to \varphi$$

This reflexive law of implication seems essential, but we note that in some paraconsistent logics, e.g. with respect to a special implication defined in Muskens [23], it does not hold, cf. [25].

The next theorems are the following:

$$\bot \to \varphi$$

$$\varphi \wedge \neg\varphi \to \psi$$

Although they look quite similar there is a big difference: the special formula for falsehood $\bot$ is not something that should be accessible for assertions by agents whereas the contradiction $\varphi \wedge \neg\varphi$ in principle could be asserted. The paraconsistent logic ∇ actually has the first law but not the second law.

The next law of classical logic we consider – which does not hold in the so-called intuitionistic logic [12] – is the law of excluded middle:

$$\varphi \vee \neg\varphi$$

This law does not hold in the paraconsistent logic ∇ – for different reasons than in the case of intuitionistic logic – but anyway it does not seem very useful to have as a theorem for assertions (of course it can be asserted; the question is whether it is important to have it as a universal truth).

We should also mention that in the paraconsistent logic ∇ the formula $\varphi \to \psi$ does not in general have the same truth value as $\neg\psi \to \neg\varphi$ (for example, if φ and ψ are ı and ıı, respectively, then $\varphi \to \psi$ is ı and $\neg\psi \to \neg\varphi$ is ıı, cf. section 3).

In summary:

- Nothing is permanently lost in the paraconsistent logic ∇ – it is just more flexible than classical logic.
- The paraconsistent logic ∇ is monotonic, and De Morgan and many other important laws hold.
- It even generalizes nicely to first order logic and higher order logic [28].

In section 3 we describe the paraconsistent logic ∇ and in section 4 we give truth tables and reduce the number of operators. We return to the case study in section 5. In section 6 we briefly compare with logics based on bilattices. In section 7 we consider the extension to predicate logic and in section 8 we discuss a translation into classical logic. Finally section 9 concludes.

3   A Paraconsistent Logic

Recall that classical logic has two truth values, namely • and ○ (truth and falsehood), and the designated truth value • yields the logical truths. But classical logic cannot handle inconsistency since an explosion occurs. In order to handle inconsistency we allow additional truth values.

The idea behind ∇ is quite simple; besides the determinate truth values $\bullet$ and $\circ$ we add an indeterminate truth value I (later we add additional indeterminate truth values). However, the semantic clause for equality is as usual.

$$[\![\varphi = \psi]\!] = \begin{cases} \bullet \text{ if } [\![\varphi]\!] = [\![\psi]\!] \\ \circ \text{ otherwise} \end{cases}$$

We are now ready for the central definitions. The motivation for the logical operators is to be found in the key equalities shown to the right of the following semantic clauses.

$$[\![\neg\varphi]\!] = \begin{cases} \bullet & \text{if } [\![\varphi]\!] = \circ \\ \circ & \text{if } [\![\varphi]\!] = \bullet \\ [\![\varphi]\!] & \text{otherwise} \end{cases} \qquad \begin{aligned} \top &= \neg\bot \\ \bot &= \neg\top \end{aligned}$$

$$[\![\varphi \wedge \psi]\!] = \begin{cases} [\![\varphi]\!] \text{ if } [\![\varphi]\!] = [\![\psi]\!] \\ [\![\psi]\!] \text{ if } [\![\varphi]\!] = \bullet \\ [\![\varphi]\!] \text{ if } [\![\psi]\!] = \bullet \\ \circ \quad \text{otherwise} \end{cases} \qquad \begin{aligned} \varphi &= (\varphi \wedge \varphi) \\ \psi &= (\top \wedge \psi) \\ \varphi &= (\varphi \wedge \top) \end{aligned}$$

In the semantic clauses several cases may apply if and only if they agree on the result. Note that the semantic clauses work for classical logic too.

To put it in words: the motivation for $\neg$ is that $\top$ and $\bot$ swap, and the motivation for $\wedge$ is that the addition of something to itself does not give anything new (known as idempotency) and that $\top$ is neutral.

We use the following standard abbreviations.

$$\bot \equiv \neg\top \qquad \varphi \vee \psi \equiv \neg(\neg\varphi \wedge \neg\psi) \qquad \varphi \neq \psi \equiv \neg(\varphi = \psi)$$

Similarly to negation $\neg$ and conjunction $\wedge$ the motivation for the definition of the biimplication operator $\leftrightarrow$ (and hence the abbreviation for the implication operator $\rightarrow$) is to be found in the key equalities shown to the right of the following semantic clause.

$$[\![\varphi \leftrightarrow \psi]\!] = \begin{cases} \bullet & \text{if } [\![\varphi]\!] = [\![\psi]\!] \\ [\![\psi]\!] & \text{if } [\![\varphi]\!] = \bullet \\ [\![\varphi]\!] & \text{if } [\![\psi]\!] = \bullet \\ [\![\neg\psi]\!] & \text{if } [\![\varphi]\!] = \circ \\ [\![\neg\varphi]\!] & \text{if } [\![\psi]\!] = \circ \\ \circ & \text{otherwise} \end{cases} \qquad \begin{aligned} \top &= (\varphi \leftrightarrow \varphi) \\ \psi &= (\top \leftrightarrow \psi) \\ \varphi &= (\varphi \leftrightarrow \top) \\ \neg\psi &= (\bot \leftrightarrow \psi) \\ \neg\varphi &= (\varphi \leftrightarrow \bot) \end{aligned}$$

As before several cases may apply if and only if they agree on the result and the semantic clause work for classical logic too.

To put it in words: the motivation for $\leftrightarrow$ is that $\top$ is neutral and $\bot$ is linked to $\neg$, and the motivation for $\rightarrow$ is that something is implied if its addition does not give anything new.

$$\varphi \to \psi \;\equiv\; \varphi \leftrightarrow \varphi \wedge \psi$$

We do not have $\varphi \vee \neg\varphi$ in ∇ since the indeterminate truth value $\mid$ is not designated (only $\bullet$ is designated). This follows from the semantic clauses and abbreviations just given (the truth tables in section 4 can also be used, but they are simply calculated from the semantic clauses). It then follows that since we obviously require that $\varphi \to \varphi$ then the usual definition $\varphi \to \psi \equiv \neg\varphi \vee \psi$ is not an alternative to the definition above. Unfortunately we would have $(\varphi \wedge \neg\varphi) \to (\psi \vee \neg\psi)$ in ∇ if the only truth values are $\bullet$, $\circ$ and $\mid$. This seems wrong – recall that we do not have $\psi \vee \neg\psi$ in ∇ – and the contradiction $\varphi \wedge \neg\varphi$ is not relevant to $\psi \vee \neg\psi$ in general.

The reason for this problem is that in a sense there is not only a single indeterminacy. Hence it make sense to consider $\parallel$ as the alternative indeterminacy. As discussed elsewhere [28] we think that in principle there should be a countably infinite number of truth values besides the two truth values of classical logic, but here it suffices to consider just these four truth values (additional truth values will not make a difference with respect to the case study).

We use the symbols $\dagger$ and $\ddagger$ for the values $\mid$ and $\parallel$, respectively, and then we use the following abbreviation.

$$\top \;\equiv\; \dagger = \dagger$$

4   Truth Tables and Reductions

Consider the following abbreviation.

$$\Box\varphi \;\equiv\; \varphi = \top$$

In classical logic the necessity operator $\Box$ as introduced above is vacuous (φ and $\Box\varphi$ are equivalent), but in ∇ we use $\Box\varphi$ to express that φ is classically true (and not contradictory). The operator $\Box$ is a so-called S5 modality [22].

We have the following truth tables – simply calculated from the semantic clauses in section 3 given that there are four truth values:

$\wedge$	$\bullet$	$\circ$	$\mid$	$\parallel$
$\bullet$	$\bullet$	$\circ$	$\mid$	$\parallel$
$\circ$	$\circ$	$\circ$	$\circ$	$\circ$
$\mid$	$\mid$	$\circ$	$\mid$	$\circ$
$\parallel$	$\parallel$	$\circ$	$\circ$	$\parallel$

$\vee$	$\bullet$	$\circ$	$\mid$	$\parallel$
$\bullet$	$\bullet$	$\bullet$	$\bullet$	$\bullet$
$\circ$	$\bullet$	$\circ$	$\mid$	$\parallel$
$\mid$	$\bullet$	$\mid$	$\mid$	$\bullet$
$\parallel$	$\bullet$	$\parallel$	$\bullet$	$\parallel$

$\neg$	
$\bullet$	$\circ$
$\circ$	$\bullet$
$\mid$	$\mid$
$\parallel$	$\parallel$

$\leftrightarrow$	$\bullet$	$\circ$	$\mid$	$\parallel$
$\bullet$	$\bullet$	$\circ$	$\mid$	$\parallel$
$\circ$	$\circ$	$\bullet$	$\mid$	$\parallel$
$\mid$	$\mid$	$\mid$	$\bullet$	$\circ$
$\parallel$	$\parallel$	$\parallel$	$\circ$	$\bullet$

$\to$	$\bullet$	$\circ$	$\mid$	$\parallel$
$\bullet$	$\bullet$	$\circ$	$\mid$	$\parallel$
$\circ$	$\bullet$	$\bullet$	$\bullet$	$\bullet$
$\mid$	$\bullet$	$\mid$	$\bullet$	$\mid$
$\parallel$	$\bullet$	$\parallel$	$\parallel$	$\bullet$

$=$	$\bullet$	$\circ$	$\mid$	$\parallel$
$\bullet$	$\bullet$	$\circ$	$\circ$	$\circ$
$\circ$	$\circ$	$\bullet$	$\circ$	$\circ$
$\mid$	$\circ$	$\circ$	$\bullet$	$\circ$
$\parallel$	$\circ$	$\circ$	$\circ$	$\bullet$

$\Box$	
$\bullet$	$\bullet$
$\circ$	$\circ$
$\mid$	$\circ$
$\parallel$	$\circ$

We next show that negation $\neg$, conjunction $\wedge$ and equality $=$ suffice. We use Δ for determinacy and ∇ for indeterminacy with the following abbreviations.

$$\Delta\varphi \;\equiv\; \Box(\varphi \vee \neg\varphi) \qquad \nabla\varphi \;\equiv\; \neg\Delta\varphi \qquad \varphi \rightsquigarrow \psi \;\equiv\; \neg\Box\varphi \vee \psi$$

We have the following truth tables – again simply calculated from the semantic clauses in section 3 given that there are four truth values:

Δ			∇			$\rightsquigarrow$	$\bullet$	$\circ$	$\shortmid$	$\shortparallel$
$\bullet$	$\bullet$		$\bullet$	$\circ$		$\bullet$	$\bullet$	$\circ$	$\shortmid$	$\shortparallel$
$\circ$	$\bullet$		$\circ$	$\circ$		$\circ$	$\bullet$	$\bullet$	$\bullet$	$\bullet$
$\shortmid$	$\circ$		$\shortmid$	$\bullet$		$\shortmid$	$\bullet$	$\bullet$	$\bullet$	$\bullet$
$\shortparallel$	$\circ$		$\shortparallel$	$\bullet$		$\shortparallel$	$\bullet$	$\bullet$	$\bullet$	$\bullet$

The abbreviation for $\leftrightarrow$ is based on its semantic clause above.

$$
\begin{aligned}
\varphi \leftrightarrow \psi \;\equiv\; & (\varphi = \psi \rightsquigarrow \top) \wedge \\
& (\varphi \rightsquigarrow \psi) \wedge \\
& (\psi \rightsquigarrow \varphi) \wedge \\
& (\neg\varphi \rightsquigarrow \neg\psi) \wedge \\
& (\neg\psi \rightsquigarrow \neg\varphi) \wedge \\
& (\nabla\varphi \wedge \nabla\psi \wedge \varphi \neq \psi \rightsquigarrow \bot)
\end{aligned}
$$

Now all truth tables are calculated from the semantic clauses of negation $\neg$, conjunction $\wedge$ and equality $=$ (well, we also need † and ‡ from which we get first $\top$ using $=$ and then $\bot$ using $\neg$ as shown in section 3).

5   Case Study

We return to the case study in section 1. Recall that classical logic explodes in the presence of the formulas $\theta_0, \theta_1, \theta_2, \theta_3$ (in other word: the formulas $\theta_0, \theta_1, \theta_2, \theta_3$ entail any formula φ). In ∇ we have several counter-examples as follows.

The reason why we do not have $(\theta_0 \wedge \theta_1 \wedge \theta_2 \wedge \theta_3) \rightarrow J$ is that $[\![L]\!] = \bullet$, $[\![I]\!] = \shortmid$, $[\![J]\!] = \circ$ is a counter-example. This can be seen from the truth tables – the result is $\shortmid$ which is not designated. The same counter-example also shows that the agent cannot conclude $\neg L$ since $[\![\neg L]\!] = \circ = [\![J]\!]$ and the agent cannot conclude J as just explained.

The agent cannot conclude L (take $[\![L]\!] = \circ$, $[\![I]\!] = \circ$, $[\![J]\!] = \shortmid$ as a counter-example) and neither I nor $\neg I$ (take $[\![L]\!] = \shortmid$, $[\![I]\!] = \shortparallel$, $[\![J]\!] = \shortmid$ in both cases).

There is quite some flexibility with respect to the formalization – as an example we consider changing θ_0 to $\Box\neg J$ where the logical necessity operator $\Box$ expresses that the fact is "really" true. Now the previous counter-example to L is no good and since it can be shown that there is no other counter-example, the agent concludes L (the agent also concludes $\neg I$, and of course still $\neg J$). Recall that classical logic is useless in this case study. The previous counter-example to $\neg L$ and J is ok, and there is a counter-example $[\![L]\!] = \shortmid$, $[\![I]\!] = \circ$, $[\![J]\!] = \circ$ to I.

In order to show that there are no counter-examples in the cases just explained the following line of reasoning is possible. Let us consider the following formula, where φ is L, $\neg I$, or $\neg J$, respectively.

$$(\Box \neg J \wedge (L \to I) \wedge (\neg L \to J) \wedge (\neg J \to \neg I)) \quad \to \quad \varphi$$

If we are going to have a counter-example where $\neg J$ is $\bullet$ (as required by $\Box\neg J$) then we can assume that $\neg I$ is $\bullet$ or $\shortmid$ (it could be $\shortparallel$ but that case is symmetric to the $\shortmid$ case). We have that assumption due to $\neg J \to \neg I$. And then from $\neg L \to J$ we have that $\neg L$ is $\circ$ or $\shortmid$, hence L is $\bullet$ or $\shortmid$. If both L and $\neg I$ are $\bullet$ we are done with the main implication (since φ is L, $\neg I$, or $\neg J$); and if at least one of them is $\shortmid$ then the left hand side of the main implication is $\shortmid$ and the right hand side is $\shortmid$ too, and we are done.

We think that the case study shows that the logic ∇ is inconsistency-tolerant in an interesting way (see also [27] for a case study in the domain of medicine).

6   Comparison with Bilattices

Muskens [23] considers a four-valued logic that has become prominent recently, namely the so-called bilattice approach for the logic that was originally developed by Belnap [7, 24].

In classical logic we have just two truth values, denoted True and False here. On the bilattice approach we move from truth values to partial truth values, namely sets of truth values, as illustrated in the third column.

$\top$	$\bullet$	{True}	**T**	Just true
$\bot$	$\circ$	{False}	**F**	Just false
$\dagger$	$\shortmid$	{}	**N**	Neither true nor false
$\ddagger$	$\shortparallel$	{True, False}	**B**	Both true and false

The fourth column shows the names used in the meta-language for the partial truth values in for example [19] and the second column shows the names that we have used (but the semantics is different). The first column shows the symbols that we use in the paraconsistent logic ∇ for the values (note that these are different from for example [19], but they correspond nicely to our names).

The idea is to have two partial orderings of these partial truth values:

– A *truth* lattice – with $\bullet$ at the top and $\circ$ at the bottom, and with $\shortmid$ and $\shortparallel$ somehow "between", because they, in a suitable sense, if assigned to φ leaves open both possibilities that φ may "really" be true or be false.

– A *knowledge* lattice – with $\shortparallel$ at the top as "over-determined" and $\shortmid$ at the bottom as "under-determined", and with $\bullet$ and $\circ$ somehow "between" corresponding to the classical truth values.

We note that the corresponding *truth* lattice operations give the same conjunction (meet), disjunction (join) and negation operators (inversion) as in ∇.

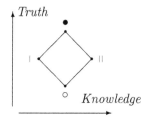

In the so-called Hasse diagram above the *truth* lattice goes "bottom-up" and the *knowledge* lattice goes "left-to-right" (the two lattices are independent of one another). Taken together the two lattices constitute a bilattice [18, 3].

There are numerous choices for the implication and biimplication operators, but they all differ from the definitions used in the paraconsistent logic ∇, cf. [19, pages 393–400] for a survey. We have not considered the notion of entailment here since in ∇ we would simply define it in the following way:

$$\varphi_1, \ldots, \varphi_n \models \psi \quad \text{iff} \quad (\varphi_1 \wedge \ldots \wedge \varphi_n) \rightarrow \psi \text{ is universally } \bullet \text{ in } \nabla$$

Muskens [23] essentially does the same, but for another implication $\twoheadrightarrow$ defined there on the bilattices and which has some problematic issues, cf. [25].

7   On the Extension to Predicate Logic

Since the paraconsistent logic ∇ is a many-valued logic it is quite straightforward to extend the propositional logic described in section 3 to a predicate logic (also known as first order logic; we have recently [28] described a sequent calculus for ∇ extended to a higher order logic that can serve as a foundation of mathematics).

We here only have space to define the syntax of ∇ extended to a predicate logic; we need to be precise since in section 8 we discuss translations of the paraconsistent logic ∇ into classical predicate logic and there we need to use classical predicate logic instead of propositional logic even for the propositional part of ∇ and therefore the predicate part of ∇ comes for free, so to speak.

We assume a countably infinite set of individual variables, a set of individual constant symbols and a set of relation symbols each having a fixed number of argument places. A term is either an individual variable or an individual constant. The set of formulas is defined with the following clauses:

1. If R is an n-ary relation symbols and $t_1, \ldots, t_n$ are terms then $Rt_1 \ldots t_n$ is an (atomic) formula.
2. If t and t' are terms then $t = t'$ is an (atomic) formula.
3. † and ‡ are (atomic) formulas.
4. If φ and ψ are formulas then $\neg\varphi$, $\varphi \wedge \psi$ and $\varphi = \psi$ are formulas.
5. If φ is a formula and x is an individual variable then $\forall x \varphi$ is a formula.

Note that equality is used both between formulas (as before) and between terms.

One reason why predicates are useful is that it enables us to treat propositional attitudes like knowledge, beliefs, and assertions in a style due originally to Hintikka [21], also known as the possible worlds approach. It is explained by Muskens [23] and we only outline the idea here by means of a tiny eample; see also [25] for a grammar formalism that takes care of both the syntax and semantics for a quite substantial fragment of English.

Consider the sentence "X asserts that Y cheats" and let x and y stand for the agents X and Y, respectively. Let A be a 3-argument relation symbol capturing assertions (the arguments are the asserting agent, the world in which the asserting takes place, and the worlds compatible with the assertions), w a constant pointing out the actual world, and C a 2-argument relation symbol capturing the property of cheaters (the arguments are the cheater and the world in which the cheating takes place). The formalization of the sentence is then essentially:

$$\forall i(Axwi \rightarrow Cyi)$$

Hence it is required that Y cheats in all possible worlds compatible with the assertions of X in the actual world. Knowledge and beliefs would use relation symbols K and B, respectively, and there are postulates about these relation symbols that give capabilities like positive introspection (if something is known then it is known that it is known and so on). Please consult the above references for further information. The main point here is that propositional attitudes can be formalized in predicate logic and that the results from the case study also hold for the possible worlds approach.

8   A Translation into Classical Logic

It is a standard for many non-classical logics to be translated into classical logic. Such translations are done for a variety of reasons [16, 4]:

- To give semantics to the logic.
- To compare it with other logics.
- To get decidability/undecidability results.
- To make use of automated deduction of classical logic.

The last item is our main motivation.

Our starting point is Muskens [23, pp. 51–55]. Although Muskens refers to the bilattice approach we are able to use a similar translation.

With each n-ary relation symbols R of the paraconsistent logic ∇ we associate two n-ary symbols R^+ and R^-. Muskens calls these the denotation and the anti-denotation, but we consider them as "shadows" in the following sense (they must agree with each other to give a determinate value):

	R^+	R^-
•	True	True
○	False	False
ı	True	False
‖	False	True

The classical logic has all individual constants of ∇ and in addition a new zero-arity relation symbol p used for the indeterminate truth values ǀ and ǁ. In the initial translation we use two temporary zero-arity relation symbols p^+ and p^- together with the following conventions:

> $\pm\varphi$ is the result of simultaneously substituting each R^+ for its associated R^- and R^- for its associated R^+ in φ (and p^+ and p^- are meant to be included here).

> $|\varphi|$ is identical to φ except that all occurrences of p^+ are replaced with p and all occurrences of p^- are replaced with $\neg p$.

With each formula φ of ∇ we associate a formula φ^μ of classical logic with the help of the following clauses:

1. $(Rt_1 \ldots t_n)^\mu = R^+ t_1 \ldots t_n$

2. $(t = t')^\mu = t = t'$

3. $\dagger^\mu = p^+ \qquad \ddagger^\mu = p^-$

4. $(\neg\varphi)^\mu = \neg \pm \varphi^\mu$

   $(\varphi \wedge \psi)^\mu = \varphi^\mu \wedge \psi^\mu$

   $(\varphi = \psi)^\mu = (\varphi^\mu \leftrightarrow \psi^\mu) \wedge \pm(\varphi^\mu \leftrightarrow \psi^\mu)$

5. $(\forall x \varphi)^\mu = \forall x \varphi^\mu$

As usual a sentence is a closed formula. The correctness of the translation is due to the following result which follows from an "Embedding Theorem" [23, p. 54] using the correspondance $\bullet \mapsto \mathbf{T}, \circ \mapsto \mathbf{F}, \text{ǀ} \mapsto \mathbf{N}, \text{ǁ} \mapsto \mathbf{B}$ and the correspondance between the truth tables for ∇ given in section 3 and the truth tables for the bilattice approach [23, p. 43] (in addition Muskens uses the axiom $(p^+ \wedge \neg p^-) \vee (p^- \wedge \neg p^+)$ instead of the replacement of all occurrences of p^+ with p and all occurrences of p^- with $\neg p$).

Theorem I

For all sentences φ of ∇, φ holds in ∇ iff $|\varphi^\mu|$ holds in classical logic.

For example, in ∇ the formula (sentence) $\dagger \vee \ddagger$ holds since it has the designated truth value $\bullet$ (cf. the truth tables); as expected the following translation of the formula holds in classical logic:

$$|(\dagger \vee \ddagger)^\mu| = |(\neg(\neg\dagger \wedge \neg\ddagger))^\mu| = |\neg(\neg p^+ \wedge \neg p^-)| = |p^+ \vee p^-| = p \vee \neg p$$

We observe that there is an asymmetry in the translation in the sense that R^+ is used (and p^+ and p^- are used for $\dagger$ and $\ddagger$, respectively). However, this is only apparent, since in the theorem above we could equally well have used $|\varphi^\mu \wedge \pm\varphi^\mu)|$ which would give a perfect symmetry.

The translation φ^μ is exponential in the size of the formula φ (due to the particular translation of $\varphi = \psi$). Since our main motivation for the translation into classical logic is to make use of automated deduction of classical logic, this is problematic. We briefly outline a solution involving another translation.

Let I and O be two new constants and let s and s' be two variables reserved for the new translation φ^τ. If α is a term we use the following abbreviation (known as a conditional expression in programming languages like Java).

$$\alpha \;?\; \varphi : \varphi' \;\equiv\; (\alpha = I \wedge \varphi) \vee (\alpha = O \wedge \varphi')$$

With each formula φ of ∇ we associate a formula φ^τ of classical logic with the help of the following clauses:

1. $(Rt_1 \ldots t_n)^\tau = s \;?\; R^+ t_1 \ldots t_n : R^- t_1 \ldots t_n$
2. $(t = t')^\tau = t = t'$
3. $\dagger^\tau = s \;?\; p : \neg p \qquad \ddagger^\tau = s \;?\; \neg p : p$
4. $(\neg \varphi)^\tau = \forall s_0 (s_0 = s \rightarrow \forall s (s_0 \;?\; s = O : s = I \rightarrow \neg \varphi^\tau))$

   $(\varphi \wedge \psi)^\tau = \varphi^\tau \wedge \psi^\tau$

   $(\varphi = \psi)^\tau = \forall s ((s = 0 \vee s = I) \rightarrow (\varphi^\tau \leftrightarrow \psi^\tau))$
5. $(\forall x \varphi)^\tau = \forall x \varphi^\tau$

The idea is that the free variable s codes the "polarity" with I corresponding to $+$ and O corresponding to $-$. The variable s_0 is used to temporary store the value of s that must be "negated" in the clause for negation. Using Theorem I we obtain the following result.

Theorem II

For all sentences φ of ∇, φ holds in ∇ iff $\forall s ((s = 0 \vee s = I) \rightarrow \varphi^\tau)$ holds in classical logic.

As before we actually only need to check that $\forall s (s = 0 \rightarrow \varphi^\tau)$ holds in classical logic (the value for s can be propagated further into φ^τ, of course).

Besides being polynomial in the size of the formula φ we find that the translation φ^τ also follows the semantics for the logic ∇ directly: A sentence φ holds if both "itself" $(+)$ and "its shadow" $(-)$ are True (p captures the indeterminate truth value since it can be True or False arbitrarily). The negation of a formula swaps $+$ and $-$ (in addition to classical negation) in order to keep the indeterminate truth value. The conjunction of two formulas does not involve $+$ or $-$ (simply the classical conjunction). The equality between formulas tests both $+$ and $-$ (with respect to classical equality).

Of course the translation of the paraconsistent logic ∇ into classical logic by no means makes ∇ superfluous; assertions in a multi-agent system must first be formalized in ∇ before the translation takes place and the tools for automated deduction of classical logic are used. It still remains to be investigated whether the translation approach as described is usable in practice. However, as listed in the beginning of this section there are several other benefits of the translation.

9   Conclusions and Future Work

We propose to use the paraconsistent logic ∇ in connection with assertions made by intelligent agents. Communication errors, inconsistent beliefs of other agents, or even dishonesty seem to require a logic that, unlike classical logic, tolerates contradictions. Of course such a logic must differ from classical logic in a number of ways. We consider additional truth values besides • and ○ (truth and falsehood; the designated truth value • yields the logical truths).

We can easily make the four-valued paraconsistent logic ∇ behave as classical logic by using the determinacy operator Δ on every propositional symbol, e.g. the following formula holds in ∇ (every interpretation would give the formula the designated truth value • since the left hand side of the main implication would be ○ for indeterminate truth values I or II for any of I, J, or L):

$$((L \rightarrow I) \wedge (\neg L \rightarrow J) \wedge (\neg J \rightarrow \neg I) \wedge \Delta (I \wedge J \wedge L)) \quad \rightarrow \quad J$$

Hence nothing is permanently lost in the paraconsistent logic ∇ – it is just more flexible than classical logic.

We recently developed a so-called sequent calculus for a higher order logic extension of the paraconsistent logic ∇ [28]. In a higher order logic it is possible to reason about many mathematical structures, including numbers, lists, trees, etc. Pre- and post-conditions of programs can be established. We are investigating how to link simple programs to plans in ordinary practical reasoning agents [29, 9] in order to obtain more advanced rational agents [26].

Fuzzy logic is widely used currently in agent research. The basic idea [30] has in the last decades been developed as a branch of many-valued logic based on the paradigm of inference under vagueness [20, 19] and a comparison and/or possible amalgamation with the paraconsistent logic ∇ is being worked on.

While it is true that $\varphi \wedge \neg \varphi$ does not entail arbitrary ψ we do have that $\neg \varphi$ entails $\varphi \rightarrow \psi$, hence we do not have a relevant logic [2] in general (but only for so-called first degree entailment). The paraconsistent logic ∇ validates clear "fallacies of relevance" like the one just noted, or like the inference from φ to $\psi \rightarrow \psi$, but these do not seem problematic for the applications we have in mind.

References

1. J. M. Abe. Some recent applications of paraconsistent systems to AI. *Logique & Analyse*, 157:83–96, 1997.
2. A. R. Anderson and N. D. Belnap Jr. *Entailment: The Logic of Relevance and Necessity.* Princeton University Press, 1975.
3. O. Arieli and A. Avron. Bilattices and paraconsistency. In D. Batens, C. Mortensen, G. Priest, and J. Van-Bengedem, editors, *Frontiers in Paraconsistent Logic*, pages 11–27. Research Studies Press, 2000.
4. O. Arieli and M. Denecker. Reducing preferential paraconsistent reasoning to classical entailment. *Journal of Logic and Computation*, 13(4):557–580, 2003.
5. R. Bagai. A query construct for paraconsistent databases. In *Proceedings of the 7th International Conference on Information Processing and Management of Uncertainty in Knowledge-Based Systems, Paris, France*, pages 428–434, 1998.

6. R. Bagai and R. Sunderraman. A paraconsistent relational data model. *International Journal of Computer Mathematics*, 55(1):39–55, 1995.
7. N. D. Belnap Jr. A useful four-valued logic. In J. M. Dunn and G. Epstein, editors, *Modern Uses of Multiple-Valued Logic*, pages 8–37. D. Reidel, 1977.
8. P. Besnard and A. Hunter. Introduction to actual and potential contradictions. In D. M. Gabbay and P. Smets, editors, *Handbook of Defeasible Reasoning and Uncertainty Management Systems: Volume II*, pages 1–9. Kluwer Academic Publishers, 1998.
9. M. E. Bratman. *Intentions, Plans, and Practical Reason*. Harvard University Press, 1987.
10. W. A. Carnielli, M. E. Coniglio, and I. M. L. D'Ottaviano, editors. *Paraconsistency: The logical way to the inconsistent*. Marcel Dekker, 2002.
11. W. A. Carnielli, J. Marcos, and S. de Amo. Formal inconsistency and evolutionary databases. *Logic and Logical Philosophy*, 8:115–152, 2000.
12. A. Church. *Introduction to Mathematical Logic*. Princeton University Press, 1956.
13. N. C. A. da Costa and V. S. Subrahmanian. Paraconsistent logics as a formalism for reasoning about inconsistent knowledge bases. *Artificial Intelligence in Medicine*, 1:167–174, 1989.
14. J. Dix, J. A. Leite, and K. Satoh, editors. *International Workshop on Computational Logic in Multi-Agent Systems*, volume 93 of *Roskilde University, Computer Science, Technical Reports*, 2002.
15. G. Evans. Can there be vague objects? *Analysis*, 38(4):208, 1978.
16. D. Gabbay, O. Rodrigues, and A. Russo. Revision by translation. In B. Bouchon-Meunier, R. R. Yager, and L. A. Zadeh, editors, *Information, Uncertainty and Fusion*. Kluwer Academic Publishers, 2000.
17. M. R. Genesereth and N. J. Nilsson. *Logical Foundations of Artificial Intelligence*. Morgan Kaufmann Publishers, 1987.
18. M. Ginsberg. Multivalued logics: A uniform approach to inference in artificial intelligence. *Computer Intelligence*, 4:265–316, 1988.
19. S. Gottwald. *A Treatise on Many-Valued Logics*. Research Studies Press, 2001.
20. P. Hajek. *Metamathematics of Fuzzy Logic*. Kluwer Academic Publishers, 1998.
21. J. Hintikka. *Knowledge and Belief*. Cornell University Press, 1962.
22. G. E. Hughes and M. J. Cresswell. *An Introduction to Modal Logic*. Methuen and Co., 1968.
23. R. Muskens. *Meaning and Partiality*. CSLI Publications, Stanford, California, 1995.
24. R. Muskens. On partiality and paraconsistent logics. *Notre Dame Journal of Formal Logic*, 40(3):352–374, 1999.
25. J. Villadsen. Combinators for paraconsistent attitudes. In P. de Groote, G. Morrill, and C. Retoré, editors, *Logical Aspects of Computational Linguistics*, pages 261–278. Springer-Verlag, 2001. LNCS 2099.
26. J. Villadsen. On programs in rational agents. In M. R. Hansen, editor, *Nordic Workshop on Programming Theory*, 2001. IMM-TR-2001-12.
27. J. Villadsen. Paraconsistent query answering systems. In T. Andreasen, A. Motro, H. Christiansen, and H. L. Larsen, editors, *International Conference on Flexible Query Answering Systems*, pages 370–384. Springer-Verlag, 2002. LNCS 2522.
28. J. Villadsen. A paraconsistent higher order logic. In *International Conference on Artificial Intelligence and Symbolic Computation*. Springer-Verlag, 2004. To appear in LNCS.
29. M. Wooldridge. *An Introduction to Multiagent Systems*. John Wiley & Sons, 2002.
30. L. A. Zadeh. Fuzzy sets. *Information and Control*, 8:338–353, 1965.

C-IPS: Specifying Decision Interdependencies in Negotiations

Kay Schröter and Diemo Urbig

Humboldt–Universität zu Berlin
Department of Computer Science
{kschroet,urbig}@informatik.hu-berlin.de

Abstract. Negotiation is an important mechanism of coordination in multiagent systems. Contrary to early conceptualizations of negotiating agents, we believe that decisions regarding the negotiation issue and the negotiation partner are equally important as the selection of negotiation steps. Our C-IPS approach considers these three aspects as separate decision processes. It requires an explicit specification of interdependencies between them. In this article we address the task of specifying the dynamic interdependencies by means of IPS dynamics. Thereby we introduce a new level of modeling negotiating agents that is above negotiation mechanism and protocol design. IPS dynamics are presented using state charts. We define some generally required states, predicates and actions. We illustrate the dynamics by a simple example. The example is first specified for an idealized scenario and is then extended to a more realistic model that captures some features of open multiagent systems. The well-structured reasoning process for negotiating agents enables more comprehensive and hence more flexible architectures. The explicit modeling of all involved decisions and dependencies eases the understanding, evaluation, and comparison of different approaches to negotiating agents.

1 Introduction

Consider having a paper presentation at a scientific conference late in the evening close to the end of the conference. Perhaps you are in conflict with several participants who leave the conference earlier, but you would like to talk to as many participants as possible. You might try to "negotiate" with them about staying until your presentation. Take care to recognize the conflict quickly; else they might already have been gone. You can also choose another negotiation issue with other partners to solve the conflict: You may negotiate with the local organizer or perhaps the session chair to assign you another time slot. Perhaps you are already in contact with the local organizer and you can take the chance to adapt the issue of conversation; hence, you do not have to set up another interaction. Again, it is important that you recognize the conflict on time.

If not the same, but similar situations associated with perceived conflicts may occur in complex multiagent systems. In high-level multiagent systems, which you can find in e-business environments as for instance Internet purchasing or supply chain management, negotiations are an often applied mechanism

G. Lindemann et al. (Eds.): MATES 2004, LNAI 3187, pp. 114–125, 2004.

to resolve such conflicts [HS99,San99]. Also in other domains negotiation is a frequently used metaphor for specific conflict resolution mechanisms. That is why analyzing and modeling negotiating agents has become an important area of research in distributed artificial intelligence and information systems engineering.

An influential conceptualization of analyzing and modeling negotiating agents distinguishes between three most important concepts: the negotiation object, the negotiation protocol, and the agent's internal reasoning process [JFL+00]. Although several authors have explored questions like which issue should be negotiated (e.g. [FWJ03]) and how are negotiation partners selected (e.g. [KL02]), these aspects have not been considered as generally important concepts in agent negotiation. A comment at an early presentation of the C-IPS framework revealed that sometimes scientists assume that the conflict itself unambiguously defines the partners that are needed to solve the conflict. But as can bee seen by our introductory example, this is not a general law. The example shows that recognition of conflicts and selection of negotiation issues and partners are important processes when dealing with negotiating agents. They become especially important for complex open multiagent systems. Therefore, when analyzing different solutions to negotiating agents the answers to questions about issue, partner, and step selection processes should be easily accessible. But the already mentioned conceptualization does not address decisions related to a negotiation partner nor does it provide an adequate structure for the agent's reasoning process. Thus, also the (dynamic) dependencies between different decisions are not explicitly specified.

The C-IPS approach that we take up in this article is a promising way to structure negotiating agents [UMS03,US04]). It distinguishes between external constraints (C) the agent has to follow and an internal reasoning process (IPS) that describes the agent's decisions. The latter deals with decisions regarding the selection of negotiation issues (I), partners (P), and particular negotiation steps (S). The interdependencies between these three decisions can be described at a new separate level, which differs from dealing with negotiation protocols or defining negotiation objects. Based on a simple example we illustrate the specification of such interdependencies. The C-IPS approach does not only provide a more sophisticated, comprehensive, and explicit perspective to negotiating agents, but also it provides a better base to compare different designs of negotiating agents.

Following this introduction, the second section provides a brief summary of the C-IPS approach. For modeling IPS dynamics the third section starts with an introduction of some general states and predicates for these states. Subsequently we apply the general ideas to a simple example: the modeling and implementation of agents in the INKA project[1]. In the fourth section we specify negotiating agents in a very idealized world, while the fifth section continuous with extending it to capture more realistic phenomenons in open multiagent system, i.e. drop out of partners or problem solution as side effects of other actions.

---

[1] The *INKA project* is funded by Deutsche Forschungsgemeinschaft (DFG) under grant 788/4-2 and 788/4-3 within the priority program *Socionics*. This priority program supports research projects that combine sociology and computer science.

2   The C-IPS Approach

A negotiation is a process by which a joint decision is reached by two or more agents, each trying to reach an individual goal or objective [HS99].

Consider an agent designer modeling a negotiating agent that should be able to solve a particular conflict. The agent might be enabled to decide everything that is necessary to solve the conflict in any way that is possible. Due to complexity reduction as well as due to the application domain this freedom is frequently restricted. Thus the C-IPS approach separates external constraints from the agent's internal reasoning process. The distinction between protocols and strategies (see [HS99,RZ94]) mirrors the same logic but claims less generality. The two driving forces of external constraints, i.e. application domain and agent designer, appear in [SW03] as exogenous and endogenous criteria.

The C-IPS approach considers decisions regarding the selection of negotiation issues, the selection of negotiation partners, and the selection of negotiation steps as separate although mutually dependent aspects of negotiating agents [UMS03,US04]. Hence, the external constraints as well as the agent's internal reasoning process contain these aspects as separate parts. The C-IPS approach encourages and requires an explicit specification of the interdependencies between these three parts. This article provides a first attempt to do this in a standardized manner. Before we specify the dynamics of our example, we briefly introduce the different parts of C-IPS. We relate them to the concepts of negotiation space and protocols and give an intuition why we believe the C-IPS approach to be more general while at the same time more specific.

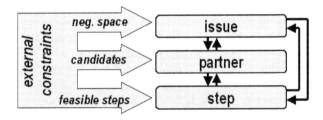

Fig. 1. C-IPS approach.

External constraints define the joint decisions agents are able to negotiate, i.e. the *negotiation space N*. If the external constraints for the negotiation issue are not too strong, then negotiating agents usually consider only subspaces in one ongoing negotiation, i.e. *negotiation issues*. For selecting a negotiation issue Huhns and Stephens suggest that agents communicate their position to identify conflicts, which then represent the issue of negotiations [HS99]. For flexible agents with large negotiation spaces a continuous broadcasting or a public knowledge of goals and objectives might be inefficient or even strategically inappropriate. Additionally, it can happen that the resulting space of possible agreements is too large, such that it should be reduced more. The reduction of large negotiation spaces, i.e. selection of issues, is a very important and not trivial aspect of an agents' reasoning process, see for instance [FWJ03]. This reduction can even change (mostly shrink) the set of negotiation partners, especially if different partners are responsible for different issues. The introductory example about the conference gives an intuition for this problem. Keep also in mind that the negotiation space does not need to be fully explored. Because negotiations are not necessarily only about making concessions but can also be about exploring the negotiation space to find currently individually unknown possible joint decisions [HS99].

An appropriate balance between external constraints and internal decision processes is also vital for the choice of *negotiation partners* from the set of *candidates C*. If *C* is restricted to agents that suffer from a conflict, then superficial solutions might be lost, i.e. not every conflict unambiguously determines the appropriate negotiation partners. Again this is exemplified by our example. It is open whether a negotiation with conference participants is more promising than a negotiation with the local chair. Sometimes it might even be more appropriate to select negotiation partners before fixing a particular issue; for instance, a provider of several products with thousands of potential buyers might select the negotiation partner before fixing the product to sell.

Beside issues and candidates, agents need *interactions* to reach a conflict resolution. Frequently these interactions are communicative acts or sequences of them. From the set of *feasible steps F* given by a protocol the agent selects the actually intended *negotiation step*. The step component may also select sequences of steps or even strategies; this depends on the specific implementation. Protocols may also restrict the set of candidates. However, one can imagine that agents think about the appropriate protocol or about the protocol a partner actually applies. The protocol and the selection of steps according to the protocol are up to now the best analyzed aspects for negotiating agents; the other aspects and especially their interdependencies are less well analyzed.

Although the C-IPS approach encourages a more precise specification of interdependencies between the selection of issues, partners, and negotiation steps, we emphasize that it does not require a specific implementation of selection processes nor of their interdependencies. The decision can follow a sequential approach or agents may be allowed to change the issue in an ongoing negotiation or to choose the partner before fixing a negotiation issue or even the other way around. The decisions themselves may be implemented following a complex BDI approach or other approaches, but this is not subject to this article. Thus C-IPS provides a level of analysis and modeling that is above designing negotiation protocols and strategies.

The C-IPS approach has been applied within the INKA project. The project aims at the development of socially intelligent agents that negotiate the exchange of shifts in a hospital. The project's objective is not to contribute to theory on scheduling but analyzes the human behavior related to the application of socially intelligent agents [MUSG03]. INKA agents can automatically initiate and perform negotiations on behalf of their users, but the users can also make all decisions themselves. During the analysis and modeling phase the C-IPS approach has successfully supported the communication between sociologists and computer scientists. Additionally, it has provided a basis for locating aspects of negotiating agents that are affected by specific sociological concepts [UMS03].

3   Specifying IPS Dynamics with State Charts

After introducing the C-IPS framework, we now come to the main contribution of this paper: the specification of interdependencies between the issue, partner and step selection processes. We will do so by defining states and transitions between these states. State charts will be used to visualize the specification. Thereby we build upon and extend the concepts developed in [US04]. Before we come to our example, we will provide some generally required states, predicates and actions.

The most prominent kind of state in our approach is an *IPS state* accumulating the decisions made by the different components. We define an *IPS state* as a three-dimensional vector $(I, P, S) \in (N \cup \bot) \times (C \cup \bot) \times (F \cup \bot)$. This state can be interpreted as the intention of the agent to act in a particular way regarding a given issue with a given partner. The three slots may have specific values or may be undefined; the latter is indicated by a $\bot$. If a specific value is set, it must be in accordance with the relevant external constraints given the other values in the *IPS state*. The different slots of an *IPS state* can be set via the actions[2] $I = SEL\_I$, $P = SEL\_P$, and $S = SEL\_S$, respectively. These actions model the different selection processes. If no decision is possible then the actions result in undefined values $\bot$.

For *IPS states* we define the predicate $DONE(I, P, S)$ that holds if the current *IPS state* represents an intention that has been already performed. The agent may realize that particular *IPS states* are – at least temporarily – impossible; it is not useful to consider these states for decisions in the near future[3]. Hence, we need a mechanism to check whether a set of *IPS states* is impossible and we need a mechanism to mark a set of *IPS states* as impossible. The predicate $IMP(I, P, S)$ holds if a state is currently impossible. The action $SET\_IMP(I, P, S, t)$ marks the state (I, P, S) impossible; this impossibility is reconsidered after a time period specified by t. An asterisk instead of a specific I, P or S value stands for an arbitrary element. Thus a whole set of states is checked or marked; for instance, $SET\_IMP(I, *, *, 20)$ sets issue I impossible with any partner and step for the next 20 time units.

4   Example: IPS Dynamics for a Sequential Approach

So far we provided generally required states, actions and conditions. We will now illustrate the specification of IPS dynamics for a sequential approach. This

---

[2] These are actions in the terms of state charts. They are not agent interactions.

[3] Imagine the agent does not find negotiation partners for a specific issue or all possible negotiations on that issue failed. Then all states comprising this issue are temporarily impossible.

approach has been used when designing our INKA system. First we will explain the effects of some external constraints we have set when designing our example. These constraints are not domain dependent and are not implied by the C-IPS framework. Rather the C-IPS framework allows specifying the negotiation process for many different constraints. Second we will give the state chart for this approach in an idealized environment. Third we extend the state chart to deal with the challenges of an open multiagent system.

4.1   External Constraints Influencing the Dynamics

As a first constraint, we follow a sequential approach in taking the three decisions regarding the negotiation. We start with selecting an issue, then we chose an appropriate partner for that issue and finally we decide on the next step in the negotiation on that issue and with that partner. This implies that all transitions between states can only change one slot of an *IPS state*. The sequential approach reduces the number and the complexity of interdependencies, which results in fewer transitions and less complex conditions for the transitions.

Second, our example requires that an agent is only engaged in one negotiation at the same time. We define an agent as engaged in a negotiation if it has selected a step S. For specifying the interdependencies we need to distinguish between *IPS states* that allow joining a negotiation and *IPS states* that do not so. That is why we introduce the two states *busy* and *¬busy*. The state *busy* comprises all IPS states where the step S is specified and the state *¬busy* comprises all other IPS states. If the agent is in state busy it will not participate in any further negotiation. As the transitions between *busy* and *¬busy* are closely related to transitions between IPS states they are not explained here, but in the following subsections.

Third, in our system the information distribution is asymmetric. The agents do not know about each other's conflicts. This requires that our agents are able to ask other agents to help them by negotiating the conflict. We term an agent that asks for a negotiation *initiator* and an agent that accepts the request *responder*. An agent must be able to request a negotiation (via step S_r) and to agree to a negotiation (via step S_a). Contrary to the initiator it is not reasonable to assume that the responder can reuse slots of the *IPS state* after the negotiation has been finished[4]. Hence the *former responder* removes all slots of the *IPS state*

Fourth, we require our agents to accept incoming requests for negotiation (RCV_REQ) except they are already handling another request. In that case the request is rejected because of becoming or being busy (SND_BUSY). We term an agent that is not yet busy and has not received a request for negotiation a *potential initiator*. An agent that is not yet busy but did receive a request is a *potential responder*.

For specifying the dynamics we define five additional states: *pot_ini*, *ini*, *pot_res*, *res*, and *frm_res*, which represent above mentioned five different roles

---

[4] While the initiator may want to try a different partner on the same issue after a failed negotiation, the responder wants to solve its own conflicts.

an agent can take: *potential initiator, initiator, potential responder, responder,* and *former responder*. We handle these states in a separate role state machine (see Figure 2). This reduces the complexity of the conditions in the negotiation state chart, which specifies the IPS dynamics.

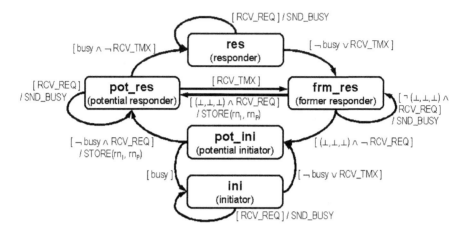

Fig. 2. The Role state chart.

Initially an agent is a potential initiator (state *pot_ini*). If it becomes busy without being requested before, then it is an initiator (state *ini*). After it is not busy anymore, e.g. the initiated negotiation has been finished, it switches back to the state *pot_ini*. If an agent in state *pot_ini* receives a request for negotiation while it is not yet busy, then it stores the information from the request ($STORE(rn_I, rn_P)$) and becomes a potential responder (state *pot_res*). Once it got busy by doing the agree negotiation step (S_a) it is in state *res*. After the accepted negotiation has been finished, the responder is not busy anymore and becomes a former responder (state *frm_res*). Finally it reaches the empty *IPS state* $(\bot, \bot, \bot)$. If there is a new request the agent stores the corresponding information and directly changes to state *pot_res*, otherwise it changes back to the initial state *pot_ini*.

Only in state *pot_ini* the agent starts handling a request for negotiation. In all other states requests are rejected. As the reception of a request in state *pot_ini* results in a state transition, it is ensured that always only one request is handled.

The condition RCV_TMX represents the reception of a timeout message from the negotiation partner. In open multiagent systems a timeout may occur because a previous message was lost, the delivery took to long, or the partner is not willing to wait any longer. A timeout may only occur in the states that relate to an active negotiation. In the states *pot_res* and *res* a RCV_TMX results in a direct change to *frm_res*. In state *ini* it causes a transition to state *pot_ini*. The timeout will become relevant only in subsection 4.3. We introduced it here to give a complete description of the role state chart.

4.2   Basic IPS Dynamics

Now we will describe the IPS dynamics of the example, i.e. a sequential approach in an idealized scenario (see Figure 3). Here we exclude any external events influencing the *IPS states* that may occur in an open multiagent system. Transitions between IPS states only happen due to negotiation related events. This restriction allows us to focus on the main path of dependencies between the negotiation decisions. The presented model is a further developed version of the one presented in [US04].

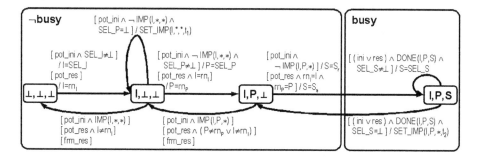

Fig. 3. Basic dynamics for the sequential approach in an idealized scenario.

If an agent is in state $(\bot, \bot, \bot)$ there are two ways to change the issue. First, if the agent is a *potential initiator*, then the agent tries to select an issue by applying the corresponding selection function $I = SEL\_I$. Second, if the agent is a *potential responder*, then it sets the issue according to the information stored, i.e. $I = rn_I$. In all other cases the agent remains in state $(\bot, \bot, \bot)$. If the *potential initiator* has already selected an issue but not a partner or a step, i.e. $(I, \bot, \bot)$, and it recognizes all states with this issue as being impossible, i.e. $IMP(I, *, *)$, then the issue is removed. The issue is also removed if the agent is a *potential responder* but the wrong issue is set[5]. Finally a *former responder* removes the issue to reach the empty *IPS state*.

In state $(I, \bot, \bot)$ there are two ways to set a partner. If an agent is a *potential initiator*, and not all states with issue I are impossible then the agent tries to select an appropriate partner. If it cannot select a partner, then the partner component recognizes states $(I, *, *)$ as impossible $SET\_IMP(I, *, *, t_1)$, otherwise the partner is set accordingly $P = SEL\_P$. If the agent is a *potential responder* and the issue has already been set accordingly, then the partner is also set, i.e. $P = rn_p$. If a *potential initiator* has a chosen issue and partner but the state $(I, P, \bot)$ is recognized to be impossible, then the partner is removed. It is also removed in case of being a *potential responder* but not having set the request-

---

[5] This happens if the request for a negotiation arrives while not all components of the agent have finished the decision process.

ing agent as partner or the requested issue as issue. Finally a *former responder* removes the partner to come closer to the empty *IPS state*.

If state $(I, P, \perp)$ is not impossible, after a *potential initiator* has chosen an issue and a partner it requests the partner to negotiate the selected issue; in fact, it sets a request for negotiation as the next negotiation step, i.e. $S = S_r$. If an agent is a *potential responder* and the issue and partner are set accordingly, then a requested agent agrees to negotiate the requested issue with the requesting agent, i.e. $S = S_a$. By following one of these two transitions the agent becomes *busy*. In state (I, P, S), where issue, partner and step have been selected, an initiator or a responder can change the step $S = SEL\_S$ after it has realized its intention, i.e. $DONE(I, P, S)$. If no new step can be found because a final step has been done, then an initiator or a responder recognizes a further negotiation with the partner on that issue as impossible $SET\_IMP(I, P, *, t_2)$ and changes to state $(I, P, \perp)$. By doing that it becomes $\neg busy$.

4.3   Extended IPS Dynamics

For this subsection on IPS dynamics we drop the restrictions made for the previous subsection: external events may now influence the IPS states. This is a realistic assumption for a complex distributed open multiagent system. It may happen that the negotiation partner or the negotiation issue disappears for some reasons[6]. For instance, the related conflict is solved as a side effect of some other action within the multiagent system. Because in such cases further negotiating this issue is useless, the agents should handle such situations in a flexible manner. The modeling of interdependencies resulting from such events requires a way to cancel a negotiation and a way to check whether a certain issue or step is still available. The first is a prerequisite for the negotiation protocol that has to enable a cancel of negotiations because of having no appropriate negotiation options S_c. The second is realized using a predicate $AV(X)$, where X is an issue or a partner. The predicate holds if the given argument is still available. The extended dynamics result from the basic dynamics only by adding some states and transitions. All states and transitions mentioned before are still included. In an open distributed multiagent system it may also happen that the potential or current negotiation partner may not want to wait any longer and sends a time-out. This has already been discussed in a previous subsection and is handled by the role state chart.

If a *potential initiator* or an *initiator* recognizes that the chosen issue is not available anymore $\neg AV(I)$, then it drops the issue. This may happen in states $(I, \perp, \perp)$, $(I, P, \perp)$, and (I, P, S). The resulting transition for the first case does already exist; we just have to add another condition for it $(\neg AV(I))$. The second case is without any problems. Because there is no ongoing negotiation, the issue component can easily remove the issue; later, also the partner will be removed. In the third case there is an ongoing negotiation. Here the agent tells the partner that it cancels the negotiation because the continuation of the negotiation makes

---

[6] A negotiation issue disappears when there is no possible agreement.

no sense, i.e. there are no alternatives to negotiate on anymore (S_c). After the cancel message has been sent, the partner component also removes the partner.

In an open multiagent system it may happen that an agent exits the system; hence it is not available anymore. In such cases, where $\neg AV(P)$ holds, the partner is removed from the IPS vector. This may happen in states $(I, P, \perp)$, (I, P, S), $(\perp, P, \perp)$, and $(\perp, P, S)$. The transition for the first case is already covered by the basic dynamics. Again, only another condition has to be added. For the second case, if the partner component realizes a loss of partner but issue as well as step is defined, then the partner and afterwards the step are removed. The last two cases result from loosing the issue before the partner. In these cases the partner can be dropped. While the agent is $\neg busy$ only a *potential initiator* may loose the partner. During an ongoing negotiation the initiator as well as the responder may loose the partner.

Before a new part of the *IPS state* is set, *potential initiators*, *initiators* and *responders* always check whether the selections of previous decision processes (according to our sequential approach) are still available. The complete dependencies of the sequential approach can be seen in Figure 4.

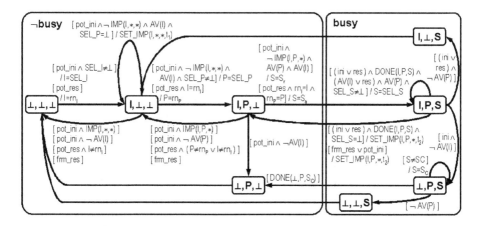

Fig. 4. Extended dynamics for the sequential approach in open environments.

5   Conclusion and Next Steps

In this article we described the specification of interdependencies between different components in a structured reasoning process for negotiating agents. We motivated the application of the C-IPS framework for structuring the reasoning process. The basic dynamics that cover only the primary state transitions where extended by transitions that enable the handling of environmental changes that have not been considered before. For instance, in our extended dynamics we consider an abrupt disappearance of negotiation partners, an unexpected loss of conflict, and a sudden inability to contribute to a conflict resolution.

Despite the C-IPS approach structures the agent's reasoning process, it abstracts from the number of partners or issues under consideration. It is also independent of the agent's characteristics. But C-IPS locates the decisions that might be affected by these parameters. Hence, the framework can serve as a frame for classifications that build on such parameters, e.g. [AWN03]. Altogether, we think that there is no comprehensive framework handling all the questions mentioned so far at an appropriate level of abstraction.

5.1   A New Level of Analysis and Modeling

The C-IPS framework together with IPS dynamics provides a new level of analysis of negotiating agents. It is above the level of negotiation mechanism design, which covers negotiation protocols and strategies. While dependencies between different aspects of the negotiation decision are frequently given only implicit, IPS dynamics make them explicit. The framework's three separate decision components also provide an interesting way of modularization of negotiating agents' internal decision processes. This eases the modeling of more flexible negotiating agents. The modularization also provides a base for exchanging single components of negotiating agents.

5.2   Further Research

Our next steps regarding the C-IPS framework aim at further exploring the advantages and the application of the framework. Because it makes comparison, evaluation, and discussion of different solutions easier we are going to do this for several influential approaches to negotiating agents. Currently, we also use the C-IPS framework for evaluating how different learning strategies can be integrated into negotiating agents. Besides mapping technologies we also map sociological concepts to the decision processes made by negotiating agents.

Because C-IPS widens the horizon, we now start exploring more deeply questions regarding different solutions for conflict identification, issue and partner selection. These solutions may also go beyond individual decisions by applying complex social interaction to establish issues and negotiation groups. Thereby we address more generally the question of agenda setting.

References

[AWN03]   R. Lomuscio A., M. Wooldridge, and R. Jennings N. A classification scheme for negotiation in electronic commerce. *International Journal of Group Decision and Negotiation*, 12(1):31–56, 2003.

[FWJ03]   S. Fatima, M. Wooldridge, and N. R. Jennings. Optimal agendas for multi-issue negotiation. In *Proceedings of 2nd International Joint Conference on Autonomous Agents and Multi-Agent Systems*, pages 129–136, Melbourne, Australia, 2003.

[HS99]   Michael N. Huhns and Larry M. Stephens. Multiagent systems and societies of agents. In Gerhard Weiss, editor, *Multiagent systems: a modern approach to distributed artificial intelligence*, pages 79–120. MIT Press, 1999.

[JFL+00]   N. R. Jennings, P. Faratin, A. R. Lomuscio, S. Parsons, C. Sierra, and
           M. Wooldridge. Automated negotiation: Prospects, methods and chal-
           lenges. *Int. Journal of Group Decision and Negotiation*, 2000.
[KL02]   K. Kurbel and I. Loutchko. Multi-agent negotiation under time constraints
           on an agent-based marketplace for personnel acquistion. In *Proceedings
           of the 3rd International Symposium on Multi-Agent Systems, Large Com-
           plex Systems, and E-Business (MALCEB2002)*, pages 566–579. Erfurt, Ger-
           many, October 2002.
[MUSG03]   M. Meister, D. Urbig, K. Schröter, and R. Gerstl. Agents Enacting So-
           cial Roles. Balancing Formal Structure and Practical Rationality in MAS
           Design. TUTS Working Papers TUTS-WP-6-2003, Technische Universität
           Berlin, Institut für Soziologie, 2003.
[RZ94]   S. Rosenschein, J. and G. Zlotkin. *Rules of encounter: designing conven-
           tions for automated negotiation among computers*. The MIT Press, Cam-
           bridge, London, 1994.
[San99]   Tuomas W. Sandholm. Distributed rational decision making. In Gerhard
           Weiss, editor, *Multiagent systems: a modern approach to distributed artifi-
           cial intelligence*, pages 201–258. MIT Press, 1999.
[SW03]   M. Ströbel and C. Weinhard. The montreal taxonomy for electronic nego-
           tiations. *Group Decision and Negotiation*, 12:143–164, 2003.
[UMS03]   D. Urbig, D. Monett Díaz, and K. Schröter. The C-IPS architecture for
           modelling negotiating social agents. In M. Schillo et al., editor, *Multiagent
           System Technologies. Proceedings of MATES 2003 (LNAI 2831)*, pages 217–
           228. Springer, 2003.
[US04]   D. Urbig and K. Schröter. C-IPS approach to negotiating agents: Specifying
           dynamics interdepencies between issue, partner, and step. In *Proceedings
           of AAMAS '04*, 2004. poster paper (to appear).

FuzzyMAN: An Agent-Based Electronic Marketplace with a Multilateral Negotiation Protocol

Karl Kurbel[1], Iouri Loutchko[1], and Frank Teuteberg[2]

[1] Department of Business Informatics, European University Viadrina Frankfurt (Oder)
POB 1786, D-15207 Frankfurt (Oder), Germany
{kurbel,loutchko}@uni-ffo.de
[2] Department of Business Administration/E-Business and Business Informatics
University Osnabrueck, Katharinenstr. 1, D-49069 Osnabrueck, Germany
frank.teuteberg@uos.de

Abstract. In this paper, conceptual foundations, the architecture, and the implementation of an agent-based electronic marketplace, FuzzyMAN (Fuzzy Multi-Agent Negotiations) are presented. Software agents on that marketplace negotiate about multiple issues according to a multilateral negotiation protocol. This protocol is based on a sequence of bilateral negotiations and on a pre-selection procedure which chooses suitable partners for negotiations first. Special attention is given to the feature that the agents' preferences are expressed in fuzzy terms. The application domain for our exemplary implementation is buying and selling "labor". Agents act on behalf of employers (looking for employees) and employees (looking for jobs). A mediator agent in FuzzyMAN supervises and coordinates the actions on the marketplace. Characteristics of the architecture and its implementation are described. Open research questions are discussed in the final section.

Keywords: Software agents, e-marketplace, multilateral negotiation, scoring functions, fuzzy logic.

1 Introduction

Software agents are applied to a wide range of commercial domains including design of production control systems [Bus+01], business process management systems [Jen+00], and electronic commerce [He+03], [KuLo03], [Ma99], [Owe+99], [SiDi01], and [YeLi01]. Characteristics like autonomy, pro-activity, cooperation, and the capability to learn make software agents a unique technology for retrieval and processing of information; searching for products, consumers or merchants; cooperation with other agents or human beings in one form or another; and personalization of information or services [NwNd99]. These functionalities are especially important for agents acting on electronic marketplaces. Here the agents can effectively support their owners when they act autonomously and pro-actively, and thus reduce the amount of human work.

Many electronic marketplaces, especially in the business-to-consumer and consumer-to-consumer fields, are in essence some kind of search engine where buyers look for the best product in a database of products offered by sellers. Usually such e-marketplaces do not use agent technology at all although agents could significantly improve the services provided both for the buyers and the sellers. One of the problems on an e-marketplace is that the situation changes very rapidly. New products may be

G. Lindemann et al. (Eds.): MATES 2004, LNAI 3187, pp. 126–140, 2004.

added, and product characteristics (like prices) may be updated. This means that customers have to visit the e-marketplaces regularly and repeat their search for appropriate products over and over again. Another problem with existing e-marketplaces is that in contrast to real life they give no room for negotiations between potential buyers and sellers.

In this paper, we demonstrate the concepts of a multi-agent approach to electronic marketplaces using a prototype of a job marketplace called FuzzyMAN (Fuzzy Multi-Agent Negotiations). On the FuzzyMAN marketplace users create their individual agents. Those agents then act in an autonomous manner and proactively. Once initialized they continuously search for new positions (employees' agents) or for new employees (employers' agents). To achieve their objectives (in our case, to find an appropriate position or an appropriate employee) the agents negotiate about the conditions of a contract according to several criteria like salary per hour, working hours per week, and social benefits. As soon as a suitable position or a suitable candidate for a vacant position is found the agents inform their owners about the conditions of the contract. Other useful features are that users can permanently monitor the performance of their agents and the situation on the marketplace, and that they may change their preferences for salary per hour, working hours per week, the negotiation tactics employed by their agents, the dates their agents expire, etc.

.The remainder of the paper is organized as follows. Section 2 discusses the architecture of FuzzyMAN's agents with special attention given to the negotiation model. Section 3 describes the overall architecture of the marketplace. In section 4, some statistical data about FuzzyMAN are presented. Section 5 gives an overview of related work. Section 6 summarizes some conclusions and open research questions.

2 Agents on the FuzzyMAN Marketplace

In this section, some essential features of the agents acting on the marketplace are discussed with special attention given to the negotiation model. Two types of agents have to be considered: a) *employees' and employers' agents* that communicate and negotiate with each other to achieve their respective objectives, and b) a *mediator agent* responsible for managing the other agents, collecting statistical information, and selecting candidate agents for a specific negotiation process. We give a short overview of both agent types.

2.1 Employees' and Employers' Agents

The architecture of employees' and employers' agents consists of three main modules: a communication module, a module for interaction with the agents' owners, and a negotiation module.

Whereas the communication module governs the exchange of messages between agents, the interaction module is responsible for communication between an agent and its owner. Interaction is bilateral: A user can manage his (her) agents through a graphical user interface, and an agent can contact its owner in certain situations (e.g. successful negotiation, approaching the deadline) through e-mail. The user interface is illustrated in figure 1. Users can manage their agents through this interface, including initializing, updating, and deleting agents.

For example, to initialize an employee's agent as in figure 1, the user has to specify the profession (e.g. "network administrator"), preferred employment dates, number of working hours per week, expectations about the salary per hour and social benefits, age, professional experience, and expiration date of the agent. Then information about professional skills (like knowledge of Unix, Java, SAP R/3) and additional skills (like foreign languages, driving license, flexibility), divided into three categories (basic, good, or excellent level of knowledge), has to be entered. Finally, the user specifies the tactic that the agent is supposed to employ in the negotiation process, and the weights for the negotiation issues, i.e. salary, employment period, working hours, and social benefits.

New Employee Profile

1. Choose a profession from the list and enter a name for your agent:

    Network Administrator ▾   *Agent name: bond007

2. Preferred employment dates:

    *Earliest start: 2003-02-01 (Use format yyyy-mm-dd)   *Latest start: 2003-02-15 (Use format yyyy-mm-dd)
    *Earliest end: 2003-05-01 (Use format yyyy-mm-dd)   *Latest end: 2003-05-20 (Use format yyyy-mm-dd)

3. Number of working hours per week:

    *Absolute minimum: 20 (A number between 1 and 40)   *Preferred minimum: 25 (A number between 1 and 40)
    *Absolute maximum: 40 (A number between 1 and 40)   *Preferred maximum: 35 (A number between 1 and 40)

4. Expectations about the salary:

    *Minimum salary: 25   €/hour   *Preferred salary: 35   €/hour

5. Expectations about social benefits:

    *Minimim benefits: 100   €/month   *Preferred benefits: 250   €/month

6. Choose the appropriate negotiation strategy:

    Linear ▾

Fig. 1. Part of the input form for initialization of a new employee's agent.

The negotiation module consists of three components: negotiation object, decision making model and negotiation protocol.

The *negotiation object* is characterized by four issues: salary per hour x_s, number of working hours per week x_h, duration of the employment x_d, and social benefits x_b. In the following we denote by $x^i = (x_s^i, x_h^i, x_d^i, x_b^i)$ an offer received by an employee's agent at time $t = t_i$, $i = 0,1,....,n$ (n = number of negotiation steps) and by $y^i = (y_s^i, y_h^i, y_d^i, y_b^i)$ an offer received by an employer's agent. We note that neither the specific types of negotiation issues nor their number are essential for the negotiation model under consideration; the same model can be used in other situations with different negotiation issues.

The *decision making model* consists of an assessment part (evaluate an offer received and determine the corresponding action) and of an action part (either generate and send a counter-offer or stop the negotiation). The assessment part is based on the fact that different values of negotiation issues are of different value for negotiating agents. The value of negotiation issues is modeled by scoring functions. The bigger the value of a scoring function for a certain value of an issue is, the more suitable is this value for a negotiating agent. The scoring functions represent private information not known by and not given to other market participants.

For illustration an example of a scoring function employed by employees' agents on the FuzzyMAN marketplace is presented in figure 2, where h^n_{Min}, h^n_{Max}, $h^n_{Opt\_Min}$, $h^n_{Opt\_Max}$ are the minimal, maximal and optimal numbers of working hours per week for an employee, respectively. The parameter n_h defines an employee's level of satisfaction with the worst case regarding the number of working hours per week.

In a real negotiation, different negotiation issues are of different importance for each partner. To model this situation, we introduce the notion of relative importance that a participant assigns to an issue under negotiation.

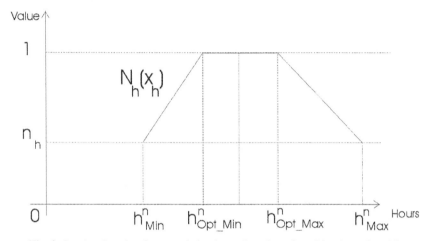

Fig. 2. Scoring function for negotiation issue "number of working hours/week".

Using such scoring functions and the relative importance of issues under negotiation, a general scoring function $G(z, \omega)$ is defined. This function depends on two arguments: z - a vector-valued offer received by an agent and $\omega = (\omega_s, \omega_h, \omega_d, \omega_b)$ - a vector of relative importance of issues under negotiation (salary per hour, number of working hours per week, employment duration, and social benefits, respectively) for a given agent. The function $G(z, \omega)$ is an additive function [BiKa03, p. 4] summing the scoring functions for individual negotiation issues multiplied by their relative importance. Weights in the vector ω of relative importance are kept in the interval [0, 1]. The sum of these weights is taken to be equal to 1. We note that this method of defining a general scoring function can only be used when the negotiation issues are independent, as they are in the FuzzyMAN marketplace.

The scoring functions are used both in the pre-selection procedure and in the negotiation process, in the latter one to evaluate the offers received from other agents. The pre-selection procedure is described in the next section. The negotiation protocols together with the action part of the decision making models are presented in section 2.3.

2.2 Mediator Agent and Pre-selection Procedure

The most important functionalities of the mediator agent are management of other agents, collecting statistical information, and pre-selection of agents for a negotiation. In this part of the paper we focus on the pre-selection procedure that plays an essential role in the negotiation protocol.

Pre-selection means selecting and ranking those agents of the marketplace that will start a specific negotiation over certain issues with a given agent. In the pre-selection process factors like profession, age, working experience, professional and additional skills of the potential employees are taken into consideration. The values of these factors are fixed on the employees' side and cannot be involved directly in the negotiation process although they are very important for the employment process.

For the ranking of employees' agents, additional scoring functions – for age, working experience, professional and additional skills – have to be constructed [KuLo02]. Then an extended set $\omega_{ext} = (\omega_s, \omega_h, \omega_d, \omega_b, \omega_a, \omega_{ex}, \omega_{ps}, \omega_{as})$ of relative importance of negotiation and pre-selection issues is defined for an employer's agent: In addition to ω_s, ω_h, ω_d, and ω_b introduced before, this set contains the relative importance of the employee's age ω_a, of his or her working experience ω_{ex}, professional skills ω_{ps}, and additional skills ω_{as}.

For evaluation of an offer $y^i = (y_s^i, y_h^i, y_d^i, y_b^i)$ received by an employer's agent from an employee's agent, the extended scoring function

$$G_{ext}(y^i, y_{fix}, \omega_{ext}) = G(y^i, \omega) + G_{fix}(y_{fix}, \omega_{fix}) \qquad (2.1)$$

is used. In the formula (2.1), $G(y^i, \omega)$ denotes the general scoring function described earlier, $\omega_{fix} = (\omega_a, \omega_{ex}, \omega_{ps}, \omega_{as})$, and $y_{fix} = (y_a, y_{ex}, y_{ps}, y_{as})$, where y_a stands for employee's age, y_{ex} for his or her working experience, y_{ps} for professional and y_{as} for additional skills, respectively. The function $G_{fix}(y_{fix}, \omega_{fix})$ is also an additive function constructed like the function $G(y^i, \omega)$.

For a given employer's agent an order of the set of all employees' agents is introduced according to the following rule:

An employee's agent y is more preferable for the employer's agent than another employee's agent z (or as well as preferable) only if

$$G_{fix}(y_{fix}, \omega_{fix}) \geq G_{fix}(z_{fix}, \omega_{fix}) \qquad (2.2)$$

where the functions and their arguments are defined as in formula (2.1). In this case, the relation between the two employees' agents is denoted by $y \succ z$ (or by $y = z$).

Using the relation (2.2) an ordered sequence n_1, n_2, n_3,..., n_l of employees' agents is determined for a particular employer's agent. This sequence is sorted according to the level of suitability as a negotiation partner for the employer's agent determined for each employee's agent:

$$n_1 \succ n_2 \succ n_3 \succ ... \succ n_l . \tag{2.3}$$

The results of the pre-selection procedure are heavily used in the multilateral negotiation protocol.

2.3 Multilateral Negotiation Model

In this section, the negotiation protocol underlying the agents' negotiation on the FuzzyMAN marketplace is presented. In general there are several employees who are interested in a position offered by an employer. Vice versa, several employers might be interested in a certain employee. So the negotiation model is a multilateral one.

First we discuss how the agents generate offers and counter-offers, i.e. the negotiation tactics. By a *negotiation tactic* we denote a vector function with four components. These components determine the way the agent changes the values of the negotiation issues (i.e. salary per hour, number of working hours per week, employment duration, and social benefits) over time.

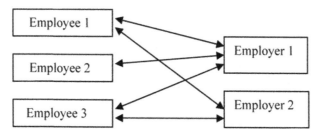

Fig. 3. Example of a multi-lateral negotiation scheme for two employers and three employees.

In the literature various cases of negotiation tactics are discussed (see for example [Far+98]). Families of tactics which can be employed by agents are time-dependent, resource-dependent, and behavior-dependent tactics. An important family of tactics consists of functions which are only time-dependent, i.e. neither the status of the marketplace nor the status of the negotiation influences the negotiation. On the FuzzyMAN marketplace agents employ time-dependent tactics in the form:

$$f(t) = f_1 + \left(\frac{t - t_{Init}}{t_{Max} - t_{Init}} \right)^{1/\beta} (f_2 - f_1), \quad f : [t_{Init}, t_{Max}] \rightarrow [f_1, f_2]. \tag{2.4}$$

Tactics of this form are often used in the literature about agents' negotiations. Other approaches to define time-dependent tactics have also been proposed, but the formula

(2.4) suited our purpose best because it describes the whole spectrum of time-dependent tactics. In formula (2.4), f_1, f_2 are user-defined values of the negotiation issue (minimal and maximal values of a certain negotiation issue for a given agent), $t \in [t_{Init}, t_{Max}]$ where t_{Init} is the time the agent was initialized by the user, t_{Max} is the time the agent has to complete the negotiation (deadline), and $\beta > 0$ is a parameter that determines how the agent changes the values for the given negotiation issue over time. The larger the value of the parameter β is, the sooner the agent is ready to make larger concessions in the negotiation process.

For multilateral negotiations in FuzzyMAN we employ a negotiation protocol based on the bilateral protocol described in [Far+98] (see also [Fat+02] for an extended version of this protocol) and a partial order of the set of all employees' agents generated by the pre-selection procedure discussed in section 2.2.

The general idea behind the bilateral negotiation protocol is that two agents participating in the negotiation sequentially send each other offers and/or counter-offers. To generate the offers negotiation tactics are used. The decision to accept or reject an offer received from the other agent is based on scoring functions constructed according to the agents' preferences, restrictions, goals, and relative importance of negotiation issues. A negotiation is completed either if an offer is accepted by one of the agents (negotiation is successful) or if one of the agents reaches its deadline (negotiation fails). For a formal presentation of the protocol for bilateral negotiation see [Far+98].

On the FuzzyMAN marketplace a multilateral negotiation is modeled as a finite set of bilateral negotiations between employers' and employees' agents. However, these bilateral negotiations are not independent but they are influenced by other ongoing bilateral negotiations, just as they would be on a real marketplace.

In the following, the general idea of the multilateral negotiation protocol for multiple issues is outlined. The interested reader is referred to [KuLo02] for details. Suppose t_{Max} is the deadline of an employer's agent and n_1, n_2, n_3,..., n_l is the ordered sequence of the employees' agents suitable for negotiation with the given employer's agent and ranked by the pre-selection procedure: $n_1 \succ n_2 \succ n_3 \succ ... \succ n_l$. The idea behind the protocol is that the total value of offers the employer's agent sends at a particular time $t = t_i$, $i = 0,1,....,n$ (n = number of negotiation steps) to the employees' agents he is negotiating with should be the same for all offers. The total value of an offer takes into consideration both the negotiation issues and the pre-selection issues (e.g. age, working experience, etc.) which are not involved directly into the negotiation. To ensure the above condition, the employer's agent starts the negotiation with all employees' agents n_1,..., n_k, $k \le l$ satisfying the condition

$$G_{fix}(n_1, \omega_{fix}) = G_{fix}(n_j, \omega_{fix}), \quad j = 1,...,l$$

by sending them an initial offer x^0 according to the bilateral negotiation protocol. A new employee's agent, n_{k+1}, gets involved in the negotiation at time $t = t_i$ only if

$$G(x^i, \omega) + G_{fix}(n_k, \omega_{fix}) \le G(x^0, \omega) + G_{fix}(n_{k+1}, \omega_{fix}), \tag{2.5}$$

where x^i is the employer's agent's offer generated according to its negotiation tactic at time $t = t_i$, and x^0 is his initial offer. The first offer sent to the employee's agent n_{k+1} at time $t = t_i$ will be x^0 and not x^i as for the employees' agents $n_1, \ldots, n_k$. Then the same procedure is repeated at every negotiation step. Condition (2.5) ensures that the total value of offers the employer's agent sends to the employees' agents he is negotiating with is the same for all of his offers at a certain negotiation step.

If a new employer's agent comes to the marketplace, the mediator agent first performs for him the pre-selection procedure. Then the newcomer starts negotiation according to the protocol described above. When a new employee's agent comes, the pre-selection procedure is performed for every employer's agent once again. As a result the newcomer possibly becomes involved into negotiations with one or several employers' agents.

In the case that an agent accepts an offer sent to him by one of the agents he is negotiating with, the agent stops negotiating with all other agents and informs those agents through a special message about the cancellation of the negotiation process. If such a cancellation message comes from one of the agents, that agent is withdrawn from the set of agents negotiating with the agent that received the cancellation message. Likewise at time $t = t_n$, $t_n \geq t_{Max}^g$ an agent stops the negotiation with all agents he was negotiating with and informs those agents about the cancellation of the negotiation process.

According to the bilateral negotiation protocol both employees' agents and employers' agents always send offers they themselves are satisfied with. Therefore, as soon as an offer is accepted by one of the agents, the agent who sent the offer and the agent who received the offer come to an agreement. Another point to mention is that the offers an agent receives are evaluated first-in-first-out: An offer received earlier than another one is evaluated first and corresponding actions are taken prior to the evaluation of the second offer.

3   FuzzyMAN's Architecture

The FuzzyMAN marketplace is a multi-agent system with architecture as shown in figure 4. In this section we describe the structure and functionality of the marketplace. The architecture includes both a specific mediator agent which plays the role of a market coordinator and agents representing individual users with their own goals and tactics. The mediator is a centralized 'super-agent' handling the communication of other agents.

Initially, all users have to register when entering the marketplace to create their own agents on the server. Employees' agents search for adequate jobs and employers' agents offer jobs. Each agent is uniquely identified by an agent-id. Users access FuzzyMAN through a web interface. Here the user can create an agent, set the agent's preferences, change personal settings, and access information provided by the agent.

An agent created by a user contacts the mediator agent to enter his profile, the user's data, and/or job offers or search requests into the databases. The agents' preferences are later used in the pre-selection procedure to find and rank agents suitable for negotiations. On the marketplace server only agents with corresponding preferences negotiate.

After several rounds of exchanging offers and counter-offers, the negotiation process will end with an agreement between an employer's and an employee's agent in the ideal case, or terminate without success. The mediator is informed and updates the database. The user then receives an automatic e-mail about the results his or her agent(s) achieved.

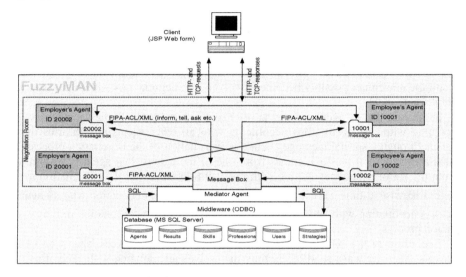

Fig. 4. Multi-agent system architecture.

The overall contracting process comprises several stages, including:

1. Discovery of potential negotiation partners in a pre-selection process with the help of the mediator agent.
2. Determination of the negotiation issues through a communication process based on FIPA-ACL/XML (FIPA-ACL = FIPA Agent Communication Language [FIPA03]; XML = Extensible Markup Language).
3. Automated negotiation by exchanging XML messages with values of negotiation issues generated with the help of agents' tactics.

FuzzyMAN is implemented in Java. So it can run on all Java-enabled platforms. In order to make FuzzyMAN widely accessible, the implementation was based on the following technologies:

- FIPA-ACL: Used as the agent communication language.
- XML: Used as the data interchange language for representing and processing fuzzy negotiation vocabulary from a syntactic and a semantic perspective. In XML domain-specific entities, attributes, and relationships between entities can be defined with tags like <salary>, <profession>, etc.
- JDBC (Java Database Connectivity): Used to access FuzzyMAN's relational database from Java.
- MS SQL Server 2000: Used as database management system.

- JSP (Java Server Pages): Used for the generation of dynamic content from the database, writing to the database, and for the web forms to enter user data.

FuzzyMAN is currently running on a server with a Windows 2000 operating system, 40 GB harddisc, Intel Pentium processor 1 Ghz and 256 MB DDR-RAM. The system was developed and tested using the following software versions: Java Software Development Kit 1.3, Tomcat Server 3.3, Internet Explorer 5.5 and 6.0.

The underlying database mainly stores information that is needed for the agents to do their work. This information includes, for example, preferences set by the users and statistical data about earlier negotiation results.

Figure 5 gives an overview of the database tables and their interrelations in UML (Unified Modeling Language) notation. The multiplicity specifications used in figure 5 indicate how many elements (entities) of one database table (relation) may be connected to the elements of another database table. Multiplicity in UML is analogous to cardinality in other modeling languages. The database contains the following tables:

- *Agent:* This table is used to store the settings of each agent initiated by a user via the web form. The *isActive* attribute is a status indicator with the following meanings:

  0 – *not loaded* (the agent has not yet been loaded for a negotiation),

  1 – *loaded* (the agent has been loaded, is active and is waiting for partners),

  2 – *negotiating* (the agent has already started a negotiation with at least one partner),

  3 – *succeeded* (a contract was achieved, negotiation is stopped),

  4 – *failed* (deadline was reached, no contract was reached).

- The attributes *PeriodFactor, HourFactor, SalaryFactor* and *BenefitFactor* are weights specifying how important the respective negotiation issue is for the user. The weights have to sum up to 1.

- *BuyAgent/SellAgent:* These two tables represent preferences of agents: the first table is for preferences of employers' agents and the second one for preferences of employees' agents.

- *Results:* Used to store the results of a negotiaton that an agent has achieved.

- *User:* Used to store passwords and e-mail addresses of users.

- *Strategies:* In this table negotiation tactics the agents can apply are stored. The *Param* attribute specifies the shape of the tactic function which determines how quickly an agent will make concessions during a negotiation process.

The other database tables are used to store professions available on the marketplace and information about professional and additional skills available or requested. Professional skills are job specific skills that an employer may require from potential employees. Each of those skills is assigned with one attribute from the set "basic", "good" or "excellent". Additional skills are not job specific and comprise things like ability to work in a team or having a driver's license.

4   Statistical Overview of FuzzyMAN

In October 2002 the FuzzyMAN marketplace was made accessible for the scientific community. Initially 200 employees' and 100 employers' agents were generated. Since then, 154 more agents were created by anonymous users from the scientific community. Table 2 gives a statistical overview of the marketplace. The results in table 1 were obtained on the basis of the 300 initially generated agents and the data the anonymous users entered in the input form for agent initialization.

116 out of 454 agents on our marketplace are successful and achieve an agreement (contract) before they reach their deadlines. The average utility value (in %) of agreements achieved by successful agents is 65 %. This low average utility value and low rate of matched agents is due to the divergent agent profiles initialized by their users. Most employees' agents failed not matching the right professions the employers' agents were searching for.

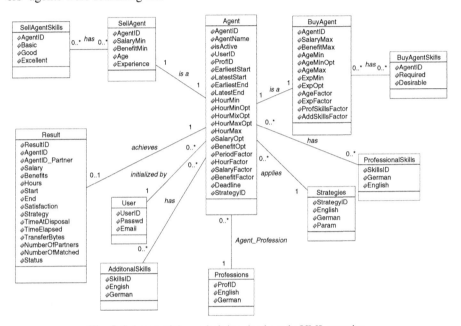

Fig. 5. Schema of the underlying database in UML notation.

Table 1. Statistical overview of FuzzyMAN (status: 5th of July, 2004).

Total number of agents	454
Total number of employees' agents	300
Total number of employers' agents	154
Agents at the following negotiation stages:	
Waiting	14
Negotiating	5
Succeeded	116
Failed	312
Deleted (by their owners)	7
Average utility value of agreements	65 %

Evaluations of the performance of the marketplace were presented in [TeKu02], with regard to the bilateral negotiation model, and in [Teu03] for multilateral negotiations. Compared with the results obtained in the bilateral model, on average more agents reach an agreement when the multilateral negotiation protocol is used, with even higher utility values. The main reason for this is that agents negotiating in a multilateral way can contact a larger number of negotiation partners within a given time frame than agents negotiating only with one partner. Therefore they have better chances to reach an agreement and to achieve higher utility values.

With regard to *computational* and *communication efficiency* the amount of data (XML messages) exchanged between agents is in the multilateral negotiation model on average three times higher than in the bilateral model. The reason for this is that agents negotiating in a multilateral way are able to negotiate with more agents simultaneously within a given time frame than agents negotiating bilaterally and thus exchange more XML messages. However, this has not shown to be a bottleneck yet. Whenever an agent failed it was due to its deadline and not due to communication overload or capacity problems of the marketplace server.

5 Related Work

Most of today's electronic marketplaces either do not use agent technology at all or they employ only restricted forms of this technology. For example, some online auctions can be regarded as multi-agent e-marketplaces. However, they are of a very simple type. The only issue under consideration is the price. Additional issues like terms and conditions, payment method, who will pay for shipment, timings, penalties, etc. are not taken into account. In the business-to-business area, for example, those issues play an essential role; sometimes they are even more important than the price. For such situations the agent models employed by today's marketplaces are not appropriate.

Several approaches to agent-mediated negotiation on electronic marketplaces have been introduced in the literature, see for example, [Ada+96], [AnJe02], [Far00], [Far+02], [Far+98], [Fat+04], [Fat+02], [Jen+01], [Kra01], [KuLo02], [San00], and [SiDi01]. In [Vei03] a multi-agent system and analysis for multidimensional matchmaking in the human resources application domain is introduced. In fact, there is no universally best approach or technique for automated negotiation. The negotiation strategies and protocols need to be set according to the situation and application domain.

In e-commerce, either auctions or bilateral negotiations are usually employed. Without any doubt, auctions are the most widely studied and used negotiation model in e-commerce today. In online auctions, the agents represent their users and are responsible for deciding when and how much to bid for the desired items. There are different types of auctions like English auction, First-price sealed-bid auction, Vickrey auction, Dutch auction, continuous double auction, etc. Depending of the auction type, agents' negotiation can be one to many, many to many or many to one negotiation. In any case, the negotiation is about only one attribute – the price of the item. For the theory and practical implementations of agent-based auctions see, for example, [AnJe02], [BeSe96] or [San99].

Bilateral negotiation is usually concerned with multi-attribute contracts covering price, quality, delivery time and date, etc. Normally the negotiation process is modeled by using the methods and techniques of game theory (see for example [Fat+04], [Jen+01], [Kra01], or [San00]). In [He+03], the following three groups of models for bilateral negotiation were introduced: 1) Decision making by explicitly reasoning about the opponent's behavior, 2) decision making by finding the current best solution, and 3) argumentation. Each of the groups was extensively studied in the literature (see [He⁺03] for numerous references).

In contrast to the extensive literature about auctions and bilateral negotiations, only few papers deal with models for automated multilateral negotiation about multiple issues. In [Lop⁺02], a generic negotiation model for autonomous agents that handles multi-party, multi-issue negotiation with single or repeated rounds was presented. The authors compare their negotiation model with the ones proposed earlier by other researchers and give an overview of the literature in this field. As to applications of automated multilateral negotiation to real-world problems, a very interesting example was presented in [Ada⁺96], where negotiation between multiple non-cooperative parties was proposed to model an application problem (California water policy). For theoretical considerations regarding n-bilateral negotiations where the negotiation involves multiple bilateral bargaining parties we refer to [Far00]. In fact, the multilateral negotiation model employed by the FuzzyMAN agents carries the ideas suggested in [Far00] further; in addition it was optimized for the specific situation and application domain of buying and selling "labor".

6   Conclusions and Questions for Further Research

FuzzyMAN is a complete, robust, and working prototype of an agent-based electronic marketplace. Nevertheless a number of starting points for improvement were observed. Some of these points are summarized in this concluding section.

Interdependence of Negotiation Issues: The negotiaton protocols in the FuzzyMAN implementation do not consider trade-offs (as, for example, shown in [Far+02]) between the issues under negotiation. In real-world negotiations, however, it is a common practice to make concessions regarding one issue if the loss in satisfaction is compensated by a better value of another issue (e.g. more working hours per week but combined with higher salary per hour).

Additional Tactics: Agents are capable of adjusting their behavior during a negotiation; however, currently they do so according to time-dependent tactic functions only. Additional tactics can be introduced to improve the results of the negotiations. Such tactics may be behavior-dependent or resource-dependent, taking situative factors into account. For example, an employer's agent might change its behavior in creating offers depending on the number of employees' agents available on the marketplace. If there are many employees' agents, then the employer's agent may be less willing to make concessions quickly because other agents are waiting as potential partners if the ongoing negotiation fails.

Learning: Like in most e-marketplace implementations, agents in FuzzyMAN still lack the capability to learn and adapt their behavior in a goal-oriented manner. Although agents are currently reacting to other agents' behavior, they do so only according to fixed tactics that were determined when the agent was instantiated. Learning from earlier negotiations might help the agents to negotiate more successfully and reach a higher level of satisfaction. For example, an agent that is able to learn from the tactical behavior of its counterpart can change its own strategy and select a different tactic for subsequent negotiation steps. Likewise, an agent in a particular situation might learn from earlier successes or failures and adapt its behavior accordingly.

Generalizing the Marketplace: The sample domain underlying the FuzzyMAN marketplace is buying and selling labor, i.e. the job market. Basic concepts and mechanisms like the negotiation processes and the protocols governing those processes are not domain-dependent. They will be valid for other application areas where goods are sold and bought as well. Generalizing the marketplace, however, would require some fundamental changes in the architecture. FuzzyMAN, like many e-marketplaces, has its own vocabulary and is not based on an explicit ontology. Prior to porting it to a different domain, an ontology needs to be developed. Agents and other objects of the implementation will then access the vocabulary specified in the ontology to do their work. Using FuzzyMAN for a different domain means basically to define and apply ontology for that domain.

Coupling Marketplaces: Chances for an employee's agent or an employer's agent to succeed would certainly increase if the agent could search for a contract not only in the FuzzyMAN marketplace but also in other job marketplaces. This feature requires two major enhancements: Agents must be capable of migrating to others marketplace sites, and they must understand the "language" spoken on those marketplaces. For the second point, crucial prerequisites are a common vocabulary for the problem domain - as for the before-mentioned topic -, implying that providers of job marketplaces agree on an ontology first, and a common understanding of the negotiation protocols. Unfortunately, such a scenario is probably unrealistic in the real world.

The FuzzyMAN marketplace has been published on the World Wide Web. Any interested researcher can create own agents, send them out to negotiate, watch their behavior, and see if they are successful in their negotiations. FuzzyMAN is available at http://www.wiwi.euv-frankfurt-o.de/wi-www/agent.htm.

References

[Ada⁺96] Adams, G., Rausser, G., and Simon, L.: Modelling Multilateral Negotiation: An Application to California Water Policy. J. Economic Behaviour and Organization, 10 (1996), pp. 97-111.

[AnJe02] Anthony, P. and Jennings, N.R.: Evolving Bidding Strategies for Multiple Auctions. In: F. van Harmelen (Ed.), Proc. 15th European Conf. Artificial Intelligence, IOS Press: Amsterdam, 2002, pp. 178-182.

[BeSe96] Beam, C. and Segev, A.: Automated Negotiation: A Survey of the State of the Art. CITM Working Paper 96-WP-1022, 1996.

[BiKa03] Bichler, M.; Kalagnanam, J.: Bidding Languages and Winner Determination in Multi-attribute Auctions, 2003. To appear in: European Journal of Operational Research. (IBM Research Report RC22478); http://ibis.in.tum.de/staff/ bichler/docs/RC22478.pdf.

[Bus⁺01] Bussmann, S., Jennings, N. R., Wooldridge, M. J.: On the identification of agents in the design of production control systems. In: Ciancarini, P.; Wooldridge, M. (Eds.): Agent-Oriented Software Engineering. Springer: Berlin et al., 2001, pp. 141-162.

[Far00] Faratin, P.: Automated Service Negotiation Between Autonomous Computational Agents. PhD thesis, Univ. of London, Queen Mary College, 2000.

[Far⁺02] Faratin, P., Sierra, C., Jennings, N.R.: Using similarity criteria to make trade-offs in automated negotiations. Artificial Intelligence 142 (2002) 2, pp. 205-237.

[Far⁺98] Faratin, P., Sierra, C., Jennings, N.R.: Negotiation decision functions for autonomous agents. Robotics and Autonomous Systems 24 (1998), pp. 159-182.

[Fat⁺04] Fatima, S., Wooldridge, M., and Jennings, N. R.: An agenda based framework for multi-issues negotiation. Artificial Intelligence Journal 152 (2004), pp. 1-45.

[Fat⁺02] Fatima, S.S., Wooldridge, M.J. and Jennings N.R.: Multi-issue negotiation under time constraints. In: Proc. 1st Int. Joint Conf. On Autonomous Agents and Multi-Agent Systems, 2002, Bologna, Italy, pp. 143-150.

[FIPA03] FIPA – Foundation for Intelligent Physical Agents. FIPA Specifications, 2003; avalable at http://www.fipa.org/specifications/index.html.

[Jen⁺01] Jennings, N. R., Faratin, P., Lomuscio, A.R., Parsons, S., Wooldridge, M.: Automated negotiation: prospects, methods and challenges. Group Decision and Negotiation 10 (2001), pp. 199-215.

[Jen⁺00] Jennings, N. R., Faratin, P., Norman, T. J., O'Brien, P., Odgers B., Alty, J. L.: Implementing a Business Process Management System using ADEPT: A Real-World Case Study. Int. Journal of Applied Artificial Intelligence 14 (2000), pp. 421-465.

[He⁺03] He, M., Jennings, N. R., and Leung H.: On agent-mediated electronic commerce. IEEE Trans. on Knowledge and Data Engineering 15 (2003), pp. 985-1003.

[Kra01] Kraus, S.: Strategic negotiation in multi-agent environments. The MIT Press, Cambridge, Massachusetts, 2001.

[KuLo03] Kurbel, K., Loutchko, I.: Towards multi-agent electronic marketplaces: what is there and what is missing? The Knowledge Engineering Review 18 (2003), pp. 33-46.

[KuLo02] Kurbel, K., Loutchko, I.: Multi-agent negotiation under time constraints on an agent-based marketplace for personnel acquisition. In: Dittmar, T.; Franzzyk, B.; Hofmann, R. et al. (Eds.): Proceedings of the 3rd International Symposium on Multi-Agent Systems, Large Complex Systems, and E-Business (MALCEB2002), 2002, pp. 566-579.

[Lop⁺02] Lopesa, F., Mamedeb, N., Novaisa A.Q., and Coelhoc, H.: A negotiation model for autonomous computational agents: Formal description and empirical evaluation. Journal of Intelligent & Fuzzy Systems 12 (2002), pp. 195–212.

[Ma99] Ma, M.: Agents in E-Commerce. Comm. ACM 42 (1999), pp. 79-80.

[NwNd99] Nwana, H. S., Ndumu, D. T.: A perspective on software agent research. The Knowledge Engineering Review 14 (1999) 2, pp. 125-142.

[Owe⁺99] Owen, M. J., Lee, L., Sewell G., Steward, S., Thomas, D.: Multi-agent trading environment. BT Technology Journal 17 (1999), pp. 33-43.

[San00] Sandholm, T.: Agents in electronic commerce: component technologies for automated negotiation and coalition formation. Autonomous Agents and Multi-Agent Systems 3 (2000), pp. 73-96.

[San99] Sandholm, T.: eMediator: A Next Generation Electronic Commerce server. In: Proc. AAAI'99 Workshop, 1999.

[SiDi01] Sierra, C. and Dignum, F.: Agent-Mediated Electronic Commerce: Scientific and Technological Roadmap. In: Dignum, F. and Sierra, C. (Eds.): Agent Mediated Electronic Commerce, Springer, 2001, pp. 1-18.

[TeKu02] Teuteberg, F., Kurbel, K.: Simulation des Agentenverhaltens auf einem elektronischen Marktplatz zur Personalakquisition. In: Weinhardt, C., Holtmann, C. (Eds.): E-Commerce: Netze, Märkte, Technologien, Heidelberg 2002, pp. 253-271.

[Teu03] Teuteberg, F.: Experimental Evaluation of a Model for Multilateral Negotiation with Fuzzy Preferences on an Agent-based Marketplace. In: Müller, J., Maass, W., Schmid, B., Pavlikova, L. (Eds.): Electronic Markets: The International Journal of Electronic Commerce & Business Media 13 (2003) 1, pp. 21-32.

[Vei03] Veit, D.: Matchmaking in Electronic Markets: An Agent-Based Approach towards Matchmaking in Electronic Negotiations. Lecture Notes in Artificial Intelligence, Vol. 2882, Springer: Berlin, 2003.

[YeLi01] Ye, Y., Liu, J. and Moukas, A.: Agents in Electronic Commerce. Electronic Commerce Research 1 (2001), pp. 9-14.

Cascaded Control of Multi-agent Systems

Karl Kleinmann

BBN Technologies
Cambridge, MA, USA
karl.kleinmann@bbn.com

Abstract. Intelligent software agents are an important enabling technology for the next generation of distributed information systems. As agent-based applications spread and enter the realm of survivable and embedded systems, the issues of control become prominent in the development of agent architectures. This paper discusses the problem of multi-level control in distributed agent systems and presents the control approach and infrastructure elements of the open source agent architecture "Cougaar". We motivate its design from a control theory perspective, discuss the characteristics of an agent system as the controlled process, and present an example of agent infrastructure-level control.

1 Introduction

Distributed multi-agent systems (DMAS) have a large number of internal states and many degrees of freedom. While these characteristics provide great benefits, like flexibility for system configuration, they also impose a complex multivariable control problem. The control goal is usually not only the optimization of the actual application but also the containment of hardware or software-related failures, which can be viewed as stochastic disturbances. In the area of survivable systems that are designed to operate under warlike conditions, robustness (which addresses intentional network and platform disruptions) and security (which addresses intentional software intrusions) become control goals of equal importance to the primary application (e.g., a planning system).

In this paper, we discuss the generic problem of multi-level control for DMAS and present concepts and infrastructure elements of the control architecture of Cougaar [1] that address the challenges above. Cougaar is an agent architecture for large-scale DMAS that has been sponsored by DARPA through the former ALP program (1996-2001) and the current UltraLog program (2001-2004). In addition, Cougaar is open source and enjoys a worldwide user community. Under the UltraLog program [2], the Cougaar software is extended to inherently ensure survivability under extremely chaotic and high-stress environments, with particular focus on robustness, security, and scalability. As a primary application, UltraLog showcases a military logistics planning and plan-execution system that implements over 500 distinct agents running on more than 100 machines.

In this context, survivability is predicated on maintaining the highest quality of service across many dimensions based on mission or application objectives. Hence, it is essential that the agents are aware not only of their own performance, but also of

G. Lindemann et al. (Eds.): MATES 2004, LNAI 3187, pp. 141–154, 2004.

the externally available resources. In addition, adaptive control must encompass optimizing cost functions describing varying emphasis across the multiple quality of service dimensions at various points in the control hierarchy.

Section 2 of this paper discusses DMAS from a control theory perspective, motivated in part by [3], [4], [5], [6]. It suggests why their characteristics constitute a hard and unusual control problem, and what makes DMAS unique as a controlled process. We also point out analogies where control theory and software engineering use different terminologies for the same abstractions.

Section 3 outlines the control objectives of DMAS and introduces the notion of application level control in contrast to agent infrastructure level control, using the UltraLog application as an example for the discussion.

Section 4 presents the concept of a hierarchical, cascaded control architecture that was designed to enable and connect application level with agent infrastructure level control.

Section 5 focuses on the specifics of agent infrastructure level control and describes control infrastructure elements of the Cougaar agent architecture in detail. An example for a implemented control strategy is given that is part of the Cougaar open source distribution.

Section 6 summarizes the current design status and discusses what we hope to accomplish with future research.

2   The Agent System as the Controlled Process

Control theory captures the fundamentals for three activities:

- *Design of the control system.* This activity defines the system boundaries of the process to be controlled (also called controlled system or plant), the control inputs by which the behavior of the process can be changed, the structure of the controller that generates these inputs, and the sensor data as input for the controller reflecting current and desired performance.
- *Initialization of control parameters.* For the controller, they are either derived from an analytic or data-driven model of the controlled process, or based on experiments and heuristics.
- *Tuning of control parameters during operation.* In the case of an adaptive control system, the controller is continually adjusted to cope with changes of the inherent process behavior over time.

Whereas parts of almost every control loop are implemented in software, in cases where the controlled process is the software system itself, the means of control theory are rarely applied. As [5] points out, "the basic paradigm of control has not found its place as a first-class concept in software engineering."

There are certain characteristics in DMAS that distinguish them from the examples of controlled processes commonly considered in control theory:

- *Dynamic system boundaries.* DMAS have typically many degrees of freedom, e.g., mobile agents can reside on various nodes over time, new communication channels are added and removed again, agents can be rehydrated elsewhere, the distribution of the application over the agents can change. This desired flexibility leads to a constantly changing topology and does not allow to assume constant system boundaries nor to partition the system statically.

- *System size.* DMAS can consist of hundreds of agents containing thousands of components to be controlled. Thus, a huge number of internal states need to be measured or monitored by separate instrumentation code. Additional sensor data are generated while monitoring the communication between peers in the network and storing these matrices including their history.

- *Type of cost functions and performance criteria.* As opposed to processes in the physical world, where every change of a control input variable adds cost, many control actions in the logical world have a strongly non-linear impact on the cost function (e.g., up to a certain point and under certain conditions, using more CPU can be done for free). Furthermore, control goals are initially described in a symbolic way, and there is often no analytic way to transform these into numeric values and map them into set points for internal states. Therefore, the set points are mostly step functions, not trajectories.

These characteristics, originating both in the nature of software and the particular design of agent-based systems, make an approach to the control of DMAS based on control theory very complex. Because of the dynamic system boundaries and the system size, it is hard to build a model of the process that is smaller than the DMAS itself. There are no good abstractions that can be analytically derived from internal states and capture the desired behavior. In addition, the number of internal states and their couplings impose a complex multivariable control problem. Since control inputs often lead to structural changes in the system, the system dynamics become nonlinear.

On the other hand, the software system can be used as a perfect model for itself and, given an automated testing environment, control approaches and control parameter variations can be simulated at almost no additional cost. The use of feed-forward controllers often avoids stability problems, with experimentally determined control parameters.

This heuristic approach is often taken in software engineering. It is reflected by the use of terminology for describing control components and measures that possess analogs in traditional control theory. Examples for these abstractions are (software engineering vs. control theory): actions or operating modes vs. control inputs; stresses vs. disturbances; control engines vs. controllers; rules or plays vs. control algorithms.

3 Concurrent Control Objectives in Multi-agent Systems

Besides the primary system function, a DMAS has to accommodate various requirements in parallel (e.g., usability, reliability, fidelity, and stability) that become additional control goals in the multidimensional control and optimization problem. Because of the distributed nature of DMAS, these generic requirements become a special meaning since communication over wide area networks, memory, CPU resources, and participating platforms are not only variable and unpredictable, but also vulnerable against kinetic or information attacks.

The primary system function of the UltraLog system is the planning and plan-execution of military deployment operations; the control goal is to build a timely plan in the face of varying workloads and system conditions. Besides this logistics application, the system has to accommodate extreme hardware- and software-related failures, motivated by the operational scenario of operating under warlike conditions. These requirements are captured under the functions of robustness and security. The control goal of robustness is to maintain a processing infrastructure despite the loss of processing resources (caused by intentional network or hardware platform disruptions). The control goal of security is to maintain system integrity despite information attacks (intentional software intrusions).

In the control hierarchy, there are two levels specifically designed to achieve these control goals:

- *Application level control.* The control inputs on this level are typically complex actions or sequences of actions composed of control primitives and designed as specific defenses against certain stresses. Examples are variable fidelity processing that requires less computing resources; load balancing by moving agents to different hosts; or reconstituting agents that were residing on destroyed hosts. These control actions are mostly initiated and implemented by manager agents within a local scope, but often have global impact. Since some complex actions can have conflicting impacts, an additional control layer for deconfliction is required that arbitrates the action selection [7].
- *Agent infrastructure level control.* The control inputs on this level are the parameters of the components within an agent, providing the agent with the autonomy to make local decisions. Examples are lowering the rate of status reports or turning on message compression when the local network load is high.

The following section presents a hierarchical, cascaded control architecture that was designed to cope with the concurrent objectives of survivability control, and that connects application level with agent infrastructure level control.

4   Hierarchical Architecture for DMAS Control

Figure 1 looks at the survivability problem from a control perspective. The DMAS delivers the application function as its primary output (e.g., the plan in a planning application) to the users. They in turn may modify the goal or the desired behavior of the application (DMAS input) at runtime, closing the loop.

During system operation a variety of hardware- and software-related disturbances affect the system. In addition to random failures that occur in every technical system, survivable systems face a broad class of intentional disruptions and intrusions ("attacks") that are difficult to model and predict.

Resource degradation attacks can be handled like random failures ("repair if it's worth it or perform your job as well as you can despite the disturbance"). The containment of information attacks (security) imposes an additional control dimension on the system, resulting in coupled control loops that cannot be independently optimized, assuming shared and constrained resources.

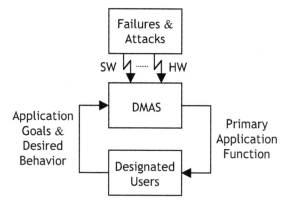

Fig. 1. Control of DMAS survivability.

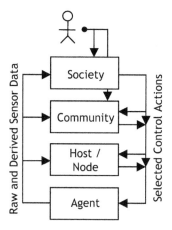

Fig. 2. Hierarchy of control loops.

A standard approach for the control of large complex systems is to set up a hierarchy of controllers, thereby cascading the lower level control actions. Figure 2 shows the principal levels for survivability control in a DMAS that correspond to the levels of resource contention where tradeoffs occur:

- *Agent level control.* This level controls the operation of individual agent subcomponents. Whereas the controllers on all higher levels can be assumed to be agents, the form of resource contention and therefore the design of the controller within an agent depend on the specific agent framework used. (Section 5 will describe the agent level control components for the Cougaar architecture in detail.)
- *Host/Node level control.* All agents on the same host share that host's resources and are controlled by one distinct node controller, managing resource allocations among enclosed agents.

- *Community level control.* Hosts on the same network partition share the same network resources, building a community (e.g., LAN) in which interactions and constraints are managed among the contained agents.
- *Society level control.* The overall system, the so-called society of agents, typically consists of multiple communities on multiple networks. The society controller is responsible for the overall system performance by integrating the various control dimensions (weighted by the users).

Several general characteristics of a hierarchical control structure also apply to our DMAS case:

- Raw sensor data are condensed and propagated up.
- In connection with a slower sampling rate, controllers on higher levels can afford more planning and reasoning (vs. reacting).
- Control inputs (decisions) on higher levels utilize underlying capabilities of higher complexity, having a more global rather than local impact.

However, there are a number of specifics that make the survivability control of a DMAS especially challenging:

- The control infrastructure is part of the DMAS and therefore exposed to attacks, and requires additional logic, sensing, and replication.
- Users are also distributed and work at multiple levels of the system. The DMAS must therefore provide a means for mixed initiative control that allows users to override control inputs from higher levels.

The rest of the section will discuss the characteristics of control actions, sensors, and controllers over the various levels of this control hierarchy in more detail.

4.1 Control Actions

Control actions that are selected, triggered, and parameterized by a controller (control decisions / inputs) are the capabilities that provide the degrees of freedom allowing a system to dynamically respond to stresses. In the context of survivability control, we note in particular those designed as explicit "defenses" against specific "attacks". Defenses can be classified according to various attributes, such as:

- *Targeted stress category* (information attack; resource degradation attack; etc.).
- *Complexity of defense* (function primitives vs. sequence of actions).
- *Causality of defense* (proactive vs. reactive).

Table 1 categorizes a few prototypical defenses that are independent of the primary application function.

4.2 Sensor Data

The control hierarchy requires the system to provide the following basic types of information by analyzing raw and derived sensor data:

- *Resource consumption.* This includes all data describing the status of low-level resources shared among the agents, such as CPU utilization, network throughput, and memory consumption.
- *Stress detection.* The defense mechanisms presented in the previous section are designed as a response to certain stress scenarios, requiring sensors and algorithms that can provide a diagnosis (e.g., tasks counts; aggregated message traffic data; health check).
- *System performance.* This includes all raw and condensed data used to quantify the overall performance of the system as defined by its users (survivability metrics). Examples from UltraLog are: correctness and complete-ness of planning; confidentiality and accountability; timely results; etc.)

A detailed description of techniques for acquiring these sensor data within DMAS is given in [8].

Table 1. Example Defense Classification.

Defense	*Classification*
Reconstitution (restarting dead agents from persistence data on a different host)	• Resource degradation (e.g., killed host) • Sequence of actions • Reactive
Load Balancing (moving agents between hosts)	• Increased workloads • Sequence of actions· • Reactive
Encryption (of messages sent between agents)	• Information attack • Underlying function primitive • Proactive or reactive

4.3 Controller Design

Since the control actions are the designated ways the system defends itself, the development of a survivable system typically starts with modeling attack scenarios and designing matching defenses. However, as complex, real-world environments continuously produce new challenges, the process of modeling and designing never completes; therefore the control infrastructure must provide both the hooks to integrate as well as the means to coordinate a large number of defense variations.

As the more sophisticated defenses involve multiple hosts, their coordination is performed by controllers on the community level, which include various responsibilities (cf. Figure 3):

- *Diagnosis to disambiguate situations.* This addresses the problem that different sensors often deliver different and contradicting outputs. Therefore, intelligent algorithms based on decision theory need to be leveraged in order to provide an unambiguous assessment of the situation.
- *Deconfliction of actions.* Due to the ongoing and independent development of defenses, there may exist redundant or even mutually incompatible defenses. The

challenge for the controller is to select the optimum action leading to the best cost-benefit ratio, given the current performance metrics. Therefore, the defenses need to publish a model of their behavior (TechSpecs, cf. section 5) that allows the controller to reason over the consequences of its selection.

- *Selection and sequencing of actions.* There are instances in which multiple defenses are applicable and their combined execution desirable. For these cases the controller needs to invoke the defenses in a compatible order.

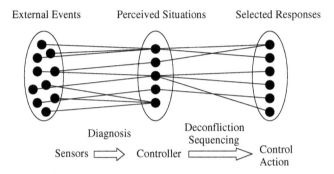

Fig. 3. Reasoning and Defense Selection on the Community Level.

The actual implementation of the controller may leverage any of a number of standard AI techniques [9]. Additionally, the necessary level of complexity varies by level in the hierarchy. Because of the independent development of the defense mechanisms, the functionality of a controller is typically distributed over several agents, which adds a significant complexity to the above task.

Figure 4 shows an abstraction of the interaction between the community level and the society controller. The details of the node and agent level control loops will follow below in section 5.

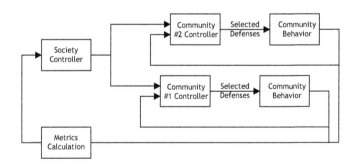

Fig. 4. Society Level Control Loop.

The overall performance is calculated from derived sensor data collected across the society and provided as input to the society controller [10]. This top-level controller may then modify the behavior of the underlying communities, by modifying the cost-benefit functions used in the controller, the allowed range of actions, or the probabilities of various threat conditions. This closes the outermost loop, and allows the society as a whole to balance the various dimensions of system survivability.

This control architecture including its generic design consi-derations for building defenses, sensors, and hierarchical controllers does not depend on the specific agent framework used. The following section will describe the specific agent level control components (realizing the innermost loop) for the open source agent architecture Cougaar.

5   Agent-Level Control in Cougaar

The agent level control mechanisms described in this section are part of Cougaar, a 100% Java agent architecture for building large distributed multi-agent systems, comprising around 500,000 lines of code. The prototype application uses over 500 distinct agents distributed over a 5-LAN network of over 100 machines. Cougaar was designed to support data intensive, inherently distributed applications, where application scalability is paramount. Intra-agent communication is accomplished via publish and subscribe to a local blackboard to reduce latency for tightly coupled component interaction. Inter-agent communication transfers locally published objects to targeted recipients to allow wide distribution of loosely coupled interactions. Communities of agents form to manage resources and provide scalable services.

Cougaar has several subsystems for collecting and measuring overlapping sets of performance data, each with different usage requirements and quality of service characterisics. These include the Metrics Service and various domain-specific sensor groups. The instrumentation is dynamic (sensor values are only measured when needed) and built into the architecture [3].

One innovation of Cougaar is its hierarchical component model, based on the JavaBeans API. This model provides unique security and composition properties for Cougaar agents. All internal system functions and application functions are added at configuration or run time into a Cougaar agent as components, where one or more binders wrap each component to mediate and secure component access to system functions.

Each Cougaar node (agent container, one per JVM) contains a Tomcat web server that provides access to the agents blackboard to external clients such as user interfaces and status monitors. Data access is provided by servlets, dynamically loadable plugins provided by the client. These servlets have full access to agent-state and load/execute only when invoked. For example, the CSMART UI for Cougaar configuration uses servlets both for system control, and runtime monitoring.

Under the UltraLog project, access control systems have been added as Cougaar components (binders) to limit component access to agent-internal data (restricted subscriptions), e.g., to restrict servlet access to Blackboard data and to restrict messaging between agents. The security subsystem can both provide performance metrics and use such metrics at runtime to tune access control policies. This security system, thereby, adaptively controls access to system data using the Cougaar agent-level control infrastructure based on feedback from performance measurements.

5.1 Agent-Level Control Components

Adaptive agent level control in Cougaar can be implemented using the inherent Adaptivity Engine (AE) mechanisms and associated components. Cougaar services are expected to have Operating Modes modes of operation that provide increased Quality of Service (QoS) with increased resource consumption or with particular dependencies on other QoS providers. The AE provides the mechanisms by which control actions (Plays) can specify QoS in multiple dimensions (Operating Modes) based on measured operating state (Conditions). Figure 5 illustrates these components and their associated data flow.

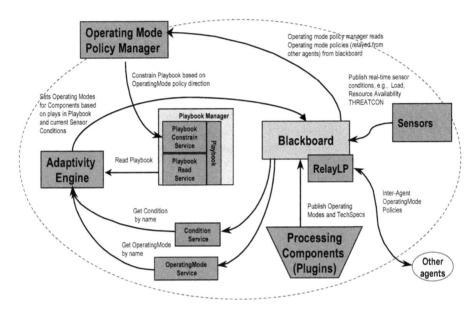

Fig. 5. Cougaar Agent-level Control Infrastructure.

The following discusses the key components, services, and objects, as well as their interactions, of the Cougaar agent-level control infrastructure. These include:

- *Operating Modes.* An operating mode is created and published by a component representing one control input dimension (out of many) of the component. An Operating Mode is a data structure with a list of ranges of values that it is allowed to have, as well as a current value. They are the control inputs ("knobs") by which the component can be controlled ("tuned").
- *Conditions.* Conditions are the generalized form of any (sensor) input information used by the controllers. Sensors can publish conditions that reflect their run-time performance measurements, and other components can aggregate measurements and state information to provide QoS values.
- *Plays, Playbook, Playbook Manager.* Plays represent the control laws; they specify restrictions or constraints on one or more Operating Modes and the Conditions under which those constraints are to be applied. A Playbook has a list of Plays that

are tested in succession for applicability to the current conditions. The Playbook manager is a component that maintains the Playbook and provides the services needed to manipulate and use the Playbook.

- *TechSpecs.* TechSpecs are published by components as a high-level model (description) of their behavior. They allow the controller (AE) to reason and predict the consequences of alternate Operating Mode settings of the Component.
- *Adaptivity Engine.* Each agent contains a component named Adaptivity Engine that acts as the controller for that agent and certain other external components. The Adaptivity Engine responds to changes in Conditions and modifications of the Playbook, evaluates the Plays, and sets new Operating Modes accordingly. By observing the system behavior and using the TechSpecs as a system model, one can use the Adaptivity Engine and associated components to implement an adaptive control approach that optimizes system behavior in accordance with specified objectives (Plays in the Playbook).
- *Operating Mode Policies and Operating Mode Policy Manager.* Higher-level system policies (set dynamically by other agents, or by a human operator) may restrict valid plays that the agent may enforce. In this way, Cougaar agents use sensors to adapt to changes in the environment and to optimize across application goals. Policies are communicated between agent blackboards via the Cougaar relay mechanism. As Operating Mode Policies can be disseminated across agents, it is the mechanism by which one can implement hierarchical control within a Cougaar agent society.

In addition to these conceptual aspects, there are various technical implementation aspects considered that are less relevant for the control issues discussed in this paper. Examples are, access to plays, conditions, and operating modes via service providers; processing order of plays; or detection of missing or overly constrained operating modes.

5.2 Example

This section provides an example that demonstrates the effective agent level control of a DMAS using these mechanisms. This example is a "toy" control problem that was developed as a "plumbing" test and demonstration of the Cougaar adaptivity engine and its associated components (and is included in the open source Cougaar distribution).

Example 1 is a two-agent system consisting of a task generator agent and a provider agent. Using a single play in its playbook, the adaptivity engine of the provider agent can modify the way tasks are processed within the provider agent. The sensor conditions are the available CPU resources (inverse to the CPU load) of the provider agent's host and the rate by which new tasks are arriving from the generator agent at the provider. The Operating Mode used in this playbook tunes the algorithm by which incoming tasks are allocated by the provider agent's allocator plugin. The quality of the allocations done by this plugin depend on how many iterations the allocation algorithm can afford. The play connects the two conditions by dividing the task rate by the CPU value, and maps this input to the Operating Mode determining the number of iteration cycles in the allocator plugin. The play represents the heuristic that if the number of incoming tasks is low and enough CPU resources are available, the task allocation can be done more precisely using many iterations of the allocation algorithm. On the other hand, if the number of incoming tasks is high or limited CPU resources are available, the allocation should be done fast using less computing resources. Figure 6 shows this nonlinear control algorithm implemented as a play in the playbook.

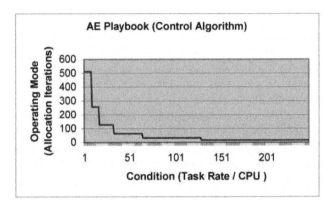

Fig. 6. Control Algorithm of the Adaptivity Engine Demonstration Example.

Figure 7 shows the dynamic behavior of the example after stimulating the generator agent via user interface (servlet). Due to the high number of incoming tasks and the decreasing CPU resources, the adaptivity engine modifies processing in the allocation plugins so that tasks can be processed faster (trading off the quality of these allocations). Once the task load is reduced and the CPU resources increase, the operating mode is set to its initial value again.

6 Conclusion

We discussed several characteristics of DMAS that make them a special case of a controlled process, to which the conventional means of control theory are hard to apply. We argued that, instead, software engineering uses a more experimentally driven approach to control, often leading to rule-based controllers parameterized by heuristics.

From a control theory perspective, the control approach presented in the previous sections has the following properties:

- The hierarchy of controllers constitutes a multi-variable cascaded control loop. In connection with a set of performance metrics it allows the system to automatically adapt to changing survivability conditions and to make local and global decisions that ensure a system performance aligned with the user specified objectives.

- The architecture allows both feedforward and feedback control, depending on the selection of conditions and operating modes.
- The modification of the control algorithm (Plays), either by using a model (Tech-Specs) or by policies constraining existing plays, constitutes for an adaptive control system.
- The Adaptivity Engine in conjunction with the Playbook constitute a rule-based controller. Theoretically, the control algorithm could be linear or nonlinear; as soon as policies impose constraints, it becomes nonlinear.

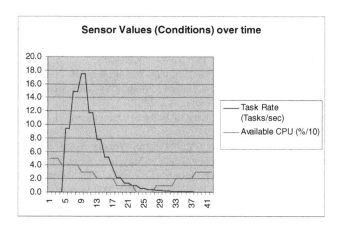

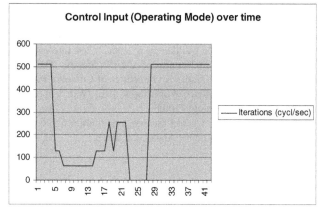

Fig. 7. Experimental Conditions and Operation Mode Values.

The Cougaar open source agent architecture provides a rich set of sensor instrumentation and a control infrastructure that is easy to adapt to various applications. Our results obtained under the UltraLog program have shown that this infrastructure is suited to support the various control goals of a survivable system.

However, in this area of multivariable control, there are still many open issues to be solved by our future research. Examples are, the proper distribution of control knowledge in order to avoid single points of failure; the systematic optimization of control parameters; or the wide use of small models for components (TechSpecs) that are currently still in the early stages of development.

Acknowledgements

This work was sponsored, in part, by the DARPA UltraLog contract #MDA972-01-C-0025. These ideas represent contributions by the many individuals who participated in the DARPA ALP and UltraLog programs.

References

1. The Cougaar Open Source Website: http://www.cougaar.org
2. The DARPA UltraLog Program Website: http://www.ultralog.net
3. Combs, N., Vagle, J., "Adaptive Mirroring of System of Systems Architectures," 1st Workshop on Self-healing Systems, Charleston, NC, 2002.
4. Valetto, G., Kaiser, G., "A Case Study in Software Adaptation," 1st Workshop on Self-healing Systems, Charleston, NC, 2002.
5. Kokar, M., Baclawski, K., Eracar, Y., "Control Theory-Based Foundations of Self-Controlling Software," IEEE Intelligent Systems, May/June, 1999.
6. Selfridge, O.G., Feurzeig, W.: Learning in traffic control: adaptive processes and EAMs", Neural Networks, 2002. IJCNN '02. Proceedings of the 2002 International Joint Conference on , Volume: 3 , 12-17 May 2002 page(s): 2598 –2603
7. Brinn, M., Greaves, M., "Leveraging Agent Properties to Assure Survivability of Distributed Multi-Agent Systems," 2nd International Conference on Autonomous Agents and Multiagent Systems (AAMAS), Sidney, 2003.
8. Helsinger, A., Lazarus, R., Wright, W., Zinky, J., "Tools and Techniques for Performance Measurement of Large Distributed Multiagent Systems," 2nd International Conference on Autonomous Agents and Multiagent Systems (AAMAS), Sidney, 2003.
9. Tianfield, H., Tian, J., Yao, X., "On the Architectures of Complex Multi-Agent Systems", Knowledge Grid and Grid Intelligence Workshop at IEEE/WIC Conference on Web Intelligence / Intelligent Agent Technology, 2003
10. Ulvila, J., Gaffney, J., Boone, J., "A preliminary draft multiattribute analysis of UltraLog metrics", Vienna, VA, Decision Science Associates, 2001

Towards a Natural Agent Paradigm Development Methodology

Fernando Alonso, Sonia Frutos, Loïc Martínez, and César Montes

Facultad de Informática, Universidad Politécnica de Madrid
28660 Boadilla del Monte (Madrid), Spain
{falonso,sfrutos,loic,cmontes}@fi.upm.es

Abstract. It is indisputable that software development using agents and, more specifically, the multi-agent systems concept has greater potential for dealing with complex problems than other more traditional approaches. The agent paradigm is acquiring the status of an engineering discipline and gradually leaving the laboratory and moving into industry. However, it has two major omissions: it is missing an agent modeling language and a consolidated development process such as the object paradigm now has. Although we do not provide a definitive answer to this question in this paper, we do try to help to solve the problem as it relates to the agent-oriented development process by considering what features an agent-based development methodology should have, pointing out the omissions of current methodologies and presenting the SONIA methodology that includes the required features.

1 Introduction

Agent-based computing has materialized as a powerful technology for developing complex software systems [1]. Having emerged, like so many other disciplines, from artificial intelligence, it is now a melting pot of many different research areas (artificial intelligence, software engineering, robotics, and distributed computing).

Agent-Oriented Software Engineering (AOSE) stems from a line of research including the *autonomous software agent* (an autonomous element, with reactive and proactive social ability, trying to accomplish its own task [2]), the *multiagent system* (MAS) (a set of autonomous agents that interact with each other, each representing an independent focus of system control [3]), and *agent societies* (where the social role of the agents and social laws delimit agent operation [4]). AOSE is well suited for tackling the complexity of today's software systems.

This line of research resulted in a new paradigm, the agent paradigm, matured in research laboratories by developing resources and applications until, with the appearance of architectures, models and methodologies, it is acquiring the status of an engineering discipline and gradually leaving the laboratory and moving into industry.

Agents, MAS and agent societies are now well enough developed for researchers and companies to be attracted by the prospects of large-scale agent engineering. The interest they are showing is actually the logical consequence of the successes

G. Lindemann et al. (Eds.): MATES 2004, LNAI 3187, pp. 155–168, 2004.

achieved in this direction, resembling the sequence of events that already took place in other development engineering disciplines (like objects, for example) [5]. This engineering approach is the key factor for the introduction of agent-based systems into industry [6].

This effort to convert agent-oriented system development into a genuine engineering discipline capable of large-scale MAS development has led to a variety of *methodological proposals* [7][8][9][10]. Although they have all played an important role in establishing this field, they have omissions that are an obstacle to the formulation of a *natural* process for developing a MAS system or an agent society from system requirements. Additionally, a good methodology should not force a given architecture (object-oriented, agent-oriented, etc.) upon developers from the beginning. It is the system specifications analysis that should point developers towards the best suited architecture for solving the problem.

In this paper, we describe a methodological approach for naturally producing a MAS or agent society from the system requirements. In section 2, we explain what problems MAS developers face. Section 3 details the omissions of current MAS development methodologies. Section 4 describes the structure of the proposed SONIA methodology. Section 5 outlines a case study: the ALBOR project. Finally, section 6 states the conclusions on the natural development of MAS.

2   Problems of Developing a Multiagent System

According to Durfee and Lesser, a MAS can be defined as "... a loosely coupled network of problem solvers that interact to solve problems that are beyond the individual capabilities or knowledge of each problem solver" [11].

From the pragmatic viewpoint, a MAS is a computer system composed of a set of agents capable of interacting with each other and with the environment in which they are located to achieve their own goals.

A MAS can be described by abstracting three underlying concepts:

- *Agents*: active system entities with the ability to sense and act in the system environment.
- *Environment* (organizational relationships): where the mutual dependencies and social relationships between agents are defined. It provides the conceptual framework for each agent to find a well-defined position (or role) in a society that stimulates and structures the interactions between agents.
- *Interaction*: this is the link element between the agents and between the agents and the objects in the environment.

The MAS-based approach is obviously not a panacea, as its use is not always justified. There are problems where the outlay and development time required by such an approach would be too costly to be acceptable for companies. It is worthwhile to employ a multiagent architecture basically [12][13]: when the environment is open, dynamic, uncertain or complex, when agents are the natural metaphor, when data, control or expertise is distributed, or when legacy systems need to be integrated.

Nevertheless, there are a series of problems and challenges that need to be dealt with to develop quality agent-based software. Seven categories of potential problems within AOSE are identified in [14]: policy, management, conceptual, analysis and design, micro(agent)-level, macro(society)-level and implementation problems.

Apart from these categories of potential problems, we have identified a set of methodological topics to be taken into account when applying AOSE to real problems [15]:

- *Reach agreement on agent theory.* This new paradigm will not be able to expand unless the agent model is standardized with respect to what characteristics define an agent, what types of architecture are available for agents, what agent organizations are possible, what types of interactions there are between agents, etc. Just as UML (Unified Modeling Language) [16] was established to model objects, a modeling language for agents needs to be agreed upon (perhaps AUML [17]).
- *Provide mechanisms for deciding whether the problem should be dealt with using a MAS.* Even if it is initially justified to conceive a multiagent solution for a given problem, a MAS could turn out to be no good in the end, because, for example, no agents can be identified or there are no interactions between the identified agents.
- *Train development team members in the field of agents and MAS.* An organization's team of developers is not usually familiar with agents and MAS these days, which means that they will have to be trained beforehand in this field if they are to be receptive to such projects and to prevent delays in project development.
- *Provide special-purpose programming languages and development tools.* Over the last few years, new languages for programming agent behavior have taken root, although general-purpose languages, like Java and C++, etc., have also been widely used. On the other hand, there are fewer development tools for representing agent structure, and they focus mainly on a particular type of agent architecture and on some specific interaction protocols.
- *Use methodologies suited to the development processes.* For organizations to adopt MAS development, the right methodology needs to be provided to guide the team of developers towards the achievement of objectives, without this requiring in-depth training in this field. A critical stage in the development of a MAS is the selection of the methodology to be followed. A good methodology should provide the models for defining the elements of the multiagent environment (agents, objects and interactions) and the design guidelines for identifying these elements, their components and the relationships between them.

Based on research and development efforts conducted in the field of AOSE, we think that an agent-oriented development methodology should have the following features [15]:

- *It should not condition the use of the agent paradigm right from analysis.* It is too risky to decide whether the system is to be designed using a multiagent architecture in the analysis or conceptualization phase, as the problem is not fully specified at this early stage of development. It is not until the design phase that enough is known about the problem specifications and architecture to make this decision.

- *It should naturally lead to the conclusion of whether or not it is feasible to develop the system as a MAS.* At present, it is the developer who has to decide, based on his or her expertise, whether or not to use a MAS to solve the problem. Because of its high cost, this is a tricky decision that cannot be made using heuristics. Note that design and implementation using a multiagent architecture has a high development cost (time, money and resources), apart from calling for experienced personnel.
- *It should systematically identify the elements of a MAS.* Current methodologies leave too much to the designer with respect, for example, to agent identification. Designer experience is therefore vital for producing a quality MAS.
- *If the problem specifications call for an agent society, it should naturally lead to this organizational model.* The development of a software system using a reductionist [18], constructivist [19] or agent society architecture [4] architecture should be derived from the problem specifications, which will lead to the best suited architecture. Current agent-oriented methodologies focus on the development of the actual agent architecture (internal agent level) and/or its interactions with other MAS agents (external agent level), but very few cover the concept of social organization.
- *It should facilitate the reusability of agents, if possible.* The concept of reuse has been one of the biggest contributions to software development. The provision of libraries has furthered procedure-, object-, or component-oriented engineering. We regard this as being a feature that is hard to achieve because of the complexity of agent architectures, but, for AOSE to advance and establish itself, its elements need to be reusable and easy to use. Current agent-oriented methodologies do not produce reusable systems.
- *It should be easy to apply and not require excessive knowledge of agent technology.* Current agent-oriented design methodologies and methods call for a high level of MAS technology proficiency for use. As MAS technology is related to many disciplines (artificial intelligence, psychology, sociology, economics, etc.), the design of these systems would be relegated to universities, research centers and companies with the latest technology.

The specific characteristics of multiagent systems and multiagent system development-related problems indicate that agent-based problem solving cannot be dealt with intuitively. It calls for a methodological process that naturally leads to the use of agents in problem solving.

3   Omissions of Current Agent Development Methodologies

On account of the advance in agent technology over the last ten years, several methodologies have emerged to drive MAS development [7][8][9][10]. These methodologies are classed according to the discipline on which they are based (Fig. 1):

- *Agent Technology-Based Approaches*: these methodologies focus on social level abstractions, like the agent, group or organization.

– *Object Orientation-Based Approaches*: these methodologies are characterized by extending object-oriented techniques to include the notion of agency.
– *Knowledge Engineering-Based Approaches*: these methodologies are characterized by emphasizing the identification, acquisition and modeling of knowledge used by the agent components.

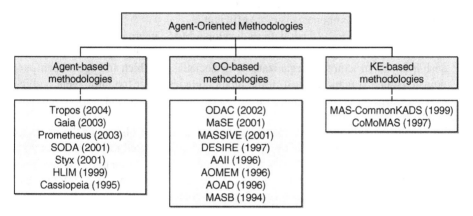

Fig. 1. Agent-Oriented Methodologies.

3.1 Agent Technology-Based Methodologies

Agent technology-based methodologies focus on agent-based system development. An agent-oriented architecture and MAS is defined from the system specification. The most representative methodologies are: Tropos [20], Gaia [21], Prometheus [22], SODA [23], Styx [24], HLIM [25] and Cassiopeia [26].

Although this methodological line is gaining in importance in agent development, the methodologies suffer from some limitations on key points:

– These methodologies propose the use of the agent paradigm as of the specification (Prometheus, HLIM, Cassiopeia) or analysis (Tropos, Gaia, SODA, Styx) phases, which they use as a starting point for design. The choice of a multiagent system should be a *design* decision. Therefore, a good agent-oriented methodology should not conduct a specific agent-oriented analysis. Indeed, an analysis that is independent of the design paradigm and can decide what design (multiagent or otherwise) is the best would be preferable. Although Tropos does not assume the choice of a MAS platform in the early phases of analysis, the decision to select a multiagent architecture is made in the analysis phase. None of the above-mentioned methodologies really account for the use of a generic analysis model that can be used to evaluate whether or not a multiagent approach is suitable.
– Most of the methodologies identify agents from social roles (Gaia, SODA, Styx, HLIM, Cassiopeia), a few from actors (Tropos, Prometheus) and none from their components. Component-driven agent identification is the most objective criterion, as it depends exclusively on the problem and eases the systematization and automation of the identification process. On the other hand, the role (or actor)-driven

criterion is more subjective, as roles or actors depend on the analyst/designer who identifies them.

- All the methodologies in this group implement a top-down agent identification process. In other words, first they identify agents from roles or actors (high level) and then their components (knowledge, behaviors, etc.) and interactions with other agents (low level). As mentioned under the last point, the process of identifying agents from their components is more efficient.

- Three aspects need to be dealt with to develop a MAS: internal agent design (intra-agent structure), design of interactions with other agents (inter-agent structure) and design of the structure of organizations or societies in which the agents can participate (social structure). Most of the methodologies cover the intra-agent and inter-agent aspects (Tropos, Gaia, Prometheus, Styx, HLIM), but only SODA accounts for social structure.

- The analysis of the environment and the identification of objects of the environment is a key point for examining problems that are intended to be solved using a multiagent architecture. SODA is the only methodology to analyze the environment, its entities and their interactions. Moreover, only a few methodologies explicitly identify environment objects (Tropos, Prometheus, Styx and SODA).

3.2 Object Orientation-Based Methodologies

Because of the similarity between the object and agent paradigms and the popularity of object-oriented methodologies in software development [27], other agent-oriented methodologies based on object orientation have emerged. The most representative are: ODAC [28], MaSE [29], MASSIVE [30], DESIRE [31], AAII [32], AOMEM [33], AOAD [34] and MASB [35].

From the viewpoint of correct agent orientation, this methodological line is beset by the following problems:

- Like the agent technology-based methodologies, it does not account for the use of a generic analysis model, which is essential for correct agent-engineered development.

- The agent concept is a design solution, which means that it should be identified in the design phase. This approach is taken by most of these methodologies, except ODAC and AOAD that do the identification during analysis, as their analysis stage is equivalent to high-level design and their design phase to low-level design.

- Only the DESIRE methodology implements a proper component-driven bottom-up agent identification process. The other methodologies implement role-driven top-down identification processes.

- Almost all the methodologies (ODAC, MASB, DESIRE, AAII, AOMEM, AOAD, MASB) cover the intra-agent and inter-agent aspects to some extent, but only MASSIVE and AOAD cover the organizational or social structure.

- With the exception of MASSIVE, none of the methodologies takes into account the environment features. The ODAC and MASB methodologies explicitly identify only the environment objects.

- These methodologies treat agents like complex objects, which is wrong, because agents have a higher level of abstraction than objects. They also fail to properly capture the autonomous behavior of agents, interactions between agents, and organizational structures [24].

3.3 Knowledge Engineering-Based Methodologies

Knowledge engineering-based methodologies are characterized by emphasizing the identification, acquisition and modeling of the knowledge that agents use. The most representative methodologies originate from the CommonKADS [36] methodology and are MASCommonKADS [37] and CoMoMAS [38].

The problems that plague these methodologies are as follows:

- Like the other approaches described earlier, these methodologies do not account for the use of a generic analysis model.
- MAS-CommonKADS identifies agents during analysis, following a role-driven top-down process (identifying actors).
- Both methodologies account for the intra-agent and inter-agent aspects, but do not cover agent-related organizational and social issues.
- Neither of the two account for the analysis of the environment, its entities and their interactions. These methodologies do not identify environment objects.

3.4 Summary of the Omissions of Current Agent Development Methodologies

The methodological approach based directly on agent technology is perhaps better than the other two approaches, because it is based on the intrinsic concept of agent and agent organization in a MAS. It basically falls down on the point that it confines problem analysis to the agent paradigm, whereas this paradigm may turn out to be unsuitable if agent technology is not a good option for dealing with the problem in question.

Briefly, we believe that a good AOSE methodology is one that defines an architecture-independent *generic analysis model* and a *design model* that can systematically identify agents following a component-driven bottom-up process, can identify the intra-agent, inter-agent and social structure of the agent, can analyze the environment and can identify environment objects.

4 SONIA Methodology

The SONIA (Set of mOdels for a Natural Identification of Agents) methodology [15] generates a multiagent architecture to solve a problem (whose conceptualization is not conditioned by the agent paradigm) according to a *Multiagent Design Model* that systemizes and automates the activities of identifying the MAS elements (Fig. 2).

Likewise, using this MAS architecture, the methodology defines an *Agent Society* that flexibly and dynamically facilitates problem solving and can be used to integrate indispensable legacy systems.

4.1 Analysis

The elicited requirements are analysed using the Set Theory Based Conceptual Model (SETCM) [39], an analysis method that was defined to combine a formal foundation with a pragmatic approach. This analysis method is design-independent: it uses a terminology other than design language to provide a real comprehension of the problem under analysis. It has been applied to develop real systems, which were finally designed using a variety of paradigms (structured, object-oriented, knowledge-based) and even a combination of paradigms.

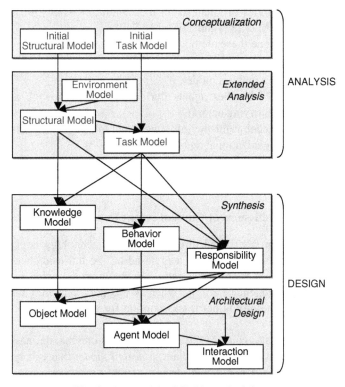

Fig. 2. Phases of the SONIA methodology.

The *Initial Structural Model* and the *Initial Task Model* are built using SETCM. The *Initial Structural Model* describes the general structure of the problem domain (based on concepts, concept attributes, associations, association attributes, concept classification and association classification), and the *Initial Task Model* describes how the problems raised in the domain are solved (based on tasks and methods).

These models are refined and expanded to capture the system environment and external entities, successively producing:

– An *Environment Model*, which defines the system external entities and their interactions with the system.

- A *Structural Model*, which includes structures from the knowledge domain of the external entities that interact with the system.
- A *Task Model*, which adds the functionalities required to interact with the system external entities defined in the Environment Model.

4.2 Design of the Multiagent Architecture

The Analysis phase is followed by the Multiagent Architecture Design, which is divided into two stages: Synthesis and Architectural Design.

The *Synthesis* stage provides for the later component-driven identification of agents (bottom-up process). The elements of the Structural Model and Task Model are grouped depending on concepts characteristic of agents, such as knowledge, behaviors and responsibilities, outputting the following models:

- A *Knowledge Model*, which identifies the knowledge components by grouping Structural Model concepts and associations. The knowledge components will be used internally or shared by the agents.
- A *Behavior Model*, produced by grouping Task Model tasks, subtasks and methods. The behaviors will be part of the agents.
- A *Responsibility Model*, output by relating knowledge components to behaviors. The purpose of this model is to be able to identify agents and environment objects.

The second stage of *Multiagent Architecture Design* focuses on the definition of the architectural elements by means of the following models:

- An *Agent Model*, which identifies and defines, from the Responsibility, Knowledge and Behavior Models, what entities should be designed as autonomous agents.
- An *Object Model*, which identifies and defines, from the Responsibility, Knowledge and Behavior Models, what passive elements are part of the environment.
- An *Interaction Model*, which identifies and defines what relationships there are in the system between agents and between agents and objects.

Not until the Agent Model is built is a decision made as to whether the architecture can be implemented by means of agents or a different paradigm needs to be used. This choice is chiefly based on whether or not agents can be identified. For an entity to be able to considered as an autonomous agent, it should have a behavior and the right knowledge components to perform the tasks of this behavior, have at least one defined goal and one utility, and perceive and act in the environment.

If no agents can be identified, another design paradigm will have to be chosen. One possible alternative would be an object-oriented design, reusing objects and interactions identified in the multi-agent architecture design stage. Another possibility would be to design the system as a knowledge-based system, reusing the knowledge components, behaviors and responsibilities output in the synthesis stage.

4.3 Design of the Agent Society

The *Multiagent Architecture Design* results in either *distributed problem solving,* in which all the agents in the system share a common goal and the problem is divided into small tasks that are shared out among agents, or an *agent society*, in which the system is designed as a set of agents embedded in a social structure.

In this case, the methodology naturally leads to an *Agent Society Model* based on the publish-subscribe paradigm. A society is composed of agents and objects (blackboards) of the environment:

- The *agents*, or active entities of the society, can be: Member-Agents, specialized in performing a given task; or Spoke-Agents, representatives of the society before other societies.
- The *blackboards*, or passive entities of the society, can be: Domain Blackboards, which describe the problem domain and its solution; Subscription Blackboards, which describe the structure of the society in terms of its member agents and the social role of each one; or Statement Blackboards, which describe society input/output knowledge.

5   Case Study

A relevant application of this methodology was the ALBOR project (Barrier-Free Computer Access) [40][41]. ALBOR was conceived as an Internet-based intelligent system designed to provide guidance on the evaluation of disabled people's computer access skills and on the choice of the best suited assistive technologies.

Each system session is divided into the three stages described below:

- *User Identification*: user personal particulars and other information are collected in order to start the session.
- *Session Preparation*: the user is informed about the goals of the questionnaire, how the session will be performed and whether any preliminary training is necessary.
- *Survey Taking*: the user is asked a series of questions, which will be depend on responses to questions already answered and will be confined to the questions strictly necessary for the evaluation of the person in question.
- *Result Evaluation*: after collecting all questionnaire data, an evaluation report is sent to the user. This evaluation contains several recommendations (sorted by priority) for the user to decide which is best suited for her/him.

Fig. 3 shows the bottom-up agent identification process of the SONIA methodology applied to the development of the ALBOR intelligent system. This case study is confined to the identification of the system multiagent architecture.

The *analysis phase*, which is independent of any paradigm, output the concepts, associations and external entities specified in the Structural and Environment Models and the tasks and methods listed in the Task Model.

Fig. 3 shows only the concepts and associations that are the source of "Questionnaires" knowledge component, and tasks and methods that are the source of "TakeSurvey" behavior.

In the *design phase*, the concepts and associations gathered were synthesized as knowledge components using a technique based on Kelly's constructs [42], and the tasks and methods as behaviors using heuristics applied to task decomposition and task dependencies. These techniques used to output the knowledge and behaviors assure highly coherent and low-coupled groupings. Then the responsibilities between knowledge and behaviors were established, from the relationships of concept/association use in tasks/subtasks. These responsibilities lead to changes in the Knowledge and Behavior Models. The models are modified according to knowledge and behavior grouping/division rules based on the cardinalities of the relationships of concept/association use of in tasks/subtasks. The final result of the synthesis stage are the Synthesis Models (Knowledge, Behavior and Responsibility Models).

Fig. 3 shows how "Questionnaire", "Section", "Question" and "Response" concepts, and "Questionnaire.hasSections", "Section.hasQuestions", "Question.hasResponses", "Question.hasMedium", "Response.nextQuestion" and "Response.hasMedium" associations have been synthesized by the "Questionnaires" knowledge component and how "TakeSurvey" behavior synthesizes the "TakeSurvey" task, its subtasks and associated methods. Finally, the responsibility between the "Questionnaires" knowledge component and "TakeSurvey" behavior was identified.

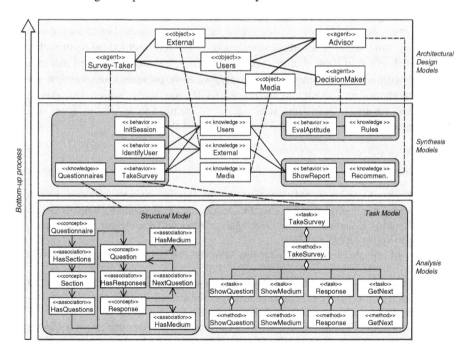

Fig. 3. Bottom-up process of the SONIA methodology in the ALBOR project.

To complete the multiagent architecture design phase, the environment agents and objects were identified. The objects were identified from the Responsibility Model, and the knowledge shared by several behaviors was chosen as environment objects. Following this criterion, we identified the "Users", "External" and "Media" objects (shows Fig. 3) in ALBOR. Agents were also identified from responsibilities. As mentioned earlier, for an entity to be able to considered as an autonomous agent, it should have a behavior and the right knowledge to perform the tasks of this behavior, have at least one defined goal and one utility, and perceive and act in the environment. For example, the responsibility between "Questionnaires" knowledge and "TakeSurvey" behavior produces "Survey-Taker" agent (shows Fig. 3). The final result of the architecture design stage are de Architectural Design Models (Agent, Object and Interaction Models).

6 Conclusions

Agent-oriented software is at a stage where, if it is to firmly establish itself as a genuine engineering discipline, it needs an agent modelling language and a consolidated agent development process, as object-oriented software has. Although there is still a lot of work to do, this should be a short-term goal if we want the agent paradigm to be incorporated into routine industrial software development processes.

This paper aims to contribute to the methodological issue of agent-based development by setting out what the basic requirements for an AOSE methodology should be and defining a new methodology that meets these requirements. For this purpose, we have listed what features an agent-oriented development methodology should have and detailed which of these features are missing from the most important methodologies used within the agent paradigm. Finally, we have presented an overview of the SONIA methodology, illustrated by the ALBOR case study, which includes these features and naturally leads from requirements elicitation to MAS and agent society development.

References

1. Zambonelli, F., Jennings, N.R., Omicini, A., Wooldridge, M.: Agent-Oriented Software Engineering for Internet Applications. In: Omicini, A., Zambonelli, F., Klusch, M., Tolksdorf, R. (eds.): Coordination of Internet Agents: "Models, Technologies and Applications". Springer-Verlag (2001) 326-346
2. Huhns, M., Singh, M. P. (eds.): Readings in Agents. Morgan Kaufmann, San Mateo, CA. (1998)
3. Wooldridge, M.: An Introduction to MultiAgent Systems. John Wiley & Sons, LTD (2002)
4. Epstein, J. M., Axtell, R. L.: Growing Artificial Societies: Social Science from the Bottom Up. The Brooking Institution Press & The MIT Press (1996)
5. Lind, J.: Issues in Agent-Oriented Software Engineering. In: Ciancarini, P., Wooldridge, M. (eds.): Agent-Oriented Software Engineering, LNAI 1957. Springer-Verlag (2001) 45-58
6. Fisher, M., Müller, J., Schroeder, M., Staniford, G., Wagne, G.: Methodological Foundations for Agent-Based Systems. Knowledge Engineering Review, Vol. 12(3) (1997) 323-329

7. Weiss, G.: Agent Orientation in Software Engineering. Knowledge Engineering Review, Vol. 16(4) (2002) 349-373
8. Wooldridge, M., Ciancarini, P.: Agent-Oriented Software Engineering: The State of the Art. In: Ciancarini, P., Wooldridge, M. (eds.): Agent-Oriented Software Engineering, LNAI 1957. Springer-Verlag, Berlin (2001) 1-28
9. Tveit, A.: A Survey of Agent-Oriented Software Engineering. First NTNU CSGSC (2001)
10. Iglesias, C.A., Garijo, M., González, J.C.: A Survey of Agent-Oriented Methodologies. In: Müller, J.P., Singh, M. P., Rao, A. (eds.): Intelligent Agents V (ATAL'98), LNAI 1555. Springer-Verlag, Berlin (1999) 317-330
11. Durfee, E. H., Lesser, V. R.: Negotiating Task Decomposition and Allocation Using Partial Global Planning. In: Huhns, M., Gasser, L. (eds.): Distributed Artificial Intelligence, Vol. 2, Pitman Publishing Ltd., London, England (1989)
12. Bond, A.H., Gasser, L.: An Analysis of Problems and Research in DAI. In: Bond, A.H., Gasser, L. (eds.): Readings in Distributed Artificial Intelligence. Morgan Kaufmann Publishers, San Mateo, CA. (1988) 3-36
13. Jennings, N. R., Wooldridge, M.: Applications of Intelligent Agents. In: Jennings, N. R., Wooldridge, M. (eds.): Agent Technology: Foundations, Applications and Markets. Springer. Berlin (1998) 3-28
14. Wooldridge, M., Jennings, N. R.: Software Engineering with Agents: Pitfalls and Pratfalls. IEEE Internet Computing, Vol. 3(3) (1999) 20-27
15. Frutos, S.: Modelo de Diseño de una Arquitectura Multi-Agente Basado en un Modelo de Sociedad de Agentes. PhD Thesis. Universidad Politécnica de Madrid, Spain (2003)
16. Booch, G., Rumbaugh, J., Jacobson, I.: The Unified Modeling Language User Guide. Addison-Wesley Longman (1999)
17. Odell, J., Parunak, H. V. D., Bauer, B.: Extending UML for Agents. In: Wagner, G., Lesperance, Y., Yu, E. (eds.): Proc. of the Agent-Oriented Information Systems Workshop at the 17th National Conference on Artificial Intelligence. ICue Publishing (2000)
18. Lesser, V.R., Corkill, D.D.: Distributed Problem Solving. In: Shapiro, S.C. (ed.): Encyclopedia of Artificial Intelligence. John Wiley and Sons (1987) 245-251
19. Wavish, P., Graham, M.: A situated action approach to implementing characters in computer games. Int. Journal of Applied Artificial Intelligence, Vol. 10(1) (1996) 53-73
20. Bresciani, P., Giorgini, P., Giunchiglia, F., Mylopoulos, J.: Tropos: An Agent Oriented Software Development Methodology. Int. Journal of Autonomous Agent and MultiAgent System, Vol. 8(3) (2004) 203-236
21. Zambonelli, F., Jennings, N. R., Wooldridge, M.: Developing Multiagent Systems: The Gaia Methodology. ACM Transactions on Software Engineering and Methodology, Vol. 12(3) (2003) 317-370
22. Padgham, L., Winikoff, M.: Prometheus: A Methodology for Developing Intelligent Agents. In: Giunchiglia, F., Odell, J., Weiss, G. (eds.): Agent-Oriented Software Engineering III, LNCS 2585. Springer-Verlag. Berlin (2003) 174-185
23. Omicini, A.: SODA: Societies and Infrastructures in the Analysis and Design of Agent-Based Systems. In: Ciancarini, P., Wooldridge, M. (eds.): Agent-Oriented Software Engineering, LNAI 1957. Springer-Verlag. Berlin (2001) 185-194
24. Bush, G., Cranefield, S., Purvis, M.; The Styx Agent Methodology. Information Science Discussion Paper Series, Number 2001/02. University of Otago. New Zealand (2001)
25. Elammari, M., Lalonde, W.: An Agent-Oriented Methodology: High-Level and Intermediate Models. Proc. of the First Bi-Conference. Workshop on Agent-Oriented Information Systems (AOIS'99). Heidelberg, Germany (1999)

26. Collinot, A., Carle, P., Zeghal, K.: Cassiopeia: A Method for Designing Computational Organizations. Proc. of the First Int. Workshop on Decentralized Intelligent Multi-Agent Systems. Krakow, Poland (1995) 124-131
27. Jacobson, I., Booch, G., Rumbaugh, J.: The Unified Software Development Process. Addison Wesley Longman. Reading, MA (1999)
28. Gervais, M.: ODAC: An Agent-Oriented Methodology Based on ODP. Journal of Autonomous Agents and Multi-Agent Systems, Vol. 7(3) (2002) 199-228
29. Wood, M. F., DeLoach, S. A.: An Overview of the Multiagent Systems Engineering Methodology. In: Ciancarini, P., Wooldridge, M. (eds.): Agent-Oriented Software Engineering,
LNAI 1957. Springer-Verlag, Berlin (2001) 207-222
30. Lind, J.: Iterative Software Engineering for Multiagent Systems: The MASSIVE method,
LNCS- 1994. Springer-Verlag (2001)
31. Brazier, F. M. T., Dunin-Keplicz, B., Jennings, N., Treur, J.: Desire: Modeling Multi-Agent
Systems in a Compositional Formal Framework. Int. Journal of Cooperative Information
Systems, Vol. 6. Special Issue on Formal Methods in Cooperative Information Systems:
Multiagent Systems (1997)
32. Kinny, D., Georgeff, M., Rao, A.: A Methodology and Modeling Technique for Systems of
BDI Agents. In: van de Velde, W., Perram, J. W. (eds.): Agents Breaking Away
(MAAMAW'96), LNAI 1038. Springer-Verlag, Berlin (1996) 56-71
33. Kendall, E. A., Malkoun, M. T., Jiang, C. H.: A Methodology for Developing Agent Based
Systems. In: Zhang, C., Lukose, D. (eds.): Distributed Artificial Intelligence - Architecture
and Modeling, LNAI 1087. Springer-Verlag, Germany (1996) 85-99
34. Burmeister, B.: Models and Methodology for Agent-Oriented Analysis and Design. In:
Fischer, K. (ed.): Working Notes of the KI'96 Workshop on Agent-Oriented Programming
and Distributed Systems, Saarbrücken, Germany (1996)
35. Moulin, B., Cloutier, L.: Collaborative Work Based on Multi-Agent Architectures: A
Methodological Perspective. In: Aminzadeh, F., Jamshidi, M. (eds.): Soft Computing:
Fuzzy Logic, Neural Networks and Distributed Artificial Intelligence. Prentice-Hall, N.J.,
USA (1994) 261-296
36. Schreiber, G., Akkermans, H., Anjewierden, A., de Hoog, R., Shadbolt, N., Van de Velde,
W., Wielinga, B.: Knowledge Engineering and Management. The CommonKADS Methodology. The MIT Press. Cambridge, MA (1999)
37. Iglesias, C.A., Garijo, M., González, J.C., Velasco, J. R.: Analysis and Design of Multi-
agent Systems using MAS-CommonKADS. In: Singh, M. P., Rao A. S., Wooldridge, M.
(eds.): Intelligent Agents IV: Agent Theories, Architectures, and Languages (ATAL97),
LNAI 1365. Springer-Verlag, Berlin (1999) 313-326
38. Glaser, N.: The CoMoMAS Methodology and Environment for Multi-Agent System Development. In: Zhang, C., Lukose, D. (eds.): Multi-Agent Systems - Methodologies and
Applications, LNAI 1286. Springer-Verlag, Berlin (1997) 1-16
39. Martínez, L.A.: Método para el Analysis Independiente de Problemas. PhD Thesis.
Universidad Politécnica de Madrid. Spain (2003)
40. Alonso, F., Barreiro, J. M., Frutos, S., Montes, C.: Multi-Agent Framework for Intelligent
Questionnaire on the Web. Proc. of the Third World Multiconference on Systemics, Cybernetics and Informatics (SCI-99) and the Fifth Int. Conference on Information Systems
Analysis and Synthesis (ISAS'99), Vol. III. Orlando, USA (1999) 8-15
41. Alonso, F., Frutos, S., Fuertes, J. L., Martínez, L. A., Montes, C.: ALBOR. An Internet-
Based Advisory KBS with a Multi-Agent Architecture. Int. Conference on Advances in Infrastructure for Electronic Business, Science, And Education on the Internet (SSGRR
2001), L'Aquila, Italy (2001) 1-6
42. Kelly, G. A.: The Psychology of Personal Constructs. Norton (1995)

Developing Tools for Agent-Oriented Visual Modeling

Anna Perini and Angelo Susi

ITC-irst, Via Sommarive, 18, I-38050 Trento-Povo, Italy
{perini,susi}@itc.it

Abstract. Most of the Agent-Oriented software engineering methodologies that
have been developed in the last years tend to propose a model-based approach
to software development. To be put into practice, this approach demands flexible modeling tools as well as tools that provide transformation mechanisms to
support the translation from one specification language to another, and finally to
code, in a transparent and simple manner. The Model-Based Architecture initiative by OMG is proposing a challenging scenario for the research in this area and
it is going to influence it providing standards.

In this paper we describe a modeling environment which integrates an Agent-
Oriented (AO) modeling tool with other tools, such as a model-checker for the
verification of formal properties of the model and a library which implements
graph transformation techniques which can be used to support model refinement
as well as model transformations. In designing it we are taking into account recommendations from the Model-Driven Architecture initiative.

A scenario is given with the aim of presenting practical motivations for supporting
a light integration of different specification languages as well as the need for
stronger synchronization mechanisms between different views on a model.

We describe the modeling environment architecture, give details on the AO modeling tool and on the components that allows for the integration with other tools.

1 Introduction

Visual modeling has been recognized a different level relevance in software development, ranging from the role of supporting activity aimed at favoring the communication
among the stakeholders involved in the development process and in the documentation of the project, to the role of a driving workflow in the model-based development
approach to software engineering.

According to the model-based development approach, a model serves as the primary
representation of a system under development. It should be able to capture different
properties of the system and of its environment, such as domain features and customer
expectations and it has to be refined and transformed to a model of the architecture and
detail design of the system-to-be, and finally to code.

Most of the proposed Agent-Oriented (AO) software engineering methodologies
tend to adopt a model-based development approach. They all define a set of models
(or views on a model) corresponding to specific steps in the analysis and design of
software. For instance, GAIA [23] considers a four stages process which starts upon
the collection of requirements, with an analysis step, followed by architectural design,
detailed design and implementation. For both the analysis and design steps, specific

G. Lindemann et al. (Eds.): MATES 2004, LNAI 3187, pp. 169–182, 2004.

models are to be defined. Differently from the process proposed in GAIA, the *Tropos* methodology prescribes a preliminary stage, called early requirements, followed by late requirements, architectural design, detailed design and implementation steps [6]. GAIA does not commit to a specific modeling language while *Tropos* builds its own notation upon the *i** framework [22]. Other AO methodologies propose their own modeling language defining appropriate UML stereotypes, for instance PASSI (Process for Agent Societies Specification and Implementation) [3] and MESSAGE [8]. More recently, the AUML [1] effort which aims at extending UML with additional abstraction and notation has been strengthened inside the FIPA initiative.

The model-based approach demands tools that support model specification providing adequate expressive power, for instance allowing the integration of specification languages which are suitable to represent dynamic properties with languages which are appropriate to model structural properties, as well as tools that provide transformation mechanisms to execute the translation steps in a transparent and simple manner.

The relevance of these issues in visual modeling have been recently pointed out also within the Model-Driven Architecture (MDA) initiative of OMG which is proposing a model-based approach to software engineering [7] and it is going to guide the development in this area by providing technological infrastructures and standards [15]. Even if the MDA initiative refers mainly to Object Oriented software development and to system design activities, we think that the emerging ideas are of interest to Agent Oriented software engineering as well.

In this paper, we describe an environment for supporting a model driven software development approach adopting an Agent Oriented methodology. Its architecture allows for a flexible integration of different tools. The current version includes a modeler that supports the analyst when building an informal specification using the *Tropos* methodology and a component that allows for its automatic transformation into a formal specification which can be verified by a model-checker. The modeling environment satisfies the requirements of a framework, that has been previously proposed [21], which rests on a light integration of informal and formal languages. Moreover, the platform includes the interface to a graph rewriting library, i. e. the Attributed Graph Grammar (AGG) system [12] that will be used to support model refinement [20]. In designing it we are taking into account basic MDA directives, such as meta-modeling standards.

The paper is structured as follows. Section 2 discusses basic motivations of this work and describes an example that will be used to illustrate how to use the modeling environment. Section 3, presents the environment architecture and its main functions. Related works are discussed in Section 4. Finally, conclusion and future work are presented in Section 5.

2   Background

Visual Modeling in *Tropos* is a core workflow which drives the software development process from early requirements to detailed design and implementation.

The *Tropos* modeling language allows to represent intentional and social concepts, such as actor and goal, and a set of relationships between them, such as actor dependency, goal decomposition, means-end and contribution relationships. A diagrammatic notation, derived from the *i** framework [22] allows to build views on the actor dependencies or on goal analysis conducted from the point of view of a specific actor (an example is given in Figure 1). The language ontology has been given in terms of common sense (informal) definitions and a subset of it (called *FT*, Formal *Tropos*) is defined in terms of typed first-order Linear Temporal Logic (LTL). *FT* specifications can be automatically verified by model-checking techniques. Using *FT* means extending a *Tropos* specification with annotations that characterize the valid behaviors of the model and are represented as temporal constraints on the evolutions of model instances. That is, an *FT* specification consists of a sequence of entity declarations such as actors, goals, and dependencies. Each declaration associates a set of attributes to the entity on which temporal constraints are given, they are expressed in LTL.

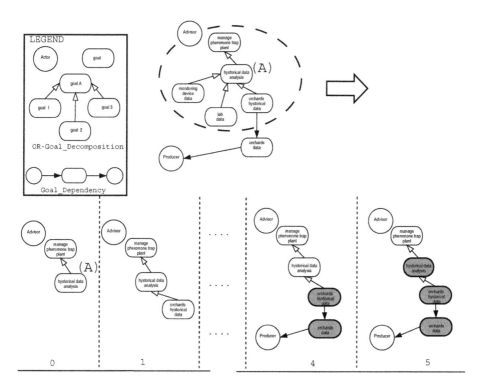

Fig. 1. The analyst builds a *Tropos* goal diagram, possibly annotated (top side) and queries a model-checker on the consistency of the resulting specification respect to the satisfiability of goal (A). The output of the model-checker can be rendered as a frame sequence where fulfilled goal are highlighted (in gray) [21].

The possibility to transform the *Tropos* specification into an *FT* specification allows to exploit automatic verification techniques to support the analyst during model refinement, as described in a previously proposed framework [21]. According to [21] the analyst performs activities such as: annotating the *Tropos* visual model with properties that can be represented in *FT* (*i*); performing the assessment of the model against

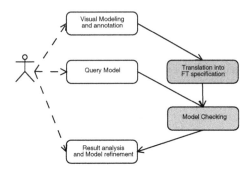

Fig. 2. A schema of the Visual Modeling process that we intend to support. Some of the activities could be completely automated, gray color, other require a mixed-initiative (analyst, tool) approach.

possible inadequacies, incompleteness and inconsistencies (*ii*); validating the resulting specification with the domain experts or the stakeholders in order to end up with an agreed set of requirements (*iii*); managing the model refinement and evolution steps (*iv*). In particular, during activities (*ii—iii*), the analyst can query a model-checker relatively to specific aspects of the model. The example below has been taken from [21] and it is proposed with the aim of illustrating the role of the environment in supporting modeling and transformations from one specification language to another.

In Figure 1, is described a *Tropos* diagram that can be extended with *FT* properties via annotations. In particular, it represents a goal decomposition of the (A)-labeled goal; this goal can be fulfilled if at least one of the goals of the decomposition is fulfilled (OR-Goal_decomposition). This static model can be checked in order to verify its properties, such as the satisfiability of the goal (A), by querying the underlying formal representation using model-checking techniques. In this case, the result of the query can be visualized as a sequence of frames that describes the fulfillment of the goal (A) as the result of the satisfiability of the subgoals that are part of its decomposition; the fulfillment of the goals in the hierarchy during the time steps $[0 \ldots 5]$ are visualized in *Tropos* notation, gray color.

This example is an instance of a more general process depicted in Figure 2, which includes activities such as: visual modeling and model annotation; translation of the resulting model into a *FT* specification. The resulting specification will be given in input to the appropriate tool. *FT* specification can be queried and validated by model-checking techniques. The output needs to be visualized in a coherent notation in order to suggest the analyst for appropriate model refinement activities. Notice that this is a recurrent process that is undertaken during the different phases of software development (i.e. early requirement, late requirement, architectural design in *Tropos*).

In developing tools for supporting the described process we are taking into account emerging guidelines and standards from the OMG' Model-Driven Architecture (MDA) initiative which proposes an approach to software development based on modeling and automated mapping of models to code. A basic motivation of MDA is that of improving quality, by allowing for the reuse of models and mappings between models, and software maintainability by favoring a better consistency between models and code.

One of the basic concepts in MDA is that of distinguishing between a software design which is platform independent (Platform-Independent Models, PIM) from a software design that includes all the platform specific details (Platform-Specific Models, PSM). The two models can be related through a transformation process which converts a PIM to its semantically equivalent PSM. A PIM model can be the result of a chain of transformations between different abstraction level PIMs, which may include, as in our case, interleaving of formal and informal specification languages. In MDA, the use of various modeling concepts and notations is foreseen with the idea to favor the exploitation of existing specification languages that are more appropriate to define views on dynamic aspects rather than of structural aspects of a given model.

From a practical point of view, the MDA initiative is proposing a standard to which the meta-models of the specification languages used in the modeling process must be compliant with, that is the Meta Object Facility (MOF), and a set of requirements for the transformation techniques that will be applied when transforming a source model into a target model, this is referred as the Query/View/Transformation (QVT) approach. The MOF version which is currently available is the 1.4 which both the *Tropos* and the *FT* modeling languages meta-models are compliant to.

For what concerns QVT, on one side OMG is working on the specification of the MOF 2.0 QVT requirements, and on the other side several techniques for model transformation have already been proposed. According to the classification proposed in [10] our approach to model transformation corresponds to a "Direct-Manipulation" approach to model transformation. More specifically, we are exploiting *Visitor* patterns implementing the structure of the models and the operations to be executed on them, in order to transform the informal *Tropos* model to the corresponding model in the target specification language (i. e. *FT* for now). In parallel, we are considering Graph Transformation techniques that have been already pointed out as a promising technology to provide mechanisms for the automatic synchronization of different views in a model or for translating a model given in a specification language to a different one. Along this line we are integrating the visual modeler with the AGG system [12], which implements graph rewriting techniques.

3   The Modeling Environment

The modeling environment that we are developing for enabling a model-based software development approach rests on a modular architecture which is sketched in Figure 3. Its main component called TAOM (Tool for Agent-Oriented Modeling), is a tool which supports the user while building a *Tropos* visual model. The tool allows to annotate each model entity with properties that can be formally represented. This core component can be integrated with other components, such as the T-TOOL [13], which is an automatic verification tool for the *FT* modeling language based on the NUSMV model checker [9]. The I2F component provides an integration between the visual modeler and the model checker. It takes in input the description of the visual model specified by TAOM and queries from the analyst. The T-TOOL produces in output a scenario stating the truth of the query or a counterexample in the case the query is false. The *Graph Transformation Interface* integrates the modeler with a library implementing

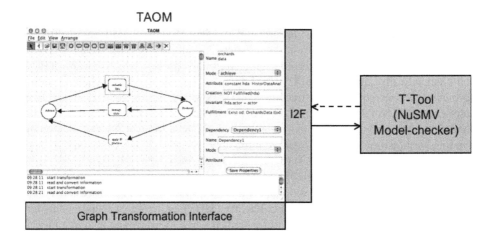

Fig. 3. The modeling environment structure: the Agent-Oriented (AO) modeling tool (TAOM) is connected to other tools, such as a model-checker for the verification of formal properties of the model (T-TOOL) through the I2F module. The *Graph Transformation interface* component integrates a graph transformation techniques library.

graph rewriting techniques. Currently we are exploiting the AGG library and we have represented correct model transformations in *Tropos* as a set of AGG rules [20]. This will allow to get a continuous verification of the model refinement process. Moreover, a complete trace of the process can be derived.

The modeling environment has been designed taking into account the following basic requirements:

– The AO modeler should support visual modeling languages whose meta-model be MOF compliant. We adapted the *Tropos* language meta-model given in [6]. The system is currently able to represent the basic entities defined in this meta-model like actor, goal, plan, resource and the relationships between them like the dependency, the and-or decomposition, the means-end and the contribution. The modeler should allow to represent new entities that could be included in the *Tropos* meta-model or in language variants, as well as to restrict the set of representable entities to a subset of the visual language, in an easy way.
– The modeling environment should be extensible and allow the integration of other tools. A modular design have been adopted so that it will be possible to add new components. A key requirement is the support of the translations of the basic *Tropos* specification into other target specifications languages in order to exploit services like automatic verification.

To allow for the sharing of the model between the environment components, the basic *Tropos* model is represented in XMI. Moreover, a basic choice was to work within an open source environment.

In the rest of this section we give more details on the modeler and on the I2F module, then we briefly illustrate how to use the modeling environment.

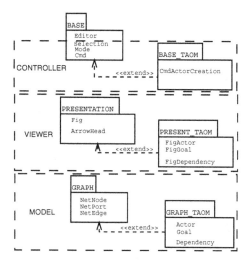

Fig. 4. The UML package diagram of TAOM.

3.1 The TAOM Component

The Agent-Oriented modeler component is based on a framework named Graph Editing Framework (GEF)[1], a library of Java classes for the visual representation and management of connected graphs which has been exploited for other modeler such as ARGO-UML[2]. The library implements the Model-View-Controller (MVC) pattern and assumes that a model can be represented as a graph composed by set of nodes, a set of ports that can be associated to a node, and a set of edges, an edge connects two ports of a given type.

The UML package diagram depicted in Figure 4 corresponds to the GEF implementation of the MVC pattern, namely:

– The package *Base* represents the controller component for the system. It is a collection of the basic classes for the application, such as the class for the editing function: the classes `Selection` and `Mode`, that combines the selection and management functionalities of the graphical objects and the classes of the type `Cmd`, that contains the functions for the editing management and for the control of the interaction with the user.
– The package *Presentation* implements the GEF viewer component. It contains the classes that define the basic graphical components of the framework. They can be grouped in two main categories, namely, the polygons and the lines that allow to build new pictures.
– The package *Graph* represents the model. It contains the definition of the basic component of the graph model, in particular it defines the classes NetNode, NetEdge and NetPort respectively devoted to the representation of the graph nodes,

---

[1] http://gef.tigris.org/

[2] http://argouml.tigris.org/

edges and ports that allow the connection via an edge to the other nodes in the graph model.

The use of the MVC pattern results in a more flexible architecture. The GEF packages have been extended to support *Tropos* visual modeling as shown in Figure 4.

In particular, the package *Presentation* has been extended with the creation of the package *Present_TAOM* to represent the visual part of the entities of the *Tropos* framework; it contains classes like FigActor, FigGoal that uses the class FigNode as a basis for the *Tropos* entity visual representation. The package *Graph* has been extended with the package *Graph_TAOM* to represent the entities of the *Tropos* meta-model and of their properties; it contains the classes Actor, Goal, and Dependency, that extend and use the classes NetNode, NetPort and NetEdges. The package *Base* has been extended in *Base_TAOM* to take care of the new functionalities. If we need to extend the visual language with a new element we simply follow these steps: the new element and the description of its relationships with the other elements is defined in the (MOF compliant) UML meta-model; the entity is then defined as a class of the package *Graph_TAOM* as an extension of classes of the package *Graph*; finally, elements for its graphical notation are defined in the *Present_TAOM* package and control functions related to the manipulation of the new entity can be defined in the package *Base*.

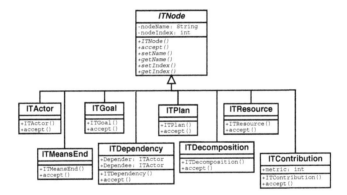

Fig. 5. The set of Informal Tropos Nodes.

3.2   The I2F Transformation Module

The I2F module is one of the bridging modules that have been implemented in the modeling environment. It allows to integrate TAOM with the T-TOOL.

The architecture of the module is based on a "Direct-Manipulation" approach to the model transformation; in particular we used a visitor to implement the transformation from the informal *Tropos* model to the *FT* one. A model developed with TAOM is saved as an XMI file containing the specification of the properties of the entities of the model and including the entity annotations which can be represented in LTL. The model's XMI file is given in input to the transformation module which produces the correspondent *FT* specification and gives it in input to the T-TOOL.

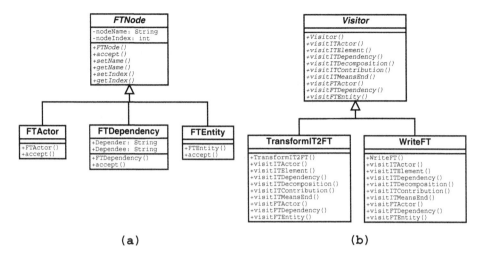

Fig. 6. The set of FT Nodes that maps the Tropos entities (a) and the set of visitor classes that implement the I2F transformation (b).

```
. . .
Goal Dependency OrchardsData
    Depender Advisor
    Dependee Producer
    Mode achieve
    Creation condition
        ∃ ohd : OrchardHistoricalData ((ohd.actor = depender) ∧¬ Fulfilled(ohd))
    Invariant
        ∃ ohd : OrchardHistoricalData (ohd.actor = depender)
```

Fig. 7. *FT* specification of the goal dependency orchards data, shown in the *Tropos* diagram in Figure 1, between the Advisor and the Producer.

Figure 5 and Figure 6 show the UML design of the transformation module which exploits the visitor pattern [14], a well known design pattern that allows to add new operations without changing the classes of the elements on which they operates; this characteristic is particularly useful in the design of a generic parsing environment, like the one we describe here, since in general the elements of a language are more stable respect to the operations executed on them. The visitor, showed in the class hierarchy in Figure 5, allows to represent the element of the *Tropos* informal model, like ITActor, ITGoal, ITDecomposition, as a realization of the abstract class ITNode. The visiting methods such as visitITActor, visitITGoal, visitITDecomposition, specified in the visitor class TransformIT2FT, shown in Figure 6(b), allow to transform the *Tropos* entities to the *FT* entities specified by the realization of the abstract class FTNode in Figure 6(a). Notice that the visit methods operates the translation according to the mapping between informal *Tropos* and *FT* concepts. Figure 7 gives an example of this mapping for the goal dependency concept. It contains several condition for the creation and fulfillment of the goal specified via first order Linear Temporal Logic (LTL) formulas.

If we need to transform a *Tropos* model (the source model) into a different target specification language, once having defined a mapping between the concepts of the source and the target specification language, we can design a new class hierarchy describing the target model entities (such as those introduced for *FT*) and a new visitor class hierarchy where the transformation operations between corresponding entities are defined.

3.3   How to Use It

Figure 8 depicts the graphic user interface of TAOM. The screen is divided in four main areas: the *Tropos* diagram palette on the top, the diagram editor, the message window at the bottom and the properties editor at the right.

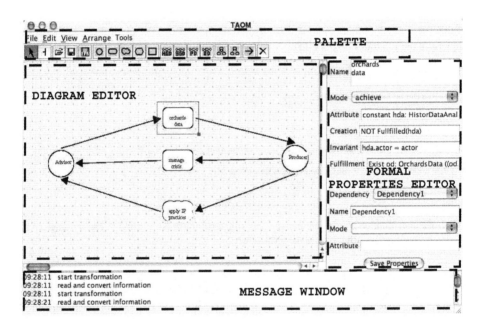

Fig. 8. The GUI of TAOM: on top of the application window the *Tropos* diagram palette, in the center the diagram editor, at the bottom the message window and the properties editor at the right.

TAOM allows the analyst to define a new *Tropos* diagram by selecting from the palette the desired *Tropos* entity and drawing it in the diagram editor. For every model refinement operation, the AGG graph rewriting system verifies its correctness against the specified rewriting rules, and send information about the validity of the operation which will be displayed in the message window. For every *Tropos* entity it is possible to specify properties that can be represented formally (i.e. conditions for goal existence and fulfillment) using the property editor; these properties can be translated into

FT specifications by selecting the corresponding command in the "Tools" menu of the TAOM Palette. The resulting *FT* specification is automatically passed to the T-TOOL for model verification.

The system allows to save and load the models in XMI format and model views in PGML, a format that maintains the graphical information on the specified model view.

4 Related Work

Relevant to the work described in the paper are the specification and technological solutions which are going to be provided by the MDA initiative of OMG [17, 7]. In particular we refer to the ongoing work on the specification of the MOF 2.0 Query/Views/Transformations (QVT) [17, 15] whose goal is that of providing a standard for expressing model transformations. Up to our knowledge, techniques and technologies that support the rigorous definition and application of model transformations, according to the MDA vision, are still under development[3].

In this context, graph grammars and graph rewriting [4] seem to offer a promising technology to support automatic transformations in a way that semantic interoperability is maintained [18]. Several tools have been developed that illustrate the practical applicability of the graph rewriting approach. These environments have demonstrated that complex transformations can be expressed in the form of rewriting rules. In a parallel work we are studying the applicability of graph rewriting techniques to support visual modeling in *Tropos* [20].

Works on CASE tools for visual modeling are worth to be mentioned. These tools are largely diffused nowadays, but most of them are not completely open-source nor provide easily extensible projects. As already mentioned we referred mainly to the ARGO-UML project, a graphical software design environment that aims at support the design, development and documentation of object-oriented software applications, that uses the GEF library, described in Section 3, as one of its components.

In the following we will describe a tool which allows to customize a modeler respect to a specific notation and a couple of tools which support methodologies for goal-analysis, from which we got interesting ideas.

The Domain Modeling Environment (DOME) [16] is a tool-set which includes model-editing, meta-modeling, and analysis tools. It has been designed to support a model-based development approach to software engineering. DOME already supports different notation, such as various OO modeling languages. Additional domain-specific notations, based on visual grammars can be easily included. DOME was written in the VisualWorks Smalltalk[4]. The latest release of DOME (5.3) dates to 2000, and no specific news on future development are available from the site.

Among the tools that support goal analysis techniques we shall mention OME3[5] which supports goal-oriented modeling and analysis within the *i** framework. It provides users with a graphical interface to develop models. OME3 is implemented in Java

---

[3] See http://www.omg.org/techprocess/meetings/schedule/
MOF_2.0_Query_View_Transf._RFP.html for request for proposal on MOF 2.0 QVT.

[4] Cincom International offers free noncommercial versions of VisualWorks for Linux and Windows.

[5] http://www.cs.toronto.edu/km/ome/

1.2 and rests upon a knowledge base which is written in Telos [19], a terminological language.

Objectiver [2] is a commercial product that supports the Kaos method [11], its graphical notations and the analysis process, which includes gathering of the information to be used as a guide for the goals to be achieved, modeling, drawing up of a report.

Finally, we shall mention the specifications provided by the ECLIPSE platform designed for building integrated development environments that can be used to create applications as diverse as web sites, Java programs, Enterprise JavaBeans and C++ programs. We are currently considering the integrability of our tools within the ECLIPSE platform.

5   Conclusion and Future Work

This paper described an AO environment which includes a visual modeling tool that supports model building in *Tropos* and integrates other tools, such as the T-TOOL, a model-checker for the verification of formal properties and AGG, a library which implements graph transformation techniques that can be used to support model refinement. We described in details the modeling environment architecture, the visual modeler and the I2F component.

Basic motivations behind this work, such as that of favoring the practical usage of AO methodologies and of supporting the model-based approach to software development proposed in *Tropos* has also been discussed.

The described environment implements a core subset of the requirements that have been identified [5]. Work is in progress to implement other requirements referring to the management of other software development artifacts, multiple views on the model and to the support of the process phases proposed by the *Tropos* methodology. Moreover, we are following the MDA initiative by OMG which is providing standards relevant for expressing model transformations (MOF 2.0 Query/Views/Transformations), and we may revise some of the design choices described in the paper in order to be compliant with the emerging standards. Graph transformation techniques have been already pointed out as a promising technology to provide mechanisms for the automatic synchronization of different views in a model or for translating a model given in a specification language to a different one. Along this line we are pursuing a parallel research [20] and extend the work on the integration of the AGG system in the environment.

Acknowledgments

The work presented in the paper is partially funded by the Italian Ministry of Research, MIUR (ASTRO project). We'd like to thank the people that contributed to the platform development: Davide Bertolini, Aliaksei Novikau, Michela Strobbe and Nicola Villa.

References

1. http://www.auml.org, 2004.
2. Objectiver 1.5. a technical overview., 2003. http://www.objectiver.com.

3. Passi documentation, 2003. http://www.csai.unipa.it/passi.
4. R. Bardohl, G. Taentzer, M. Minas, and A. Schürr. Application of Graph Transformation to Visual Languages. In *Handbook of Graph Grammars and Computing by Graph Transformation*, volume 2: Application, Languages and Tools. World Scientific, 1999.
5. Davide Bertolini, Paolo Bresciani, Alessandro Daprá, Anna Perini, and Fabrizio Sannicoló. Requirement specification of a case tool supporting the tropos methodology. Technical report, IRST Technical Report 0204-02, Istituto Trentino di Cultura, April 2002.
6. P. Bresciani, P. Giorgini, F. Giunchiglia, J. Mylopoulos, and A. Perini. Tropos: An Agent-Oriented Software Development Methodology. *Journal of Autonomous Agent and Multi-Agent Systems*, 8(3):203 – 236, May 2004.
7. Alan Brown. An introduction to Model Driven Architecture Part I: MDA and today's systems. *The Rational Edge*, January 2004.
8. Giovanni Caire, Wim Coulier, Francisco J. Garijo, Jorge Gomez, Juan Pavon, Francisco Leal, Paulo Chainho, Paul E. Kearney, Jamie Stark, Richard Evans, and Philippe Massonet. Agent oriented analysis using message/uml. In *Revised Papers and Invited Contributions from the Second International Workshop on Agent-Oriented Software Engineering II*, pages 119–135. Springer-Verlag, 2002.
9. A. Cimatti, E. M. Clarke, E. Giunchiglia, F. Giunchiglia, M. Pistore, M. Roveri, R. Sebastiani, and A. Tacchella. NUSMV 2: An opensource tool for symbolic model checking. In *Computer Aided Verification*, number 2404 in LNCS, Copenhagen (DK), July 2002. Springer. http://nusmv.irst.itc.it.
10. Krzysztof Czarnecki and Simon Helsen. Classification of Model Transformation Approach. In *Proc. of OOPSLA'03 Workshop on Generative Techinques in the Context of Model-Driven Architecture*, 2003.
11. Robert Darimont, Emmanuelle Delor, Philippe Massonet, and Axel van Lamsweerde. Grail/kaos: An environment for goal-driven requirements engineering. In *Proceedings of ICSE 1997, Boston*, pages 612 – 613, Boston, MA, USA, 1997. ACM Press.
12. C. Ermel, M. Rudolf, and G. Taentzer. The AGG approach: Language and environment. In *Handbook of Graph Grammars and Computing by Graph Transformation*, volume 2: Application, Languages and Tools. World Scientific, 1999. See also AGG site: http://tfs.cs.tu-berlin.de/agg/.
13. A. Fuxman, L. Liu, M. Pistore, M. Roveri, and J. Mylopoulos. Specifying and analyzing early requirements: Some experimental results. In *IEEE Int. Symposium on Requirements Engineering*, Monterey (USA), September 2003. IEEE Computer Society. http://dit.unitn.it/ ft/ft_tool.html.
14. E. Gamma, R. Helm, R. Johnson, and J. Vlissides. *Design Patterns*. Addison Wesley, Reading, MA, USA, 1995.
15. Trecy Gardner, Catherine Griffin, Jana Koehler, and Rainer Hauser. A Review of OMG MOF 2.0 Query/View/Transformations Submission and Recommendations towords the final Standard. Technical report, 2003.
16. Honeywell, Inc. *DOME Guide 5.2.2*, 1999.
17. Sheena R. Judson, Robert B. France, and Doris L. Carver. Specifying Model Transformations at the Metamodel Level, 2004. http://www.omg.org.
18. G. Karsai, A. Agrawal, and F. Shi. On the Use of Graph Transformations for the Formal Specification of Model Interpreters. *Journal of Universal Computer Science*, 9(11):1296 – 1321, January 2003.
19. J. Mylopoulos, A. Borgida, M. Jarke, and M. Koubarakis. Telos: a language for representing knowledge about information systems. *ACM Trans. Information Systems*, 8(4), 1990.
20. Aliaksei Novikau, Anna Perini, and Marco Pistore. Graph Rewriting for Agent Oriented Visual Modeling. In *Proc. of the International Workshop on Graph Transformation and Visual Modeling Techniques, in ETAPS 2004 Conference*, Barcelona, Spain, 2004.

21. A. Perini, M. Pistore, M. Roveri, and A.Susi. Agent-oriented modeling by interleaving formal and informal specification. In *Agent-Oriented Software Engineering IV(AOSE 2003). 4th International Workshop AOSE03, Melbourne, Australia - July 2003*, LNCS 2935, pages 36–52. Springer-Verlag, 2004.
22. E. Yu. *Modelling Strategic Relationships for Process Reengineering*. PhD thesis, University of Toronto, Department of Computer Science, University of Toronto, 1995.
23. F. Zambonelli, N. R. Jennings, and M. Wooldridge. Developing Multiagent Systems: The Gaia Methodology. *ACM Transactions on Software Engineering and Methodology*, 12(3):317 – 370, July 2003.

Towards a Component-Based Development Framework for Agents*

Gaya Buddhinath Jayatilleke, Lin Padgham, and Michael Winikoff

School of Computer Science and Information Technology
RMIT University
GPO Box 2476V, Melbourne, VIC 3001, Australia
Tel: +61 3 9925 3781
{gjayatil,linpa,winikoff}@cs.rmit.edu.au

Abstract. Developing agent-oriented systems is still a difficult task. However, a component-based approach can help by supporting both modular modification of existing systems and construction of new systems from existing parts. In this paper we develop a foundation (conceptual model) for a component-based agent development framework by extending the concepts of the SMART framework. We apply our definitions to an existing agent application in order to both refine the definitions, and to evaluate the extent to which the model is able to support modification of existing systems.

1 Introduction

Agents are a powerful technology with many significant applications, both demonstrated and potential [12, 13]. However, building and modifying agent systems require substantial expertise. Unfortunately, the complex domains where agents are used often have requirements that change as the understanding of the system grows. Often domain experts (e.g. meteorologists, scientists, accountants) or users identify and require these changes. Therefore the need for expert agent developers hinders the evolutionary development and makes it costly to maintain agent systems. Further the notion of code reuse (as in components) is not well established within Agent Oriented Software Engineering (AOSE).

In order to make it simpler to build and modify agent systems, we have started developing a component-based approach for agent systems, with structured support for building and modifying components. Our objective is to define a framework where an agent system is developed as a composition of well-defined components (building blocks), which can then be modified in specified ways. However it is important to note here that our view of components is somewhat different to how they are viewed in traditional software engineering. Components in Object Oriented Software Engineering are viewed as binary units of composition with specified interfaces, which can be used in a suitable component infrastructure [10, 22]. We require components that are easily modifiable (hence not binary) by non-experts. Further the components need to be defined

---

* This work was supported by the Australian Research Council (Linkage Grant LP0347025) in collaboration with the Australian Bureau of Meteorology and Agent Oriented Software Pty. Ltd.

G. Lindemann et al. (Eds.): MATES 2004, LNAI 3187, pp. 183–197, 2004.

at a granularity that is sufficiently fine to allow easy modelling and implementation of agent systems with various behaviors.

For example, assume that we have a definition for a goal, which is based on a description of the world in terms of a set of attributes. A developer wishing to add a new goal could then be presented with a menu of the attributes from which to choose a combination that specifies the goal state. In order to build plans to achieve this goal, the developer can be presented with the set of existing actions and (sub)goals which affect the relevant attributes. Development of the application in terms of well structured components aids in making the application easier to understand, as well as making it more likely that some components can be re-used.

Our primary goal is enabling domain experts to modify an existing application. Supporting reuse is of lesser importance, and supporting a "component market place" where components are bought and sold in binary form is not a goal of this research.

2   Background

Component Based Software Engineering is a well-established technology within object-oriented software engineering [10], and has also been explored in relation to Agent Oriented Software Engineering. However none of the approaches that we have seen have provided the right combination of simplicity and expressivity to support non-experts in modification of evolving agent applications in the way that we envision.

Agent component systems such as PARADIGMA [1], DESIRE [3], JAF [23], JadeX [17] and others [8, 20] have focused on making agent *architectures* modular, rather than on making applications developed using these architectures modular. These approaches make it easier to change the core functionality of the agent architecture such as how the agent selects actions and how the agent perceives the world. However, they do not support domain-oriented structuring and changes of an agent application through components as in developing a weather event monitor agent from existing weather-related components. In other words they are not intended for non-experts. Another common problem faced in using these systems is the loosely defined nature of components such as *actions*. While most of these systems use *actions* as the primitive atomic behaviors used by agents (frequently contained in Plans), they do not clearly define what constitutes an *action* at the implementation level. Another aspect that needs highlighting is the use of XML in our framework and in JadeX. JadeX uses XML in defining the structure of the Java code that implements each component. This is significantly different to our use of XML where it defines the implementation independent (inherent) structure of the component. This allows for easy comprehension for the non-experts while keeping the implementation independent of the component definition.

The SMART framework [15] on which PARADIGMA [1] is based provides an extensive set of components for defining an agent. However we find that some of these are not relevant for our purpose, as they define the underlying infrastructure components such as *AgentPerception* and *AgentState*, rather than those required for a particular application. Other components are not defined in sufficient detail, or in a way that facilitates their use for building and modifying applications. These include components such as *Actions*, *Plans* and *Events*. We have however taken aspects of the SMART framework as a starting point and further developed or modified these in line with what we perceive as necessary for providing the concrete implementation support desired.

Another category of work has focused on providing agent toolkits with general purpose agent components for expert agent programmers. This category includes toolkits such as ABLE (Agent Building and Learning Environment) [2] and ZEUS [6]. Both these tools provide graphical interfaces with an extensive set of components mostly comprising core processing elements such as communication, learning and planning based on Java. ZEUS provides more support for multi agent communication and collaboration while ABLE specialises in agent learning. These prepackaged components help the rapid development of agent systems via component reuse. However they can only be used by expert programmers who are skilled in object-oriented languages such as Java and agent concepts. Therefore these tools do not provide an answer to our problem of supporting non-expert users.

The only work that we are aware of that develops a component framework aimed at applications, rather than agent architectures, is [9]. This work views each agent as consisting of a number of Activity components, where an activity is basically a tree of Decision components leading to a Behaviour component. Although this work is promising, defining an agent with only Activity, Decision and Behavior components seem too limited in implementing complex agent systems. For example, it is not clear how agent beliefs (i.e. agent's view of the world) are maintained and also how proactive (goal-oriented) behavior can be implemented. As a whole, it is not clear how the three component types can be used to implement flexible behaviors as supported by architectures such as Belief Desire Intention (BDI) architecture [18].

3   Approach

In this work we are interested in defining components with the right granularity to support non-expert users with limited programming knowledge in modifying agent behavior. It is essential that the component model support implementation, not just design. In particular, we are interested in implementation using a particular style of agent systems, namely Belief, Desire, Intention (BDI) [18] systems such as JACK [4], PRS [11] and dMARS [7]. In this paper we provide details of a conceptual component model which is a result of our initial work towards achieving the aforementioned goal.

As a starting point we used the SMART framework [15] to identify the potential building blocks of an agent system. The reasons for selecting SMART are two fold. Firstly SMART is precisely defined (using the Z formal specification notation). Secondly SMART has been used to formalise the operation of the dMARS agent platform [7] which suggests that the SMART model is compatible with the use of a BDI implementation platform.

Some of the component types defined in SMART correspond to core functions of an agent platform, for example the action selection function. These components are provided by the agent platform and are not usually modified by application developers. For example, the mechanism by which an agent selects which plan to use or which event to process next will not be changed by the designer of a particular agent application. These "core platform components" are not the focus of our work since they are not the focus of an application developer, but of a platform developer.

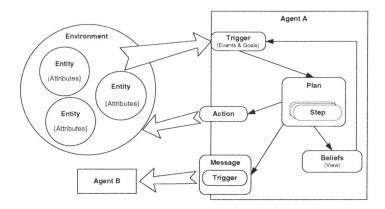

Fig. 1. Simplified model of an agent in our framework

Other component types *are* application-specific. For example, the entities that a particular application domain deals with, or the goals that an agent achieves. These component types are the focus of our investigation. Figure 1 shows an overview of how these descriptive components are structured within an agent.

In order to investigate the suitability of the descriptive components identified in SMART and to find what other component types are required, we applied these to an existing agent application. We used the weather alert system at the Bureau of Meteorology in Melbourne [16] for this purpose. We now briefly describe this application.

3.1 Meteorology Alerting System

Currently, human forecasters receive a large range of information from many sources such as radar, automated weather stations, lightning, and volcanic ash advisories. The weather alert system[1] [16] aims to reduce the information overload experienced by human forecasters by filtering information and automatically generating a range of alerts.

The system receives events from a range of sources including:

– Automated Weather Stations (AWS) which produce regular readings including temperature, pressure, and wind speed and direction.
– Terminal Aerodrome Forecasts (TAF) which are regularly-issued forecasts for airports, and contain pressure and temperature predictions.
– Thunderstorm alerts.

The system is structured as an open agent system implemented in JACK^{TM} [4] where each agent subscribes to events. For example, one of the agent types subscribes

[1] The weather alert system is part of the research project *Open Agent Architectures for Intelligent Distributed Decision Making* which is funded by the Australian Research Council (Linkage Grant LP0347025, 2003-2005) and is joint work with the Australian Bureau of Meteorology (Australia's national weather service, *www.bom.gov.au*) and Agent Oriented Software Pty. Ltd. (*www.agent-software.com*).

to AWS and TAF events and checks for consistency between the forecasts (TAF) and the actual weather readings (AWS). If a significant inconsistency is detected it sends an alert event. Forecasters' GUIs subscribe to alert events. Currently there are agents that check for inconsistencies between forecasts (TAF) and data readings (AWS) and agents that check for extreme weather conditions (e.g. high wind speed, thunderstorms).

The key issues include ensuring that the system is resilient to various forms of failure (i.e. is robust); reducing "alert pollution", that is trying to avoid overloading the human forecasters with too many alerts whilst ensuring that essential information is delivered; and ensuring that the system is extensible.

4 Component Model

Our exploration using the weather application yielded a basic set of component types which we believe are sufficient to describe an agent application. This set of components comprise: *attribute, entity, environment, goal, event, trigger, plan, step, belief* and *agent* (see Figure 1).

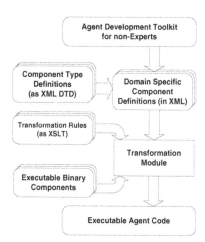

Fig. 2. An Overview of the Component Framework

These *Component Types* define the generic types of agent building blocks which can be used to create domain specific component types. The use of these *Component Types* are done in three "levels" and it is important to avoid confusion. The first level includes the domain-independent generic component types mentioned above. The second level uses these as the basis for defining component types that are domain-specific; for example, *FireMonitorAgent* or *AlertPlan*. We call these *Type Instances*. Finally, the third level is the run-time instances of the domain-specific entities, for example *FireMonitorAgentSydney*. In this paper we will focus on the first two levels, the relationship between the second and third level is straight forward instantiation. These levels resemble the levels M0, M1 and M2 of the Model Driven Architecture (MDA) of the Object Management Group (OMG). However we have not defined our levels using the Meta Object Facility (MOF) which the MDA is based on [14]. A rigorous comparison of the MDA levels and our levels are out of the scope of this paper and we leave it as future work.

We use XML as a language for defining the components and hence use an XML DTD specification to provide the meta level definitions of component types. The reasons for selecting XML as the definition language for components are three fold. As stated earlier, our interest is in defining components at a descriptive level rather than at a platform level. For this XML provides an inherently structured language for specifying the anatomy of each component. This is also one of the reasons for deciding against a formal language such as Z ("Zed") [21] (used by SMART for defining it's components) which is more suitable for defining process than structure. Secondly, using technologies such as XSLT (XSL-Transformations) it is easier to transform the XML definitions of the components to executable code. This process is shown in Figure 2. The XML component definitions generated by the top level development tool can be converted into executable code of an existing agent programming language by the *Transformation module*. This way we are able to leverage an existing agent platform for executing our component agents. For example, in our initial implementation, we are transforming the component definitions to JACK agent language [4] code. Thirdly, XML is heavily supported by tools and also well established in mainstream software engineering.

In the rest of section 4 we define the component types found in our study.

4.1   Attributes, Entities and Environments

A defining characteristic of agents is that they are situated in an environment (usually highly dynamic). For example, in the meteorological alerting domain the environment is dynamic in (at least) two ways:

1. The Environment generates a continuous flow of sensory data (e.g. weather related readings from automated weather stations).
2. The Environment may add/remove sensory data sources with or without prior notice (e.g. an automated weather station might go down due to a technical fault).

Therefore we need an effective way to model and represent the Environment. The SMART model is sufficient for our needs. SMART provides two ways of viewing the environment: as a set of Attributes, where an *Attribute* is defined as a "perceivable feature"; or as a set of Entities, where an *Entity* is a set of Attributes. Using Entities rather than attributes gives a more structured view of the environment. We extend this model by adding identifiers (unique names).

Since the environment is dynamic, attributes are not simply mappings of names to values, but fluents [19] – the value of a given attribute depends on the situation. Hence, in some situations it may be useful to explicitly attach state references (for example time stamps) to Attributes.

Based on the above we define an Attribute type as a tuple:

```
<!ELEMENT Attribute (%ID;)>
<!ATTLIST Attribute Type CDATA #REQUIRED>
<!ENTITY % ID "(#PCDATA)">
```

Where *ID* refers to a *unique identifier* used to identify an Attribute. *Type* refers to the domain the Attribute value belongs to. As Attributes are used to hold values and also references to other components, *Type* can contain regular data types such as integer, real etc and also identifiers of other components such as Entities, Events etc.

Using the Attribute definition we can define an Entity as being a collection of Attributes:

```
<!ELEMENT Entity (Attribute)+>
<!ATTLIST Entity ID CDATA #REQUIRED>
```

Where *ID* refers to a *unique identifier* used to identify an Entity.

While Environment and View are not implementable components in our model, the above definitions show that Attributes and Entities can be used to define the environment an agent is situated in. This helps in defining environment related constructs such as percepts and beliefs.

Our view of an Attribute is an elaboration of the SMART definition which does not specify any structure on Attributes (and as a result avoids requiring meta types).

The meteorology domain has entities such as Automated Weather Station (AWS) readings which contain attributes such as temperature, pressure, wind direction and wind speed. Following is an attribute definition for a temperature reading.

```
<Attribute Type="READING">temperature</Attribute>
```

Note that we use a Type called "READING" to denote the domain of the *temperature* values where READING can be any of the possible data types such as real, integer etc. At runtime an instance of the *temperature* attribute will be bound to a value from the *READING* domain.

Formally, an AWS reading is a Type Instance of the Entity Component Type (referred to as *awsreading*). The definition for the *awsreading* entity is given below:

```
<Entity ID="awsreading">
   <Attribute Type="STRING">location</Attribute>
   <Attribute Type="READING">temperature</Attribute>
</Entity>
```

At runtime an instance of the *awsreading* entity will have its *location* and *temperature* attributes bound to values (e.g. *location="Melbourne"* and *temperature=18.4*).

4.2 Goals

Being proactive is an important property of agents and consequently, goals are a crucial concept for agents [24]. Simply, a goal can be seen as a set of attributes that describes a desired state of the world.

In addition to the desired state of the world, [25] argues that goals should include a failure condition which describes when the goal should be abandoned; as well as an indication of how the goal could be achieved (the *procedural* aspect of the goal). However, from an implementation point of view linking goals to the process of achieving them (called a *Plan*) can lead to problems when a priori knowledge of the relevant plans is not available and the agent has to formulate a plan using a planner. Hence in our model we bind a plan to a goal rather than a goal to a plan. Based on the above we define a Goal as:

```
<!ELEMENT Goal (Attributes, Success?, Failure?)>
<!ELEMENT Attributes (Attribute+)>
<!ELEMENT Success (#PCDATA)>
<!ELEMENT Failure (#PCDATA)>
<!ATTLIST Goal ID CDATA #REQUIRED>
```

Where *ID* is a "Goal Identifier" used to identify a goal and *Success* and *Failure* are (optional) boolean expressions formulated with Attributes that state the success and failure conditions of the Goal respectively.

A distinction not made in this definition is between different types of goals such as achievement and maintenance. A formal definition for a goal that takes this aspect into consideration is given in [7] in formalizing the dMARS agent architecture. However, we regard the distinction between achievement and maintenance goals to be a part of the goal processing rather than to be a part of the goal definition itself. In other words we are able to define both types of goals with the definition given above while the processing of the two types would be different. For example the same goal g could be fired as *achieve(g)* and *maintain(g)* where the definition of g would be the same (using our definition) while the resulting process would be different.

An example for a Goal from the application domain we are working with is given below. The purpose of the goal in this case is to find a weather station which is responsible for monitoring a given region. We assume that this mapping is not available in the agent's internal beliefs and that the agent has to consult an external agent or a directory service to obtain this information. Therefore due to the absence of a provider service, the agent might fail in achieving this goal. The goal also assumes the existence of an attribute called *GoalSeekTime* and a BeliefBase query (see section 4.7) *queryws*. *GoalSeekTime* is a time counter that keeps track of the time since the generation of the goal and *queryws* queries the agents beliefs for a weather station for a given region.

```
<Goal ID="FindEffectiveWS">
   <Attributes>
      <Attribute Type="STRING">region</Attribute>
   </Attributes>
   <Success> queryws(region) </Success>
   <Failure> goalSeekTime >= 5 </Failure>
</Goal>
```

Based on our definition of a goal, the above states that the goal with an identifier *FindEffectiveWS* has a success condition (*Success*) which says that once the goal is achieved the Belief set query *queryws* should return *true* for the given *region* and a failure condition (*Failure*) that says the goal needs to be achieved within five seconds.

4.3   Events

An Event is a notification of a certain state of the internal or external environment of the agent. Based on our definitions, an Event type can be defined as:

```
<!ELEMENT Event ((Attributes|Entities)+, Step?)>
<!ELEMENT Attributes (Attribute+)>
<!ELEMENT Entities (Entity+)>
<!ELEMENT Step (#PCDATA)>
<!ATTLIST Event ID CDATA #REQUIRED>
```

where the *Attributes* and *Entities* describe the state being notified by the Event and the optional Step (see section 4.6) provides a way to specify a reflexive action. A reflexive action is when an action is executed directly as a result of an event occurrence without invoking a plan.

An Event is similar to a goal in that once an event is generated, it needs to be handled by an Event Handler (similar to a Plan). However an event describes a current actual situation whereas a goal describes a desired situation that needs to be brought about. Hence an event does not state success or failure conditions. Further, by including a single Step, the event provides a way to execute a mandatory action before any plans are processed. This helps in implementing reflexive behavior and also when a single action is sufficient to handle the event. A good example is 'percept events' that are generated as a result of sensing actions of the agent. Most of the percept data are written to the agent's Beliefs before they are handled by any plans. By including a write action in the event, an agent is able to easily achieve this, without executing any plans.

For example, an event type instance *awsdatareceipt* is generated when an agent receives data from an Automated Weather Station. This event is defined below:

```
<Event ID="awsdatareceipt">
   <Attributes>
      <Attribute Type="STRING">location</Attribute>
      <Attribute Type="READING">temperature</Attribute>
      <Attribute Type="READING">pressure</Attribute>
   </Attributes>
   <Step>insertInto(awsData)</Step>
</Event>
```

Attributes *location, temperature* and *pressure* define the data being passed on by the *awsdatareceipt* event. As it is a percept event that is generated by the environment, we include a step that writes the event data onto a Belief set called *awsData*.

4.4 Triggers

A Trigger is an Event or a Goal, which invokes a plan (see section 4.5 for the definition of a plan).

```
<!ELEMENT Trigger (Goal|Event)>
```

Defining a Trigger allows us to give a common definition to a Plan as a process that handles Triggers (i.e. Events or Goals). However a Trigger is only an addition to our terminology and not a component in its own right. By defining a Trigger we provide flexibility and expressiveness in the modeling process when it is not clear if an Event or a Goal is to invoke a Plan. This can be expressed as a Trigger and later can be implemented as an Event or a Goal.

4.5 Plans

A Plan responds to a predefined Trigger (i.e. achieves a Goal or handles an Event) by sequentially executing a set of "steps" (a step is a generalized form of an action defined in section 4.6), after checking whether a predefined state of the Environment (known as a Context) is satisfied. This is similar to the notion of a Plan definition given in [24]. Based on this definition we represent a Plan as:

```
<!ELEMENT Plan (Context, Steps)>
<!ELEMENT Context (#PCDATA)>
<!ELEMENT Steps (Step+)>
<!ATTLIST Plan ID CDATA #REQUIRED>
<!ATTLIST Plan Trigger_ID CDATA #REQUIRED>
```

Where *Context* is a boolean expression that specifies the state in which this plan is applicable and *Steps* specify the sequence of steps to be executed by the plan. The parameters *ID* and *Trigger_ID* refer to the identifier of the plan and the identifier of the Trigger (i.e. Goal or Event) being handled by the plan respectively.

Example: The plan type instance *FindAWS* handles the *FindEffectiveWS* goal defined in section 4.2.

```
<Plan ID="FindAWS" Trigger_ID="FindEffectiveWS">
   <Context> queryws(region) = NULL </Context>
   <Steps>
      <Step> QueryAWSServer(region, wsName) </Step>
      <Step> wsName != NULL </Step>
      <Step> UpdateWSBeliefs(region, wsName) </Step>
   </Steps>
</Plan>
```

The action *QueryAWSServer(region, wsName)* queries from an external server the AWS name for the given region. The internal action *UpdateWSBeliefs(region, wsName)* updates the agent's belief set with the new data.

4.6 Steps

Actions are defined as primitive elements in many agent platforms and frameworks. In SMART, actions are defined as operations that change the state of the external Environment. However, from an implementation point of view where we consider actions to be the steps of a plan, it is useful to also allow for "internal actions" that affect the agent's internals rather than its environment. In order to avoid confusion, we retain the term "action" for an operation that affects the environment, and view actions as being one type of *step*. Some of the other types of steps (apart from actions) include:

– *sense*: changes attributes in the agent's beliefs that reflect the external Environment.
– *trigger*: generates a *Trigger*. Note that the step type *trigger* is not a *Trigger* itself but a process that instantiates a *Trigger*.
– *message*: this is similar to generating a *Trigger*, however in this case the generated *Trigger* is sent to another agent. This is a very important step type for an agent in a multi agent system.
– *belief*: reads or updates Attribute values in the agent's beliefs. In other words *sense* steps are a special type of belief steps.
– *logical*: These are logical expressions that evaluate to *true* or *false*. This is a special type of step defined to make the plan formulation simpler. This type of step does not change the internal or external environments. By including logical steps an agent can test various conditions within the plan execution and abandon the plan as being failed if a logical step evaluates to *false*.

Based on the above, we attempt to provide an implementation-oriented specification for a *step*, which when implemented will lead to easier formulation of plans. For example, we believe that with the right tool support, a non-expert will be able to use existing step components in creating plans easily.

A step can be formalized as below:

```
<!ELEMENT Step (Input*, Output*, Instructions, Outcome*)>
<!ELEMENT Input (Attribute+)>
<!ELEMENT Output (Attribute+)>
<!ELEMENT Instructions (#PCDATA)>
<!ELEMENT Outcome (#PCDATA)>
<!ATTLIST Step ID CDATA #REQUIRED>
<!ATTLIST Step Type (action | sense | trigger | belief
            | logical) #REQUIRED>
```

Where, *ID* refers to the "Step Identifier". *Input* specifies which Attributes are required to carry out the step. *Output* specifies a set of attributes that will be bound to values as a result of the step execution. *Outcome* is a boolean expression based on Attribute/Value pairs that specifies the state of the Environment/View after the execution of the step. In other words *Outcome* can be used to verify whether the step has succeeded or failed. *Instructions* specify the execution process of the step. From an implementation point of view *Instructions* will include the code that implements the step.

4.7 Beliefs

An agent's Beliefs are responsible for storing the agents view of the internal and external environments. In their simplest form Beliefs can be represented as a set of Attribute tuples. However in our model, Beliefs are extended further by introducing Keys which make them closer to a *relation* in a relational database model. The relational model is sufficient for most data (belief) descriptions and it is also simple to use. Extending this model to support more complex structures such as storing objects instead of atomic values would be part of our future extensions. The current definition of a Belief set is given below:

```
<!ELEMENT Belief (Attribute+, Keys)>
<!ELEMENT Keys (Key+)>
<!ELEMENT Key (#PCDATA)>
<!ATTLIST Belief ID CDATA #REQUIRED>
```

Where the set of *Attributes* (denoted by *Attribute+*) defines a tuple in the Belief set and the *Keys* define a subset of the attributes that acts as a unique identifier for each tuple instance.

Example: The Belief set used in section 4.3 called *awsData* is defined below.

```
<Belief ID="awsData">
   <Attribute Type="DATETIME">timestamp</Attribute>
   <Attribute Type="STRING">location</Attribute>
   <Attribute Type="READING">temperature</Attribute>
   <Attribute Type="READING">pressure</Attribute>
   <Keys>
      <Key> timestamp </Key>
   </Keys>
</Belief>
```

An implementation of a belief set would need to provide a means to *update*, *query* and raise triggers on its beliefs. The *update* and *query* operations can be seen as *belief steps* defined in section 4.6. An *update* step changes the state of the Belief set. A *query* step returns a set of Attribute instances with the values set to values taken from the Belief set. By raising triggers we refer to the ability of the Belief set to generate events or goals when predefined conditions are met by the current beliefs. While existing database concepts can be used to implement these functions, tuple spaces [5] are perhaps more suitable due to the associative nature of data storage and logical querying.

4.8   Agent

An agent in our framework is a collection of triggers (goals and events), plans and beliefs. In other words, an agent type in our model can be defined as below:

```
<!ELEMENT Agent (Triggers+, Plans+, Beliefs+)>

<!ELEMENT Triggers (Handles*, Posts*)>
<!ELEMENT Handles (Event_ID | Goal_ID)+>
<!ELEMENT Posts (Event_ID | Goal_ID)+>
<!ELEMENT Event_ID (#PCDATA)>
<!ELEMENT Goal_ID (#PCDATA)>
<!ELEMENT Plans (Plan_ID)+>
<!ELEMENT Plan_ID (#PCDATA)>
<!ELEMENT Beliefs (BeliefSet_ID)+>
<!ELEMENT BeliefSet_ID (#PCDATA)>

<!ATTLIST Agent ID CDATA #REQUIRED>
```

The set of triggers include all the goals and events used by the agent. The distinction between the Triggers *handled* and *posted* by the agent could be derived from the Plans used by the agent as only a plan can handle or post a trigger. However specifying them explicitly help in detecting errors by cross checking between Triggers specified in the agent definition (intended events) and events used by the plans (used events).

5   Using the Component Model

The components identified above were used to model the weather alert system (see section 3.1) in order to evaluate the effectiveness of the framework. We found that structuring the agents as consisting of the aforementioned components made it easier to modify and add new behaviors to agents. These included operations such as adding new plans and creating triggers which were identified as frequent changes by the meteorologists who use the system. We also found that it is essential to define Attributes and Steps carefully as the other component types are based on one or both of these *base* component types.

Here we describe two scenarios of modification and addition. In these examples we assume the existence of the necessary Attributes, Steps and an agent platform required to process the descriptions.

Example 1: When a marked difference is detected between a forecast and a current weather station reading, the *TAFMonitorAgent* sends a "TAFAlert" event to subscribed agents. The simplest form of $TAFAlert$ would be to include a *message* attribute which includes a warning[2]. The definition for this type of $TAFAlert$ is given below:

```
<Event ID="TAFAlert">
   <Attributes>
      <Attribute Type="STRING">message</Attribute>
   </Attributes>
</Event>
```

An example message would look like: "Temperature higher than predicted by $4°C$". A disadvantage of this specification is that, except for displaying, it is difficult to process the message (e.g. to identify whether the alert is about temperature, pressure etc is not straight forward). Therefore if one wants to modify this event to be more flexible, it can be easily achieved within the framework. This is possible due to the structured nature of the framework, as once the Attributes are clearly defined, they can be easily reused in other definitions. Hence we could replace the *message* attribute of the $TAFAlert$ by two new attributes, namely $readingType$ and $deviation$ to show how much the forecast has deviated from the actual weather reading:

```
<Event ID="TAFAlert">
   <Attributes>
      <Attribute Type="STRING">readingType</Attribute>
      <Attribute Type="READING">deviation</Attribute>
   </Attributes>
</Event>
```

From an implementation perspective this change would only require a user to select the attributes $readingType$ and $deviation$ from a list of available *attributes* as the new attributes of *TAFAlert* event. While the plan handling the event $TAFAlert$ will also have to be changed accordingly, the strict structure of the Event based on Attributes will make the plan update much simpler.

Example 2: The alerts generated by the different alerting agents such as *TAFAlertAgent* and *VaacAlertAgent* [16] are visually displayed by an "AlertGUIAgent". The component description required to add an agent of the type "AlertGUIAgent" is given below:

```
<Agent ID="AlertGUIAgent">
   <Triggers>
      <Handles>
         <Event_ID>eventAlertReceipt</Event_ID>
         <Goal_ID>goalNotifyCritical</Goal_ID>
      </Handles>
   </Triggers>
   <Plans>
      <Plan_ID>planHandleAlert</Plan_ID>
      <Plan_ID>planHandleCriticalAlert</Plan_ID>
   </Plans>
</Agent>
```

---

[2] In the actual development process this would represent an early primitive version of the event with further refinements later on.

The specific contents of the *beliefs*, triggers and plans are not given here due to space limitations. However it is evident from the component definitions in section 4 that they would contain Attributes, Steps and component specific parameters. Hence it shows that creating new agent types within the framework is straight forward once the Attributes and Steps are specified.

6   Conclusion and Future Work

This paper described a conceptual framework of domain independent component types that can be used to formulate and modify an agent system. We used SMART concepts as a starting point in analyzing an existing agent application for generating weather alerts. This process yielded a set of component types, namely *attribute, entity, environment, trigger (goal, event), plan, step, belief* and *agent* that can be used to build an agent system. While some of these are identified as building blocks in SMART, the definitions and usage are different in our framework. For example a *plan* is not a basic construct in SMART. Another difference is the definition of an *action* in specifying a *step*. We have attempted to define our components to make the description of an agent simpler from an implementation perspective. This is one of the key differences between our work and some of the other work on component based agents. Some of the key issues yet to be resolved in our work include the lack of of a structured representation for condition statements (as in Plan Context), a richer plan language (set of operators for steps) and a representation for the start up configuration of the agent system.

As a continuation of this work we intend to complete the framework outlined in figure 2. We have already started implementing the "Transformation Module" which is based on XSLT and Java generating JACK agent language code. Further we plan to re-build the weather application using our components. By reproducing the evolution of the weather application within the component framework, we intend to evaluate the effectiveness of the components and also refine the framework.

References

1. R. Ashri, M. Luck, and M. d'Inverno. Infrastructure support for agent-based development. *Foundations and Applications of Multi-Agent Systems, LNAI2403*, pages 73–88, 2002.
2. J. Bigus, D. Schlosnagle, J. Pilgrim, W. Mills, and Y. Diao. ABLE: A toolkit for building multiagent autonomic systems. *IBM Systems Journal*, 41(3):350–371, 2002.
3. F. M. Brazier, C. M. Jonker, and J. Treur. Principles of component-based design of intelligent agents. *Data Knowledge Engineering*, 41(1):1–27, 2002.
4. P. Busetta, R. Rönnquist, A. Hodgson, and A. Lucas. JACK Intelligent Agents - Components for Intelligent Agents in Java. Technical report, Agent Oriented Software Pty. Ltd, Melbourne, Australia, 1998. Available from http://www.agent-software.com.
5. N. Carriero and D. Gelernter. Linda in Context. *Communications of the ACM*, 32(4):444–458, 1989.
6. J. Collis and D. Ndumu. The zeus agent building toolkit: Zeus technical manual (release 1.0). Technical report, British Telecommunications PLC, 1999.
7. M. d'Inverno, D. Kinny, M. Luck, and M. Wooldridge. A formal specification of dMARS. In M. Singh, A. Rao, and M. Wooldridge, editors, *Intelligent Agents IV: Proceedings of the Fourth International Workshop on Agent Theories, Architectures, and Languages*, pages 155–176. Springer-Verlag LNAI 1365, 1998.

8. K. Erol, J. Lang, and R. Levy. Designing agents from reusable components. In *Proceedings of the Fourth International Conference on Autonomous Agents*. Barcelona, Spain, 2000.
9. H. J. Goradia and J. M. Vidal. Building blocks for agent design. In *Fourth International Workshop on AOSE*, pages 17–30. AAMAS03, July 2003.
10. G. T. Heineman and W. T. Council. *Component-Based Software Engineering: Putting the Pieces Together*. Addison-Wesley Publishing Company, ISBN: 0-201-70485-4, 2001.
11. F. F. Ingrand, M. P. Georgeff, and A. S. Rao. An architecture for real-time reasoning and system control. *IEEE Expert*, 7(6), 1992.
12. N. Jennings and M. Wooldridge. Applications of intelligent agents. In N. R. Jennings and M. J. Wooldridge, editors, *Agent Technology: Foundations, Applications, and Markets*, chapter 1, pages 3–28. Springer, 1998.
13. N. R. Jennings. An agent-based approach for building complex software systems. *Communications of the ACM*, 44(4):35–41, April 2001.
14. A. Kleppe, J. Warmer, and W. Bast. *MDA Explained, The Model Driven Architecture: Practice and Promise*. Addison-Wesley Publishing Company, ISBN: 0-321-19442-X, 2003.
15. M. Luck and M. d'Inverno. *Understanding Agent Systems*. Springer, ISBN 3540419756, 2001.
16. I. Mathieson, S. Dance, L. Padgham, M. Gorman, and M. Winikoff. An open meteorological alerting system: Issues and solutions. In *Proceedings of the 27th Australasian Computer Science Conference*, Dunedin, New Zealand, Jan. 2004.
17. A. Pokahr and L. Braubach. Jadex: User guide (release 0.92). Technical report, Distributed Systems Group, University of Hamburg, Germany, 05 2004.
18. A. S. Rao and M. P. Georgeff. BDI-agents: from theory to practice. In *Proceedings of the First Intl. Conference on Multiagent Systems*. San Francisco, 1995.
19. S. Russell and P. Norvig. *Artificial Intelligence A Modern Approach*. Prentice Hall, ISBN 0 13 080302 2, 2003.
20. N. Skarmeas and K. L. Clark. Component based agent construction. *International Journal on Artificial Intelligence Tools*, 11(1):139–163, 2002.
21. J. M. Spivey. *The Z Notation: A Z Reference Manual*. Prentice Hall International, 1989.
22. C. Szyperski. *Component Software: Beyond Object Oriented Programming*. Addison-Wesley Publishing Company, ISBN: 0-201-17888-5, 1998.
23. T. Wagner, B. Horling, V. Lesser, J. Phelps, and V. Guralnik. The Struggle for Reuse: Pros and Cons of Generalization in TÆMS and its Impact on Technology Transition. *Proceedings of the ISCA 12th International Conference on Intelligent and Adaptive Systems and Software Engineering (IASSE-2003)*, July 2003.
24. M. Winikoff, L. Padgham, and J. Harland. Simplifying the development of intelligent agents. In *proceedings of the 14th Australian Joint Conference on Artificial Intelligence (AI'01)*, pages 557–568. Adelaide, 2001.
25. M. Winikoff, L. Padgham, J. Harland, and J. Thangarajah. Declarative & procedural goals in intelligent agent systems. In *Proceedings of the Eighth International Conference on Principles of Knowledge Representation and Reasoning (KR2002)*, Toulouse, France, Apr. 2002.

Visualizing a Multiagent-Based Medical Diagnosis System Using a Methodology Based on Use Case Maps

Tawfig Abdelaziz[1], Mohamed Elammari[2], and Rainer Unland[1]

[1] University of Duisburg-Essen
Institute for Computer Science and Business Information Systems (ICB)
Data Management Systems and Knowledge Representation
Schützenbahn 70, D-45117 Essen
{Tawfig,unlandr}@informatik.uni-essen.de
[2] Garyounis University
Faculty of Science, Department of Computer Science
Benghazi, Libya
elammari@ccs.carleton.ca

Abstract. Multi-agent systems are realized as a practical solution to the problem of constructing flexible and dynamic environments. Understanding such systems needs a high-level visual view of how the system operates as a whole to achieve some application related purpose. In this paper, we demonstrate how a visual high-level view called Use Case Maps (UCMs) may help in visualizing, understanding, and defining the behaviour of a Multi-agent medical diagnostic system.

1 Introduction

Nowadays, the concept of agent represents an important revolution and new approach to the development of complex software systems. There are many definitions of agents and multi-agent systems. However, we have chosen what we found most suitable to our problem domain.

An agent is an encapsulated software system that is intelligent and capable of actively performing autonomous actions in order to meet its objectives [7]. Multi-agent systems are collections of autonomous agents that interact or work together to perform tasks that satisfy their goals [6]. A methodology is a software engineering method that spans many disciplines, including project management, analysis, specification, design, coding, testing, and quality assurance. All of the methods guiding this field are usually mixtures of all of these disciplines. To understand and model agent systems some methodologies were proposed like *Agent-oriented methodology HIM* [1], *Gaia methodology* [12], *The Styx Agent methodology* [13], *PASSI methodology* [14], *Tropos methodology* [15], *AgentUML* [16], ... *etc.* Developing agent systems requires suitable methodologies and good software development techniques.

A lot of different Agent Oriented Software Engineering (AOSE) methodologies have been compared in [17, 18], including the AAII methodology, AgentUML, Gaia, MaSE, Tropos, Prometheus and ROADMAP. Each methodology has it is strong and weak points, and each included features which are tailored for a specific application domain. It is clear that there is no methodology, which can do it all. We suggest the use of the HIM methodology to develop a powerful multi-agent medical diag-

G. Lindemann et al. (Eds.): MATES 2004, LNAI 3187, pp. 198–212, 2004.

nostic system, because it captures the most shared elements of the existing methodologies, such as cooperation and interaction, organizational design, communication, collaboration, and coordination.

The HIM methodology is especially tailored for agent systems; it provides a systematic approach for generating implementable system definitions from high-level designs. The methodology captures effectively the complexity of agent systems through depicting the internal structure of agents, relationships, conversations, and commitments. Also HIM contributes to the development of agent-oriented programming as a discipline. One of the system views suggested by the methodology is the *Agents System view*. This view is represented by a high level visual view, which is realized by use case maps (UCMs) [1,2,3,4]. The view enables the understanding of agent systems and shows how all system components work together to achieve some application related purpose. HIM confirms that any design process that is tailored to agents should provide support for the following:

System View: Understanding agent systems requires a high-level visual view of how the system works as a whole to accomplish some application related purpose. It is difficult to express this understanding if the only models available are low-level design diagrams, such as object interaction diagrams, and class inheritance hierarchies [1]. We need a macroscopic, system-oriented model to provide a means of both visualizing the behaviour of systems of agents and defining how the behaviour will be achieved, at a level above such details.

Structure: The internal structure of agents consists of some aspects such as goals, plans, and beliefs. This structure should help to discover other agents in the system and their internal structure

Relationships: An agent has dependencies and jurisdictional relationships with other agents. An agent might be dependent on another agent to achieve a goal, perform a task or supply a resource. A process should capture the different inter-agent dependencies and jurisdictional relationships.

Conversations: Agents must cooperate and negotiate with each other. When agents communicate, they engage in conversations. A process should capture the conversational messages exchanged and facilitate the identification of conversational protocols used in communication.

Commitments: Agents have obligations and authorizations about services they provide to each other. A process should capture the commitments between agents and any conditions or terms associated with them.

Systematic Transitions: A good design process should provide guidelines for model derivations and define traceability between the models.

In this paper, we describe a process for designing agent systems in which a visual technique is used to provide a general view of the system as a whole and to provide a starting point for developing the details of agent models and software implementations to satisfy the requirements. A new aspect in this methodology is that systems are developed through a series of levels of abstraction in which humans, with machine assistance, can manipulate abstractions at one level into abstractions at the next lower level. HIM methodology consists of two phases the *discovery* and *definition* phases. *The discovery phase* guides the identification of agent(s) (types) and their high-level behaviour. The ultimate goal of this phase, apart from discovering the agents and their relationships, is to produce models that capture the high-level structure and behaviour of the system. *The definition phase* produces implementable definitions. The goal is to get a clear understanding of the behaviours, the entities that participate in exhibiting these behaviours and their interrelationships, as well as inter-agent conversations and commitments.

2 HIM Methodology

We have five models that are generated by the HIM methodology. Figure 1 shows these models and the traceability between them.

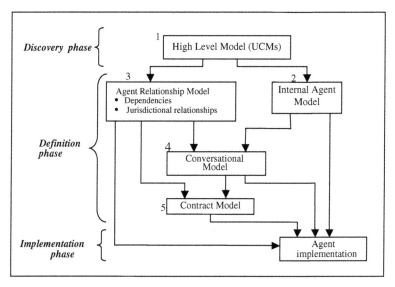

Fig. 1. Models of The HIM methodology.

The *high-level model* identifies agents and their high-level behaviour. It gives a high-level view of the system and provides a starting point for developing the details of the other models. Tracing application scenarios that describe functional behaviour, discovering agents and behavioural patterns along the way generates it. The *internal agent model* describes the agents in the system in terms of their internal structure and behaviour. It captures agent aspects such as goals, plans, tasks and beliefs. The internal agent model is derived directly from the high level model. The *relationship model* describes agent relationships: *dependency* and *jurisdictional*. The *conversational model* describes the coordination among the agents. The *contract model* defines a structure that captures commitments between agents. Contracts can be created when agents are instantiated or during execution as they are needed.

The high-level model is the only model that is associated with the discovery phase. The rest of the models are associated with the definition phase, which is not the topic of this paper.

3 Medical Diagnosis System

The diagnostic process is a distributed and cooperative work involving many different specialists, departments, and knowledge sources.

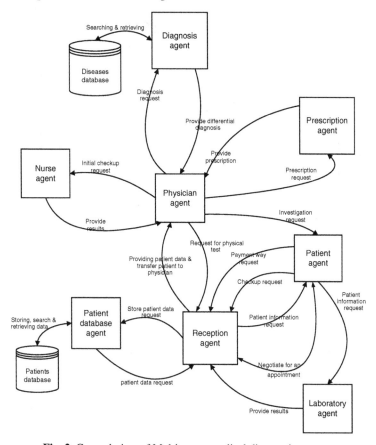

Fig. 2. General view of Multi-agent medical diagnostic system.

Before analyzing the cooperative relations in medical diagnosis, we should first describe the agent system as a whole and then we should discuss the diagnostic process. Figure 2 describes a general view of Multi-agent medical diagnostic system. It consists of set of agents, which cooperate together to achieve the diagnosis process. Behind the practice of medical diagnosis is the theory of *differential diagnosis*. Differential diagnosis operates within an uncertainty-based theoretical framework. It is a highly developed theory and is also frequently used. There are two important phases to the diagnostic procedure: hypothesis formation and evidence gathering. The hypothesis formation phase begins as soon as the patient enters the doctor's office. The patient may complain of more than one key symptom.

However, the selection of the key symptoms is tentative, because evidence gathered further along the diagnostic process may cause the doctor to rethink the selection. It is important to emphasize that a key symptom is usually caused by more than one disease. In fact, a one to one relationship is rare. Because of its rarity, diagnosis is fundamentally a process of finding evidence to distinguish a probable cause of the patient's key symptoms from all other possible causes of the symptom.

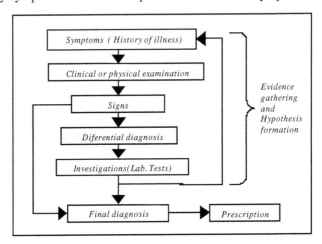

Fig. 3. Summary of the differential diagnosis.

This process is called *differential diagnosis*. The differential diagnosis may have more than one disease as a working hypothesis. In this case, extra investigations are needed to confirm which one is established as a final diagnosis. With a key symptom in hand, the doctor refers to a medical textbook, which leads the doctor to have a set of disorders. In turn, each disorder has a set of possible hypotheses as to the cause of the disease. In choosing one cause from the set or list, the doctor sets one disease or cause apart as the most likely cause of the symptom. This becomes the doctor's working hypothesis, and it is a tentative designation.

The doctor then starts to gather evidence in support of the working hypothesis, always keeping in mind the set of alternative hypotheses. The *evidence-gathering* phase is divided into three parts: *history, physical examination* and *investigations such as (laboratory tests, X-rays, MRI and so on)*.

The history of the illness involves the doctor questioning the patient about the history of the symptoms, the medical history of the patient, and other factors.

During *the physical examination* part, the doctor looks for *signs* of the disease, which are obtained through a physical examination of the patient. *Signs* are manifestations of the disease, which the doctor can see or feel.

If the evidence is not conclusive, the doctor may call for investigations such as *laboratory tests,* (both tests of body tissues, fluids etc.) and photographic monitoring such as (*X-rays, computed tomography, image scans* and the like). This step-by-step procedure in differential diagnosis allows the doctor to establish a *working hypothesis*, thus giving the procedure a structure and a direction for evidence gathering.

The gradual step-by-step decrease in the number of hypotheses the doctor considers keeps the doctor's mind open to all the evidence from the beginning to the end of the procedure. The diagnostic procedure is based on maximizing uncertainty so that all options are considered in the diagnosis. Figure 3 illustrates the summary of the differential diagnosis steps.

4 Agent System View (High Level Model)

Developing and understanding complex systems is not easy to achieve by traditional software systems that concentrate on low level details. The main goal of the use of a high level view is to understand the entire system and its structure without referring to any implementation details. We use Use-Case Maps, which are suitable for high-level visual representations, as a starting point for generating more detailed visual descriptions. UCMs are used to model the high-level activities because of their ability to simply and successfully depict the design of complex systems, and provide a powerful *visual* notation for a review and detailed analysis of the design.

4.1 Use Case Maps (UCMs)

UCM notation helps persons to visualize, think about and explain the overall behavior of a whole system. The center of attention of UCM is not the details. It describes scenarios in terms of causal relationships between responsibilities. It also emphasizes the most relevant, interesting and critical functionalities of the system.

UCMs describe the complex systems at a high level of abstraction. The complex system requirements are captured as UCM scenarios integrated in one model with stubs and plug-ins. Table 1 shows basic UCM symbols [4] of the type that are used within this paper.

4.1.1 UCM Notation with a Simple Example

UCMs are precise structural entities that contain enough information in highly condensed form to enable the visualization of system behavior. It provides a high level view of causal sequences in the system as a whole, in the form of paths. The causal sequences are called scenarios. In general, UCMs may have many paths. The figures in this paper only show one, for reasons of simplicity. Figure 4 shows an example of UCMs. The simple example is called "**Money withdrawal using ATM** *Automatic Teller Machine*" where a scenario starts with a triggering event or a pre-condition (filled circle labeled *Customer wants to withdraw money)* and ends with one or more resulting events or post-conditions (bar labeled *logon rejected, withdraw rejected, slip printed* and *money withdrawn*). The path starts with a filled circle, which indicates a starting point of a path, the point where stimuli occurs causing movement to start progressing along the path until the end point of a path is reached. Paths define causal sequences between start and end points. The causal sequences connect stubs and responsibilities, indicated by named points along the paths *Insert card, Ask PW, Enter PW, Validate, Enter amount, Chk, Debit, Print, Notify and Provide.* Think of responsibilities as tasks or functions to be performed, or events to occur.

In this example, the activities can be allocated to abstract components: *Customer, ATM interface, Account, Printer* and *Dispenser,* which can be seen as objects, agents, processes, databases, or even roles or persons. Paths may cross many components and components may have many paths crossing them. When maps become too complex to be represented as one single UCM, UCM may be decomposed using a generalization of responsibilities called stubs. *Stubs* link to sub-maps called *plug-ins.* Stubs may be positioned along paths like responsibilities but are more general than responsibilities in two ways: they identify the existence of sub-UCMs and they may span multiple paths (not shown). A stub can be static or dynamic.

Table 1. Basic UCM symbols.

UCM Notation	Notation Explanation
Start point — End point — Path	**Path:** Represents flow of events in the system, path, connects start points, stubs, responsibilities, forks, and end points of UCM. The start-point represents preconditions. The end-point represents post-conditions.
Do something — ✕ —	**Responsibility point:** Represents the functions to be accomplished by the system at that point of the path.
⟨	**Or Fork:** An OR fork means the path proceeds in only one out of two or more directions.
⟩	**Or Join:** it means two or more paths merged it in one single path.
⊨	**And Fork:** it means that a single path is distributed at the same time into many concurrent paths.
⊨	**And Join:** it means that several concurrent Paths merged at the same time into a single path.
◇	**Static stub:** associated with one plug-in (Sub UCM) as task to be achieved by the system, used as decomposition of complex maps.
◇ (dashed)	**Dynamic stub:** associated with several plug-ins, whose selection can be determined at run-time according to selection policy (often described with preconditions). It is also possible to select multiple plug-ins at once (sequentially or parallel).
a ——●—— (b)	**Wait point:** Path a waits for an event from path b.
□	**Agent:** Software component representing a software agent.

Static stubs contain only one plug-in and enable hierarchical decomposition of complex maps. *Dynamic stubs* are shown as dashed outline to distinguish them from stubs that are used for static stubs. Dynamic stubs may represent several plug-ins, whose selection can be determined at run-time according to a selection policy often described with pre-conditions.

It is also possible to select multiple plug-ins at once sequentially or in parallel. A plug-in may involve additional system components not shown in the main UCM. Start points may have pre-conditions attached, while responsibilities and end points can have post-conditions.

In Figure 4, the *Validate* stub has two outgoing ports **a** and **b**. Port **a** which means authentication was accepted. Port b means authentication was not accepted. There are two plug-ins associated with the *Validate* stub: *Fingerprint* and *Password*.

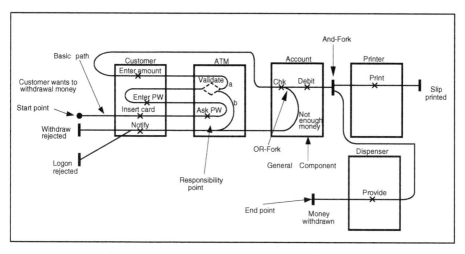

Fig. 4. UCM scenario for money withdrawal with stubs.

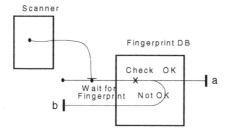

Fig. 5. Fingerprint plug-in for the validate stub.

The *Fingerprint* plug-in illustrated in Figure 5 describes the behavior when the validation is performed by fingerprint. The plug-in starts with a *wait* for *fingerprint*, which waits till the customer enters his fingerprint.

Then the path proceeds to the *Check* task, which is followed by an or-fork in the path if the entered fingerprint was found to match the stored fingerprint, the path labeled *Ok* is followed to the end point **a**. Otherwise, the path labeled *not Ok* is followed to the end point **b**.

The other plug-in is the *Password* plug-in shown in Figure 6, which is used when the customer enters his password instead of his fingerprint. The plug-in starts with *Wait for PW*, which waits for the customer to enter a password and then the *Check PW* task is performed. The path is split into three paths after the *Check PW* responsibility. The first fork (labeled *PW OK*) is followed when the entered password matches the customer's stored password. The second fork (labeled *PW Not OK*) is followed when the entered password is incorrect. The third fork is followed if the customer is allowed to retry to enter the password after it is found to be incorrect.

4.1.2 High-Level Model (Medical Diagnostic System Scenarios)
In the high-level model, we describe use case maps of the medical diagnostic system and we state how UCMs can be used to represent agent systems. Also we apply

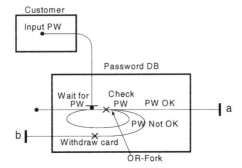

Fig. 6. Password plug-in for the validate stub.

UCMs to capture an agent based disease diagnosis system and explain how UCMs describe the system scenarios in visual views. The following scenarios represent interactions between some agents in the system. Examples of interactions shown are patient agent with reception agent, patient agent with physician agent and physician agent with diagnosis agent. By tracing application scenarios the high-level model is derived. These scenarios describe functional behavior, as UCM paths within the system. This discovers agents, responsibilities, and plug-ins along the way. Generally, one starts with some use cases and some knowledge of the agents required to realize them. This model maintains the most important steps:

- Identify scenarios and major components involved in the system.
- Identify roles for each component.
- Identify pre-conditions and post-conditions to each scenario.
- Identify responsibilities and constraints for each component in a scenario.
- Identify sub scenarios and replace them with stubs.
- Identify agent collaborations for the major tasks.

4.1.2.1 Patient Agent and Reception Agent UCM

The UCM, shown in Figure 7 represents a basic scenario between a patient agent and a reception agent in our system. Patient agent represents the patient in the application environment, and the reception agent represents the reception. The precondition for the patient agent and reception agent scenario is that the patient needs a checkup. The scenario starts with the *Checkup Request* stub, which hides the detailed information of the checkup request process.

Preconditions:	*Postconditions:*
• Patient needs a checkup.	• Patient transferred to physician.|
	• Patient refused

The checkup request can be achieved in several ways. For example, it can be done by phone call or by Email. Therefore, the *Checkup Request* stub is represented as a dynamic stub. Figure 8 illustrates the plug-ins for the *Checkup Request* stub.

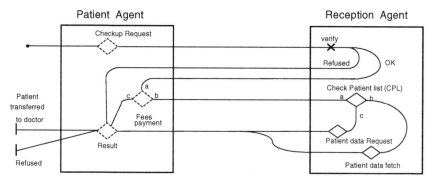

Fig. 7. UCM scenario between Patient agent and Reception agent.

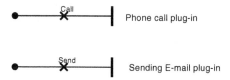

Fig. 8. Plug-ins for *Checkup Request* stub.

After all responsibilities for the checkup request process are performed, the path leads to the reception agent where there is a responsibility called *verify* which verifies whether the specialist whom the patient requests is available or not. Then the path leads to an or-fork immediately after the *verify* responsibility which indicates alternative scenario paths. One path leads to refuse the checkup request, e.g. because there is no specialist available who can examine the patient. Then the path leads to the result stub to inform the patient that the checkup is refused.

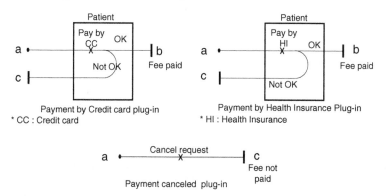

Fig. 9. Plug-ins for Fees payment stub.

The other path leads to accept the checkup request and the path proceeds to the Fees payment stub, which is concerned with the payment of the checkup fees. The *Fees payment* stub has two outgoing ports b and c. When fees are not paid, Port c is followed. In this case the path leads to the result stub to confirm that the checkup request is refused. Port b is followed when the fees are paid.

There are three plug-ins associated with the *Fees payment* stub illustrated in Figure 9: *Payment by Credit card* plug-in, *Payment by the Health Insurance* plug-in *and Payment canceled* plug-in.

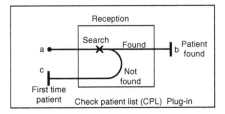

Fig. 10. Check patient list Plug-in.

After that the path leads to the *Check patient list* CPL stub, which is responsible for searching the patient database to find the history of the patient and all related information.

The CPL stub has two outgoing ports. If the patient is found, port b will be followed, which means that there is no need to enter the patient information again. Otherwise port c is followed, which means that this is the first visit of the patient. And then the path leads to the result stub, which is responsible to inform the patient about the results by sending E-mail or by a phone call. The result stub has two plug-ins shown in Figure 11: *Notify by phone* plug-in and *Notify by E-mail* plug-in.

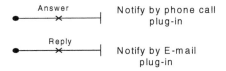

Fig. 11. Plug-ins for Result stub.

4.1.2.2   Patient Agent and Physician Agent UCM

In figure 12, the UCM shows the scenario between patient agent and physician agent. The physician agent represents the physician in the application environment. The precondition for starting the scenario is that the patient is transferred to the physician.

This scenario starts at the physician agent with the *Review History* (RH) stub. In this stub, the physician agent performs a review of the patient history in order to get the process of disease diagnosis started.

After that the path leads to the *ask* responsibility in the physician agent in which the physician agent starts to ask the patient agent about the symptoms the patient is aware of. The patient agent replies to the physician agent by the *answer* responsibility in the patient agent. After that the path leads to the *eval* responsibility in the physician agent, which causes the evaluation of the patient answers.

Pre-conditions:
Patient transferred to physician.

Post-conditions:
Patient successfully diagnosed and informed.

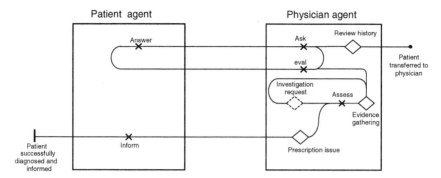

Fig. 12. Patient agent and Physician agent UCM.

After the *eval* responsibility there is an or-fork, which indicates alternative scenario paths. One fork path leads again to the cycle of the *ask* responsibility in case the physician agent wants to ask more questions.

When the physician agent determines that no further questions are needed, the other fork path leads to the *Evidence gathering* stub is followed. In this stub, the physician agent collects all evidence related to the disease to form the possible hypothesis of the disease. Also the *Evidence gathering* stub hides the connection between the physician agent and the diagnosis agent. Figure 13 shows the *Evidence gathering* plug-in. The plug-in starts with the *Diagnosis request* responsibility, which asks the diagnosis agent to examine the current patient case. Then the path leads to the stub "hypothesis formation" in the diagnosis agent, which is responsible for searching in the disease database for a match for the patient case symptoms.

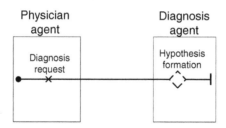

Fig. 13. Evidence gathering plug-in.

After that, the path leads to the *assess* responsibility which assesses whether the collected evidence is enough. If it is, the path leads to the *prescription* stub, which is responsible for issuing a prescription to the patient agent, and then informs the patient what the problem is, which is the post-condition of this scenario.

If the collected evidence is not enough, the path leads to the *Investigation request* stub, which performs some investigations that are required by the physician agent. Figure 14 shows the plug-ins for the *Investigation request* stub: *appointment for physical exam* plug-in, *Lab-work* plug-in and *X-Ray* plug-in. After the investigations, the path leads again to the *Evidence gathering* stub to assess whether the collected evidences are not enough.

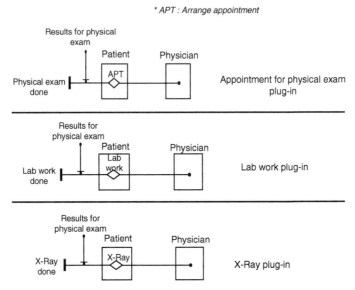

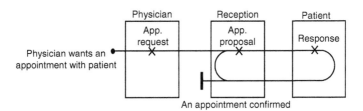

Fig. 14. Plug-ins for Investigation request stub.

Fig. 15. Patient agent, Reception agent and Physician agent UCM.

4.1.2.3 Patient Agent, Reception Agent and Physician Agent UCM

This scenario starts when the physician wants to meet the patient to make a physical exam.

The physician agent asks the reception agent for an appointment request with the patient agent. The path leads to the reception agent, which negotiates with the patient agent for an appointment. Figure 15 shows the UCM scenario for that.

5 Conclusion

In this paper, we developed a Multi-agent medical diagnostic system using a notation called use case maps. The notation was found to be one of the most significant techniques for the process of developing complex systems. The approach chosen for the development is proven to be a practical solution for the problem of constructing systems, which are required to be flexible and working in dynamic environments. We have shown that the visual high-level view helps in visualizing, understanding, and defining the behaviour of a Multi-agent medical diagnostic system.

Currently we are developing models that capture the internal details of agents and their relationships. The models being developed capture the goals, beliefs, plans, relations, conversations, and agent commitments.

6 Future Work

In this paper, we described the high-level model that captures the high level behaviour of agent systems. In the future, we will try to develop the definition phase, which produces intermediate models that facilitate the implementation of a multi-agent system. And how we map from UCMs to the internal agent model and agent relationship model in straightforward manner. The high-level model, supplemented by other information, is used to generate these models. These models express the full functional behaviour of an agent system by identifying aspects of agents such as goals, beliefs, plans, jurisdictional and dependency relationships, contracts, and conversations.

References

1. Elammari, M. and Lalonde, W., *An Agent Oriented Methodology: High Level and Intermediate Models*, in Proceedings of the 1'st International Workshop on Agent Oriented Information Systems (AOIS 99), Heidelberg, Germany, June 1999.
2. Gunter Mussbacher, Daniel Amyot, *Acollection of patterns for Use Case Maps*, Mitel Networks, 350 Legget Dr., Kanata (ON), Canada.
3. D. Amyot, L. Logrippo, R.J.A. Buhr, and T. Gray (1999), *Use Case Maps for the Capture and Validation of Distributed Systems Requirements.* In: Fourth International Symposium on Requirements Engineering (RE'99), Limerick, Ireland, and June 1999.
4. R.J.A. Buhr, D. Amyot, M. Elammari, D. Quesnel, T. Gray, and S. Mankovski (1998), *High Level, Multi-Agent Prototypes from a Scenario-Path Notation: A Feature-Interaction Example. In: H.S. Nwana and D.T. Ndumu (Eds),* Third Conference on Practical Application of Intelligent Agents and Multi-Agent Technology (PAAM'98), London, UK, pp. 255-276
5. R.J.A. Buhr, M. Elammari, T. Gray, S. Mankovski, *A High Level Visual Notation for Understanding and Designing Collaborative, Adaptive Behaviour in Multi-agent Systems,* Hawaii International Conference on System Sciences (HICSS'98), Hawaii, January 1998.
6. Timothy Finin, CFP: 1st Int. Conference on Multi-agent Systems - ICMAS '95 Fri, 5 Aug 1994.
7. Jennings, N., Sycara, K., and Wooldridge, *M. A Roadmap of Agent Research and evelopment.* Int. Journal of Autonomous Agents and Multi-Agent Sys tems, l(l):7-38 (1998).
8. Use Case Maps Web Page and UCM User Group, 1999. http://www.UseCaseMaps.org
9. Buhr, R.J.A.: *"Use Case Maps as Architectural Entities for Complex Systems".* In: Transactions on Software Engineering, IEEE, December 1998, pp. 1131-1155. http://www.UseCaseMaps.org/UseCaseMaps/pub/tse98final.pdf
10. R.J.A. Buhr, R.S. Casselman, *Use Case Maps for Object-Oriented Systems,* Prentice Hall, 1996.
11. J.A. Barondess, C.C.Carpenter. *Differential Diagnosis,* Lea and Febiger, Philadelphia, PA, 1994.
12. M. Wooldrige, N. R. Jennings and D. Kinny, *The Gaia Methodology for Agent-Oriented Analysis and Design, Autonomous Agents and Multi-Agent Systems,* volume 3, pp 285-312, Kluwer Academic Publishers, The Netherlands, 2000.
13. G. Bush, S. Cranefield and M. Purvis: *The Styx Agent Methodology.* In The Information Science Discussion Paper Series, Number 2001/02, January 2001, ISSN 1172-6024 http://citeseer.nj.nec.com/bush01styx.html

14. P. Burrafato, M. Cossentino - "*Designing a multi-agent solution for a bookstore with the PASSI methodology*" - Fourth International Bi-Conference Workshop on Agent-Oriented Information Systems (AOIS-2002) - 27-28 May 2002, Toronto (Ontario, Canada) at CAiSE'02 (www.csai.unipa.it/cossentino/paper/AOIS02.pdf)
15. Tropos web site http://www.cs.toronto.edu/km/tropos/
16. AgentUML web site http://www.auml.org/auml/
17. Iglesias, C., Garijo, M., and Gonzalez, J. *A Survey of Agent-Oriented Methodologies*. In Intelligent Agents V - Proceedings of the Fifth International Workshop on Agent Theories, Architectures, and Languages (ATAL-98), Lecture Notes in Artificial Intelligence. Springer-Verlag, Heidelberg. 1999
18. Wooldridge, M. and Ciancarini, P. Agent-Oriented Software Engineering: The State of the Art. In Agent-Oriented Software Engineering. Ciancarini, P. and Wooldridge,M. (eds), Springer-Verlag Lecture Notes in AI Volume 1957, 2001.

From Modeling to Simulation of Multi-agent Systems: An Integrated Approach and a Case Study

Giancarlo Fortino, Alfredo Garro, and Wilma Russo

D.E.I.S. - Università della Calabria, Via P. Bucci, cubo 41C
87036 Rende (CS), Italy
{fortino,garro,russow}@deis.unical.it

Abstract. In this paper, an integrated approach for the modeling and the validation through simulation of multi-agent systems is proposed. The approach centers on the instantiation of a software development process which specifically includes a simulation phase which makes it possible the validation of a multiagent system before its actual deployment and execution. The approach uses the Gaia methodology for the analysis and the design, the Agent UML and the Distilled StateCharts for the detailed design, the MAO Framework for the neutral-platform implementation of software agents, and a Java-based discrete-event simulation framework for the simulation. The proposed approach is exemplified by defining and simulating a multi-agent system concerning with an agent-mediated consumer-driven e-Marketplace which offers mobile agent-based services for searching and buying goods.

1 Introduction

Recently, several methodologies supporting analysis, design and implementation of Multi-Agent Systems (MAS) have been proposed in the context of Agent Oriented Software Engineering (AOSE) [17]. Some of the emerging methodologies are Gaia [22], MaSE [7], Prometheus [19], Tropos [1], Message [5], Passi [4], and Adelfe [2]. These notable efforts basically provide a top-down and iterative approach for the modeling and the development of agent-based systems. Although, from the software development life-cycle point of view, such methodologies fully cover the requirements, architectural design and detailed design, the implementation phase is not well supported [6]. In fact, the design models are hard to map to different target agent platforms since a seamless translation process is usually not provided. Furthermore, none of them supports validation through simulation of the MAS under-development before its actual deployment and execution. Validation through simulation or through formal methods can demonstrate that a MAS correctly behaves according to its specifications. In particular, discrete-event simulators are highly required to evaluate how complex MAS work on scales much larger than the scales achievable in real testbeds [21].

This paper proposes an integrated approach for the modeling and the validation through simulation of MAS. The approach centers on the instantiation of a software development process which specifically includes a simulation phase which makes it possible the validation of a MAS before its actual deployment and execution. In the

G. Lindemann et al. (Eds.): MATES 2004, LNAI 3187, pp. 213–227, 2004.

proposed approach, requirements capture is supported by a goal-oriented approach [1], the analysis and design phases are supported by the Gaia methodology [22], the detailed design phase is supported by Agent-UML [3] and the Distilled StateCharts formalism [11], the implementation phase is supported by the MAO Framework [9, 11], and the simulation phase is enabled by a Java-based event-driven framework [10].

The proposed approach is exemplified by defining and validating through simulation a consumer-driven e-Marketplace model which offers mobile agent-based services for searching and buying goods. The e-Marketplace consists of a set of stationary and mobile agents, which provide basic services such as secure access to the e-Marketplace, discovery of vendors of a given product, selling of products, and product payment through e-cash. In particular, two models of mobile consumer agents, namely itinerary and parallel, which are able to search for and buy products on behalf of users, were defined.

The remainder of the paper is organized as follows. In section 2, the proposed integrated approach is presented. Section 3 describes the case study and details the work products outcoming from the development phases. Finally, conclusions are drawn and directions of future research delineated.

2 An Integrated Approach for Modeling and Simulating Multi-agent Systems

In this section an integrated approach which allows to fully and seamlessly support the modeling and simulation of MAS is proposed.

The approach centers on the instantiation of the process, shown in Figure 1 using the SPEM notation [20], which completely covers the development of MAS. An instance of the process can be obtained by exploiting in each phase a methodology or a methodology fragment chosen from agent-oriented methodologies proposed in the literature [22, 7, 19, 1, 5, 4, 2] or ad-hoc defined.

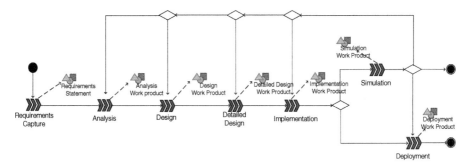

Fig. 1. The reference development process.

In the following, the proposed approach is illustrated by describing each phase along with the adopted methodology.

Requirements Capture. The requirements are captured using a goal oriented approach [1] and reported in a *Requirements Statements* document which represents the work product of this phase.

Analysis. The analysis phase, which is aimed at developing an understanding of the system and its organization, is supported by the Gaia methodology [22]. The work products of this phase (the *Prototypical Roles Model*, the *Interactions Model* and the *Roles Model*) are obtained in the following steps:

1. Identification of the *roles* in the system to build a list of the key roles that occur in the system, each of them with an informal, unelaborated description (*Prototypical Roles Model*);
2. Identification and documentation of the *protocols* associated to each role to capture the recurring patterns of inter-role interaction (*Interactions Model*);
3. Full elaboration of the roles in the *Prototypical Roles Model* on the basis of the *Interactions Model* (*Roles Model*). The *Roles Model* documents the *Roles* occurring in the system, their *Responsibilities* and *Permissions*, and the *Protocols* and *Activities* in which they participate. *Responsibilities* are the key properties associated with a role and are divided into two types: *(i) liveness properties* which describe those states of affairs that an agent must bring about, given certain environmental conditions; (ii) *safety properties* which are invariants and state that an acceptable state of affairs is maintained across all states of execution. *Permissions* are the rights associated with a role and identify the resources that are available to that role in order to realize its responsibilities. *Protocols* defines how a role can interact with other roles. Finally, the *Activities* of a role are computations associated with the role that may be carried out by the agent without interacting with other agents.

Design. The aim of the design phase is to transform the analysis models into a design which is concerned with the cooperation in a society of agents and the services offered by each individual agent to realize the system-level goals. The work products of this phase, which is also supported by the Gaia methodology, are the *Agent Model*, the *Services Model* and the *Acquaintance Model*. This phase is structured in three main steps:

1. Aggregation of roles into *Agent Types*, so forming an agent type hierarchy and establishing how many agent instances could be instantiated for each type (*Agent Model*).
2. Identification of the main *Services* that are required to realize the agent's role by examining activities, protocols, and safety and liveness properties of roles (*Services Model*). A service is a coherent block of activity in which an agent will engage. Inputs, outputs, pre-conditions, and post-conditions are to be identified for each service.
3. Documentation of the relationships of communication between the different agent types (*Acquaintance Model*). The *Acquaintance Model* does not define what messages are sent or when messages are sent, it simply indicates that communication pathways exist.

Detailed Design. The objective of this phase is to obtain a detailed specification, seamlessly translatable into code, of the behaviors of the *Agent Types* defined in the *Agent Model*. The work products of this phase are the *Agent Interactions Model* and the *Agent Behaviors Model*. This phase is carried out by means of:

1. Agent-UML interaction diagrams [3] to thoroughly specify the patterns of interaction between the *Agent Types* of the *Agent Model* (*Agent Interactions Model*);
2. The Distilled StateCharts (DSC) formalism [11] to specify the dynamic (proactive, active and reactive) behavior of each *Agent Type* (*Agent Behaviors Model*) on the basis of the *design work product* and the *Agent Interactions Model*. DSC were derived from Statecharts [15] and allow to model the behavior of lightweight agents, i.e. event-driven, single-threaded, capable of transparent migration, and executing chains of atomic actions. A DSC specification of an agent is done according to the template of a FIPA agent [12].

Implementation. The aim of the implementation phase is to obtain the code of the agent behaviors from the *Agent Behaviors Model*. This code, which represents the work product of this phase, can be used both in the simulation phase and in the deployment phase. The implementation phase is supported by the Mobile Active Object (MAO) Framework [9] by which a DSC specification can be seamlessly translated into a composite object (called "*MAOBehavior object*") representing an agent behavior and into a set of event objects (or simply *Events*) representing interactions. The obtained code, before its deployment and execution, should be adapted to the target agent platform. The adaptation can be carried out by means of the customization of the Mobile Agent Adaptation Framework (MAAF) [11] for a given agent platform. In [11] the customization for the Voyager ORB system is reported.

Simulation. The strategic goal of the simulation phase is the validation of the MAS under-development before its actual deployment by providing, as work product, both qualitative and quantitative information about correctness and efficiency. This information can be exploited for the reformulation, modification and/or refinement of some choices carried out in the previous phases of the development process. The simulation phase is supported by a Java-based, discrete-event simulation framework [10] for stationary and mobile agents. Using this framework, an agent-based complex system can be easily validated and evaluated by defining suitable test cases and performance measurements. In particular, the simulation engine of the framework allows for the: (i) execution of agents by interleaving their event processing, (ii) exchange of events among agents, (iii) migration of agents, and the (iv) clustering of agents into agent servers connected by a logical network. The basic simulation entities offered by the framework are:

- the *AgentServer*, which is an object representing the agent server hosting mobile and stationary agents;
- the *Agent*, which is an object representing a stationary or a mobile agent and including a pair of objects: <MAOId, MAOBehavior>, where MAOId is the agent identifier and MAOBehavior incorporates the dynamic behavior of an agent type obtained in the implementation phase;

- the *MAOEvent*, which represents an event object;
- the *VirtualNetwork*, which represents the logical network of hosts on which an *AgentsServer* is mapped;
- the *UserAgent*, which is an object representing a user. A *UserAgent*, which is directly connected to an *AgentServer* and can create, launch and interact with *Agents*;
- the *UserAgentGenerator*, which is an object modeling the process of generation of *UserAgents*.

3 A Case Study: An Agent-Based, Consumer-Driven Electronic Marketplace

3.1 Requirements of a Consumer-Driven e-Marketplace

An e-Marketplace is an e-commerce environments which offers new channels and business models for buyers and sellers to effectively and efficiently trade goods and services over the Internet [16]. A consumer-driven e-Marketplace is an e-Marketplace in which the exchange of goods is driven by the consumers that wish to buy a product [18]. The consumer browses the e-Marketplace, evaluates the vendors' offers, contracts with the vendors the product price and decides to buy the product from a selected vendor. The case study is based on the application scenario presented in [23]. The buying process within the e-Marketplace can be described in the following sequence of phases:

1. *Request Input.* When users wish to buy a product, they identifies a set of product parameters (product description, maximum price P_{MAX}, etc), log into the e-Marketplace and submit a request containing the product parameters. The Authentication Authority of the e-Marketplace checks if users are trustworthy (i.e. from a commercial and security viewpoint) and decides if their requests can be accepted. If a user request is accepted the Consumer Assistant System (CAS) of the e-Marketplace starts satisfying the user request;

2. *Searching.* The CAS obtains a list of locations of vendors by using the Yellow Pages Service (YPS) of the e-Marketplace. The YPS is a federation of autonomous components to which vendors register to advertise the products they offer. In particular the following YPS organizations were established:
   - *Centralized*: each YPS component stores a complete list of vendors;
   - *One Neighbor Federated*: each YPS component stores a list of vendors and keeps a reference to only one other YPS component;
   - *M-Neighbors Federated*: each YPS component stores a list of vendors and keeps a list of at most M YPS components.

   Searching can be carried out by adopting one of the following searching policies:
   - ALL: all the reachable YPS components are contacted;
   - PARTIAL (pa): a subset of YPS components are contacted;
   - ONE-SHOT (os): only one YPS component is contacted.

3. *Contracting & Evaluation.* The CAS interacts with the found vendors to request an offer (Poffer) for the desired product, evaluates the received offers, and selects an

offer, if any, for which the price is acceptable (i.e., Poffer$\leq$PMAX) according to the following buying policies:

- Minimum Price (mp): the CAS first interacts with all the vendors to look for the vendor offering the desired product at the lowest acceptable price and then purchases the product from this vendor;
- First Shot (fs): the CAS interacts with the vendors until it obtains an offer for the product at an acceptable price; then, it buys the product;
- Fixed Trials (ft): the CAS interacts with a given number of vendors and buys the product from the vendor which offers it at the best acceptable price;
- Random Trials (rt): the CAS interacts with a random number of vendors and buys the product from the vendor which offers it at the best acceptable price.

4. *Payment.* The CAS purchases the desired product from the selected vendor using a given amount of e-cash (or bills). The following steps are performed to execute the money transaction between the CAS and the vendor: (i) the CAS gives the bills to the vendor; (ii) the vendor sends the bills to its bank; (iii) the bank validates the authenticity of the bills, exempts them from reuse, and, finally, issues an amount of bills equal to that previously received to the vendor; (iv) the vendor notifies the CAS. Transactions among the CAS, vendor and bank can be encrypted using public/private keys to avoid bills interceptions.

5. *Reporting.* The CAS reports the buying result to the User.

3.2 The Analysis Phase

The Roles Model. On the basis of the process-oriented description of the system functionalities obtained during the Requirements Capture phase (see Sect. 3.1), the following key roles were identified:

- *User Assistant*, which involves assisting a user in looking for and buying a specific product that meets her/his needs;
- *MPEntryPoint*, which involves granting the access to the services of the e-Marketplace;
- *Consumer*, which involves searching and buying of goods;
- *Directory*, which involves the management and the provision of a catalogue of vendors of specific products;
- *Vendor*, which involves selling of goods;
- *Bank*, which involves the management of e-cash transactions.

According to the Gaia methodology each role was represented using a Role Schema. As an example, the Role Schema for the *Consumer* is reported in Fig. 2.

The Interactions Model. The identified interaction patterns are reported in Table 1. Using such patterns the protocols associated to the Roles were defined. For example, the *SearchForVendor* protocol (see Fig. 2) associated to the *Consumer* role, is obtained by composing the *VendorListQuery* and the *VendorListResponse* interactions.

Role Schema: CONSUMER

Description: *This role involves searching and buying of goods*

Protocols and Activities:
SearchForVendor, VendorListConstruction, ContractingForProduct, OfferEvaluation, ProductPayment, BuyingResultReport

Permissions:
reads   supplied userInformation, supplied productParameters, supplied vendors, supplied offers
generates *vendorList*
changes *userCredit*

Responsibilities
Liveness:

CONSUMER=(SearchForVendor·VendorListConstruction)$^{+}$·

(ContractingForProduct·OfferEvaluation) $^{+}$· ProductPayment · BuyingResultReport

Safety:
- *vendorList* not empty;   *userCredit* >0

Fig. 2. The Role Schema for the *Consumer.*

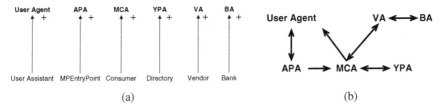

(a)   (b)

Fig. 3. The Agent Model and the Acquaintance Model.

Table 1. Interaction patterns among roles.

INITIATOR ROLE	INTERACTION	RESPONDER ROLE	COMMUNICATIVE ACT
User Assistant	BuyingRequest	MPEntryPoint	Task Execution Request
MPEntryPoint	MPAccessGranting	User Assistant	Request Notification
Consumer	VendorListQuery	Directory	Information Request
	PriceQuery	Vendor	Information Request
	PayFor	Vendor	Task Execution Request
	BuyingResultReport	User Assistant	Result Notification
Directory	VendorListResponse	Consumer	Result Notification
Vendor	PriceQueryResponse	Consumer	Result Notification
	BillVerifyRequest	Bank	Task Execution Request
Bank	BillVerifyResponse	Vendor	Result Notification

3.3   The Design Phase

The Agent Model. The defined Agent Model is shown in Fig. 3a. There is a one-to-one correspondence between the roles defined in the *Roles Model* and the identified *Agent Types*: User Agent (UA), Access Point Agent (APA), Mobile Consumer Agent (MCA), Yellow Pages Agent (YPA), Vendor Agent (VA), and Bank Agent (BA). Each agent type can be instantiated one or more times at run time.

The Acquaintance Model. The communication links existing between the agent types defined in the Agent Model are shown in Fig. 3b.

Table 2. The Services Model for the *Consumer* role.

SERVICE	INPUTS	OUTPUTS	PRE-CONDITION	POST-CONDITION
Searching for vendors	*productParameters*	*vendorList*	true	true
Contracting and evaluation offers	*vendorList*	*selectedVendor*	*vendorList* not empty	true
Payment of goods	*selectedVendor*	*paymentResult*	*selectedVendor* available *userCredit* >= *Poffer*	*userCredit* -= *Poffer*
Reporting the buying result	*paymentResult*		true	true

The Services Model. A *Services Model* for each role was specified. Because of space limitations only the *Services Model* for the *Consumer* role is reported (Table 2).

3.4 The Detailed Design Phase

The *Agent Interactions Model* is reported in Fig. 4. The interactions in the *Searching* and the *Contracting & Evaluation* phases (see Sect. 3.1) are not detailed in the figure since they depend on the behavior model of the MCA agent which is employed.

The *Agent Behaviors Model* is composed of a set of DSC specifications which are associated to each *Agent Type*. In particular, in the following, only the behavior models of the MCA agents are discussed.

Mobile Consumer Agent Models. A behavior model for the MCA agent can be defined on the basis of a tuple: <SP, BP, MD>, where SP is a searching policy in {ALL, PA, OS}, BP is a buying policy in {MP, FS, FT, RT}, and MD is a task execution model. Two different task execution models were defined:

– *Itinerary*: the Searching and Contracting & Evaluation phases are performed by a single MCA agent which fulfils its task by sequentially moving from one location to another within the e-Marketplace;
– *Parallel*: the Searching and Contracting & Evaluation phases are performed by a set of mobile agents in parallel. The MCA agent is able to generate a set of children (generically called *workers*) and to dispatch them to different locations; the workers can, in turn, spawn other workers.

An MCA model is chosen by the APA agent when it accepts a user input request. The DSC specification of the defined *Parallel Consumer Agent* (PCA) model is detailed in the following. The defined *Itinerary Consumer Agent* (ICA) model can be seen as a particular case of the PCA model.

A Parallel Consumer Agent Model. The DSC specification of the PCA agent is reported in Fig. 5. With reference to Fig. 5, it is worth pointing out that:

– events are asynchronously received and processed according to a run-to-completion semantics (i.e. an event can be processed only if the processing of the previous event is fully completed);
– the received events can be asynchronously generated by the agent itself (internal events) or by other agents (external events) through the primitive gener-

`ate(<mevent>(<param>))`, where `mevent` is an event instance and `param` is the list of formal parameters of `mevent` including the identifiers of the event sender and of the event target, and (possibly) a list of event parameters.

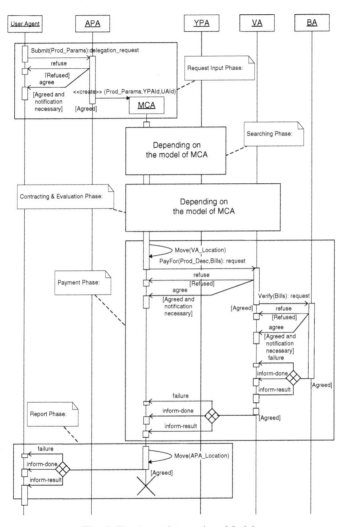

Fig. 4. The Agent Interactions Model.

The PCA agent fulfills the searching phase in the SEARCHING state. In particular, as soon as the PCA agent is created, it moves (ac1) to the first YPA location and locally interacts (ac2) with the `YPATarget` by sending it the *VAListQuery* event. The `YPATarget` replies to the PCA agent with the *List* event which can contain a list of VA agents with the linked YPA agents. After processing the reply (ac3), the PCA agent can do one of the following:

- create an Itinerary Searcher Mobile Agent (ISMA), which sequentially moves from one YPA location to another, if the YPS organization is of the One-Neighbor Federated type, and pass (ac4) into the contracting phase as soon as a *PList* event sent by the ISMA agent is received;
- create M Spawning Searcher Mobile Agents (SSMAs), if the YPS organization is of the M-Neighbors Federated type and pass (ac4) into the contracting phase when all the *PList* events sent by the directly created SSMA agents are processed. In particular, a SSMA agent moves to the assigned YPA agent and, in turn, creates a child SSMA agent for each reachable YPA agent. This parallel searching technique generates a spawning tree with SSMA agents as nodes and rooted at the PCA agent. If a SSMA agent interacts with a YPA agent which has already been visited by a SSMA agent belonging to the same spawning tree, the YPA agent notifies the SSMA agent which comes back to its parent;
- directly pass into the contracting phase if the YPS organization is of the Centralized type;
- report an unsuccessful search to the UA agent.

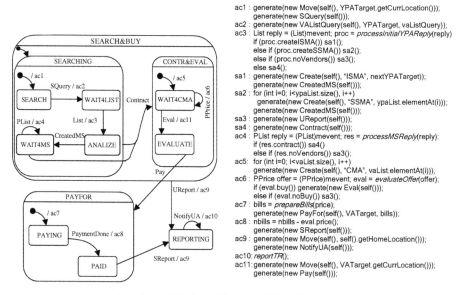

Fig. 5. The DSC specification of the PCA agent.

The contracting phase accomplished in the CONTRANDEVAL state involves the creation of a Contractor Mobile Agent (CMA) for each VA agent in the `vaList`. Each CMA agent moves to the assigned VA location, contracts with the VA agent, and finally returns to the PCA location to report the offer. The `evaluateOffer` method, which embeds the buying policy, evaluates the VA offers (*PPrice* events) reported by the CMA agents and generates (ac6) a decision about when and from which VA agent to purchase. In the PAYFOR state the PCA agent pays (ac7) the VA agent using the *PayFor* event which contains the bills. After receiving the *Payment-*

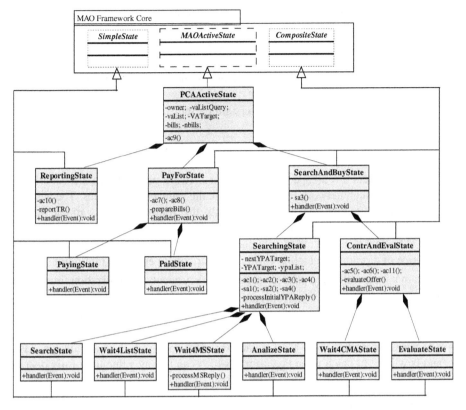

Fig. 6. Class diagram of the PCA agent behavior.

Done event, the PCA agent passes (ac8) to the REPORTING state from where it moves back (ac9) to the original APA location and finally reports (ac10) to its UA agent.

3.5 Implementation Phase

Each agent behavior defined in the previous phase has been seamlessly translated into Java code using the MAO Framework [9, 11] so obtaining a set of classes which represent the behaviors of the agent types and the inter- and intra-agent interaction events which are associated to the behaviors. In Fig. 6 the simplified UML class diagram of the PCA agent behavior is reported.

3.6 Simulation Phase

The primary goal of the simulation phase which was performed was to validate (i) the behavior of each type of agent, (ii) the different models of MCA agents on the basis of the different YPS organizations, and (iii) the agent interactions.

The second goal of the performed simulation phase was to better understand the effectiveness of the simulation for evaluating MAS performances. To this purpose, the evaluation of the completion time of the buying task of the ICA agent and the PCA agent was carried out. Such evaluation also allowed to validate an analytical model proposed in [23] regarding the sequential and parallel dispatching of mobile agents.

The simulation and analysis parameters are presented in Table 3. The simulated e-Marketplace was set up as follows:

- each stationary agent (UA, APA, YPA, VA, BA) executes on a different agent server;
- the agent servers are mapped onto different network nodes which are completely connected through network links which have the same characteristics. The network link delay (δ) is modeled as a lognormally distributed random variable with a mean, μ, and standard deviation, σ [8];
- each UA agent is connected to only one APA agent at the same time;
- the price of a product, which is uniformly distributed between a minimum (PP_{MIN}) and a maximum (PP_{MAX}) price, is set in each VA agent at initialization time and is never changed; thus the VA agents adopt a fixed-pricing policy to sell products;
- each YPA agent manages a list of locations of VA agents selling available products.
- a UA agent searches the e-Marketplace for a desired product which always exists and is willing to pay a price P_{MAX} for it which can be any value uniformly distributed between PP_{MAX} and $(PP_{MAX}+PP_{MIN})/2$.

In order to analyze e-Marketplaces having different structures and dimensions, the simulations were run by varying the organization of YPS (Centralized, 1-Neighbour and 2-Neighbour organized as a binary tree), the number of the YPA agents in the range [5..40] and the number of VA agents in the range [5..640]. These ranges were chosen for accommodating small as well as large e-Marketplaces.

Table 3. Simulation and Analysis parameters.

N_{VA}	Number of VAs
N_{YPA}	Number of YPAs
YPO	Yellow Pages Organization type: {Centralized, 1-Neighbour, 2-Neighbour}
δ_{MSG}	Link delay between two adjacent nodes for transmitting a message
δ_{agent}	Link delay between two adjacent nodes for transmitting a mobile agent
T_{VA}	Service time of VA
T_{YPA}	Service time of YPA
T_{APA}	Service time of APA
T_{BA}	Service time of BA
$T_C = T_{REPORT} - T_{CREATION}$	Completion time of the MCA, where $T_{CREATION}$ is the time of the MCA creation and T_{REPORT} is the time of the MCA report

The performance evaluation focused on the <ALL, MP, *> MCA models (see Sect. 3.4) since they are the only MCA models which guarantee both a successful purchase and the best purchase since they are successful at identifying the VA selling the desired product at the minimum price.

The results obtained for the <ALL, MP, *> MCA models over an YPS organization of the binary tree 2-Neighbour type are reported in Fig. 7. The results shown in Fig. 7a were obtained with $N_{YPA}=10$ and by varying N_{VA}, whereas, the results shown in Fig. 7b were obtained with $N_{VA}=80$ and by varying N_{YPA}. In agreement with the analytical model reported in [23], the PCA agent, due to its parallel dispatching mechanism, outperforms the ICA agent when N_{VA} and N_{YPA} increase.

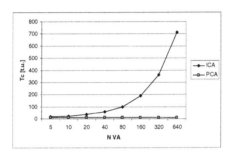 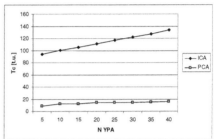

Fig. 7. Performance evaluation of the <ALL, MP, *> MCA models for an e-Marketplace with YPO=2-Neighbour of the binary tree type: (a) $N_{YPA}=10$ with variable N_{VA}, (b) $N_{VA}=80$ with variable N_{YPA}.

4 Conclusions

Flexible processes, methodologies and tools for the modeling and the simulation of agent-based systems are highly required to effectively support agent-oriented software development in emerging and complex application domains such as e-Commerce, e-Learning, and e-Science.

This paper has proposed an integrated approach which supports the modeling and simulation of MAS. The efficacy of the proposed approach has been highlighted through a case study concerning with an agent-based consumer-driven e-Marketplace.

The distinctive features of the proposed approach are:

1. *Integration.* The integrated use of existing methodologies, method fragments and tools for driving the software development phases of MAS is now widely recognized also in the 'Agents' research area as it is witnessed by the fervent activity in the Modeling and Methodology Technical Committees of FIPA;

2. *Seamless code generation and adaptation.* The detailed design is seamlessly translatable into a platform-neutral code by means of the MAO Framework. The obtained code can be used for feeding both the simulation phase and, notably, the deployment phase after adaptation of the code to the target agent platform;

3. *Simulation.* The use of the simulation to validate the modeled MAS before its actual deployment and execution, is strategic. In fact, the simulation, particularly if

event-driven, is the only viable means for the validation of large-scale and complex MAS.

Current research efforts are devoted to:

- improving the integration among the phases of the proposed approach and, in particular, between the design phase and the detailed design phase. The chosen technique is based on the extraction of methodology fragments and on the representation of these fragments using a SPEM-based common notation. In particular, the extraction and representation of fragments of the Gaia methodology is an on-going activity in the context of the Methodology TC of FIPA [13];
- simulating agent-mediated e-Commerce scenarios more complex than the scenario of the presented case study for the purpose of (i) validating and evaluating new business models, strategies, and systems and (ii) gaining insights into how different market mechanisms and business models might play out in real e-Marketplaces [14].

References

1. P. Bresciani, P. Giorgini, F. Giunchiglia, J. Mylopoulos and A. Perini. TROPOS: An Agent-Oriented Software Development Methodology, Journal of Autonomous Agents and Multi-Agent Systems, 8(3):203-236, 2004.
2. C. Bernon., M.P. Gleizes, G. Picard, and P. Glize. The Adelfe Methodology For an Intranet System Design. In Proc. of the Fourth International Bi-Conference Workshop on Agent-Oriented Information Systems (AOIS), Toronto, Canada, 2002.
3. B. Bauer, J.P. Muller, and J. Odell. Agent UML: A Formalism for Specifying Multiagent Interaction. In Paolo Ciancarini and Michael Wooldridge, editors, Agent-Oriented Software Engineering, pages 91-103. Springer-Verlag, Berlin, 2001.
4. M. Cossentino, P. Burrafato, S. Lombardo, and L. Sabatucci. Introducing Pattern Reuse in the Design of Multi-Agent Systems. In Ryszard Kowalczyk, Jörg P. Müller, Huaglory Tianfield, Rainer Unland, editors, Agent Technologies, Infrastructures, Tools, and Applications for E-Services, LNAI 2592, pages 107-120. Springer-Verlag, Berlin, 2003.
5. G. Caire, F. Leal, P. Chainho, R. Evans, F. Garijo, J. Gomez, J. Pavon, P. Kearney, J. Stark, and P. Massonet. Agent Oriented Analysis using MESSAGE/UML. In Proc. of the Second International Workshop on Agent-Oriented Software Engineering (AOSE), LNCS 2222. Springer-Verlag, Berlin, 2002.
6. K.H. Dam and M. Winikoff. Comparing Agent-Oriented Methodologies. In Proc. of the fifth International Bi-Conference Workshop on Agent-Oriented Information Systems (AOIS), Melbourne, Australia, 2003.
7. S. A. DeLoach, M. Wood, and C. Sparkman. Multiagent system engineering. International Journal of Software Engineering and Knowledge Engineering, 11(3):231–258, April 2001.
8. S. Floyd and V. Paxson. Difficulties in simulating the Internet. IEEE/ACM Transations on Networking, 9(4):392-403, 2001.
9. G. Fortino, W. Russo, and E. Zimeo. A Framework for Design and Implementation of Mobile Active Objects. In Proc. of IASTED Internationall Conference on Software Engineering and Applications (SEA), Marina del Rey, CA, pages 635-640. Acta Press, 2003.
10. G. Fortino and W. Russo. A Statecharts Based Methodology for the Simulation of Mobile Agents. In Proc. of the EUROSIS European Simulation and Modeling Conference (ESMC), pages 77-82, Naples, Italy, October 2003.

11. G. Fortino, W. Russo, and E. Zimeo. A Statecharts-based Software Development Process for Mobile Agents. Information and Software Technology, 2004. to appear.

12. Foundation of Intelligent and Physical Agents (FIPA), http://www.fipa.org.

13. A. Garro, P. Turci, and M.P. Huget. Expressing Gaia Methodology using Spem. FIPA Methodology TC, working draft v. 1.0/04-03-15, http://fipa.org/activities/methodology.html.

14. M. Griss and R. Letsinger. Games at Work – Agent-Mediated E-Commerce Simulation. In Proc. of ACM Autonomous Agents, Barcellona, Spain, Jun. 2000.

15. D. Harel and E. Gery. Executable Object Modelling with Statecharts. IEEE Computer, 30(7): 31-42, 1997.

16. R. Kowalczyk, M. Ulieru, and R. Unland. Integrating Mobile and Intelligent Agents in Advanced e-Commerce: A Survey. In Ryszard Kowalczyk, Jörg P. Müller, Huaglory Tianfield, Rainer Unland, editors, Agent Technologies, Infrastructures, Tools, and Applications for E-Services, LNAI 2592, pages 295-313. Springer-Verlag, Berlin, 2003.

17. J. Lind. Issues in Agent-Oriented Software Engineering. In Proc. of the First International Workshop on Agent-Oriented Software Engineering (AOSE), LNCS 1957, pages. 45-58. Springer-Verlag, Berlin, 2001.

18. P. Maes, R.H. Guttman, and A. Moukas. Agents that buy and sell: Transforming commerce as we know it. Communications of the ACM, 42(3): 81-91, 1999.

19. L. Padgham and M. Winikoff. Prometheus: A methodology for developing intelligent agents. In Proc. of the Third International Workshop on Agent-Oriented Software Engineering (AOSE), LNCS 2585. Springer-Verlag, Berlin, 2003.

20. Software Process Engineering Metamodel Specification, Version 1.0, formal/02-11-14. Object Management Group Inc. , November 2002.

21. A.M. Uhrmacher, M. Röhl, and B. Kullick. The Role of Reflection in Simulating and Testing Agents: An Exploration Based on the Simulation System James. Applied Artificial Intelligence (9-10):795-811, October-December, 2002.

22. M. Wooldridge, N. R. Jennings, and D. Kinny. The Gaia methodology for agent-oriented analysis and design. Journal of Autonomous Agents and Multi-Agent Systems, 3(3):285–312, 2000.

23. Y. Wang, K-L. Tan, and J. Ren. A Study of Building Internet Marketplaces on the Basis of Mobile Agents for Parallel Processing. World Wide Web: Internet and Web Information Systems 5(1): 41-66, 2002.

Coupling GIS and Multi-agent Simulation – Towards Infrastructure for Realistic Simulation

Michael Schüle, Rainer Herrler, and Franziska Klügl

Dept. of Artificial Intelligence, Universität Würzburg, Würzburg, Germany
{schuele,herrler,kluegl}@ki.informatik.uni-wuerzburg.de

Abstract. Based on the agent paradigm highly realistic simulation models can be formulated. However, the richness of the environment and its spatial representation are a basic ingredient for such models that cannot be easily modelled with the simple spatial representations usually used in Multi-Agent Simulation. An interesting solution is coupling a Multi-Agent Simulation tool and a geographical information system. Based on such a coupling existing map data can be used for realistic Multi-Agent Simulations.

In this contribution we are presenting several ways of coupling Multi-Agent Simulators and geographical information systems. Several important aspects are tackled, like correspondence between agents and their shape as well as possible perceptions and actions. The concepts are exemplified in a coupling between SeSAm and Arcview and demonstrated using a simple traffic simulation.

1 Motivation

Modelling and simulation are important and well established methods in scientific and industrial applications. They help to improve understanding and to increase the quality of design and control of complex systems e.g. traffic simulation [9] or suburban spawl development [18]. Multi-Agent Systems provide an attractive modelling paradigm that enables to overcome several shortcomings of traditional approaches: especially concerning the representation of variable structures, flexible interaction and a greater level of detail related to intelligent behavior.

This greater level of detail corresponds also to detailed models of the Multi-Agent System's environment. In most cases Multi-Agent Simulations are placed in an artificial environment. This may consist of 2- or 3- dimensional maps with discrete or continuous positions. A map provides a mean for determining the spatial position of the agents. An important point is that this environment – as the virtual time – is completely controllable by the modeler. The modeler may fix influences that he cannot control in real life, e.g. available resources in non-laboratory experiments.

However, the more details are captured by the agents model, the richer its environment has to be. If realistic human decision making has to be modelled, then, the environment where this is happening should also be as realistic as necessary. Realistic models are effortful, especially because of the complex design and programming tasks, but also due to the exploding amount of assumptions that influence the model and have to be documented and justified e.g. by empirical findings. The environmental model is critical for the Multi-Agent System as it stongly affects the agents decision

G. Lindemann et al. (Eds.): MATES 2004, LNAI 3187, pp. 228–242, 2004.

making and behavior. Thus, it has to be carefully elaborated and tested. This would be extremely facilitated if real-world data could be directly fed into the simulation model. Spatial real-world data is commonly organized using Geographic Information System (GIS). Therefore it would be good, if GIS data would be accessible by the simulated Multi-Agent System.

Although Geographic Information Systems are highly elaborated tools for managing spatial information and provide powerful support in manipulating data about position, shape, extensions, etc., they lack capabilities for representing dynamics. Simulation and especially Multi-Agent Simulation provides a way to express dynamics related to spatial elements. This can be achieved by the agents' local perception and action capabilities.

Therefore coupling Multi-Agent Simulation with information from GIS is highly attractive for both, applications in the simulation area as well as in geographic data processing. There are several Multi-Agent Simulation applications, that already combine these techniques [5][4]. However, it is mostly handmade and without support provided by Multi-Agent Simulation tools. The basic aim of this contribution is to show systematic ways of coupling a Multi-Agent Simulation tool with a GIS and present a prototype implementation. Therefore we proceed in the following way: after giving a short introduction to Multi-Agent Simulation and tools for their development, we discuss in section 3 four ways of connecting GIS and Multi-Agent Simulation models. After that we show an existing file-based coupling that is integrated into a process model for developing Multi-Agent Simulation with a GIS-based environmental representation. In section 5 a short example model is given that indicates the usability of the presented approach. The contribution ends with a short conclusion.

2   State of the Art: Components for Realistic Simulation

2.1   Multi-agent Simulation

Multi-Agent Simulation applies the concept of Multi-Agent Systems to the basic structure of simulation models. Active components are identified as agents and programmed using agent-related concepts and technologies. A Multi-Agent Simulation consists of simulated agents that "live" in a simulated environment. The environment may play an important role as it frames the agent behaviors and interactions. The individual environment of an agent may consist of other agents and contain spatially distributed objects or resources.

The particular environmental model is highly relevant, especially when using adaptive agents. Little modelling errors may result in a completely unexpected system behaviour and potentially in an useless agent model. An important cause for errors is a sloppy handling of the environmental model – consisting of some form of map and additional dynamics that are not directly triggered by agents actions. The highly relevant role of environment for Multi-Agent Systems in general is documented by the E4MAS Workshop at the AAMAS 2004 (http://www.cs.kuleuven.ac.be/~distrinet/events/e4mas/).

2.2   Tools for Multi-agent Simulation – SeSAm

Because building realistic model is a very difficult task, powerfull tools for simulation and building models are required. Several tools became popular in the last years. Most referenced is Swarm [13] a Objective C programming framework for agent based simulation. Another upcoming tool is the "Shell for Simulated Agent Systems" (SeSAm), that provides a generic environment for modelling and experimenting with agent-based simulations. Its development was specially focused on providing a completely visual tool for the construction of complex agent-based models [10].

Based on a framework for the representation of agents and their behavior a specification language and a software environment for modelling and simulation were developed (see [15]). The specification framework focuses on the representation of agent behavior based on UML-like activity graphs and also allows to express relations to other agents and resources. In SeSAm the user is able to design the behavior of agent classes visually without programming in a traditional programming language. Analogous mechanisms are provided for specifying the static structures of an agent, an agent system or the environmental elements and their configuration. So the complete agent-based simulation model, even very complex ones, can be created, executed and analized within SeSAm.

SeSAm[1] is publicly available for more than two years now and is updated peridically. Realized simulations models and reach from the simulation of social insects and traffic simulation to coordinating treatment tasks in hospitals. Scientists from many application domains have implemented own models.

2.3 Geographic Information Systems

Geographic information systems (GIS) allow to administrate and manipulate general information together with geographical data respecting its complexity and spatial relations. In addition they can be used to extract new information based on spatial analysis, like intersection, etc. GIS today are highly relevant for several application domains, ranging from ecological modelling to urban development. Decisions in policy, economy and administration, that are based on spatial information, are increasingly often made with the support of GIS software. More details about GIS can be found in one of the many text books about GIS, like [2].

The main components of geographic information systems are software – instruments for analysis and adminstration of data – and the geographic data base. Most GIS also posses graphical user interfaces for visualization increasing the usability for users.

Important in the context of this contribution is to understand how geographic objects are usually represented in a GIS. Every entity stands for a concrete physical, geometric or conceptual unity of the real world. Objects always have geometrical information which is given by its position, data and shape.

Basically there are two formats for geometric information. Information can be represented using vector or raster data format. Vector data is particularly useful for representing lines and line-like structures (e.g. streets and rivers). Raster data is quite commonly used in processing satellite pictures, e.g. climate data. Both representations have advantages and disadvantages. This concerns memory consumption, possible elegance and performance of manipulation and analysis algorithms. Some particular GIS systems are restricted to only one representation, others support both types of representation.

---

[1] SeSAm: *http://www.simsesam.de*

Additionally, spatial entities may be augmented with thematic information (statements, attributes) and topological information (nodes, edges, areas). The thematic information also can be used for classification and grouping of entities. Thus, entities of same thematic layer are stored with only one thematic dimension (see figure 1).

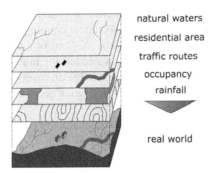

natural waters

residential area

traffic routes

occupancy

rainfall

real world

Fig. 1. Examples for thematic dimensions of a GIS [2]

2.4   Existing Approaches for Coupling

There are several examples for different environmental models used in Multi-Agent Systems and Simulations. It would be beyond the scope of this paper to enumerate them all. The most prominent are discrete two-dimensional maps where agents may occupy a cell and interact with items that are positioned in the same cell or the neighboring cells. Such spatial representations can already be found in early testbeds like MICE [12]. Simple forms of environmental models are developed further basing environmental representation and dynamics on Cellular Automata. A prominent example is the Sugarscape model[1] with its resulting tool Ascape [17]. Combining an agent-based model with a cellular automation forms an approach that can be observed quite often and especially in agent-based land use models (see [16] for a review).

Elaborated environmental models including sophisticated sensor and effector models canbe found in simulation tools for robots as well as in early test beds for Multi-Agent Systems, like DVMT[2] with screenshots) for vehicle monitoring or Phoenix [3]. Here a detailed spatial model of the Yellowstone National Park was used for testing cooperative problem solving in fire fighting.

However, all these spatial models are implemented directly in the simulator. That means, they are tightly coupled to the simulator and the simulation model. Therefore, they can basically serve as a motivation for providing a flexible and standardized way of coupling tools for Multi-Agent Systems and Simulation with standardized GIS for developing realistic models.

Although the idea of coupling Multi-Agent Simulations and GIS is quite obvious, when aiming at a realistic level of model details, there exist not many solutions. Basically one may identify two attempts for a generic coupling:

---

[2] DVMT: *http://dis.cs.umass.edu/research/dvmt/*

InterGIS and iEPISIM^2 [5]: The coupling of InterGIS and iEPISIM^2 provides a tool for individual-oriented modelling und simulation together with methods and technics for knowledge discovery in databases. The application area is restricted to environmental epidemiology. The C++ simulation system iEPISIM^2 executes simulation models developed in the modelling language iEPISIM-ML. Concerning the GIS-side of the coupling InterGIS is based on a client-server architecture. It allows different clients to use InterGIS like an internet service. The technical coupling between the two systems is realized using a C++ interface and an ActiveX-Control. Summarized the simulation component iEPISIM^2 is not as powerful as needed for multi-agent simulations. The main focus are methods and technics for knowledge discovery in databases. The aspect of combining dynamics of multi-agent models with geographic information systems was secondary.

Another Multi-Agent Simulation system, that already has been connected to a GIS, is RePast. The RePast library for Multi-Agent Modelling^3 has been augmented with several tools for visualizing vector GIS data, like Geotools or Java Topology Suite. The simulation system with its GIS enhancements provides support for loading standard data files and displaying the vector data. Further integration has to be made on basic code level for manipulating the spatial data structure.

3   Ways of Coupling Multi-agent Simulations and GIS

Before we continue with a generic coupling between a Multi-Agent Simulation environment and GIS data, different ways of couplings are described in a systematic way.

3.1   Ontological Coupling as Prerequisite

An essential prerequisite for coupling a GIS and a Multi-Agent Simulation consists in establishing a terminological relation between both, model and spatial data. Because geological data is usually saved in thematic dimensions on a layer, knowledge about the meaning of the layers should be available throughout the complete environmental model. However, the explicit representation of spatial entities with attributes is more relevant for simulation aspects. Additional information is especially available for vector data where a line object may contain attributes describing the depth of the river or the mean flow of vehicles on this line. Such data is highly relevant for simulation as not only the existence of the entities in space is important, but also their properties.

The solution for this problem is to use a common ontology in order to establish a shared comprehension of spatial (and non-spatial) entities and their properties. That means that "river" denoting some lines in the GIS system can be associated with such lines in a model that describes fishes and fishermen.

For coupling of Multi-Agent Simulations and GIS the ontology may be realized as a class structure containing attributes for the classes. All objects of a layer are associated with instances of a particular object class. The attribute declarations of spatial objects are inserted as attributes of this class. Figure 2 gives an example of an object catalogue, which can be used for developing an ontology.

---

^{3} RePast: *http://repast.sourceforge.net/index.php*

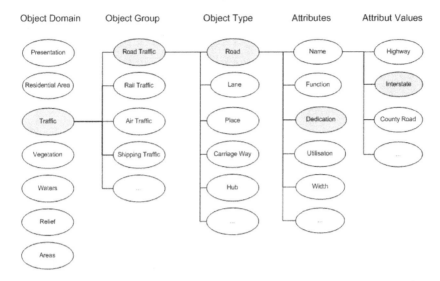

Fig. 2. Part of standard object catalogue in GIS as an example for an ontology of geographical data [19]

This form of ontological knowledge is very common for geographical data and is built-in to several existing GIS systems. Thus, what remains to be done is to make this knowledge explicit and to reuse the ontological data in a Multi-Agent Simulation. This facilitates modelling and especially coupling between model and GIS data.

In analogy to technical possibilities for coupling of two information systems (see [11]), we identify four architectural categories for coupling Multi-Agent Simulation systems and GIS. In the following we describe those approaches together with some short notions of consequences.

3.2   Loose Coupling

Loose coupling of GIS and Multi-Agent Simulation means that data between the systems is exchanged using a data file in a format that both systems are able to tackle. Although there is no official standard for storing geographical data, there are established formats, that are widely used Geographic Information Systems and can so be seen as a defacto standard. Obviously it is advantageous to ground this file-based loose coupling on such an existing format.

Thus, loose coupling means that data is generated using a GIS and then imported to the Multi-Agent Simulation platform. The data is stored in the internal representation of the Multi-Agent Simulation where it may be manipulated by the agents during the simulation run. Finally, the simulation system exports the resulting situation into a file that again follows the geographical standards and be further processed using a GIS. Figure 3 shows schematic representation of this form of coupling.

The most important advantage of this approach is that its implementation seems to be quite straight forward. If the simulation system should provide animation facilities,

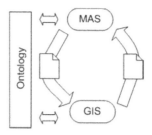

Fig. 3. Schematic representation of a loose coupling between Multi-Agent Simulation and GIS. The connection is implemented using a file in a format that can be handled by both system

at least a visualization of geographical data has to be provided in the simulation system. Nevertheless, both systems maintain their independence.

The main disadvantage is efficiency and the need of handling additional data files. For example, when generating output data for every time transition, the file-based handling becomes quite cumbersome. Thus, depending on the application area a tighter coupling with dynamic data exchange might be more desirable.

3.3   Tight Coupling

Tight coupling between GIS and Multi-Agent Simulation is reached by embedding one system into the other. Either a GIS can be embedded in a Multi-Agent Simulation system or vice versa. The important point is to consider, which one of the systems is supposed to have the control of the coupled system. It may result in a GIS with Multi-Agent Simulation facilities or a Multi-Agent Simulation environment that also provides functionality of a GIS beyond pure visualization.

Both system components work on the same internal spatial representation. This requires a high degree of integration. The two configurations work in the following ways:

 - If a GIS is integrated in a Multi-Agent Simulation system as a sub-component (like depicted in figure 4), it makes the GIS functionality available at runtime. Map situations can be edited directly in the simulation environment using the sophisticated GIS features. In addition simulated agents may perform high-level interaction with the spatial entities they perceive in their simulated surroundings. E.g. an agent may use intersection of two perceived areas for determining the best locations for positioning itself or an entity that it generates. Thus, reasoning about spatial relations is supported by operations provided by the GIS component.
 - If Multi-Agent Simulation system is part of a GIS system, the simulation is triggered compute dynamics of spatial data. A impotant criteria refers to the accessibility of the simulated agents and their behavior description for manipulation in the user interface. Is the modelling environment also integrated to the GIS or just a simulation runtime engine? In the latter case the agents and their interactions with their environment have to be modelled outside of the GIS.

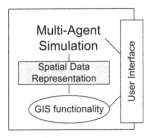

Fig. 4. Schematic representation of an example for a tight coupling: the integration of GIS functionality into a Multi-Agent Simulation system

In principle, the possibility to work on the same data representations and structures and thereby to access functionalities from both systems may provide interesting facilities. Depending on the overall user interface the integration of the functionalities from both systems can be transparent and hopefully easy to use. However, the effort of developing such a coupled system is very high. Especially the design of a common user interface may be demanding as it should hide the currently not required complexity of the overall system from the user. Moreover, the resulting complex system may have the negative properties of monolithic software systems. The question which of the alternatives of tight coupling is preferable, depends on the main focus of your intended projects. From a general point of view there is no "better" alternative.

3.4 Direct Cooperative Coupling

The third form of coupling is based on a common interface to two separated systems. In accordance to [11] we call this form of coupling "Direct cooperative coupling". Generally such a system can be distributed over a network. One of the components acts according to the "role" server and the other one as client (see fig. 5). Like in the other cases, communication of the components requires standardized protocols and ontologies.

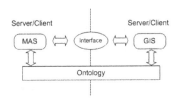

Fig. 5. Schematic representation of direct cooperative coupling

Both systems must support a client-server architecture. The integration of the systems just based on a common interface is weaker when compared to *tight coupling* since both applications remain independent. Explicit task sharing ensures transparency and flexibility for the experienced user. Also like in the other cases there are quite hard requirements to the user interface. Usability may be facilitated if there is a higher degree of integration.

3.5 Indirect Cooperative Coupling

In the last form of coupling, an additional software system controls both, Multi-Agent Simulation and GIS: Indirect cooperative coupling of the systems is managed by introducing a third application (see fig. 6). This mediating application controls of the overall workflow and information exchange between Multi-Agent Simulation and GIS. It can be implemented for example using a shell or a script language.

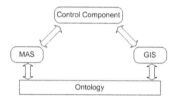

Fig. 6. Schematic representation of indirect cooperative coupling

However, like in the approaches described above, the interfaces – languages and protocols – between the controlling and the serving applications have to be defined carefully. This approach allows to use standardized user interfaces. The extensibility of the total system is very good. GIS and Multi-Agent Simulation components may be exchanged easily. The high development effort of a third component is a disadvantage of such a solution.

In the following we selected the first of these possibilities not only due to the effort of developing such a system, but also due to maintaining the independence of the simulation system.

4   Coupling SeSAm and ArcView via ESRI Files

In the following section a practical implementation for coupling a Multi-Agent Simulation system and a GIS is presented. As an implementation basis on the simulation side we used the open source Multi-Agent Simulation environment SeSAm that was developed at the University of Würzburg. We decided on "loose coupling" as SeSAm offers open well defined interfaces for such plugins and is therefore easily extendable. As basis for our development on the GIS side, we decided to ground on the shape file (.shp) data format provided by ESRI This verctor format is used by many authorities and is very widespread so it can be seen as an established data format for spatial vector data. It's export and import is supported by many GIS.

Before going into technical details of the SeSAm plugin, first two general issues have to be tackled. First the relevance of high-level spatial representations in SeSAm is discussed and then a process for developing geographic simulation models is introduced. This shows the general integration of the coupling into work with SeSAm.

4.1   High-Level Spatial Representations

The original form of spatial representation used in SeSAm is a two-dimensional continuous map of a limited size. The map can either be treated as a torus or as a limited map with fixed boundaries. Every entity – agent or resource object – may have the following attributes related to its spatial representation: position (2-d coordinates), direction (2-d), speed, extension radius and a graphical image (a sprite). The shape of an agent basically resembles a circle although sometimes the associated figures show more complicated shapes. Primitive functions are provided to manipulate these spatial attributes (e.g. for movement).

The main goal was to give SeSAm the possibility to deal with agents that have a more sophisticated spatial context. Shapes in the vector data model can be points, lines and polygons. In principle an agent or resource object can be associated with every kind of those shapes.

The perceptive abilities of agents should be independent from their shape, except if local perception is based on neighborhood relation. Then, the shape would determine which other agents or resources the agent would be able to perceive.

Agents with sophisticated shapes are supposed to be endowed with additional capabilities for changing their state and environment. Point-agents for example may move along a line, line-agents may intersect or connect to other lines and so on.

A combination of those agents can be used for quite speculative simulation models with agents that connect to form new shapes. However, in realistic GIS-based simulation it is quite valuable that e.g. a pre-defined land area (polygon-agents) may change their cultivation or coverage, a line-agent may count point-agents moving along and point-agents may send messages to polygon-agents in their neighborhood denoting gathering advertisements or spending money.

In the current prototype agents are represented only by points, resources might be have the shape of points, lines and polygons. The other shapes for agents will be added in future.

4.2   Process Model for Realistic Simulations

Until now we described possible approaches and extensions of existing tools basically for implementation of Multi-Agent Simulation models with standard geographic data. In this section we want to provide a process model for creating realistic Multi-Agent Simulations that rely on real-world geographic data. This process is also depicted in figure 7

1. **Ontology modelling**: Creating a simulation model and using the implemented coupling begins with the development of an ontology. This is based on available real-world geographical data and empirical findings that are also represented as attributes in the GIS data. In most times the complete geographical object catalogue will not be required for a model that resembles a part of the real world. Thus, the ontology needed for simulation does not necessarily contain the complete set of geographical data.

2. **Agent and resource modelling**: In the next step agent and resource classes have to be created in the simulation environment. The ontological concepts can be used

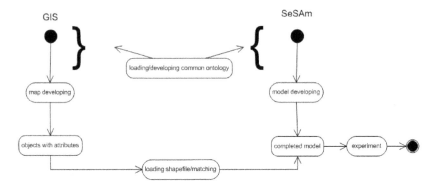

Fig. 7. Schematic representation of the different activities for developing a Multi-Agent Simulation with a real-world GIS data

to generate entity classes for agents and resources in a very generic manner. The attributes of ontology have to be matched to corresponding attributes of the simulation model. Ontologies of geographic data can be reused and imported to SeSAm by a previously developed Ontology-Import Plugin (see [7]).

3. **Behavior modelling**: The next step is to extend the static simulation model structures with dynamic behaviour of the agents. This can be easily done in SeSAm, as it provides visual tools for activity-based behavior modelling. In addition the global dynamics of the "world" can be defined.

4. **Creating start situations**: A start situation can be seen as an initial "map" or "configuration" for a simulation. After implementing the the entities of simulation and repecting their attributes and behaviour, the number of agents and their positions can be read from the GIS data. The generated maps are a basis for simulation experiments. Every shapefile that represents a thematic layer is assigned to an agent or resource class. Class attributes of both representations can be assigned automatically due to the used common ontology. In ambiguous situations a manual assignment may be required. For every object definition in the shapefile an instance of the agent or resource classes is created and positioned in the considered situation. This is repeated until the situation contains all relevant entities and all situations for the intended simulation experiments are defined.

5. **Running the experiments**: When the start situations have been generated from the GIS data, the simulation runs can be started. During and after the simulation run modified situation generated by the model can be exported to the GIS again, to save different snapshots of the dynamic situation.

6. **Analyzing the generated simulation data**: After simulation the shapefiles generated during the simulation runs can be accessed by GIS again for reasons of analysis with GIS functions. Depending on the results new situations can be generated and again be input to the modelling and simulation process.

4.3 SeSAm GIS Plugin

As mentioned above, for the capability of importing and operating on spatial data from shapefiles, some extensions in SeSAm had to be developed. This refers basically to the data structures for dealing with spatial information and an animation component that allows users to observe agent system and environmental dynamics in an appropriate way.

The implementation of those GIS functionalities in SeSAm is realized by a SeSAm extension called "GISPlugin". This plugin is not part of the core modelling and simulation environment, so it can be dealt with separately. SeSAm in fact is not dependent on any kind of spatial representation. However if the plugin is available in a particular SeSAm installation, it is completely integrated from the users' point of view. The GIS-Plugin substitutes the standard SpatialPlugin of SeSAm that provides all related aspects to a 2-d continuous spatial map and position representation. The grahical visualization of the GIS maps was realized by integrating the open source Java library GeoTools for rendering (*www.geotools.org*).

The GISPlugin itself consists of four parts:

- The *ShapeInfoFeature* has to be assigned to objects that have a spatial representation. The ShapeInfoFeature is responsible for the administration and the representation of all geometrical data of the related object. Thus, it provides geographic coordinates for the individual agent (latitude, longitude), stores its shape, etc.
- The *ShapeMapFeature* is assigned to a world class and contains and manages all entities with a spatial representation in form of a *ShapeInfoFeature*. The ShapeMap-Feature is also responsible for the projection of the sphere onto a plane and the rendering of the map.
- A set of behavior primitives for sensing (eg. perception of nearby agents) and action (e.g. movement) is provided for modelling. The primitives ca be executed by the agents with *ShapeInfoFeature*.
- The *GISConnector* is an extension that allows to import shapefiles and converts the information from those files to the spatial representation provided by the GISplugin (*ShapeInfoFeature* and *ShapeMapFeature*) Another function of this component is to export a shapshot of the simulated situation.

5   Evaluation Scenario

As evaluation of the coupling of SeSAm and ArcView via ESRI files a microscopical traffic simulation based on the Nagel-Schreckenberg model was chosen ([6], [14]). Traffic simulation is one major application for simulations with a real-world spatial context. The original Nagel-Schreckenberg model is a Cellular Automaton. In this model time and road network are made discrete. One timestep corresponds to one second, a cell of the road network to 7,5m. Every road user represented as vehicle-driver unit has a maximum speed. There are four rules that guide the behavior of the vehicles. Three rules control acceleration when there is enough space in front of the vehicle to speed up, deceleration when there is not enough distance and a randomizing component for decreasing the speed. The forth rule controls the actual locomotion. Thus, the speed is always calculated based on the current speed and the distance to the preceding vehicle. This simple traffic flow model is able to reproduce real-world traffic phenomenons like stop and go traffic or traffic jams without particular reasons like accidents or road works. We adapted this simple model for an agent-based simulation model where the vehicles correspond to agents for demonstrating the usage of our coupling. One can easily image that more sophisticated and intelligent agents may also populate such a traffic worlds.

In contrast to the original Nagel-Schreckenberg model, which is defined for a single track, the implemented model adapts the rules of the Nagel-Schreckenberg model to a road network. Both, the research groups of Nagel and Schreckenberg apply this automaton currently to road networks. The advantage of our approach is that the road network is directly imported from GIS data without any manual or automatic discretization step. The existence of cells, discrete velocities, etc. is just present as a parameter in the agents behavior model and can be changed easily.

The data for the experiment were pre-defined examples from ATKIS, a GIS developed and used by German authorities. An ontology can directly created from the given object catalogue of ATKIS (see fig. 2). The driver-vehicle units are represented by agents with a punctual shape. Agents are capable of moving only on a road. The roads are interpreted as resources, that means they are just there with some attributes like maximum allowed velocity, but without behavior e.g. that could for example represent road surface degradation. Agents are generated at several source positions and leave the network at designated exit positions. At the beginning an agent chooses a general direction. At crossings it always changes direction towards that overall goal direction. Figure 8 shows a screenshot from an example simulation run.

This implementation of the Nagel-Schreckenberg model reproduces the same phenomena like the original and other properties, like reduced average speed at crossings.

6   Conclusion and Further Work

The Multi-Agent Simulation paradigm is able to capture necessary details of models that should resemble real-world scenarios. It is suited better than any other simulation and modelling paradigm. Flexible interactions with partners that are not pre-defined, but selected during a simulation run, is just one of the large set of advantages. However, there are several drawbacks, like a large number of parameters and assumptions, high sensitivity due to possible feedback loops between the different levels of observation, etc. This contribution tackles a step towards integrating real-world data from measurements and empirical surveys. Thus we are able to apply this data directly without abstractions or other mappings to simplified environmental characteristics. This again reduces the amount of incertain assumptions influencing the simulation model and decreases the modelling effort.

We presented a generic solution to a coupling between GIS and a general purpose Multi-Agent Simulation system that can be used for many applications that require treatment of real-world geographic data. Currently, the implementation of the GISPlugin is finished and should be available for download at the SeSAm site in summer 2004. But also further developments that support realistic large scale simulation models are

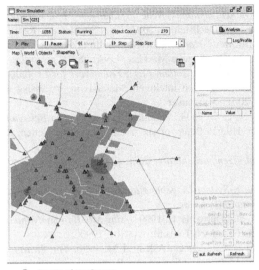

⬤ Agents of typ Source
⬤ Characteristic volume of traffic at crossroads

Fig. 8. Screenshot of a running simulation

planned: Vector data based GIS are mainly distributed in the traffic area, other application areas, like e.g. ecology rely more on raster data. Such an extension for SeSAm is quite straight forward, as it can be based on the original spatial representation and just generate objects based on the characteristics given in the input files. A plugin for database connectivity and for importing csv-style tables with row-wise object descriptions are already available. Thus, the basic infrastructure for real-world Multi-Agent Simulation models will be available in short future. Then, we will probably have to tackle different problems concerning data management and simulation performance. For being prepared, we are also working on optimization techniques for Multi-Agent Simulation.

References

1. Axtrell R. L. and Epstein J.M. 1996. *Growing Artificial Societies: Social Science from the Bottom Up*. Brookings Institution Press/MIT Press.
2. Bill R. 1999. *Grundlagen der Geo-Informationssysteme Band 1 Hardware, Software und Daten*. Wichmann.
3. Cohen P. R. ,Greenberg M. L. ,Hart D. and Howe A. 1989. *TRIAL BY FIRE. Understanding the Design Requirements for Agents in a Complex Environment*. In: AI Magazine, 10.
4. Dibble C., Feldman P.G. 2004. *The GeoGraph 3D Computational Laboratory: Network and Terrain Landscapes for RePast* Journal of Artificial Societies and Social Simulation,Vol. 7.
5. Friebe J. und Köster F. 2001. *Die Nutzung des internetbasierten geographischen Informationssystems InterGIS als Grundlage fr räumlich explizite Simulationen am Beispiel des individuenorientierten Simulationssystems i EPISIM²*.

6. Helbing D. 1997. *Verkehrsdynamik Neue physikalische Modellierungskonzepte.* Springer.
7. Klügl F., Herrler, R. and Oechslein C. 2003. *From Simulated to Real Environments: How to use SeSAm for software development* In: M. Schillo et al. (eds) Multi-Agent System Technologies - 1st German Conferences MATES. (LNAI 2831). pp 13-24.
8. Klügl F. 2001. *Simulated Ant Colonies as a Framework for Evolutionary Models* Proc. Of the International Conference on Intelligent Methods in Processing and Manufacturing of Materials (IPMM 2001), Vancouver
9. Klügl F., Bazzan, A. L. C. 2003. *Simulated Route Decision Behaviour: Simple Heuristics and Adaptation* In: Human Behavior and Traffic Networks; Selten, R.; Schreckenberg, M. Springer.
10. Klügl F. 2001. *Multiagentensimulation Konzepte, Werkzeuge, Anwendungen.* Addison Wesley.
11. Mandl P. 1996. *Fuzzy-System-Umgebung als regelgesteuerte Simulationsmaschinen für Geographische Informationssysteme.*
12. Montgomery T. A. and Durfee E. H. 1990. *Using MICE to Study Intelligent Dynamic Coordination.* Proc. IEEE Conf. on Tools for AI. Nov. 1990
13. Minar N.,Burkhart R.,Langton C., Askenazi M. 1996, *The Swarm Simulation System, A Toolkit for Building Multi-Agent Simulations* Report
14. Nagel K. 1995. *High-Speed Microsimulations of Traffic Flow.* PhD thesis. Universität Köln.
15. Oechslein, C. 2004. *A Process Model with Integrated Specification- and Implementation Language for Multi-Agent Simulation.* PhD Thesis. University of Wüburg. Institute for Computer Science.
16. Parker D. C., Manson S. M., Janssen M. A., Hoffmann M. J. and Deadman P. 2001. *Multi-Agent Systems for the Simulation of Land-Use and Land-Cover Change: A Review.* CIPEC Working Paper CW-01-05. Bloomington: Center for the Study of Institutions, Population, and Environmental Change, Indiana University.
17. M. T. Parker, 2001, *What is Ascape and Why Should You Care?.* Journal of Artificial Societies and Social Simulation vol. 4, no. 1.
18. Torrens P. 2001. *SprawlSim: Modeling Sprawling Urban Growth using Automata-Based Models.* Proceedings of a Special Workshop on Land-Use/Land-Cover Change, Irvine, California
19. Bayerische Vermessungsverwaltung. URL: *http://www.geodaten-bayern.de* (01.01.2004).

Spark – A Generic Simulator
for Physical Multi-agent Simulations

Oliver Obst and Markus Rollmann

Universität Koblenz-Landau, AI Research Group, D-56070 Koblenz
{fruit,rollmark}@uni-koblenz.de

Abstract. In this paper we describe a new multi-agent simulation system, called Spark, for physical agents in three-dimensional environments. Our goal in creating Spark was to provide a great amount of flexibility for creating new types of agents and simulations. To achieve this, we implemented a flexible application framework and exhausted the idea of replaceable components in the resulting system. In comparison to specialized simulators, users can effortlessly create new simulations by using a scene description language. Spark is a powerful and flexible tool to state different multi-agent research questions. It is used as official simulator for the first three-dimensional RoboCup Simulation League competition. We present the concepts we used to achieve the flexibility in our system and show how we seamlessly integrated the different subsystems into one user-friendly framework.

1   Introduction

Simulated environments are a commonly used method for researching artificial intelligence methods in physical multi-agent systems. Simulations are especially useful for two different types of problems: (1) to experiment with different sensors, actuators or morphologies of agents and (2) to study team behavior with a set of given agents. Additionally, the connection between both types of problems is an interesting research problem.

To address each of these problem types without simulators, the actual hardware would have been to be built and set up in several experiments. Doing so with a number of real robots is often an expensive and also a difficult task because of the amount of parameters generally involved. For many approaches, like for instance in machine learning, experiments have to be repeated a great number of times.

In this paper we describe a multi-agent simulation system, called Spark, for physical agents in three-dimensional environments. Spark is a generic tool for creating simulations that can be used to address all of the above mentioned problem types. It was our goal to provide a great amount of flexibility, so that for somebody creating new simulations it is possible to choose how much attention should be paid to each of these problems. We show how we achieved this flexibility by exhausting the idea of replaceable components in the underlying framework.

G. Lindemann et al. (Eds.): MATES 2004, LNAI 3187, pp. 243–257, 2004.

For simulation designers, this flexibility comes together with a user-friendly way to create simulations by using a scene description language and pluggable components. For users of the system creating agents for a given simulation it is interesting that they do not need to know internals of the system because agents are decoupled from the simulator. To achieve reliable and reproducible results, we built Spark integrating prior work in both physical and multi-agent simulation.

2   Related Work

A large number of simulators has been developed in both multi-agent and robotics research. From the multi-agent perspective, the primary interest is usually to study team behavior. In this domain, RoboCup Simulation League [12] is a prominent benchmark. One of the landmark goals for RoboCup is that by mid-21st century, a team of fully autonomous humanoid robot soccer players shall win against the champion of the most recent World Cup. In Soccer Simulation League competitions, two teams of 11 autonomous agents, represented as circles, compete in a two dimensional, discrete-time simulation. From the first official RoboCup competition[1] up to now the simulator [11] has continuously been enhanced. However, its limitation to a two dimensional world remained. In order to accomplish the vision of the RoboCup Initiative, it is absolutely necessary to move the simulation into a three-dimensional world (cited from [8]). Beyond this, a physical multi-agent simulator can be useful for example to research the interdependency between single agent abilities and team behavior, for instance when a group of robots has to move in areas with obstacles which can be avoided or removed cooperatively. A sample application would be a rescue scenario where different robots collect information about the status of collapsed buildings.

On the RoboCup 2003 Symposium, we proposed a new approach to a three-dimensional physically realistic soccer simulator [9]. This system was a prototype of the simulator we describe in this paper and not specially designed to simulate only soccer competitions, but a universal system for simulation of physical agents. However, the specific features for reproducible and distributed simulations, simple construction of articulated bodies and the scene description language we describe here were missing.

Despite this, in a road map discussion for Soccer Simulation League on RoboCup 2003, a huge majority of participants voted for adding the three-dimensional simulation to the competitions; this year a simulation built on top of Spark was used for the first three-dimensional RoboCup Simulation League competition. In contrast to the two-dimensional simulation, our implemented three-dimensional simulation possesses a higher complexity with respect to the possible team behavior while it maintains a good degree of abstraction with respect to the possible agent actions and sensations.

---

[1] The first Robot World Cup Soccer Games and Conferences were held in conjunction with the International Joint Conference on Artificial Intelligence (IJCAI) in 1997.

An entire different tool to study the behavior of a large number of agents in two- or three-dimensional continuous virtual worlds is XRaptor [2]. For XRaptor, an agent is either a point, a circular area or a spherical volume. A detailed physical simulation is not supported by XRaptor, though in principle possible. The agent processes are not entirely decoupled from the simulation loop, unlike in Spark. Consequently, XRaptor is primarily useful for reactive agent types.

For roboticists, the primary purpose of a simulation system is often to set up reproducible experiments and provide prototyping environments for mobile robots. Some of the existing simulators are tailored to specific robots platforms, most however address a number of robot types. The simulators below fall more or less into this category.

Webots [4] is a commercially available mobile robotics simulation software that is intended as a rapid prototyping environment for modeling, programming and simulating mobile robots. It includes robot libraries that allow the direct transfer of control programs to existing mobile robots platforms. Like Spark, it uses the ODE library for accurate physics simulation. It comes with tools for visualization and for editing properties of objects in the world. The focus of Webots is the accurate modeling of existing robot platforms. This affects the level of abstraction of the provided sensors and effectors. These are low level in order to match their real life counterparts. In this type of simulation a major part of the robot's job is the classification of sensor data for self-localization and obstacle avoidance. In comparison the focus of Spark is more towards general principles of multi-agent research as for example coordination or learning in multi-agent systems.

Übersim [1] is a simulator specifically designed as a robot development tool for the RoboCup small-size soccer league. It uses a fixed level of abstraction to model the perception and action interfaces for the simulated robots. It provides a set of predefined robot models and can be parameterized only at compile time. Like Spark, Übersim is an Open Source project and uses the ODE physics library.

M-ROSE [3] is a 2D simulator used for the rapid development of robot controllers. It features a three step approach for learning a desired controller behavior. First the individual motion profile of a robot is learned using a neural net. The learned profile is then the basis for a simulator specialized for this robot type, in which the controller learning tasks are performed. The trained controller is then transfered to the real robot to validate its performance. This simulator is specialized for the development of controllers for robots with realistic sensor inputs. The approach is quite different to ours in that it lacks features like for instance a full physical collision detection.

The ultimate simulation system addresses all of these questions, and in fact this at least the direction Spark is aiming for. Admittedly, it does so from the multi-agent side of the spectrum, because with RoboCup Soccer Simulation League as one implemented application this is where its origin lies. With our underlying physics system and the way sensors and effectors are realized, simulations built with Spark are not constrained to high-level abstractions of multi-agent systems.

The remainder of this paper is organized as follows: The following section describes the application framework we created as base for the whole simulation system. In Sect. 4, we explain the functionality and integration of the core simulator engine. Section 5 shows how we integrated the underlying physics engine and provided a user-friendly way to access it by introducing the idea of connecting different simulation primitives via path expressions through a scene graph. Section 6 gives some details of the way network support has been added to the simulator, while Sect. 7 introduces a scene description language for setting up different kinds of simulations. Finally, Sect. 8 concludes the paper.

3   The Zeitgeist Application Framework

One of the first implementation steps was to create a flexible application framework, called Zeitgeist. Zeitgeist was invented[2] as application framework for the simulator, but has also been used successfully to create other applications such as software agents and monitors for the simulation. The flexibility of Zeitgeist was one of the the key reasons why it was possible to refactor and build upon the prototype implementation instead of starting from scratch again. A variant of the reflective factory design pattern can be identified as key element for the flexibility of Zeitgeist. The reflective factory pattern was extended with methods supporting an object hierarchy of both created objects and factories in the same tree. We describe this pattern in the subsequent paragraphs. To our knowledge, a description of this element as design pattern cannot be found elsewhere, even though it is very likely that this pattern also occurs in other applications. We believe that it is also useful for other applications which have to provide a system of exchangeable and scriptable components.

3.1   Reflective Factory Pattern

The reflective factory pattern [7] is also known as the Class Object pattern. It allows the factory based instantiation of objects at runtime, given the class name as a string. Products of the factory, i.e. instantiated classes, maintain references to the factory that created them.

The property that each instantiated object has the knowledge which factory created it distinguishes the reflective factory pattern from the abstract factory pattern [5]. It enables every object to access meta data stored in the associated class object at runtime. Zeitgeist exploits this to store class names and information about supported interfaces in the class objects, allowing for queries about the class type and supported interfaces at runtime. By using this information we made all objects in the simulator accessible to a scripting language. The availability of this kind of meta data is native to object oriented programming languages, such as Objective C, Smalltalk or Ruby, but not to C++. We have chosen C++ as primary implementation language and adding this information

---

[2] Original implementation by Marco Kögler, see also [9].

"by hand" anyway, because it provided the most freedom in integrating external libraries. For instance the agent middleware system we are using (SPADES, see also below) offers only a C++ interface.

3.2   Reflective Factory with Object Hierarchy

In combination with the reflective factory pattern, Zeitgeist organizes factories and objects created by factories in a tree like structure, comparable to a virtual file system. To this end, each object stores its node name along with references to its parent and its child nodes. Based on these means we have a flexible mechanism to locate and reference objects at runtime: Given a path expression, similar to that used in a UNIX like file system, Zeitgeist is able to retrieve the corresponding object instance.

The object hierarchy is useful for implementation of a concept called pathname space mapping. Pathname space mapping appeared already in the QNX operating system and has been used to realize the QNX resource manager concept [13]. Resources are addressed by a path through the hierarchy given as string. The managed resources here are Spark services, called *servers* in our terminology. Servers are simply objects installed somewhere in the object hierarchy; they expose their functionality at locations which are known to applications. Applications can get services at runtime by querying the known location.

Zeitgeist itself relies on the combination of the reflective factory in conjunction with the object hierarchy for the following reason: The factories themselves are installed at determined locations in the hierarchy. This can be used to create objects of classes that are unknown at compile time of the simulation system. This feature is useful because additional functionality can be added to the system with no recompilation of the whole system, but just by adding plugins. From these custom classes realized as plugins, it is possible to get instances via configuration scripts and install the instances as servers again. Zeitgeist makes further use of the pathname space mapping concept when the implementation of services is delegated to helper classes. In the object hierarchy, these helper classes are installed immediately below the server node. This leaves the server object as a lean mediator to several exchangeable sub-services with one common interface.

An example application is the file server in Spark, a service that provides access to various mounted file systems. File systems are realized by objects implementing the file system interface used to access different file stores, like the standard file hierarchy of the operating system or like a file archive contained in a zip file. The file server implementation provides a single interface to transparently access different file system objects. During simulator run time, it is possible to create the file server and required file systems by using the file server factory and file system factories. The created file server is linked into the object hierarchy at a known location and the created file systems are installed directly below the file server. The great flexibility of the Spark system stems from the fact that all services have been implemented in this fashion. Adding this kind of flexibility does not add much overhead to the system: the lookup of the objects in our framework usually happens during initialization time and is cached by ordinary pointers.

4   Core Simulator

For an entire simulation, the simulator, agents, and monitors to watch simulations are all different processes that have to work together. The core of our simulator is the part of the system that contains the run loop and does the event management. It cares for the timing, and controls the communication between the simulator and external processes.

4.1   Run Loop

The core part of the system is realized in the same spirit as other services described in the previous section. Thus even the run loop of the simulator is replaceable. We realized two different kinds of run loops, which users of the Spark simulation system can choose for their simulations: a straightforward implementation that realizes agent actions in the order in which they arrive at the simulator, and an implementation that cares for maximum reproducibility of distributed simulations. With the straightforward implementation, simulations and agents can be realized easily. The other implementation was implemented using SPADES [14], a middleware system for agent-based distributed simulations. This system provides an abstraction that allows world model and agent designers to ignore machine load on different machines, networking issues and reasoning about distributed event realization.

4.2   System Overview

Both run loops described above rely on the same set of generic simulator services. These services comprise agent and simulation management, monitor management and the physics system.

The agent management, implemented as part of the so called game control server, is responsible to construct and maintain the internal agent representation. We call the internal representation of an agent in the simulator an agent proxy, as it carries out actions and collects sensor data on behalf of a connected remote agent. Agent proxies are a part of the internal scene graph. A designated agent root node, called *agent aspect* identifies a sub tree of the scene as an agent. The physical and visual representation of an agent however is not further differentiated from other objects in the simulation.

Agent proxies possess sensor and actuator nodes that reflect the capabilities of the represented agent type. On receipt of action messages from a connected agent the game control server parses it into a fixed internal representation, that resembles a nested list of parameterized predicates. The server dispatches the messages parts to the different agent actuators, that then act on behalf of the agent on the simulated world. Simulated sensors are implemented in a analogous way. The agent management periodically queries the perceptor nodes of the managed agent proxies to collect sensor data in the fixed internal representation. From this data the game control server generates sensor data for the remote agent in a the sensor data format of the particular agent.

The second responsibility of the game control server is the game management, that is the implementation of rules in a simulation, called *game control aspects* in our terminology. They implement aspects of a simulation that do not immediately follow from the physical simulation of the environment. Examples are performance measures of participating agents, like their score count in the soccer simulation. Game control aspects are implemented as a set of plugin that are registered to the game control server. The runloop triggers the update of the control aspects after each simulation step. Control aspects have complete control over simulation as they can access the scene graph. The game control server provides additional services to locate and access agent aspect nodes in the simulation. Further, the monitor management is realized in the same spirit as the control aspects as a replaceable plugin. It delegates all of its tasks to a plugin that is installed below the monitor server node. This allows for the easy customization of the monitor protocol in the same spirit as the parser plugin of the game control server described above.

4.3   SPADES-Based Simulations

SPADES operates on simulation events that are sequentially realized. Agents simply receive sensations and send actions. For a simulation designer, two kinds of latencies are of interest: firstly, the latency inherent in the communication between agents and simulator, and secondly the modeled latency (dead time) of real sensors and effectors. SPADES is able to address both kinds of latencies. It hides away the network latency using simulation time stamps, so that this kind of latency is non-existent from the agents point of view. It further allows for explicitly modeling the dead times of sensors and effectors, addressing the second kind of latency.

The system models agents as computational entities that receive sensation events from the simulation and return actions to be executed after some computation. Apart from the requirement that an agent can read and write to UNIX pipes, its internal architecture is not constrained in any way. In particular it is not required that agents are written in a special programming language or linked against a specific library. Agents are not executed as part of the simulator loop. This means that actions of agents do not have to be synchronized with the simulator. Therefore no single joint operation of agent and simulator is required at any particular time.

4.4   System Structure

SPADES is one of the possible instantiations of the simulator run loop. From the SPADES point of view, a simulation is structured into several groups of components: These are a simulation engine, a world model, one or more communication servers, agents participating in the simulation and possibly some connected monitors. The simulation engine contains the main run loop of the SPADES system. It implements the event system and coordinates all network communication with connected monitors and communication servers. A communication server must be run on each machine on which agents run. It connects via TCP to the simulation engine and manages the communication with agents on the host machine through a Unix pipe as well as tracking their CPU usage to calculate their thinking latency.

The world model holds the state of the simulated world and advances it up to the time of the next event as requested by the simulation engine and is further responsible to realize events. The most common source of an event is an act event in order to carry out an agent action. Finally, the world model generates sensations that are sent to participating agents. These events carry perception data about the current state of the world.

4.5   Event Processing

In the interaction with the world model, SPADES advances the world model several time quanta until the next pending event. In the interaction with the agents, SPADES is a discrete event simulator, following its model of agents. After a sensation is sent to an agent, the corresponding communication server tracks the machine time used until it receives a **done thinking** message. The total amount of machine time used in the think cycle is then translated into simulation time. By correlating the consumed machine time with the corresponding simulation time SPADES assures that the simulation is reproducible and unaffected by network delays or load variations among machines hosting the agents.

SPADES exploits concurrency by overlapping of events. It guarantees however that the order of event realization will not violate causality. That means no causally related events are realized out of order, for example like a sensation and a subsequent act event of an agent. In many cases however, the sense, think and act components can be overlapping in time.

4.6   Spades Integration

In order to build a simulation, SPADES expects an implementation of a world model and custom event realizations for sense and act events. Both, the simulation engine and the custom world model become part of the same process.

In this way the Spark simulator implements the SPADES world model interface. We attached great importance to the separation between SPADES specific code and other Spark components so that SPADES can be replaced by other simulation engines easily. Currently the user can choose between SPADES, providing reproducibility with high accuracy and a custom simulation server focusing on raw speed. Here, we drop the reproducibility SPADES provides with the remaining concepts being similar. We implemented this engine because we think that it will be useful in application domains where a large number of agent configurations and control parameters have to be evaluated, as for example in genetic evolution or machine learning.

5   Physical Simulation

Another equally important part is the physical simulation of the system. Instead of implementing an own physics subsystem, we integrated ODE [15], the Open Dynamics Engine. ODE is a free, high quality library for simulating articulated rigid body dynamics.

5.1   Basic Concepts

Rigid bodies are the basic entity of the physical simulation. They have several constant properties like mass, their center of mass and mass distribution. Other properties change over time. These are their position and orientation in space and further linear and angular velocity.

Without any external influences a rigid body keeps its properties unchanged, resulting in a monotonous movement over time. ODE provides forces and torques as the two basic concepts used to act on rigid bodies. These two concepts model all interesting properties one expects from a physical simulation.

A good example for properties that are modeled using forces are shape and extent of a simulated object. These are not direct properties of rigid bodies and are irrelevant to their simulation unless two objects collide. In this case they should influence each other, which can be accurately described in terms of forces and torques that are applied on the two colliding bodies. ODE models shapes of a simulated objects with a so called collider. It represents a geometric object whose only purpose is to detect intersections with other colliders. A collider does usually not model the exact shape of the associated visible object but a computationally less expensive shape. ODE supports boxes, spheres, capped cylinders and planes as collision primitives. Technically it is also possible to detect collisions with arbitrary shapes and extents. Though not yet supported by Spark, we are currently about to implement this.

5.2   Articulated Bodies and Joints

When a collision is detected it must be resolved. The correct forces that prevent the objects to interpenetrate must be applied to the bodies. This is done with the help of contact joints that are generated in response to a detected collision. Joints are used to actively enforce a relationship between two connected bodies. Supported joint types of ODE are ball and socket joint, hinge joint, two-hinge joint, slider joint and universal joint. These joints constrain the relative movement of the two connected bodies along one or more axes. Additionally joints can act as motors by enforcing the movement along the non-restricted axes. A set of bodies that are connected with joints form an articulated structure, used to simulate vehicles or legged creatures.

5.3   Agents as Objects in the Simulation

Agent programs are external processes for the simulator. The representation of the agents properties inside the simulator is almost equal to the representation of all other objects in the simulation. There are bodies (i.e. mass and a mass distribution) for the physical simulation, colliders to implement the shape of objects to handle collisions with other objects, ODE joints to connect single bodies and colliders to compound objects. Additionally, agents possess perceptors and effectors. Perceptors provide sensory input to the agent program associated with the representation of the agent in the simulator, and the agent program uses the effectors to act in its environment. Other objects in the simulation and the physics of the system can affect the situation of agents; this is reflected in the respective aspects by changing the positions or velocities. The way agent programs get their input is described in Sect. 6.

5.4   Enhanced Usability of ODE Concepts

ODE is a library with a plain C interface. Spark provides easy object oriented access to all ODE concepts, implemented on top of the Zeitgeist framework. All ODE concepts, rigid bodies, colliders and joints, are encapsulated by C++ objects. Instances of these objects are installed into the scene graph. Specific groupings of objects express their responsibility for each other. This enables the objects to automatically care for the proper interaction. This concept is more natural for an object-oriented framework and hides the handle-based ODE interface. In Spark, all created objects are stored in a tree of objects. By accessing well-defined locations of objects, it is possible to exchange different implementations of components with equal interfaces easily. The objects that are used to describe a scene are located below the scene server node, and are referred to as scene graph. In the scene graph, objects maintain a relative position to their parent node. This feature is useful to arrange groups of objects.

To relate arbitrary objects in the scene graph, for example to install joints between bodies, we use path expressions in the scene graph. This dramatically simplifies the construction of articulated bodies in comparison to the original handle-based ODE approach. As these expressions are relative to the joint node, they further support the reuse of construction scripts and scene description languages that build upon them, as we show in one of the next sections.

Spark also uses an object-oriented approach to handle the collisions occurring in a simulation. These are handled by collision handler classes grouped to colliders of simulated objects in a similar fashion as we implemented the native ODE concepts. This allows simulation dependent reactions when two objects collide. Examples are playing a sound if a body touches the ground or triggering special simulation events. The latter approach is used in the RoboCup soccer simulation to detect if a goal is scored: this is the case if the ball collides with the goal box collider of the opposite team.

The default reaction to a collision however is to resolve it. As described above, contact joints are used to prevent the bodies from interpenetrating each other.

A contact joint takes several parameters that describe the contact surface: The resulting friction, if and how the two bodies slide along the contact surface and the "bouncyness" are some example parameters. Spark associates a surface description with each collider holding these parameters. When two objects collide, a resulting contact surface description is automatically calculated and applied by a contact joint handler.

6   Network Support

Spark supports both the separation of the simulation core from the connected monitoring applications and from agents participating remotely in the simulation. The network implementation focuses on modularity and reusability and a strict separation of protocol layers.

Each monitor protocol implementation is contained within a single class that implements the monitor interface. It is responsible to generate updates for and parse commands from a connected monitor. The monitor update protocol implementation itself does not know about further network details, for instance which transport and which meta protocol is used. The meta protocol is responsible to classify and assemble the different message fragments received via the transport protocol. Conversely it is also responsible to prepare messages to be dispatched over the network. One possible meta protocol is to treat messages as strings that are prefixed with their type and length.

A similar concept applies to the communication with agent processes. An independent meta protocol identifies messages received from an agent. A parser plugin is then responsible to convert these messages into an internal fixed representation. This is a nested list of named predicates, each with an arbitrary number of typed parameters. The parser plugin we currently use supports an external language based on S-expressions [10]. All perceptor and effector plugins within the simulator that act on belhalf of an agent only work on the internal representation. This effectively separates their implementation from varying protocol details between the simulator and connected agents and allows them to be reused with different agent types. The external protocol is not constrained by the simulator. By simply exchanging the parser plugin, it is possible to switch for instance to an XML-based language. This parser can be implemented without regard to any other network detail. For custom simulations however, this should generally not be necessary as S-expressions can be used to encode arbitrary (also binary) data. For a diagram on the data flow between agents and simulator, we refer to Fig. 1.

7   Scene Description Language

Spark provides access to the managed scene graph in several ways. Besides the internal C++ interface and external access via script language, an extensible mechanism for scene description languages is implemented. This allows for both a procedural and a description-based scene setup.

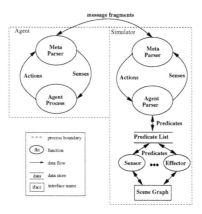

message fragments

Fig. 1. Data flow between agents and simulator

A scene is imported using one of any number of registered scene importer plugins, each supporting a different scene description language. Currently one S-expression-based importer is implemented. The language we implemented as reference language, called *RubySceneGraph*, maps the scene graph structure to the nesting of Lisp-like expressions. A node in the scene graph is described with the (`node <ClassName>`) expression. The importer relies on the Zeitgeist class factory services to create an object of the requested type. A node expression can further be parameterized with function calls in order to access properties of a scene node. A function call expressed as S-expression is realized using the script function exported from corresponding the C++ class.

An example of the two concepts combined is the setup of a transform node. These node types are used to position and orient nodes along a path in the scene graph relative to their respective parent node. The transform node therefore provides a method `SetLocalPos` to set the offset to the parent node.

```
(RubySceneGraph 0 1)
((node Transform (setName myTransform)
      (setLocalPos 10 20 5)
      (node Box (setExtents 1 1 1))))
```

Listing 1. A minimal RubySceneGraph example

Listing 1 starts with the RubySceneGraph header giving the version number. It then creates a single transform node `myTransform`, and sets its offset relative to the parent node. This node is not explicitly given in the above example. In the hierarchy below the transform node a box node is constructed. This is a node that simply renders a box with the extents in the subsequent `setExtents` function call.

A second more elaborate example demonstrates two additional concepts available in this language. It allows the definition of scene graph templates, that take parameters to construct a set of similar scenes. The demo graph in Listing 1 is not complete as it omits two additional aspects of the box that are needed for it to take part in the physical simulation. These are a collider and an associated rigid body. All three properties are usually aligned to each other, concerning their extents and assigned mass. This repetitive task can be expressed using a template, as shown in Listing 2.

```
(RubySceneGraph 0 1)
((template $lenX $lenY $lenZ $density $material)
 (node Box (setExtents $lenX $lenY $lenZ)
           (setMaterial $material))
 (node Body (setName boxBody)
            (setBox $density $lenX $lenY $lenZ))
 (node BoxCollider (setBoxLengths $lenX $lenY $lenZ)))
```

Listing 2. A RubySceneGraph template

The language further allows the reuse of scene graph parts, that are not necessarily templates, in a macro like fashion. This enables the construction of a repository of predefined partial scenes, or complete agent descriptions. The macro concept is not part of the language itself but implemented as a script function called `importScene`. It delegates its task to the generic scene graph importer, from where scenes are imported with one of the registered plugins. This allows the nesting of scene graph parts expressed in different graph description languages. An example application of this feature is that parts of a scene could be created by application programs to create 3D models. By now, we do not exploit this feature yet.

```
(RubySceneGraph 0 1)
((node Transform ; create the char chassis
       (setName chassis)
       (setLocalPos 0 0 0.5)
       (importScene box.rsg 1 3 0.8 10 matRed)
       (node Transform (setLocalPos 0 1.3 0.55)
             (node Box (setMaterial matBlue)
                       (setExtents 1 0.1 0.3)))))
 (node Transform   ; install the left back tire
       (setName leftBack)
       (setLocalPos -0.5 -1.5 0)
       (importScene sphere.rsg 0.4 2 matWhite)
       (node Transform (setLocalRotation 0 180 0)
             (node Hinge2Joint ; install the joint
                   (attach ../../sphereBody ../../../chassis/
                       boxBody)
                   (setAnchor 0 0 0)
                   (setMaxMotorForce 1 4000) ; enable joint
                       motor
                   (node Hinge2Perceptor)
                   (node Hinge2Effector)))))
 ; [...]
```

Listing 3. Buggy Construction Example (partial)

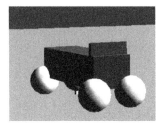

Fig. 2. Constructed buggy from Listing 3

Listing 3 is a partial example constructing a simple buggy that consists of a box connected to four spheres as its wheels. Each tire is connected to the buggy chassis using a two-hinge joint. This joint type behaves like two hinges connected in series. The framework facilitates the straight forward installation of joints, as two connected bodies are referenced with path expressions relative to the joint node. The joint anchor is given in coordinates relative to the joint. The resulting buggy can be seen in Fig. 2. The buggy is further equipped with a motor that controls the left front wheel, together with a perceptor that reads back the current orientation of the wheel. Connecting this buggy scene to a controlling agent process using Spark gives a good example for the construction of agents featuring articulated bodies.

8   Results and Conclusions

In this paper we introduced Spark, a generic three-dimensional physical simulation system. Spark is built as an extensible set of plugins on top of Zeitgeist, an application framework that brings features of scripting languages to C++. As fundamental concept in Zeitgeist, we identified reflective factories used together with an object hierarchy as implementation pattern, which we believe to be useful for creating other applications as well. Spark features a scene graph language and network support, delivering a simulator that is ready for usage in research and education. Spark can be used to address problems of both multi-agent researchers like team behavior as well as research questions like the influence of changes in the morphology of single agents.

However, even if simulations can facilitate experiments in many cases, they are abstractions of other systems and usually cannot totally replace an implementation on the target system [6]. Consequently, a goal of simulation is not specialized solutions but the identification of general principles [2]. For this, creating reproducible experiments is of great value, which is supported through the integration of the SPADES middleware into Spark. An alternative simulation engine focuses on speed, giving up the exact reproducibility. Both engines come with full network support. Our system already shows its real world applicability as the official simulator of RoboCup Simulation League 2004. Because we are using simple types of agents in this first competition, interesting questions will be if approaches previously successful in two-dimensional soccer are still applicable despite the higher complexity of the environment.

We also started some work in developing wheeled and legged robot models so that we hope to be able to introduce a legged simulation league to RoboCup. The necessary primitives to do this are already implemented in our framework. In the current 3D soccer simulation, the agents' sensor data describe the complete object type and position of sensed objects. To address problems other than team behavior alone it is however possible to implement a realistic distance sensor or a camera. For future work we hope to be able to support description languages of other, more specialized simulators. There is already some interest from people doing research using real robots.

References

1. Brett Browning and Erick Tryzelaar. Übersim: a multi-robot simulator for robot soccer. In *Proceedings of AAMAS 2003*, pages 948–949, 2003.
2. Günter Bruns, Daniel Polani, and Thomas Uthmann. Eine virtuelle kontinuierliche Welt als Testbett für KI-Modelle. *Künstliche Intelligenz*, (1):60–62, 2001.
3. Sebastian Buck, Michael Beetz, and Thorsten Schmitt. M-ROSE: A multi robot simulation environment for learning cooperative behavior. In H. Asama, T. Arai, T. Fukuda, and T. Hasegawa, editors, *Distributed Autonomous Robotic Systems 5*. Springer, 2002.
4. Cyberbotics Ltd. *Webots User Guide*, April 2004.
5. Erich Gamma, Richard Helm, Ralph Johnson, and John Vlissides. *Design Patterns - Elements of Reusable Object-Oriented Software*. Addison-Wesley, 1995.
6. Erann Gat. On the role of simulation in the study of autonomous mobile robots. In *Proceedings of the AAAI 1995 Spring Symposium*, pages 112–115, 1995.
7. Chris Hargrove. Reflective factory.
   http://www.gamedev.net/reference/articles/article1415.asp,
   December 2000.
8. Hiroaki Kitano and Minoru Asada. RoboCup humanoid challenge: That's one small step for a robot, one giant leap for mankind. In *Proceedings of IEEE/RSJ International Conference on Intelligent Robots and Systems*, pages 419–424, 1998.
9. Marco Kögler and Oliver Obst. Simulation league: The next generation. In D. Polani, A. Bonarini, B. Browning, and K. Yoshida, editors, *RoboCup 2003: Robot Soccer World Cup VII*, Lecture Notes in Artificial Intelligence. Springer, Berlin, Heidelberg, New York, 2004. To appear.
10. John McCarthy. Recursive functions of symbolic expressions and their computation by machine, Part I. *Communications of the ACM*, 3(4):184–195, April 1960.
11. Itsuki Noda. Soccer Server: A simulator of RoboCup. In *Proceedings of AI symposium '95*, pages 29–34. Japanese Society for Artificial Intelligence, 1995.
12. Itsuki Noda, Hitoschi Matsubara, Kazuo Hiraki, and Ian Frank. Soccer Server: a tool for research on multi-agent systems. volume 12, pages 233–250, 1998.
13. QNX Software Systems Ltd. *QNX Neutrino Realtime Operating System: System Architecture*, 2003.
14. Patrick Riley and George Riley. SPADES — a distributed agent simulation environment with software-in-the-loop execution. In S. Chick, P. J. Sánchez, D. Ferrin, and D. J. Morrice, editors, *Winter Simulation Conference*, volume 1, pages 817–825, 2003.
15. Russell Smith. *Open Dynamics Engine (ODE) User Guide*, May 2004.

Simulating Agents' Mobility and Inaccessibility with $\mathcal{A}$-GLOBE Multi-agent System

David Šišlák, Michal Pěchouček, Milan Rollo, Martin Rehák, and Jan Tožička

Department of Cybernetics
Czech Technical University in Prague
Technická 2, Prague 6, 166 27 Czech Republic
sislakd@feld.cvut.cz
pechoucek@labe.felk.cvut.cz

Abstract. People use multi-agent systems for three kinds of activities – (i) integration (ii) simulation (iii) complex problem solving. In this contribution we describe architecture of a newly developed multi-agent platform that supports real world simulation, with particular emphasis to all kinds of mobility and communication inaccessibility. $\mathcal{A}$-GLOBE performance benchmarks compared against other agent platforms are also stated in this paper.

1 Introduction

The reason why people use multi-agent systems for modelling and simulation (in contrary to classical mathematical and symbolic modelling techniques) is easy and natural transition from the modelling process into the real distributed operation. For distributed operation (e.g. control, diagnostics, planning, ...) can be deployed the same set of agents that are used in the modelling phase. Industrial partners often require substantial testing and experimental verification of the advanced AI systems before they are ready for industrial deployment. Agent technology is an ideal concept for this.

At present several Java-based multi-agent platforms from different developers are available, but none of them fully supports agent mobility and communication inaccessibility. They are thus no suitable for experiments with real-world simulation. In this paper we describe architecture of newly developed agent platform $\mathcal{A}$-GLOBE. It is fast and lightweight platform with agent mobility support. Beside the functions common to most of agent platforms it provides Geographical Information System service to user, so it can be used for experiments with environment simulation and communication inaccessibility. $\mathcal{A}$-GLOBE performance benchmarks compared against other agent platforms are also stated in this paper.

$\mathcal{A}$-GLOBE is an agent platform designed for testing experimental scenarios featuring agents' position and `communication inaccessibility, but it can be also used without these extended functionalities [1]. The platform provides functions for the permanent and mobile agents, such as communication infrastructure, store, directory services, migration function, service deployment, etc.

G. Lindemann et al. (Eds.): MATES 2004, LNAI 3187, pp. 258–272, 2004.

Comparing to the classical agent platforms and development environment, $\mathcal{A}$-GLOBE is lightweight and is optimized in order to consume just a limited amount of resources. Communication in $\mathcal{A}$-GLOBE is very fast. Comparison with the others agent platforms can be found in Section 3. The price we have to pay for this is the fact that $\mathcal{A}$-GLOBE platform is not fully compliant with the FIPA [2] specifications. This is why it does not support communication between different agent platforms (e.g. with JADE, JACK, FIPA-OS, etc). Technically, it is not a very difficult problem and custom tailored interoperability can be implemented upon request. Once we are ready to sacrifice interoperability we can significantly improve ease of communication, stability of the system and overall lightweightness. For large scale scenarios the problems with system performance (memory requirements, communication speed) that interoperability brings are not negligible. Interoperability is also unnecessary when developing closed systems, where no communication outside these systems is required (e.g. agent-based simulations).

$\mathcal{A}$-GLOBE is suitable for real-world simulations including both static (e.g. towns, ports, etc.) and mobile units (e.g. vehicles). In such case the platform can be started in extended version with Geographical Information System (GIS) services and Environment Simulator (ES) agent. The ES agent simulates dynamics (physical location, movement in time and others parameters) of each unit. In Section 4 we present two different simulation scenarios where the $\mathcal{A}$-GLOBE system has been deployed.

2   System Architecture

The system integrates one or more agent platforms. The $\mathcal{A}$-GLOBE design is shown in Figure 1. Its operation is based on several components:

- **agent platform**[1] – provides basic components for running one or more agent containers, i.e. container manager and library manager (section 2.1);
- **agent container** – skeleton entity of $\mathcal{A}$-GLOBE, ensures basic functions, communication infrastructure and storage for agents (section 2.2);
- **services** – provide some common functions for all agents in one container;
- **environment simulator (ES) agent** – simulates real-world environment and controls visibility among other agent containers (section 2.4);
- **agents** – represent basic functional entities in specific simulation scenario.

Simulation scenario is defined by a set of actors represented by agents residing in the agent containers. All agent containers are connected together to one system by the GIS services. Beside the simulation of dynamics the ES agent can also control communication accessibility among all agent containers. The GIS service applies accessibility restrictions in the message transport layer of the agent container.

---

[1] We shall distinguish between the agent development (or integration) platform such as JADE and the agent platform used in this context. The agent platform here is a highest level component of the system architecture and resides on one Java Virtual Machine (JVM). Communication between these platform is obviously possible.

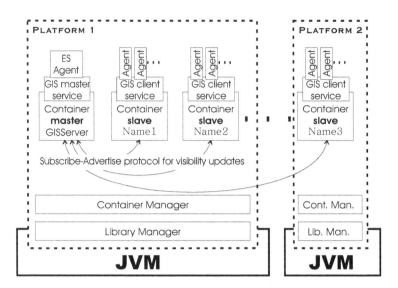

Fig. 1. System Architecture Structure

2.1   Agent Platform

The main design goals were to develop the platform as lightweight as possible and to make it easily portable to different operating systems and devices (like PDA). The platform is implemented as an application running on Java Virtual Machine (JVM version 1.4 or higher is required). Several platforms can run simultaneously (maximum 1000) on one computer, each in its own JVM instance. When new agent container is started, it can be specified in which platform it will be created and running.

The platform ensures the functionality of the rest of the system using two main components:

- **Container Manager.** In one agent platform can run one or more agent containers. Container Manager takes care of starting, execution and finishing these containers. Containers are mutually independent except for the shared library manager. Usage of one agent platform for all containers running on one computer machine is beneficial because it rapidly decreases system resources requirements (use of single JVM), e.g. memory, processor time, etc.
- **Library Manager.** The Library Manager takes care of the libraries installed in the platform and monitors which agents/services use which library. Descriptor of each agent and service specifies which libraries the agent/service requires. The Library Manager is also responsible for moving libraries of any agent migrating to other platform when required libraries are not available there. Whenever an agent migrates or agent/service is deployed, Library Manager checks which libraries are missing on the platform and obtains them from the source platform. The inter-platform functionality of the Library Manager is realized though the service `library/loader` (this service

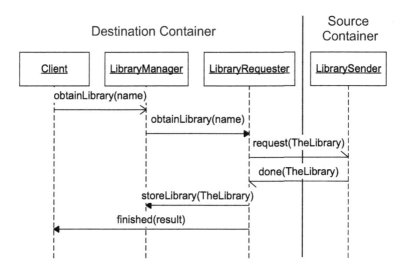

Fig. 2. Library Deployment Sequence Diagram

is present on every agent container). Library deployment sequence diagram is shown in Figure 2. The user can add, remove and inspect libraries using the container GUI.

2.2 Agent Container

The agent container hosts two types of entities that are able to send and receive messages: agents and services. Agents do not run as a stand-alone applications, but are executed inside the agent containers, each in its own separate thread. Container provides the agents and services with several low level functions (message transport, agent management, service management). Most of the higher level container functionality (agent deployment, migration, directory facilitator, etc.) is provided as standard container services.

The agent container components are:

- **Container Core.** The Container Core starts and shuts down all container components.
- **Store.** The purpose of *Store* is to provide permanent storage through interface which shields its users from the operating system filesystem. It is used by all container components, agents and services. Each entity in the agent container (agent, service, container components) is assigned its own virtual storage, which is unaffected by the others. Whenever an agent migrates, its store content is compressed and sent to the new location.
- **Message Transport.** The Message Transport is responsible for sending and receiving messages from and to the container.
- **Agent Manager.** The Agent Manager takes care of creation, execution and removal of agents on the container. It creates agents, re-creates them

after platform restart, routes the incoming messages to the agents, packs the agents for migration and removes agent's traces when it migrates out of the platform or dies.

– **Service Manager.** The Service Manager takes care of starting and stopping the services present in the agent container and their interfacing to other container components. The user can start, stop and inspect the services using GUI. There are two types of services – user services and system services. The system services are automatically started by the container and form a part of the container infrastructure (agent mover, library deployer, directory services etc.). The system services cannot be removed. The user services can be started by user or any agent/service. The user services can be either permanent (started during every container startup) or temporary (started and stopped by some agent).

The *container name* must be unique inside one system build from several containers. This name is also used for determination specific store subdirectory for the agent container and registered to the *Environment Simulator Agent*.

Message Transport: The message transport is responsible for sending and receiving messages. Shared TCP/IP connection for message sending is created between every two platforms when the first message is exchanged between them. The message flow inside the platform is shown on figure 3.

The message structure respects FIPA-ACL [2]. Messages are encoded either in XML or Byte64 format. Message content can be in XML format or String. The structure of each message content in XML format is described by Document

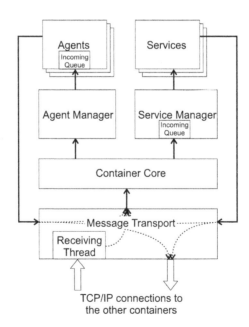

Fig. 3. Message Flow

Type Definition (DTD). For coding and decoding XML messages the Java APIs for XML Binding (JAXB) [3] package is used. For transport, all binary data (e.g. libraries, serialized agents, etc.) are encoded using the open source Base64 coding and decoding routines. Agent may receive messages without using conversation discrimination (all messages incoming to this agent are processed in one method), otherwise it must use **conversation manager** with tasks.

Conversation Manager and Tasks: Usually, an agents deals with multiple jobs simultaneously. To simplify a development of such agents, the $\mathcal{A}$-GLOBE offers *tasks*. A task is able to send and receive messages and to interact with other tasks. The Conversation Manager takes care of every message received by the agent to be routed to the proper task. The decision, to which `Task` a message should be routed, depends on the massage `ConversationID`. The `ConversationID` should be viewed as a 'reference number'.

Agents: The agents are autonomous entities with unique name and ability to migrate. There is a separate thread created for each agent. A wrapper running in the thread executes the agent body. Whenever an agent enters an error state or agent body exits, the control is passed back to the wrapper, which handles the situation. The return value of the agent state is used to determine agent's termination type (die, migrate, suspend). Therefore potential agent failures are not propagated to the rest of the agent container. Agents could be deployed on remote containers.

Services: The services are bound to particular container by their identifier. There could be the same service on several containers. Services do not have their own dedicated thread and are expected to behave reactively on response to incoming messages and function calls. Services can be deployed to remote container. The agents (and services or container components) have two ways how to communicate with a service. Either via normal messages or by using the *service shell*. The service shell is a special proxy object that interfaces service functions to a client.

The advantage of service shell is an easy agent migration (for migration description see section 2.3): while the service itself is not serializable, the service shell is. When an agent migrates, the shell serializes itself with information what service name it was connected to. When the agent moves to the new location, the shell reconnects to its service at the new location. When a service is shut down, it notifies it's shells so that they refuse subsequent service calls. There are several common services such as remote command execution, searching agents/services directories, service deployment, etc. These services are automatically started by the agent container and provide common functions for all agents.

Agent Name: The agent name is globally unique and is normally generated by platform during agent creation. The service name is unique only within one agent container (services cannot migrate) and is specified by the service creator. An address has the following syntax:

```
aglobe://platform_ip:port/[agent|service]/name.
```

2.3   Migration Procedure

In order to successfully migrate, the agent has to support serialization. The migration sequence is shown in Figure 4.

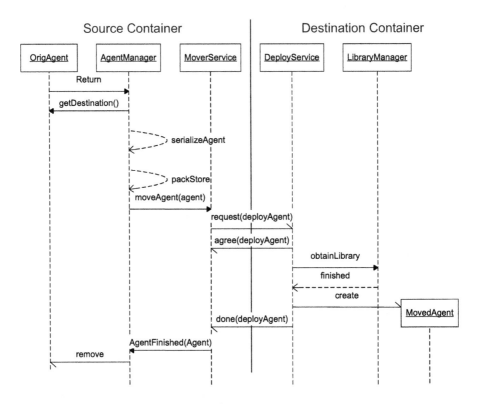

Fig. 4. Agent Migration

All exceptions that might occur during the process are properly handled and the communication is secured by timeouts. If the migration cannot be finished for any reason, the agent is re-created in its original container.

If the **done** message is successfully sent by the agent destination container but never received by the source container, two copies of the agent emerge. If the **done** message is received by the source container, but the agent creation fails at the destination container, the agent is lost. These events can never be fully eliminated due to the possible communication inaccessibility, but maximum caution was given to minimize their probability.

2.4   Environment Simulator

The purpose of ES is to simulate the real world environment. More specifically the ES models the platform mutual accessibility and informs each container about other platforms inside its communication range. Besides visibility, the ES can inform the containers about any other parameters (eg. position, temperature, ...). The ES consists of two parts:

- **ES Agent**, which generates the information and
- **GIS services** that are present at every platform connected in the scenario.

Presence of the ES agent allows the container freely communicate with all other containers. The ES agent architecture allows simulation of complicated container motion and environment dynamics. There are two ES agents implemented:

- Manual (Matrix) ES Agent This agent provides simple user-checkable visibility matrix. The user simply checks which containers can communicate together and which can not.
- Automatic ES Agent This agent is fully automatic environment simulator. It moves mobile agent containers representing mobile units in virtual world and automatically controls accessibility between them. The visibility is controlled by means of simulation of the short range wireless link. Therefore each container can communicate only with containers located inside predefined radius limit. As the containers move, connections are dynamically established and lost.

GIS services distribute visibility information to all container message transport layers. There are two types of GIS services - one for server side and one for client side, as presented in Figure 1.

Server side is container where ES Agent and `gis/master` service are running. On the client side `gis/client` service is running. After the container startup, the service subscribes with the `gis/master` to receive the environmental updates (visibility, etc) and this information is than accessible to any container component (agent or service) interested in it. This client services are connected to the message transport layer and control message sending (when agent tries to send message to agent whose container is not visible, this message is returned as undeliverable). If no ES Agent is started, all platforms are connected without any restrictions.

2.5   Sniffer Agent

The Sniffer Agent is an on-line tool for monitoring all messages and their transmission status (delivered or not-reachable target). This tool helps to find and resolve communication problems in system during development phase.

The sniffer can be started only on an agent container where GIS/*master* service is running. After the sniffer starts, all messages between agents and services inside any container or among two agent containers are monitored. Messages can be filtered by the sender or receiver of the message. All messages matching the user-defined criteria are shown in the sniffer gui. The message transmission status is emphasized by type of line. The color of the message corresponds to the message performative.

Table 1. Message delivery time results for selected agent platforms

JAVA-based Agent Development Toolkits/Platforms - Benchmark Results					
April 2004, Rockwell Automation in Prague					
PIII, 600MHz, 256MB	Message sending - average roundtrip time (RTT)				
Agent Platform	agents: 1 pair messages: 1.000 x ⇆		agents: 10 pairs messages: 100 x ⇆		agents: 100 pairs messages: 10 x ⇆
	serial [ms]	parallel [s]	serial [ms]	parallel [s]	serial [ms]	parallel [s]
JADE v3.1	0,8	0,36	7,5	0,19	76,3	0,49
JADE v3.1 1 host, 2 JVM, RMI	10,3	4,92	111,9	6,35	1 190,5	7,14
JADE v3.1 2 hosts, RMI	5,79	3,30	68,8	3,71	770,3	2,48
FIPA-OS v2.1.0	28,6	14,30	607,1	30,52	2 533,9	19,50
FIPA-OS v2.1.0 1 host, 2 JVM, RMI	20,3	39,51	205,2	12,50	x	x
FIPA-OS v2.1.0 2 hosts, RMI	12,2	5,14	96,2	5,36	x	x
ZEUS v1.04	101,0	50,67	224,8	13,28	x	x
ZEUS v1.04 1 host, 2 JVM, ?	101,7	51,80	227,9	x	x	x
ZEUS v1.04 2 hosts, TCP/IP	101,1	50,35	107,6	8,75	x	x
JACK v3.51	2,1	1,33	21,7	1,60	221,9	1,60
JACK v3.51 1 host, 2 JVM, UDP	3,7	2,64	31,4	3,65	185,2	2,24
JACK v3.51 2 hosts, UDP	2,5	1,46	17,6	1,28	165,0	1,28
A-Globe v1.0	0,3	0,10	2,8	0,04	28,4	0,09
A-Globe v1.0 1 host, 2 JVM, TCP/IP	2,4	0,33	24,6	0,88	242,7	0,98
A-Globe v1.0 2 hosts, TCP/IP	2,2	0,33	13,9	0,31	96,5	0,44

3   Platform Comparison

This section presents the results of comparison of available JAVA-based agent development frameworks evaluated by an independent expert Pavel Vrba from Rockwell Automation Research Center in Prague [4], which were carried out in a cooperation with the Gerstner Laboratory.

These benchmarks were focused especially on the platform performance which is a crucial property in many applications. Detailed description of the particular features is beyond the scope of this paper. Firstly, the particular benchmark criteria, which the agent platform should provide are identified (e.g. small memory footprint and message sending speed). These benchmarks were carried out for following agent platforms[2] - JADE [5] [6], FIPA-OS [7], ZEUS [8], JACK [9] and A-GLOBE [10].

3.1   Message Speed Benchmarks

The agent platform runtime, carrying out interactions, should be fast enough to ensure reasonable message delivery times. The selected platforms have been put

---

[2] GRASSHOPPER's licence does not allow to use it for benchmarking and other comparison activities.

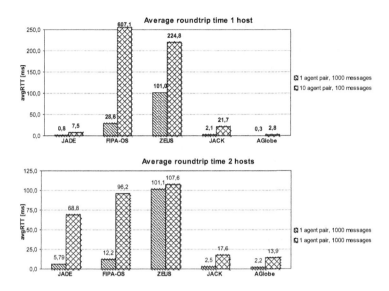

Fig. 5. Message delivery time - serial test results

through a series of tests where the message delivery times have been observed under different conditions.

In each test, so called *average roundtrip time* (avgRTT) is measured. This is the time period needed for a pair of agents (let say A and B) to send a message from A to B and get reply from B to A. The roundtrip time is computed by the agent A when a reply from B is received as a difference between the receive time and the send time. This message exchange was repeated several times (depending on the type of experiment) and the results were computed as an average from all the trials.

The overall benchmark results are presented in the table 1. More transparent representation of these results in the form of bar charts is depicted in Figure 5. Three different numbers of agent pairs have been considered: 1 agent pair (A-B) with 1000 messages exchanged, 10 agent pairs with 100 messages exchanged within each pair and 100 agent pairs with 10 messages per pair. Moreover, for each of these configurations two different ways of executing the tests are applied.

In the *serial* test, the A agent from each pair sends one message to its B counterpart and when a reply is received, the roundtrip time for this trial is computed. It is repeated in the same manner N-times (N is 1000/100/10 according to number of agents). The *parallel* test differs in such a way that the A agent from each pair sends all N messages to B at once and then waits until all N replies from B are received.

Different protocols used by agent platforms for the inter-platform communication are mentioned: Java RMI (Remote Method Invocation) for JADE and FIPA-OS, TCP/IP for ZEUS and $\mathcal{A}$-GLOBE and UDP for JACK. Some of the tests, especially in the case of 100 agents, were not successfully completed mainly because of communication errors or errors connected with the creation of agents. These cases are marked by a special symbol.

3.2   Memory Requirements Benchmark

This issue is mainly interesting for running thousands of agents on the one computer at the same time. Approximate memory requirements per agent can be seen in Figure 6.

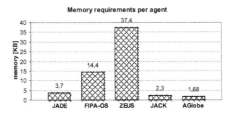

Fig. 6. Approximate memory requirements per agent

4   Simulation

The functionality and usefulness of the $\mathcal{A}$-GLOBE approach to agent modelling and simulation has been tested on two different scenarios, that we will describe briefly below:

4.1   NAIMT – Underwater Mines Detection

Features of the $\mathcal{A}$-GLOBE platform were verified on the simulation of identification/removal of mines situated in given area using a group of autonomous robots. This simulation was developed within the Naval Automation and Information Management Technology (NAIMT) project. This software simulation of real-life hardware robots was required to enable scalability experiments and efficient development and verification of embedded decision making algorithms.

The goal of the group of robots is to search the whole area, detect and remove all mines located there. To allow mine removal a video transmission path must be established between the base (operated by human crew that gives the robot a permission to remove the mine) and the robot who has found the mine. Typically, relying via the other robots is necessary, because the video transmission range is limited (e.g. wi-fi connection or acoustic modems in underwater environment). Figure 7 shows an example of robots transmitting a video to base. In this scenario two types of communication accessibility are included:

- **High bandwidth** accessibility, necessary for video transmissions, is limited.
- **Signaling** accessibility, used for coordination messages and position information, is currently assumed to be perfect.

All robots in the simulation are autonomous and cooperative. Their dedicated components (coordinators) negotiate in peer-to-peer manner when preparing the

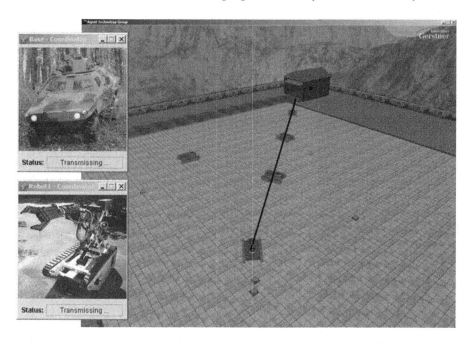

Fig. 7. Relayed communication (link between the robot and base through 3 relays)

transmission path. $\mathcal{A}$-GLOBE ES agent and GIS services are utilized during this phase to inform the robot about others within its video transmission range.

Each robot consists of several components, implemented as $\mathcal{A}$-GLOBE agents running within one agent container:

- **Robot Pod** simulator, computing robot moves and updating its position with GIS server via GIS service.
- **Mine Detector** simulator, providing the decision making components with information about found mines.
- **Video** data acquisition and transmission element. This subsystem creates the data feed form the source provided by the simulation and prepares transmission path by remotely spawning one-use transmission agents along the path. Video is then transmitted as a stream of binary encoded messages.
- **Robot Coordinator** implementing search algorithm, transmission coalition establishment and negotiation.

Next step within the NAIMT project would be integration of this $\mathcal{A}$-GLOBE simulator with the KAoS policy and domain services [11]. This system (developed at Institute for Human and Machine Cognition [12]) provides an organizational structure to an agent community which facilitates policy management of agent actions. It structures the groups of agents into domains (e.g. dynamic task-oriented teams like in this case). KAoS policy services than allow specification, management, conflict resolution and disclosure of policies within these domains.

The goal is especially the automatic conflict resolution (e.g. the potential deadlock problem solving when several robots find mine simultaneously). In current version the human crew in base station decides about resolution of all conflict situations, which could be heavily time consuming in complex scenarios.

4.2   Ad-Hoc Networks – Distribution of Humanitarian Aid

The second scenario has been motivated by another real-life situations and was developed within InX (Inaccessibility in Multi-Agent System) project supported by EOARD – European Office for Airspace Research and Development. Let us assume that several delivery vehicles are operating in an area without available communication infrastructure (e.g. land lines, cellular phone infrastructure, etc.). In the scenario we have three kinds of actors:

- **ports** – areas where the humanitarian aid is located and distributed from
- **villages** – locations in where the humanitarian aid is required
- **trucks** – autonomous vehicles that dispatch the humanitarian aid upon request from the ports to the villages

These are represented in the 𝒜-GLOBE system by *containers*, each located on one of physically distributed platforms. Communication between the platforms is possible, while within a limited range. Communication is reliable (with no lags or dropouts) and complete (at all times) among the agents residing on one agent container, while communication across the agent containers is implemented by means of the short range radio links (for example IEEE802.11 [6]). Therefore each agent container can communicate only with containers located within its radio range.

Specific experiment scenario is shown in Figure 8. There are five villages, six ports and six trucks. Positions of villages and ports in the agents' world are chosen in such a way that no village can directly communicate with any port. They can communicate only by sending information over trucks. A truck can communicate with villages, ports and other trucks only if they are within the reach of the simulated radio link. There is at least one truck going from each village where some resource is needed to some port where this resource is distributed from. In other words there is no need for some middle storehouse to transfer the commodities through, but under special occasions the resource can be delivered into target village through others villages or ports.

Three specific sets of experiments have been carried out:

- agents that are planning the port-to-village humanitarian aid provision reside each on one truck and they collect requests when at the village and then travel to port for supplies
- on each of the vehicles we have a **relay agent** that broadcasts the request for aid to all 'visible' agents in hope to be forwarded to the right recipient (once the right couple of trucks will meet)

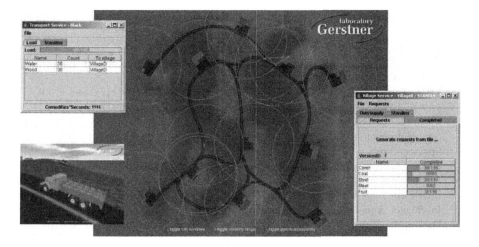

Fig. 8. Humanitarian Relief Scenario

– introducing the community **stand-in** agents that represent and act on behalf of the village; the stand-in agents swarm in the environment so that soon a stand-in agent from each of the village is located at each vehicle and each port. Non-trivial techniques of knowledge synchronization have been put in place.

5 Conclusion

$\mathcal{A}$-GLOBE agent platform supports communication inaccessibility, agent migration and deployment on remote containers. These features make $\mathcal{A}$-GLOBE well suited platform for simulation and implementation of physically distributed agent systems with applications ranging from mobile robotics to environmental surveillance by sensor networks. $\mathcal{A}$-GLOBE was designed as stream line lightweight platform which will operate on classical (PC) as well as mobile devices (PDA).

As can be seen, $\mathcal{A}$-GLOBE has the best results in all message sending speed benchmarks (table 1) from all selected agent platforms. In comparison with its main competitors, JADE and FIPA-OS, the $\mathcal{A}$-GLOBE is at least two times faster than JADE and six times faster than FIPA-OS. $\mathcal{A}$-GLOBE has not any communication errors. Also in memory benchmark (Figure 6) $\mathcal{A}$-GLOBE has one of the smallest memory requirement per agent.

Acknowledgement

Authors wish to express acknowledgement to Rockwell Automation Research Center in Prague for mutually beneficial cooperation in the platform evaluation process. $\mathcal{A}$-GLOBE agent platform was developed within the project "Inaccessibility in Multi-Agent Systems" (contract no.: FA8655-02-M-4057). The NAIMT deployment has been supported in part by ONR project no.: N00014-03-1-0292.

References

1. Pěchouček, M., Mařík, V., Šišlák, D., Rehák, M., Lažanský, J., Tožička, J.: Inaccessibility in multi-agent systems. final report to Air Force Research Laboratory AFRL/EORD research contract (FA8655-02-M-4057) (2004)
2. FIPA: Foundation for intelligent physical agents. http://www.fipa.org (2004)
3. JAXB: JAVA API for XML Binding. http://java.sun.com/xml/jaxb (2004)
4. Vrba, P.: Java-based agent platform evaluation. In Mařík, McFarlane, Valckenaers, eds.: Holonic and Multi-Agent Systems for Manufacturing. Number 2744 in LNAI, Springer-Verlag, Heidelberg (2003) 47–58
5. JADE: Java Agent Development Framework. http://jade.tilab.com (2004)
6. Bellifemine, F., Rimassa, G., Poggi, A.: Jade - a fipa-compliant agent framework. In: Proceedings of 4th International Conference on the Practical Applications of Intelligent Agents and Multi-Agent Technology, London (1999)
7. Poslad, S., Buckle, P., Hadingham, R.: The fipa-os agent platform: Open source for open standards. In: Proceedings of 5th International Conference on the Practical Applications of Intelligent Agents and Multi-Agent Technology, Manchaster (2000) 355–368
8. Nwana, H., Ndumu, D., Lee, L., Collis, J.: Zeus: A tool-kit for building distributed multi-agent systems. Applied Artificial Intelligence Journal **13** (1999) 129–186
9. Fletcher, M.: Designing an integrated holonic scheduler with jack. In: Multi-Agent Systems and Applications II., Manchaster, Springer-Verlag, Berlin (2002)
10. A-Globe: A-Globe Agent Platform. http://agents.felk.cvut.cz/aglobe (2004)
11. Bradshaw, J.M., Uszok, A., Jeffers, R., Suri, N.: Representation and reasoning for daml-based policy and domain services in kaos and nomads. In: Autonomous Agents and Multi-Agent Systems (AAMAS 2003), Melbourne, Australia, New York, NY: ACM Press (2003)
12. IHMC: Institute for Human and Machine Cognition. http://www.ihmc.us (2004)

On the Definition of Meta-models
for Analysis of Large-Scale MAS*

Adriana Giret and Vicente Botti

Departamento de Sistemas Informáticos y Computación
Universidad Politécnica de Valencia, Spain
46020 Valencia, Spain
Phone: +34 96 387 7000
{agiret,vbotti}@dsic.upv.es

Abstract. Multi Agent Systems (MASs) are undergoing a transition
from closed monolithic architectures into open architectures composed
of a huge number of autonomous agents. Large-scale MASs involve hundreds or perhaps thousands of agents to share a common goal. However,
the current practice of MAS design tends to be limited to individual
agents and small face-to-face groups of agents. With this kind of approaches it is very difficult to model large-scale MAS. To cope with this
limitation an Abstract Agent can be used as a modelling artifact for
MAS analysis and design. An Abstract Agent may represent, at modelling stage, groups of agents (MAS, organization, federation, etc.) which
can take on the qualities of being an agent. An Abstract Agent acting
in organizational structures can encapsulate the complexity of group of
agents (simplifying representation and design) and modularize its functionality. In MAS analysis and design there are some models commonly
used to specify MAS. In this work we present extensions to these models
in order to include the Abstract Agent into them.

1   Introduction

A large-scale Multi Agent System (MAS) encompasses multiple types of agents
and may, as well, encompasses multiple MASs, each of them having distinct
agency properties. A large-scale MAS needs to satisfy multiple requirements such
as reliability, security, adaptability, interoperability, scalability, maintainability,
and reusability. But, how can we specify and model the agency properties of a
MAS made up of others MASs?

MAS offers powerful tools to realize complex problem spatialized solving or
simulations systems. Some of these problems present hierarchical and multi-
scale requirements and evolve in structured environments which posses recursive
properties. In the intelligent manufacturing field, the need for some kind of hierarchical aggregation in real world systems has been recognized. These systems

---

* This work is partially supported by research grants TIC2003-07369-C02-01 from
the Spanish Education Department, TIC2001-5108-E from the Spanish Science and
Technology Department and CICYT DPI2002-04434-C04-02.

G. Lindemann et al. (Eds.): MATES 2004, LNAI 3187, pp. 273–286, 2004.

have to remain readable while they are expanded in a wide range of temporal and spatial scales. For example, a modern automobile factory, incorporates hundreds of thousands of individual mechanisms (each of which can be an agent) in hundreds of machines which are grouped in to dozens or more production lines. Engineers can design, build, and operate such complex systems by shifting from the mechanism, to the machine or to the production line (depending on the problem at hand) and by recognizing the agents of higher levels as aggregations of lower-level agents. Also, in e-commerce applications, an enterprize is a legal entity which is independent of the individual people whose are its employees and directors.

In the agent-specialized literature, we have found very little work about approaches which allow us to model large-scale MAS made up in turn of MASs. Parunak and Odell, in [1], proposed UML conventions and AUML extensions to support nested agents' groups. Wagner, in [2], models an institutional agent which is made up of agents themselves. In [3], Occello proposes a recursive approach to build hybrid Multi Agent Systems. However, the current practice of MAS design tends to be limited to individual agents and small face-to-face groups of agents. With this kind of approaches it is very difficult to model large-scale MAS which encompasses multiple types of agents and may, as well, encompasses multiple MASs, each of them having distinct agency properties.

We believe that an Abstract Agent [4] can be used as a modelling artifact for analysis and design of large-scale MAS. To this end we are working on the definition of a methodology for large and complex MAS using Abstract Agents as the major conceptual entity. Our methodology is an extension of the INGENIAS methodology [5, 6]. In this work we present the extended INGENIAS' meta-models we have defined. This is a continuation of the work we have presented in [7].

The paper is structured in the following way. Section 2, introduces the Abstract Agent notion. Section 3, outlines the intended methodology we are working on. Section 4, presents the extended meta-models. Finally, in Section 5, we draw some conclusions and future works.

2   Abstract Agent

An extremely useful feature in terms of reduction of complexity for the designer of a MAS is that an overall task can be broken down into a variety of specific sub-tasks, each of which can be solved by a specific agentified problem solver. Divide and conquer is a widely accepted problem solving paradigm of computer science. We are working on the definition of a MAS methodology which will provide to the designer modelling artifacts and guidelines to apply divide and conquer paradigm to the analysis of large-scale MASs.

In our approach the major modelling entity is the Abstract Agent. We have proposed an Abstract Agent in [4] as a notational entity for representing groups of agents that work together to fulfil some goal. That is, groups of agents which can take on the qualities of being an agent. An Abstract Agent has agency properties, it is autonomous, reactive and pro-active [8].

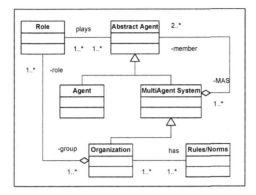

Fig. 1. Abstract Agent

Figure 1 illustrates the essential structure of an Abstract Agent. An Abstract Agent can be seen as a MAS, an organization, a federation or an institution with the added value that it can also be a composition of all this abstraction models. An Abstract Agent will exist only at modelling stages, in the end (at coding stages) it will be replaced possibly by a group of agents or also by a single agent. Our definition extends the traditional notion of MAS when indicating that a MAS is made up of MASs. This will allow us to build large-scale systems in which the building blocks are interacting MASs that work together to reach one or several goals.

An Abstract Agent acting in organizational structures can encapsulate the complexity of subsystems (simplifying representation and design) and modularize its functionality (providing the basis for integration of pre-existing Multi Agent Systems and incremental development). The Abstract Agent notion facilitates the modelling of organization of organizations (as well as, Multi Agent Systems of Multi Agent Systems).

An Abstract Agent is specially tailored for: specification of interaction between groups of agents, integration of pre-existing Multi Agent Systems and modelling of Holonic Manufacturing Systems [9], among others.

3 Methodology

Our approach tries to reduce the complexity of large-scale MAS, dividing the domain problem in simpler sub-problems and considering every sub-problem as an Abstract Agent. Every such Abstract Agent can in turn be decomposed in simpler interacting Abstract Agents. Until we reach an abstraction level in which there is no more subdivision, that is all the constituent members of the MAS are agents. We can think of the methodology as a MAS-driven methodology.

The MAS is specified dividing it in more concrete aspects that form different *views* of the system. This idea already appears in the work of Kendall [10], MAS-CommonKADS [11], and later in GAIA [12, 13]. The way in which the views are defined is inspired by INGENIAS methodology [5,6]. In our work, as in INGENIAS, there are five views (see Section 4): the agent model, the organization model, the task-goal model, the interaction model and the environment model. The definition of the behaviour of the MAS is carried out following the work presented in [4].

The software development process guided by this methodology will be a recursive, incremental and concurrent MAS driven process, see Figure 2. It will have as many iterations as Abstract Agents (constituent MASs) are identified. The result of each iteration will be a MAS made up of interacting Abstract Agents (MASs) or agents. In each new iteration there will be as many concurrent processes as non-defined Abstract Agents of the previous iteration (because in each iteration we can end up with some Abstract Agents which are already defined, for example pre-existing MASs). Each iteration will be a recursive, incremental and concurrent process.

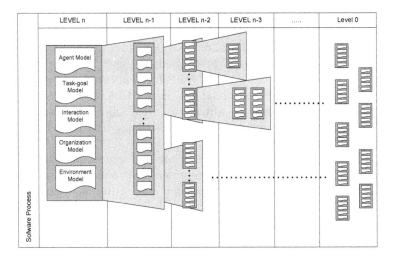

Fig. 2. Software Development Process

Every iteration will be conducted in the following way. In the analysis phase, organization models will be produced to sketch how the MAS looks like. In this step, we can identify potential constituent Abstract Agents (that is, group of agents with close interaction, with an identified functionality or goal, in which every member interacts to solve some problem, and with self-regulating rules of actions) or pre-existing constituent MASs. The models obtained in this phase will be refined later to identify common goals and relevant tasks to be performed by each Abstract Agent (task-goal model and environmental model). More details will be added specifying Abstract Agent interactions with interactions models and environmental models, and, as a consequence, refining Abstract Agents's mental state with agent models. For each emerged MAS a new process is started, until we reach a step in which there are no more non specified MASs.

To outline the idea behind our approach we present a simple example of the domain of mobile physical cooperating robots. Let's suppose a postal service system in which the robots are the postmen. Mail can arrive at any moment, each piece of mail has an addressee and a priority (normal, urgent, etc.). The team of postmen has to determine a good way to deliver the mail on a building floor according to the priority, the addressee, the team members, their current positions, their skills and environment obstacles (a closed door, a barrier in their path, etc.).

We can model this domain as a traditional MAS made up of agents which are robots that have to cooperate to fulfill a given MAS goal. However, current robot architectures are very complex. In such an architecture, a robot is made up of multiple processing units, each of which is an autonomous entity. Therefore, we have to model each robot as a system made up of cooperating agents. In a first step we can model each robot as an Abstract Agent and the postal service system as a Multi Agent System.

First iteration. The problem is to study the PostMen Team. Let's suppose we have three robots: *Robot-1*, *Robot-2* and *Robot-3* and the role *PostMan* which is played by the three robots. The goal of each PostMan is *To cooperate, if possible, with other PostMen to deliver mail in a good way*. The environment of the Robots are defined by the following resources: the *mail*, the *map* of the building floor and *obstacles* in their path. At this level of abstraction the only Abstract Task of the Robots is *Deliver mail*. The robots of the PostMen Team maintain the social relation of *cooperation*.

At this point we are interested in the inner structure of each robot. We can take every robot in isolation and study it as a Multi Agent System.

Second iteration. The problem is to study the group of agents that made up one robot of the PostMen Team. Let's suppose we have the following agents in *Robot-1*: *navigation Agent*, *planner Agent* and *battery saving Agent*. Each of these agent has its owns goals. These goals are combined to achieve the goal of *Robot-1*. The tasks of the *navigation Agent* are: *move, turn, stop, avoid collision* and *set velocity*. The other agents has also their own tasks. All these tasks are combined and sequenced to define the Abstract Task of *Robot-1*.

We can follow this analysis until we reach some point in which every agent identified in the system is indivisible. The conjunction of all the specifications obtained in every abstraction level will model the entire Postal Service System.

4   Meta-models for Modelling Large-Scale MASs

In this section we present the extensions we have made to the meta-models proposed by the INGENIAS methodology [5, 6]. These extensions deal with the addition of the Abstract Agent, the redefinition of some relations to conform with the new modelling entities and the dependencies between them. The meta-models presented in this section are in GOPRR language (Graph, Object, Property, Relationship, and Role) [14]. We have unified the two mayor entities (agent and organization) of INGENIAS into a single mayor entity, Abstract Agent. For space reason we use A-Agent instead of Abstract Agent in the figures. Also, the extensions we have made are marked with gray colors.

4.1   Agent Meta-model

The Agent Model is concerned with the functionality of each Abstract Agent: responsibilities and capabilities (what roles it may play, what goals it is committed to pursue and what task it is able to perform). Figure 3, shows the posible relations between goals and Abstract Agent. It may pursue A-Goals (Abstract Goals) and may play Roles. An A-Goal may be a Group Goal or a Goal (the A-Goal is presented in the Task-Goal Model). The light gray boxes are redefinitions of the relationships WFPursues (from the Organization Model) and GTPursues (from the Task-Goal Model). They are included to constraint these relationships when the participant entity is a single Agent. Since, an Agent can not pursue a goal it is not able to reach. A Role may pursue either a Group Goal or a Goal. An Agent can not play a Role which pursues a Group Goal.

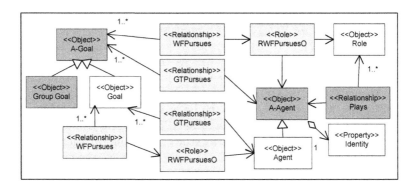

Fig. 3. Goals of an Abstract Agent

Figure 4, shows the relationships between the Abstract Agent and its Mental State, and between the Abstract Agent and the Tasks it is able to perform. We have defined an A-Task (abstract task) which may be a Task (an action which may be performed by a single agent) or a Work Flow (a sequence of actions in which a group of agents is involved). Again, the light gray boxes are redefinitions of relations when the participant entity is an Agent.

In Figure 5, we can see the mental entities an Abstract Agent may have. We have added to the INGENIAS agent model the entities A-Goal, A-Commitment and A-Belief. As with the A-Task all these entities are generalization of its single and group corresponding entities.

When modelling a MAS the designer will specify the functionality of an Abstract Agent in terms of A-Goals, A-Task, A-Commitments and A-Beliefs without worrying whether it is a single agent or a group of interacting agents. In subsequent analysis steps the designer may need to see "inside" the Abstract Agent

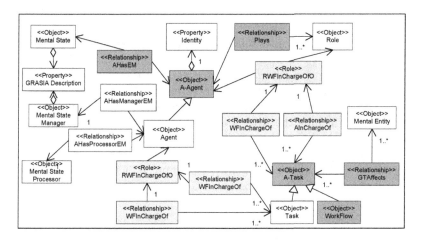

Fig. 4. Mental States and Tasks of an Abstract Agent

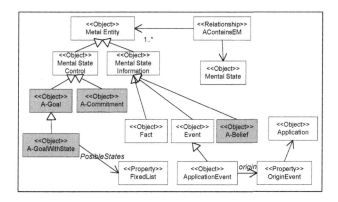

Fig. 5. Mental Entities of an Abstract Agent

to specify its internal structure. It is in this moment when he has to decide if the Abstract Agent is an Agent or an Organization. If he chooses to model it as an Agent, the abstract entities will be changed to single entities. To complete the definition of the agent functionality the designer has to provide a Mental State Processor and a Mental State Manager. On the other hand, if the designer chooses to implement the Abstract Agent as an Organization, the abstract entities will be transformed into its corresponding group entities (Group Goal, Work Flow, Group Beliefs, etc.). To complete the definition of the organization he has to start a new iteration of the methodology. In this iteration the organization will be fully specified developing the five models corresponding to its constituent members.

4.2   Task-Goal Meta-model

The Task-Goal Model describes relationships among goals and tasks, goal structures, and task structures. It is also used to express which are the inputs and outputs of the tasks and what are their effects on the environment or on the Abstract Agent's mental state. We have extended the Task-Goal meta-model of INGENIAS redefining the relationship between task and goals (how a task affects a goal) to include the Abstract Agent which pursues an A-Goal and performs an A-Task. We have adopted the task specification defined in INGENIAS to describe the inputs and outputs of the A-Task. We have extended the goal decomposition and goal dependencies (see Figure 6) with A-Goal, Group Goal and the relationships GTDecomposes and GTDepends for these goals.

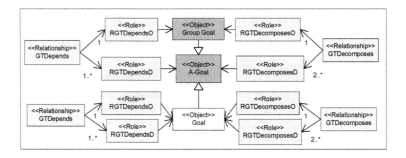

Fig. 6. Goal Decomposition and Dependencies of the Task-Goal Meta-model

4.3   Interaction Meta-model

The Interaction Model describes how interaction among agents and Abstract Agents takes place. Each interaction declaration includes involved actors (Abstract Agent, Role), goals pursued by interaction, and a description of the protocol that follows the interaction. An abstract interaction is an interaction in which at least one of the speakers is an Abstract Agent.

Figure 7 shows the ways an Abstract Agent (and a Role) can participate in an interaction. An Abstract Agent can starts an interaction, IStarts, in order to pursue (GTPursues from the Task-Goal meta-model) some A-Goal. The relationship ICooperates allows an Abstract Agent to participate in an interaction cooperating with other Abstract Agents. The definition of an Abstract Agent as a participating entity in an interaction is of especial value for the analysis of large-scale MAS. With this approach the designer can use interacting entities of different levels of abstraction. Let's suppose a MAS in which there are pre-existing MASs and autonomous entities which have to be developed from scratch. In early analysis fases the designer can abstract away from the internal structures of the participating entities and considers every such entity as an Abstract Agent. He can define interaction scenarios with Abstract Agents, modelling all the necessary details of the particular level of interaction without worrying about lower level details (agent level). The interaction scenarios

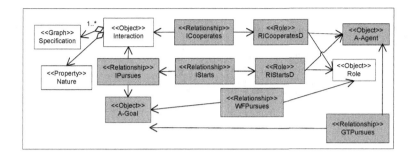

Fig. 7. Interaction Meta-model

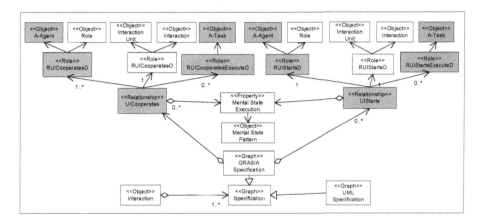

Fig. 8. Interaction Units, Abstract Tasks, Roles and Abstract Agents

obtained are conceptual models of the integration of MASs, organization, federation, etc. Later, on subsequent analysis fases, these interactions can be used as requirement inputs for the specification of more detailed models.

An Interaction Unit (see Figure 8) represents messages or protocols depending on the abstraction level. An Interaction Unit relates who starts it? (UIStarts - an Abstract Agent or a Role), who cooperates? (UICooperates), and what A-Tasks are executed.

In Figure 9 we can see the relationships between an interaction and the organization in which it is executed. These relationships comes from other meta-models and altogether allow the designer to build up the MAS architecture in a consistent way.

4.4 Environment Meta-model

The Environment Model defines agent's and MAS's perception in terms of existing elements of the system. These elements are resources and applications. Figure 10 presents the relationship between A-Tasks, Resources and Applications. From the relationships defined in the Task-Goal Meta-model and the Organiza-

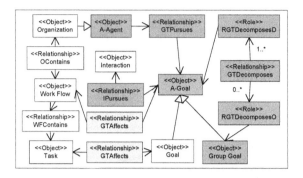

Fig. 9. Relationship between Interaction and Organization

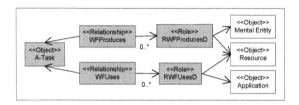

Fig. 10. Environment Meta-model. Abstract Tasks, Resources and Applications

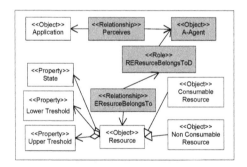

Fig. 11. Environment Meta-model. Resources

tion Meta-model, we have that an A-Task uses resources and applications, and affects Mental Entities.

Figure 11 shows the relationship BelongsTo between Resources an Abstract Agents. This relationship represents the fact that a Resource is used by an Abstract Agent. When the Abstract Agent is an organization it is interpreted that the Resource is owned by a single agent of the organization.

4.5 Organization Meta-model

The Organization Model describes how system components (agents, Abstract Agents, roles, resources, and applications) are grouped together, which are executed in common, which goals they share, and what constraints exists in the interaction among agents and among Abstract Agents. The specification of the relationships among the entities is very simple thanks to the Abstract Agent.

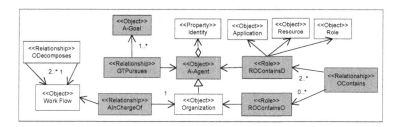

Fig. 12. Organization Structure

Figure 12 illustrates the structural view of an organization. In our approach, there is no need to define a different modeling construct to represent members of an organization which are in turn groups of agents. We can group Abstract Agents (relationship OCantains) to build organizations, no mater how is the internal structure of the Abstract Agent (an organization, a Multi Agent System, or some group of them). Since an Organization is an Abstract Agent it may pursues (GTPursues) A-Goals. Relationship AInChargeOf (from Agent Meta-model) is a redefinition to impose the constraint that an Organization is in charge of a Work Flow not a task. When an Abstract Agent is used to represent an organization it may contain, in addition to other Abstract Agents, Resources, Applications and Roles.

Figure 13 shows that an A-Task may be decomposed in Tasks and/or Work Flows. By inheritance a Work Flow can be decomposed in the same way. But a Task can be only decomposed in Tasks, due to the redefinition of relationship WFDecomposes.

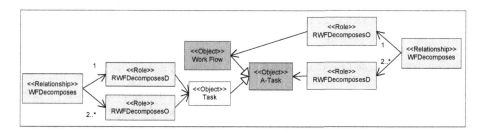

Fig. 13. Abstract Tasks, Tasks and Work Flows

We have extended the social relations defined in INGENIAS redefining the relationship AGORelationship (see Figure 14). With this extensions it is posible to define hierarchies, holarchies [9] and heterarchies. Since, in contrast to INGENIAS, we do not restrict the social relations to entities of the same type.

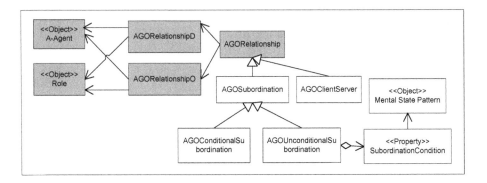

Fig. 14. Social Relationships among Abstract Agents

5   Conclusion

The current practice of MAS design tends to be limited to individual agents and small face-to-face groups of agents. With this kind of approaches it is very difficult to model large-scale MAS which encompasses multiple types of agents and may, as well, encompasses multiple MASs, each of them having distinct agency properties. To cope with this limitation we propose an Abstract Agent to develop large-scale MASs as systems in which their components may be MASs themselves. An Abstract Agent is specially tailored for: specification of interaction between groups of agents, integration of pre-existing Multi Agent Systems and modelling of Holonic Manufacturing Systems [9], among others. An Abstract Agent can be thought of as a virtual entity which may be a single agent, or a set of agents that interacts with other sets of agents. An Abstract Agent acting in organizational structures can encapsulate the complexity of subsystems (simplifying representation and design) and modularize its functionality (providing the basis for integration of pre-existing Multi Agent Systems and incremental development). The Abstract Agent facilitates the modelling of organization of organizations (as well as, Multi Agent Systems of Multi Agent Systems).

In this work we have presented the meta-models we propose for the definition of a methodology for large-scale MASs. These meta-models are extensions to the five models proposed by INGENIAS [5, 6]. These extensions include:

- Unification of the two mayor entities (agent and organization) for Multi Agent System modelling in a single mayor entity - Abstract Agent.
- Abstract entities for: goals, mental entities, mental state, believes, task, etc.
- New relationships between Abstract Agents, abstract entities and the traditional entities.

The Abstract Agent is a very useful modeling artifact for complex Multi Agent Systems. With this structure and the five models presented in this work we can develop very complex systems applying divide and conquer paradigm. The overall task of a MAS can be broken down into a variety of sub-tasks, each of which can be solved by a specific agentified problem solver, an Abstract Agent. No mater if the Abstract Agent is a single agent or another MAS or organization. The idea is as follows. When we begin to analyze a group of agents (MAS) A, abstraction level 1, we identify the Abstract Agents $\{a_1, a_2, ..., a_n\}$ which execute certain functions. These Abstract Agents may encapsulate individual persons, physical, or software entities (agents). They may also be other groups of MAS, say B, so we can have $a_i = B_i$, which we treat as black boxes. We can take this perspective as long as our analysis can ignore the internal structure of the member groups (MAS). For every such 'level' of abstraction we can specify the system with the five models presented in the previous sections. However, subsequent analysis generally needs to 'open' these black boxes and look inside them to see the agent components and their corresponding functions; for example, when analyzing B we have that $B = \{b_1, b_2, ..., b_m\}$, abstraction level 2.

In this paper we have also presented an outline of the methodology we are working on. To complete the definition of this methodology we are working on the formalization of the data flows relations among the five models. We are experimenting with case studies from the academic and industrial field. We are defining guidelines for the development process of the large-scale MAS Methodology.

References

1. Parunak, V.D., Odell, J.: Representing social structures in UML. In Agent-Oriented Software Engineering II, M. Wooldridge, G. Weiss, and P. Ciancarini, eds. Springer Verlag (2002) 1–16
2. Wagner, G.: Agent-oriented analysis and design of organizational information systems. in J. Barzdins and A. Caplinskas (Eds.), Databases and Information Systems. Kluwer Academic Publishers. (2001) 111–124
3. Occello, M.: Towards a recursive generic agent model. In Proceedings of International Conference on Artificial Intelligence (2000)
4. Giret, A., Botti, V.: Towards an abstract recursive agent. Integrated Computer-Aided Engineering. IOSPRESS. ISSN: 1069-2509 **11** (2004) 165–177
5. Gomez, J., Pavon, J.: Meta-modelling in agent oriented software engineering. 8th Ibero-American Conference on AI (Iberamia 2002) : F.J. Garijo, J.C. Riquelme, M. Toro. Advances in Artificial Intelligence, LNAI 2527 (2002) 606–615
6. Pavon, J., Gomez, J.: Agent oriented software engineering with INGENIAS. 3rd International Central and Eastern European Conference on Multi-Agent Systems (CEEMAS 2003) : V. Marik, J. Müller, M. Pechoucek:Multi-Agent Systems and Applications II, LNAI 2691 (2003) 394–403
7. Giret, A., Botti, V.: Towards a recursive agent oriented methodology for large-scale MAS. P. Giorgini, J. Müller, and J. Odell (Eds.), Agent-Oriented Software Engineering IV. Springer Verlag. ISSN: 0302-9743 **LNCS 2935/2003** (2004) 25–35
8. Wooldridge, M., Jennings, N.R.: Intelligent agents - theories, architectures, and languages. Lecture Notes in Artificia Intelligence, Springer-Verlag. ISBN 3-540-58855-8 **890** (1995)
9. HMS, P.R.: HMS Requirements. HMS Server, http://hms.ifw.uni-hannover.de/ (1994)

10. Kendall, E.: Developing agent based systems for enterprise integration. IFIP Working Conference of TC5 Special Interest Group on Architectures for Enterprise Integration (1995)
11. Iglesias, C., Garijo, M., Gonzalez, J., Velasco, J.: Analysis and design of multi agent systems using MAS-CommonKADS. In Singh, M. P., Rao, A., and Wooldridge, M.J. (eds.) Intelligent Agentd IV LNAI, Springer Verlag **1365** (1998)
12. Wooldridge, M., Jennings, N.R., Kinny, D.: The Gaia methodology for agent-oriented analisys and design. Journal of Autonomous Agents and Multi-Agent Systems **15** (2000)
13. Zambonelli, F., Jennings, N.R., Wooldridge, M.: Developing Multiagent Systems: the Gaia Methodology. ACM Transactions on Software Engineering and Methodology (TOSEM).ISSN:1049-331X **12** (2003) 317–370
14. Lyytinen, K.S., Rossi, M.: METAEDIT+ - A Fully Configurable Multi User and Multi Tool CASE and CAME Environment. Springer Verlag LGNS 1080 (1999)

ExPlanTech: Multi-agent Framework for Production Planning, Simulation and Supply Chain Management

Michal Pěchouček[1], Jiří Vokřínek[1], Jiří Hodík[1], Petr Bečvář[2], and Jiří Pospíšil[2]

[1] Gerstner Laboratory, Czech Technical University in Prague
Technická 2, 166 27 – Prague 6, Czech Republic
{pechouc,vokrinek,hodik}@labe.felk.cvut.cz
[2] CertiCon, a.s. Václavská 12, 120 00 – Praha 2, Czech Republic

Abstract. We present a unified multi-agent technology for decision making support in production planning and scheduling, manufacturing simulation in and supply chain management. The technology has been tested on several industrial cases and is used in a daily production planning processes of one important automobile industry supplier in the Czech Republic.

1 Introduction

In the cases of highly flexible production process, the proper production planning can highly increase its effectiveness. On the other hand, the high flexibility makes the production planning and acquisition of relevant data quite complicated.

There is strong demand for universal and flexible tool for the production planning that is able to increase utilization of resources and supports a decision making in a selection of orders. The flexibility of the tool should allow to adapt the system to changes in the production structure, or to allow using the system by another customer. The system should use a universal description for all resources, including product design and development, production, stores and transport. The system has to be able support not only internal production processes, but also integration of external business processes and universal secure access to the data.

We focus the production planning having a need of following elements:

- **Existing software integration** – the already existing software solutions, which can be still exploited, can be integrated into new system.
- **Complex data representation, collection and maintenance** – the production data and its flow are complex process. There is strong demand to collect, store and use existing data in the most suitable way.
- **Extra-enterprise access** – the need of access the production data anytime from anywhere is required.
- **Supply-chain integration** – not only access, but also integration of the outside processes is needed. Linking the suppliers, customers and other collaborators is very crucial problem.
- **Security** – all the parts of the system have to use the appropriate security politics. The factory business data are very important and have to be properly secured.
- **Visualization** – complex data and production processes generates the need of centralized view. This view has to be adjustable to the user and have to be accessible from the place, where the user needs to see the information.

G. Lindemann et al. (Eds.): MATES 2004, LNAI 3187, pp. 287–300, 2004.

- **Emulation and simulation** – not just planning problem is solved in the complex production. The simulation of the processes helps to find better configuration of the production, and recognize and analyze the possible problems.

The needs of the nowadays enterprises cannot be covered by classical solutions anymore. New technologies that deal with all the requests described above have to be adapted. In the next part of the text we present the ExPlanTech multi-agent technology of the production planning.

1.1 Multi-agent Technology

Agent technologies and the concept of multi-agent systems is coming from the field of artificial intelligence and computer science, using principles of component-based software engineering, distributed decision making, parallel and distributed computing, autonomous computing, advanced methods of interoperability and software integration. Operation of an agent-based system is based on interactions of autonomous and loosely coupled software or hardware entities – agents. The computational processes which are characterized by natural decomposition or possible computation distribution can be solved by multi-agent systems very well [4]. Moreover, the multi-agent system offers superb run-time integration capacity and dynamic reconfiguration, and autonomous delegation abilities. They are robust and provide easy integration of humans, existing software and hardware.

Agents technologies are suitable for domains that posses either of the following properties:

- highly complex problems need to be solved or highly complex systems to be controlled,
- the information required for solving problems or controlling systems is distributed and is not available centrally,
- in domains with dynamically changing environment and problem specification, or
- high number of heterogeneous software (and possibly hardware) systems needs to be integrated in an open and heterogeneous way.

There are several typical application areas of the agent technologies that relate to manufacturing [8]. In production we need highly complex planning problems to be solved, we need to control dynamic, unpredictable and unstable processes. In production there is also a potential for agent-based diagnostics, repair, reconfiguration and replanning. In the domain of virtual enterprises [1] and supply chain management there are requirements for forming business alliances, planning long-term/short-term cooperation deals, managing (including reconfiguration and dissolving) supply chains. Here we also can use various agent technologies for agents' private knowledge maintenance, specification of various ontologies and ensuring service interoperability across the supply chain. In the domain of internet-base business agent technologies can be used for intelligent shopping and auctioning [5], information retrieval and searching, remote access to information and remote system control. An important application domain is logistics. Multi-agent systems can be used for managing transportation and material handling, optimal planning and scheduling, especially in cargo transportation, public transport but also peace-keeping missions, military maneuvers, etc. There is a nice match of the agent technologies and managing of the utility networks such as energy distribution networks, mobile operators networks, cable provider networks. Here the concept of distributed autonomous computation can be used for simulation and predication of alarm situations, prevention to black-out and overload and intrusion detection.

2   ExPlanTech Technology

ExPlanTech is a consolidated technological framework that is an outcome from the series of European Union RTD and Trial projects in the area of agent-based production planning [10]. ExPlanTech is a collection of different components, which can be put together in order to develop a custom-tailored system for supporting user's decision making in different aspects of production planning.

From the user perspective the system is supposed to provide the support to the human user when sizing resources and time requirements for a particular order, creating the production plans, optimizing manipulation with material resources, managing and optimizing the supply chain relationships, visualizing and analyzing the manufacturing process in middle and long terms and accessing the data from outside the factory.

ExPlanTech system provides technological support for easy software integration, complex data representation, data-collection, maintenance, extra-enterprise access, supply-chain integration, security handling, visualization and emulation/simulation, while it does not feature at the moment any agents or components for control and real-time diagnostics.

As a result of used multi-agent architecture, each software system based on ExPlanTech concept is component-based, flexible, and reconfigurable and allows distributed computation and flexible data management. Each component has been integrated in an agent wrapper that complies with the FIPA (Foundation for Intelligent Physical Agents) standard for the heterogeneous software agents [3] and can be used in a variety of configuration or independently as a standalone application. System configurations can contain various planning, data-management or visualization agents. An agentification process can be also used for an integration of the software and hardware equipment already existing in the enterprise.

Another advantage of agent-based approach is its ability to process relevant production data, distributed across the entire enterprise. The classical approach when data are collected and processed centrally is difficult especially in situations where the production planning data are voluminous and changes frequently. Agent approach allows to process data proactively at the place of their origin and to exchange only necessary results. The agent-based technology certainly does not provide an uncomplicated solution of NP-hard planning problems. However the concept allows integration of heavy-duty AI problem solver (such as constrain satisfaction systems, linear programming tools, genetic algorithms, etc.)

An agent technology is also suitable paradigm to integrating the manufacturing enterprises into a supply chain. From the planning perspective it is irrelevant whether the system reasons about in house manufacturing workshop or about a subcontracted company.

Production managers are often interested in modeling and simulation of the production process. Experimenting with changes in production lines, and how they affect the manufacturing process as a whole, is not a trivial task but it can be simplified by ExPlanTech build in simulation environment.

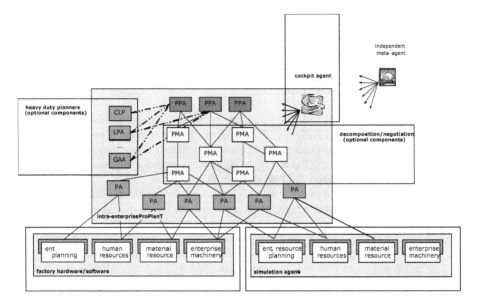

Fig. 1. ExPlanTech Intra-Enterprise Architecture.

2.1 ExPlanTech Architecture

The ExPlanTech framework is build on top of JADE (Java Agent Development Environment) [6,2], the most wide spread agent integration platform that provides full FIPA interoperability [3]. An appropriate ontology for semantic interoperability in manufacturing domain has been developed within the ExPlanTech development. Fig. 1 shows ExPlanTech intra-enterprise architecture and the following part describes the most remarkable agents present in that architecture.

Planning Agent
The core of the any ExPlanTech based system is a community of appropriate planning agents. The planning agent is in charge of making production plans for individual orders, taking care of conflicts and managing re-planning and plan reconfiguration. For different types of production, different planning engines are available or can be developed:

- **Linear planning:** For planning problems with limited computation requirements, caused by limited plan variability, or restrictive external constrains (e.g. predefined priorities or ordering), a backward/forward chaining based planning engine exists.

- **Mathematical programming:** For cases with an explosive variability of possible plan configurations, an existing engine based on the linear programming method can be extremely efficient under specific situations. For other hard problems, constrain-satisfaction or genetic-algorithm based planning engines can be developed. These methods and engines are however very specific and would need to be redeveloped for new planning cases.

– **Distributed planning:** At the same time planning can be implemented collectively by a community of simple planning agents. The plan (especially if multi-criteria optimization needs to employed) would be constructed by be sophisticated auction-based negotiation based on use of the social knowledge and acquaintance models.

Resource Agents
Typically, there are many resource agents running in the system that carry out data gathering and specific data pre-processing and that directly interact with the planning agent. We provide two types of agents for an integration or representation of manufacturing resources. ExPlanTech features (i) agents that integrate/simulate a specific machine, workshop or department (e.g. CNC machine, CAD department) and (ii) agents that integrate a factory software system (e.g. an implemented bridge to MRP system that administers material resources handling in the factory).

Cockpit Agents
There may be several different users interacting with the planning agent at the same time. In order to allow such an access and to control possible conflicts, we have developed a specific agent – a cockpit agent. The cockpit agents presents the user in a user friendly way with the state of production processes, plans, loads of given resources etc. Cockpit agent also provides a possibility to interact with the system, and according to access rights change the plans or resources parameters.

Extra-Enterprise Agent
While Cockpit Agents are intended to be used inside the factory (and inside a security firewalls of the factory), the Extra-Enterprise agents allow an authorized user to access the system from outside using a thin client technology (see Fig. 2). As the environment outside the factory is variable, also the technology for Extra-Enterprise access must be very flexible and platform independent. To satisfy this requirement, an Extra-Enterprise agent has been developed [11], that can, in cooperation with application server, made ExPlanTech system accessible via the WEB browser, PDA device or WAP-enabled phone. Secure connection protocol and a system of user access rights protects the system against an unauthorized access [7].

Enterprise-to-Enterprise Agent
As the Extra-Enterprise agent makes the system accessible for authorized human users outside the factory, the Enterprise-to-enterprise agent makes it accessible for external software systems (see Fig. 2). These external systems can be for example Remote Cockpit Agents that represents thick clients for a remote access. In addition, the Enterprise-to-enterprise Agent (E2E agent) can proactively connect external agents (such as similar E2E agents in another factories or agents of material resources suppliers), exchange data with them and use them for decision support. This technique can help to find possibilities of tasks outsourcing in case of exhausted local resources, can advertise local free capacities to the cooperators or can search for optimal suppliers of material resources.

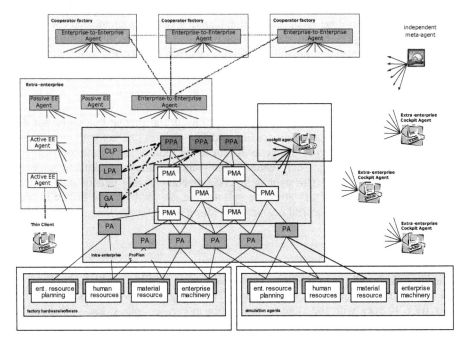

Fig. 2. ExPlanTech Extra-Enterprise Architecture.

Simulation Agent (ExPlanTech Real-Time Planning Simulation)

For the purpose of evaluation of plans by modeling a feedback from a plan realization, it is possible to simulate the behaviour of the real production. The simulation agent represents an interface between the planning system and a community of emulation agents. The emulation agents substitute the real machine or human resources and model their properties such as production times or failure rates. They follow production schedule defined by plans while adhering to the common simulation times and speeds defined by the user. Consequently they provide a feedback to the planning system by means of the simulation agent, announcing the actual time spent on a plan realization to the planner. If the actual time differs from the plan, the planner initiates a re-planning. The agent-based architecture of the simulation offers modularity of the whole model, so it is possible to replace each emulation agent by an agent with another parameters or by a binding to the real resources. On the other hand it is possible to provide the same emulation with another scheduler.

Meta-agent

Meta agent operates differently on different levels of the system operation. Within the intra-enterprise level the meta-agent carries out sophisticated methods of meta-reasoning in order to independently monitor the information flow among the agents and suggest possible operation improvements (e.g. workflow bottlenecks, inefficient or unused components in the production process, carry put long term performance measurements, etc.) On the extra-enterprise level the meta-agent is designed to provide centralized knowledge about communication among selected extra-enterprise agents – companies integrated in the supply chain. Its goal is to ask other agents for their communication logs on regular basis, to store the collected information in its local database and thereby to provide an entry point to a further analysis or visualization in the attached user interface. The meta-agent employs the same security module as ordinary extra-enterprise agents, thus it strictly conforms the same security rules.

2.2 On Implementation

As mentioned above, the ExPlanTech system is implemented using the JADE multi-agent development environment. This decision affects many features of the system and implicates many assets of the ExPlanTech platform. In the following some examples of these assets will be briefly discussed.

The first advantage of the JADE platform mentioned is not directly visible to the end user, although it influences whole the system – JADE development environment is easy to use and allows rapid development of sophisticated and reliable multi agent system. Predefined agent core with already implemented control and message transport protocols frees the author of MAS from low-level programming and resource management. The designer can focus on high level functions and can easily build user targeted application.

The second advantage has also been already mentioned. Any application build on JADE platform complies with FIPA interoperability standards for implementing of independent software agents [3]. This feature facilitates an easy integration of new and third party components to the system as well as use of independent meta-agents for communication evaluation and optimization.

JADE platform and thus whole ExPlanTech system is implemented in JAVA2 language which gives to it a platform independence and openness. Agents can run on different platform (MS Windows, Windows CE, LINUX, even PLC) and cooperate without care of low level platform specific problems. The same implementation of the agent can be used on different platform.

JADE platform contains sophisticated open system for communication support. Agents can use various message content languages to serialize interchanged data. In ExPlanTech system, three different languages are used for different purposes: JADE native SL0 language is used for common intra enterprise communication. XML language is used for extra-enterprise communication, where the human readability is more important and bit efficient BEC language is used for communication with embedded devices, where the amount of transmitted data must be kept low. JADE also uses two models of addressing – intra-platform and inter-platform. When the intra-platform addressing is used, the agent is identified by its unique name and the AMS (Agent Management System) agent is responsible for finding of the receiver on computers, connected to the agent platform. When the inter-platform addressing is used, the agent's identification must contain a valid address in some message transport protocol (IIOP, HTTP, etc.) and AMS agent uses an appropriate protocol to deliver the message to an computer outside the agent platform. In ExPlanTech system, all computers inside one factory are organized as one agent platform and so all intra-enterprise communication uses intra-platform addressing. Extra-enterprise communication uses inter-platform addressing and HTTP protocol.

For an implementation of application server for ExPlanTech thick clients, a Tomcat server developed within Jakarta project of The Apache Software Foundation was used. Tomcat server uses so called Servlets or a JSP (Java Server Pages) technology to generate documents. Servlets are special Java classes, that are invoked when a request for a document comes, and those generate the document. ExPlanTech thin client Servlets utilizes the JADE agent ability to directly communicate with another application, running in the same JVM (Java Virtual Machine).

3   ExPlanTech Use Cases

There is a set of the most usual ways, how to utilize ExPlanTech based system:

3.1   Production Planning, Dynamic Re-planning

The most obvious use case is intra-enterprise planning production planning. The Ex-PlanTech provides sets of linear and non-linear plans and schedules of in-house manufacturing activities that are to be carried out so that the requested orders and tasks are achieved while utilization of the enterprise resources is optimized. Given the fixed deadlines the system provides the user with resource requirements and an appropriate manufacturing schedule. If there are insufficient resources available in order to meet the deadline, the users get notified, and a supervised process of re-planning and re-scheduling is initiated. Re-planning in ExPlanTech is often a reaction to the situation when the planning problem dynamically changes (e.g. by malfunction of the manufacturing machinery). Re-planning thus solves existing or potential conflicts in production plans. ExPlanTech provides sophisticated tracking of interdependence among the particular tasks which makes re-planning process very fast and prevents from planning again from scratch.

   ExPlanTech continually analyses the production data in order to give a feedback to the project planner and to keep the plans up-to-date. Task specifications and resources capacities can be changed any time and new plans are re-computed and displayed in real time. A so-called "competitive planning" allows examining of several possible orders, testing their feasibility and choosing of the best one.

3.2   Supply Chain Management

In order to solve a complicated task of an automated supply chain management, many technical and commercial difficulties have to be overcome. Unlike in the case of the intra-enterprise planning, ExPlanTech has not a complete knowledge about supplier's parameters and capacities. This is why the simplest "master-slave" interaction approach is not sufficient and classical auctioning techniques (e.g. contract-net-protocols) are provided by ExPlanTech system. In addition ExPlanTech handles secure and authenticated communication by the X-Security component, and it uses the concept of acquaintance models in order to handle temporal suppliers inaccessibility. For supply chain integration and management ExPlanTech provides the **extra-enterprise** agents, **enterprise-to-enterprise** agents and **material-resources-provision** (MRP) agents.

3.3 Simulation

Simulation can support decision-making process in two wais. First of them is a simulation of a new factory or of an overhauled or upgraded existing factory. The simulation tool supports a high-fidelity analysis of what the performance of the investment alternative will be. The second way to use a simulation tool is a decision support in factory control to test how changes in performance of key machines would affect the manufacturing process as a whole. ExPlanTech provides an integrated simulation environment that allows simulation of different manufacturing scenarios in order to make technology changes and control safer.

3.4 EE Access

It is possible to access the planning system remotely using the **thin client** or the **thick client** technology. The former approach requires merely an appropriate browser on client's side whilst the second one assumes installation of software based on Java and JADE technology on a user's computer but the latter provides user with more comfortable way to handle the planning system. The remote users exploit the functionality ranging from a passive observation of the system to active interventions (e.g. planning custom orders), which is determined by level of their access rights. Big stress is put on the security of extra-enterprise communication: public key cryptography in common with the secure JADE platform is employed to provide the maximal security level.

4 ExPlanTech Implemented

There are several industrial partners whom we have deployed the ExPlanTech solution with. They did not use all of them the identical collection of software system, while the solution for each of them has been custom tailored.

4.1 ExPlanTech in Modelarna Liaz

Modelarna Liaz spol. s r.o is middle size pattern shop enterprise in the Czech Republic. The customers of the enterprise are mainly from automotive industry from Czech Republic, Germany, Belgium and others. The patterns shop specializes on a single part production of pattern equipments, permanent moulds and dies, measuring and gauging devices, welding, cooling, positioning and machining fixtures and cubings (see an example of a production on Fig. 3).

ExPlanTech was adapted on the planning level. The main goal was to improve middle-time and long-time horizon efficiency. The important criterion was the load of the strategic departments (machines) and delivery times. The multi-agent decomposition based planning within the ExPlanTech was implemented. The factory information system has been agentified and the Resource Agents are updated with real-time production feedback. One Planning Agent is responsible for whole planning course. On the other hand, several Cockpit Agents have been implemented for parallel connection to the system.

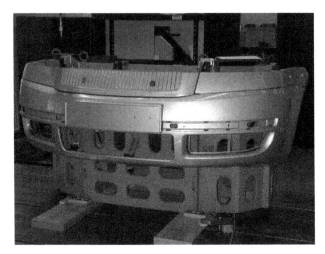

Fig. 3. An example of Modelarna Liaz product.

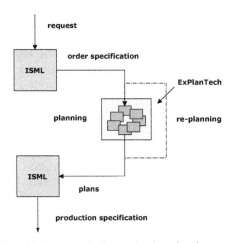

Fig. 4. The role of ExPlanTech system in the production planning process at Modelarna Liaz.

Upon the order specification in the company ERP system (denoted in Figure 4 as ISML) the ExPlanTech system produces a complete set of production plans that are again shipped to the ERP system. Planning a new order as much as a change in the factory shop-floor represented by the resource agents triggers a re-planning process of the all pre-committed plans within the ExPlanTech system.

Besides production planning the ExPlanTech technology supports the factory management with the extra-enterprise access to the planning data and automation of its supply chain management. The complete solution helps to find more efficient plans on the intra-enterprise level and improve the extra-enterprise activities. The faster and more precise cooperation with the suppliers and selling the free capacities can shorten the production lead-time and higher utilization of the factory. After several months of testing the system proved its potential by improving the machine utilization by 30% and due time reduction by 5.3%.

Fig. 5. An example of an engine produced at SkodaAUTO.

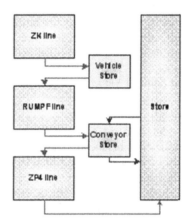

Fig. 6. Motor manufacturing process at SkodaAUTO.

ExPlanTech in SkodaAUTO

The concept of the ExPlanTech technology has been successfully applied in design of the robust planning system for car engines manufacturing [9] in the new SkodaAUTO motor factory in collaboration of GEDAS, s.r.o and CertiCon, a.s. This is an example of a high volume production with few thousands of engines manufactured daily (see an example of an engine on Fig. 5). Given a high variability in types of motors to be manufacturing the planning problem is not a trivial task. The planning system was required to provide us with hourly plans for the period of six weeks. The production process (see Fig. 6) involves three production lines and three different part buffer stores.

The agent technology provided a great help in solving a highly complex problem of planning assembly line production. Planning has been designed to carry out on two independent levels:

- On a higher level a rough plan has been produced. This plan specifies an approximate amount of engines to be produced each day so that all the requested constraints are met. We have used a linear programming based heavy-duty agent for elaborating this higher level plan.

- On a lower level the agents (each representing either a line or a buffer store) analyze the provided higher-level plan and check for conflicts. In an ideal situation the amount of conflicts is reasonable so that the agents can negotiate and solve the conflicts by swapping the tasks within days. The performance of this activity is given primarily by the higher level planning algorithm. Besides solving the conflicts, the lower level planning also provides ordering of tasks within a day.

ExPlanTech in BEHR

The use case of The BEHR GmbH & Co., an automotive supplier in the field of Cooling and Air conditioning systems, employs mainly the production simulation part of the ExPlanTech framework, supported by simplified planning and special Cockpit Agents and Meta-agents. The main purpose of the simulation is comparison of long-term effectiveness of several shop floor layouts. Simulation also allows finding of production bottlenecks, optimal position of product buffers and it can evaluate impacts of important machines failures. These results are very important in decision support during design of new or reconfiguration of an existing factory or even during an important control decisions.

From the implementation point of view, there are two main tasks for the ExPlanTech system:

- For a given shop floor configuration and for a given set of task find a possible sub-optimal production plan. The main goal is to produce tasks on time while keeping the resources utilization balanced. The planning algorithm re-plans the production using spare resources in case of machine failure or overload.
- To simulate a production of particular plans with respect to production time deviations, probability of production of defect products, machines failure rates, human operators accessibility etc. While the planning agent uses one common production model with average production times, the simulation agents can contain particular detailed model of the machine containing many possibilities and events.

The planning and simulation components of ExPlanTech closely cooperate during the simulation. The simulation agents read processes the plans and try to execute them. The planning agent processes the results from the production process and continuously updates the plans so that they comply with an actual situation.

To obtain a meaningful simulation results, it is crucial to set a parameters of production models precisely. If the parameters with some systematical error are used, simulation results cannot fit a real production. In general, the most important are results of simulation of rare and critical situations. Unfortunately, the parameters necessary to emulate such situations are usually very difficult to measure.

ExPlanTech in CHATZOPOULOS

Hatzopoulos S.A. GR is one of the biggest company in Greece in its sector , and it is also one of the 5 largest companies at European level, having a market share of more than 26%. Its clients include amongst others: Chipita, Unilever, Procter & Gamble, PepsiCo Greece, PepsiCo Hungary, PepsiCo Cyprus, Nestle Greece, Nestle Bulgaria, Bic, Warner Lambert, etc. Big multinational clients of CHATZOPOULOS have repeatedly evaluated the company and included it in their accredited suppliers' short-lists.

Within the IST EC take-up action technology transfer project the ExPlanTech technology has been evaluated at the CHATZOPOULOS production site (in close collaboration with CertiCon and UniSoft S.A.). The production planning capacity of ExPlanTech has been exploited primarily for optimization of the production load at two different factory sites. For any new incoming order ExPlanTech provides the user with an estimate of the promised delivery date, taking into account the production place (whether it will be Plant #1 or #2 that will be responsible for the production), and allocating the required time for the construction of the required cylinders or the cliches (which are subject to the particular production "route" to be decided i.e. plant #1 or #2).

5 Conclusion

This contribution has illustrated the potential of the agent-based decision support technology in various fields of manufacturing – planning, supply chain management, simulation, extra-enterprise access, etc. The integration exercise that we have carried out at different industries validated that the agent based technology is viable in situations where the planning problem is dynamically changing – e.g. project driven production, and needs frequent and continuous re-planning. In these situations the collective aspects of the agent technology have been exploited. At the same time we have identified a great potential of the technology in situations where the planning problem is inherently complex but it features some of the internal logic. This has been case of the high volume production, where not only collective aspects of agent technology have been used but also the integrative capabilities of agents have been exploited (e.g. integration of the linear programming heavy-duty solver). Obviously in situations where the planning data are widely distributed and not fully available the agent technology provided an elegant integrative and distributed planning framework. This was the case of the supply chain management and virtual enterprises integration. It has been shown that the multi-agent approach provides a specific modeling and simulation alternative to the known mathematical and system science modeling technologies for simulating the manufacturing process.

References

1. Afsarmanesh, H., Camarinha-Matos, L.M.: Collaborative Networked Organizations / A research agenda for emerging business models. Norwell, MA: Kluwer Academic Publishers, 2004, s. 77-90. ISBN 1-4020-7823-4.
2. Bečvář P., Charvát P., Pěchouček M., Pospíšil J., Říha A., Vokřínek J.: ExPlanTech/ExtraPLANT: Production planning and supply-chain management multi-agent solution, EXP in search of innovation, Special Issue on JADE. Vol. 3, No. 3, pp. 116-125, 2003
3. FIPA: Foundation for Intelligent Physical Agents organization, http://www.fipa.org/
4. Fischer, K., Müller, J. P., Heimig, I., and Scheer, A.W.: Intelligent agents in virtual enterprises. In Proceedings of the First International Conference on Practical Applications of Intelligent Agents and Multiagents (PAAM'96), London, 1996
5. Hodík, J. - Rollo, M. - Novák, P. - Pěchouček, M.: Agent Exchange - Virtual Trading Environment. In: Holonic and Multi-Agent Systems for Manufacturing. Heidelberg : Springer, 2003, p. 179-188. ISBN 3-540-40751-0.

6. JADE: Java Agent Development Framework, http://sharon.cselt.it/projects/jade/
7. Novák, P., Rollo, M., Hodík, J., Vlček, T.: Communication Security in Multi-agent Systems. In: Mařík, V., Muller, J., Pěchouček, M.: (Eds.): Multi-Agent Systems and Application III, LNAI 2691, Springer Verlag. 2003, pp. 454-463.
8. Pěchouček, M., Říha, A., Vokřínek, J., Mařík, V., Pra ma, V.: ExPlanTech: applying multi-agent systems in production planning. In: International Journal of Production Research. 2002, vol. 40, no. 15, p. 3681-3692. ISSN 0020-7543.
9. Rehák, M., Charvát, P., and Pěchouček, M. : Agent System Application In High-Volume Production Management In Proceedings of BASYS'04 6th IFIP International Conference on Information Technology for BALANCED AUTOMATION SYSTEMS in Manufacturing and Services, Vienna, September 2004
10. Říha, A. - Pěchouček, M. - Vokřínek, J. - Mařík, V.: ExPlanTech: Exploitation of Agent-Based Technology in Production Planning. In: Multi-Agent Systems and Applications II. Berlin : Springer, 2002, vol. 1, p. 308-322. ISBN 3-540-43377-5
11. Vokřínek, J. - Říha, A. - Pěchouček, M. - Mařík, V.: Extra-Enterprise Production Planning in ExPlanTech System. In: Thirteenth International Workshop on Database and Expert Systems Applications. Los Alamitos: IEEE Computer Society Press, 2002, p. 628-632. ISBN 0-7695-1668-8.

Towards an Approach for Debugging MAS Through the Analysis of ACL Messages

Juan A. Botía, Juan M. Hernansáez, and Fernando G. Skarmeta

Universidad de Murcia
{juanbot,juanma,skarmeta}@um.es

Abstract. Multi-agent systems (MAS) are a special kind of distributed systems in which the main entities are autonomous in a proactive sense. These systems are special distributed systems because of their complexity and hence their unpredictability. Agents can spontaneously engage in complex interactions, guided by their own goals and intentions. When developing such kinds of system, there are many problems the developer has to face. All these problems make it virtually impossible to totally debug a quite complex multi-agent system (i.e. a MAS in which hundreds or even thousands of agents are involved). In this article we present a debugging tool we have developed for the JADE agents platform. Hence, it is a FIPA technology based tool and seeks to alleviate typical debugging problems derived from distribution and unpredictability.

1 Introduction

To follow the global behavior of information systems which have control, data and processes and all organized in a distributed fashion is a hard task [13, 3, 11]. Each entity of the system usually has to have a local view or the organization and to integrate all limited views coming from each entity is a work which depends on the user (i.e. the programmer). Moreover, due to the complexity of interactions between many entities, a really effective visualization is even more important than in monolithic systems. The main reason for the high complexity in debugging these kinds of systems is that the source of errors is twofold. On the one hand, each independent entity (i.e. agents) can be a source of functional errors. These kinds of errors are derived from a bad design of the methods used to carry out an internal task. These errors are also typical in monolithic systems. On the other hand, in distributed systems there is also another typical source of errors, those derived from coordination and cooperation tasks. These kinds of errors are even more subtle to discover, diagnose and solve. Moreover, multiagent systems are autonomous and their interactions can be even more complex and unpredictable than the typical processes we can find in *conventional* distributed systems.

In this paper we propose a tool devoted to assisting in debugging both functional and coordination/cooperation related errors. From our perspective, such a tool should fulfil the following requirements:

G. Lindemann et al. (Eds.): MATES 2004, LNAI 3187, pp. 301–312, 2004.
© Springer-Verlag Berlin Heidelberg 2004

1. For each entity (i.e. agent) of the system, the tool must allow us to revise its behavior during the whole execution of a trial. It must keep a register of the actions (i.e. in the sense of communicative acts [1] in this case) along with the time they were executed and the appreciable effects they caused.
2. An important requirement is that the register needs a global time reference. In order to analyze an isolated interaction between two or more agents, it would be enough to keep a local time reference, just to order into a correct sequence all the exchanged messages. However, when all the systems have to be analyzed, it is crucial to obtain a global time stamp. In the case of having that global time reference, it is possible then to check if some actions had effects on others within a global context.
3. The analysis tool must be capable of not only registering but distinguishing all the different interactions carried out in the trial, for each interaction it should register also the protocol used, the agents implied, the time sequence of interactions and results for all agents. In order to correctly detect some undesirable behaviors in agents implied at the interaction, the tool must be capable of deciding if a sequence of messages, supposed belonging to a concrete interaction protocol, really adjust to it.
4. When hundreds or even thousands of agents are involved in a trial, other problems arise like, for example, how can we move through really populated groups of agents without losing the global perspective. Such a tool should also allow the debugger to perform some kind of zoom in/out operation, in a visual and comfortable way.
5. Also the global perspective of the trial would not be complete if some statistically descriptive measures where not used. The tool has to show statistics for each kind of interaction protocol, number of successful/unsuccessful conversations, statistics by kind of performative, and also graphs showing the number of messages sent over time.

Requirements 1 and 2 are addressed in section 2.1. Requirement 3 is addressed in section 2.2. The accomplishment of requirement 4 is explained in section 2.3 and some of the measures mentioned in requirement 5 are shown in section 3.

The rest of the article is structured as follows: section 2 will introduce the tool from an architectural and functional perspective. We will demonstrate the usefulness of the tool in section 3 with a working example. Finally, section 4 will summarize lessons learned and mention some future works.

2   The ACLAnalyser Tool

The ACLAnalyser tool has been designed to analyze runs on the JADE (Java Agents Development Environment) platform. Hence, it is useful for debugging FIPA compliant MAS [2]. It is coded in Java and it is available as an add-on of JADE from the platform web page[1].

---

[1] http://jade.tilab.com

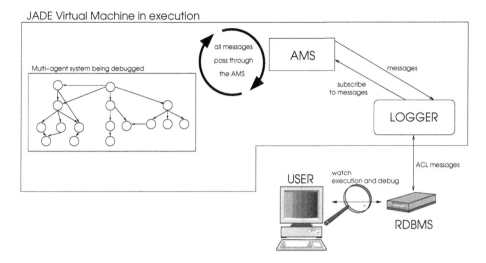

Fig. 1. Architecture for the ACLAnalyser tool

2.1   The Architecture

The architecture of the ACLAnalyser appears in figure 1. In the figure, there are four main elements. These are the JADE execution environment, a logger, a relational database and the user module.

The JADE environment represents the multi-agent system being debugged. It has to be executed and, in turn, it will generate the messages exchanged by all the agents of the system.

The logger is actually another JADE agent (i.e. a spy agent), which is not part of the MAS being debugged. In order to start using it, the JADE platform must be launched, along with the spy agent. This agent is really like the Sniffer which comes with the JADE distribution. Its purpose is to intercept all the messages exchanged between agents. However, instead of simply reproducing it like the Sniffer does, this spy agent has two main tasks: (1) to keep track of all the interactions being performed in the run currently executing and (2) to store all messages in the third element of the architecture, a relational database. Communication between the spy agent and the database is done through a JDBC connection.

In Figure 2 appears the entity-relationship model used for the relational tables used in the database. The main element of the database is a session. A session represents the set of all messages generated in a run of the MAS being debugged. Obviously, a session can be compounded of many different conversations. And a conversation corresponds to a concrete interaction between an initiator and one or more agents, but always following a concrete interaction protocol which can be a FIPA standard or user-defined. The use of a relational database to store all interactions has a number of advantages. One of them is that the system should be capable of storing a virtually unlimited number of

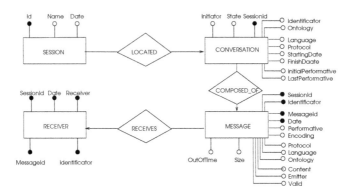

Fig. 2. Entity-relationship model for the log of messages

messages corresponding to complex interactions for the case of runs where thousands of agents are implied. Connection to the database from the Spy agent is done through a remote JDBC connection. This implies that the debugger has a minimal impact in terms of resources consumption as, for each message, the only thing to do is send it to the database which, in turn, can be located in a different machine than the one running the system being debugged. Another important benefit of using a relational database through a JDBC connection is that all the software, except the Spy agent, can be reused for another FIPA compliant platform rather than JADE like, for example, FIPA-OS or ZEUS. The only additional work for integration into other platforms is to habilitate the mechanism in charge of sending all messages to the Spy agent. Moreover, the tool also offers the possibility of showing the effectivity of the debug process, during the lifetime of the development stage as the database stores results for all the sessions performed during the whole process.

Finally we have the user module. This is in charge of presenting results to the user in order to help keep track of all events produced in the execution. This module is the most important part of the tool because it shows the user all the information needed to be checked if something went wrong in the execution of the MAS and, in such case, to make an appropriate diagnostic. User module functionality will be shown in sections 2.3 and 3.

2.2   Interaction Protocols

We have already mentioned that, in a run of the MAS being debugged, all the messages are organized into conversations, and all conversations belong to a session. A session is the compendium of all the messages exchanged in a run.

Since the user module must represent any conversation produced in a run, the tool needs a way of representing interaction protocols and a method to match a sequence of messages with a concrete interaction protocol. Examples of FIPA [7] interaction protocols are `fipa-request` [6], `fipa-query` [5] and the well known `fipa-contract-net` [12, 4].

In ACLAnalyser, an interaction protocol has an internal representation as a finite state automaton. When a new conversation is initiated between agents, an automaton is created for all the participants as they become known for the tool. In this way, the state of the automaton represents the state of the conversation for the corresponding agent. When a new message is received by the spy agent, the roles for the sender and receiver of the message are obtained. Once these roles, state of each participant and the performative of the message exists then transitions are made for all automatons.

At each instant of the run, all participants are in a specific state. There are four kind of states. The first is the initial state, let it be denoted by $q_{0,i}$, for the i−th participant. The second is the final state, let it be denoted by $q_{f,i}$ for the i−th participant. If its automaton is in this state, the conversation has ended for the participant i (i.e. if more messages are received, corresponding to the same interaction, these messages are incorrect). The third kind of state is the error state, let it be denoted by $q_{e,i}$ for the participant i. This state represents a situation in which the agent i has passed a timeout before which it should have sent a message or received it. The fourth state if the so called *possible final*, let it be denoted by $q_{p,i}$ for the agent i. If an agent is in this state, it can be considered as a final one but, however, more messages of a concrete kind can still be received (sent), and the state would not be erroneous.

2.3   Zooming out

The ACLAnalyser tool can show a view consisting of a directed graph of all the agents implied in a run (i.e. a concrete session) or a graph of all the agents implied in a simple interaction (i.e. a conversation). In this graphical view, both nodes of the arc are agents and if there is an arc from the agent i to the agent j, it means that agent i has sent one or more messages to agent j, and also that messages have been received by j. Also, each arc is labeled with the number of messages sent and the total number of bytes transferred. This basic view of the whole system has the following applications: detection of no communication, when expected, between two or more agents, detection of excessive number of bytes exchanged between two or more agents and detection of unbalanced execution configurations in which agents from a specific group (or machine) show an amount of activity disproportionate to the rest.

An interesting point of this kind of view of the system is that it is still useful when hundreds or even thousands of agents are implied, because it is possible to make a zoom out. It is possible to apply a clustering process on the messages to detect groupings of agents, and present them as such.

The clustering process is based on the ROCK [8] clustering algorithm. Conventional clustering algorithms detect spontaneous groupings on data [9]. This grouping is based on a distance measure, typically the Euclidean distance. This basic clustering works on continuous data. However, we have categorical data (i.e. messages exchanged between agents in a MAS). Which was what led us to use ROCK. This clustering algorithm works with boolean and categorical (i.e. symbols) data. Instead of using a distance, ROCK uses the concept of link. This term is, in turn, based also in the concept of neighbor. Two items of data are considered as neighbors if they share some degree of similarity, whose definition depends on each problem. The number of neighbors between two entities corresponds to their number of links. Once the links have been calculated, groupings are determined between entities which share a high number of links. The number of groups detected is a configuration parameter of the algorithm. Hence, the lower the number, the higher the abstraction level we are using to look at the agents society.

With respect to this concrete problem (i.e. the application of ROCK to messages exchanged between agents) two agents will be considered as neighbors if they exchanged some messages. The zooming process is represented in the graph (a) in Figure 3; where we can see, in the lower layer, the whole agents society and the links between the agents. We can easily check that there are three different groups of agents in terms of neighborhood. Should we apply the ROCK clustering algorithm, with the number of groups set to 3, then we obtain the three clusters of the higher level. As a particular example of using the tool, in graph (b) of Figure 3, it appears represented a graph corresponding to a hundred agents. By applying the zoom out, we can obtain graph (c) of the same figure with ten groups, which correspond to the example in the next section.

3   A Concrete Example of Use

We will now show the use of the tool with a concrete example. To do so, all the agents will execute the task of deciding which agent will be the leader for the group. This is a well known problem in distributed systems when spontaneous centralized coordination is needed between a group of entities. We will use the algorithm proposed in [10], pag. 101. The following is its pseudo-code, given that I is the ID of the corresponding agent:

```
M = I;
send I to all neighbors
on reception of message J do
  if M < J then
    M = J;
    send J to all neighbors;
  end
on message from each neighbor received do
  if M = I then return leader else return follower
```

It assumes that all agents have a numeric ID and the selection process ends when the agent with the highest ID assumes the leadership (i.e. it is not necessary for the process to be fair in any sense).

There will be a *launcher* agent, in charge of creating the rest of the agents which will compound a group of one hundred. Each agent will have an unique ID and an unique random number to be used for the leadership selection. Both are generated by the launcher agent.

In this example, agent i will recognise the agent $i - 1$ and the agent $i + 1$. Now, we define a new interaction protocol, called protocolo-lider using

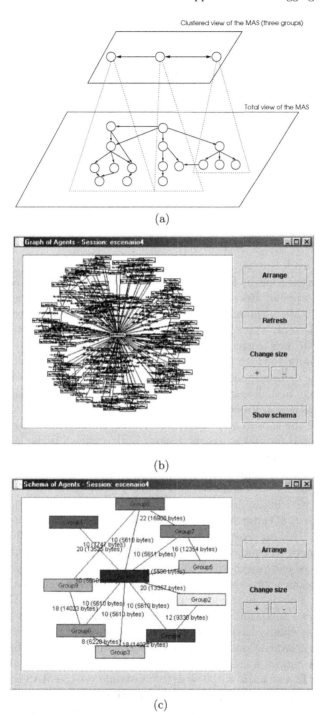

Fig. 3. Different levels of abstraction for a MAS through categorical clustering

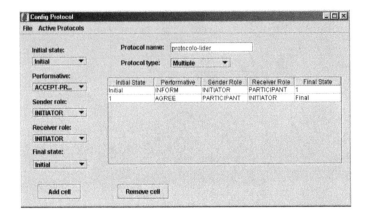

Fig. 4. Definition of the `protocolo-lider` interaction protocol

the window appearing in Figure 4. In this figure, two different cells (i.e. rows in the table) appear. Each cell refers to a kind of message. The first column indicates the state of the automata from which the transition is generated when the message is sent. The second indicates, the kind of performative. The third and the fourth ones correspond, respectively, to who sends and who receives messages. Finally, the fifth column shows to which state the transition generated on sending the message goes. The protocol type is `multiple` because the initiator sends a message in multicast mode (i.e. to all its neighbors) and has to wait until all `agree` messages are received from the participants. The buttons on the left are used to fill the gaps in new cells. But a further interaction protocol is needed. This will be used for all the agents when it is clear which is the leader, and will be called `protocolo-resultado`. It will consist of an `inform` performative sent to the launcher. When all these messages are received, the final result will be shown to the user by the launcher.

The error we will simulate is a coordination error, and it will consist of killing the agent with 20 ID after some seconds of live. After running the simulation, the launcher will show an error window because it did not receive all the necessary `inform` messages to compound the final result after a timeout. Once the error is produced, we can use the tool to generate general statistics by means of the statistics window appearing in Figure 5, where two different data are marked with a circle. The one in the lower part of the window indicates that a total of 99 conversations following the `protocolo-resultado` protocol were performed when the value should have been 100. Also, in the upper part of the window we can see that 9 conversations did not totally follow their corresponding interaction protocol. How can we determine which agent did not send the `inform` message to the launcher? In a scenario with few agents we could use the MAS communication graph (see Figure 3, graph (b)). But this is not the case here. Fortunately, there is an alternative manner. We can search for the unsuccesful conversations of session `UNKNOWN22` by using the conversations search window of the tool and obtain the list of convesations appearing at the window of Figure 6. From a glance at the

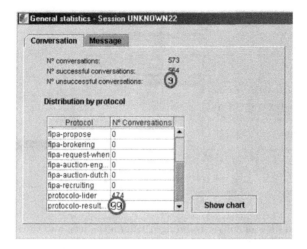

Fig. 5. General statistics window for the coordination error scenario

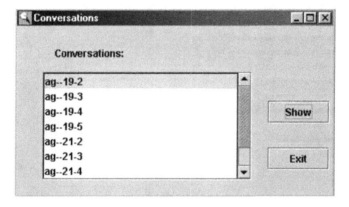

Fig. 6. List of uncorrect conversations for the session `UNKNOWN22` used in the coordination error scenario

window, we can see that all unsuccessful conversations were performed by agents 19 and 21. We can get more detail in, for example, the first conversation labeled with `ag-19-2` and obtain the window on the left of Figure 7, in which it can be seen that the first and last performative is a single `inform`, from which we can conclude that the agent 20 did not respond with the required `agree` message. We can also confirm this by the sequence diagram we can obtain by clicking at the `Show Diagram` button. It also appears in Figure 7 on the right. We can also have a look at the rest of the unsuccessful conversations, and conclude likewise.

We can get more details of the error by using the view of the agent 20, appearing in Figure 8. This agent did not send any message to the launcher, as can be seen by looking at the `Output graph` window. Moreover, we can check,

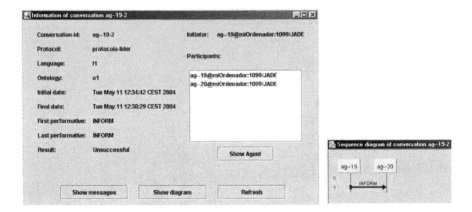

Fig. 7. A detailed view of conversation `ag-19-2`, on the left, and the sequence diagram on the right

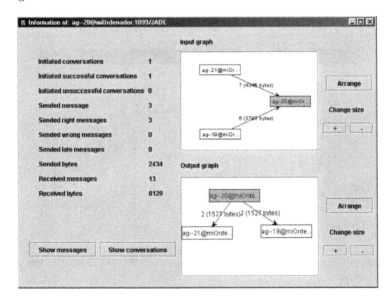

Fig. 8. Detailed view of the activity of `ag-20`

by using the `Show messages` button, when this agent sent its last message (with label (a) in Figure 9) and when it received the first unanswered one (with label (b) in Figure 9). From this we can conclude that `ag-20` died some time between 12:34:32 and 12:34:38.

4   Conclusions and Future Works

In this paper, some of the many functionalities of the ACLAnalyser have been shown. Its strengths are the use of a relational database which allows storage of

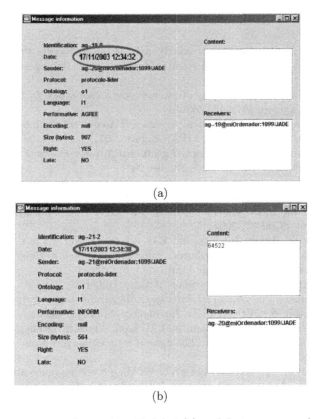

(a)

(b)

Fig. 9. Last message sent by `ag-20` with label (a) and first unanswered message with label (b)

any number of complex multi-agent interactions, views of the MAS at different abstractions levels by using categorical clustering, and a complete and versatile window system which allows accessing any information available for a run. This, as a whole, is a powerful debugging system for complex multiagent systems. Future works will include investigating the application of OLAP (On-line Analytical Processing) techniques for visualizing the database and a tighter integration with the execution system (i.e. JADE platform). Another issue which is still pending is to check the ongoing work in MDP (Multi-threaded, Parallel and Distributed) application systems as one of the reviewers suggested.

Acknowledgements

Part of this work has been funded by the Spanish Science and Technology Ministry (MCYT) by means of the *TIC-2002-04021-C02-02* project.

References

1. J.L. Austin. *How to Do Things with Words*. Oxford University Press, 1962.
2. J Dale and E. Mamdani. Open standards for interoperating agent-based systems. *Software Focus*, 2(1), 2001.
3. David W. Flater. Debugging agent interactions: a case study. In *Selected Areas in Cryptography*, pages 107–114, 2001.
4. Foundation for Intelligent Physical Agents. FIPA contract net interaction protocol specification. Technical report, FIPA, August 2001.
5. Foundation for Intelligent Physical Agents. FIPA query interaction protocol specification. Technical report, FIPA, August 2001.
6. Foundation for Intelligent Physical Agents. FIPA request interaction protocol specification. Technical report, FIPA, August 2001.
7. Foundation for Intelligent Physical Agents. FIPA Communicative Act Library Specification. SC00037, 2002.
8. Sudipto Guha, Rajeev Rastogi, and Kyuseok Shim. ROCK: A robust clustering algorithm for categorical attributes. *Information Systems*, 25(5):345–366, 2000, (citeseer.nj.nec.com/guha00rock.html).
9. Tom M. Mitchell. *Machine Learning*. McGraw-Hill, 1997.
10. Jorg P. Muller. *The Design of Intelligent Agents. A Layered Approach*, volume 1117 of *Lecture Notes in Artificial Intelligence*. Springer, 1996.
11. David Poutakidis, Lin Padgham, and Michael Winikoff. Debugging multi-agent systems using design artifacts: The case of interaction protocols. In *AAMAS'02*, Bologna, Italy, July 2002.
12. Reid R. Smith. The contract net protocol: High-level communication and control in a distributed problem solver. In A. H. Bond and L. Gasser, editors, *Readings in Distributed Artificial Intelligence*, pages 357–366. Morgan Kaufmann Publishers, Los Altos, CA, 1988.
13. Marc H. Van Liederke and Nicholas M. Avouris. Debugging multi-agent systems. *Information and Software Technology*, 37(2):103–112, 1995.

Implementing Norms in Multiagent Systems

Javier Vázquez-Salceda, Huib Aldewereld, and Frank Dignum

Institute of Information and Computing Sciences
Utrecht University, The Netherlands
{javier,huib,dignum}@cs.uu.nl

Abstract. There is a wide agreement on the use of *norms* in order to specify the expected behaviour of agents in open MAS. However, current norm formalisms focus on the *declarative* nature of norms. In order to be implemented, these norms should be translated into *operational* representations. In this paper we present our preliminary work on implementation of norm enforcement and issues on verifiability that highly affect this enforcement. We propose some mechanisms to be included in agent platforms in order to ease the implementation.

1 Introduction

In open societies, where heterogeneous agents might deviate from expected behaviour, mechanisms are needed in order to systematize, defend and recommend right and wrong behaviour, along with safe environments to support those mechanisms, thereby inspiring trust into the agents that will join such an environment. Some foundational work in this direction has been done in the ALFEBI-ITE project [13], in particular in [1]. An Electronic Institution [9] [11] is a safe environment mediating in the interaction of agents. The expected behaviour of agents in such an environment is described by means of an explicit specification[1] of norms, which is a) expressive enough, b) readable by agents, and c) easy to maintain.

Current work on normative systems' formalization (mainly focused in Deontic-like formalisms [14]) is declarative in nature, focused on the expressiveness of the norms, the definition of formal semantics and the verification of consistency of a given set. In previous work [8] [10] we have focused on the formal definition of norms by means of some variations of deontic logic that includes conditional and temporal aspects [4] [7], and we provided formal semantics. Although the declarative aspects of norms are important, norms should not only have a *declarative* meaning but also an *operational* one in order to be used in MAS. This means that, to be used in practice, norms should be operationally implemented.

---

[1] The main reason for having explicit representations of norms is that norms may change over time. If norms are embedded in the agents' design and code, all the design steps have to be checked again and all the code verified to ensure compliance with new regulations.

G. Lindemann et al. (Eds.): MATES 2004, LNAI 3187, pp. 313–327, 2004.

Implementing norms is not implementing a theorem prover that, using the norms semantics, checks whether a given interaction protocol complies with the norms. The implementation of norms should consider a) how the agents' behaviour is affected by norms, and b) how the institution should ensure the compliance with norms. The former is related to the *implementation of norms from the agent perspective*, by analyzing the impact of norms in the agents' reasoning cycle (work on this perspective can be found in [2] [3] [6]). The latter is related with the *implementation of norms from the institutional perspective*, by implementing a safe environment (including the enforcing mechanisms) to ensure trust among parties. As far as we know, the most complete model in literature considering some operational aspects of norms for MAS is the extension of the SMART agent specification framework by López y López, Luck and d'Inverno [15] [16]. The framework aims to represent different kinds of agent societies based on norms. However, no implementation of the architecture applying it to a real problem has been reported in literature, there are no tools to support the development and implementation of a normative multiagent system, and there are no mechanisms defined from the institutional perspective in order to enforce the norms.

In this paper we complement our previous work on norm formalization by focusing on how norms should be operationally implemented in MAS from an institutional perspective (i.e. How to check a norm? How to detect a violation of a norm? How to handle it?). In order to analize the problem we categorize norms depending on a) whether they are restrictive (norms permitting/forbidding actions or situations) or impositive (norms forcing an entity to do an action or to reach a state), b) how the start and end of an obligation are detected, c) the different aspects of the norms to be specified, and d) who is responsible for norm enforcement.

We will also propose a first draft of a machine-readable format for expressing norms, which is not only expressive enough for complex norms (such as those present in *e*Commerce, *e*Government or *e*Care domains) but also useful for implementation in MAS. Our implementation guidelines use the ISLANDER framework for institutions and platform as a starting point.

There are two main assumptions in our approach. First of all we assume that norms can sometimes be violated by agents in order to keep their autonomy, which can also be functional for the system as a whole as argued in [5]. The violation of norms is handled from the organizational point of view by violation and sanction mechanisms. Secondly we assume that from the institutional perspective the internal state of the external agents is neither observable nor controlable (external agents as black boxes). Therefore, we cannot avoid a forbidden action to be in the goals and intentions of an agent, or impose an obligatory action on an agent to be in their intentions.

The paper is organized as follows. In the next section we discuss how normative specification is currently done in the ISLANDER formalism, being the most appropriate for defining institutions. Then, in §3, we discuss the different types of norms one can distinguish, as well as implementation related issues. In

§4 we discuss how violations are managed by means of plans of action. We end this paper with our conclusions and outline future lines of research. To illustrate that our approach is quite general and can be used on several domains, we use examples of norms throughout this paper coming from three different domains (electronic auction houses such as Fishmarket, organ and tissue allocation for human transplantation purposes and the access to Dutch police criminal registers).

2   Norms in ISLANDER

The ISLANDER formalism [11] provides a formal framework for institutions [18] and has proven to be well-suited to model practical applications (e.g. electronic auction houses). This formalism views an agent-based institution as a *dialogical system* where all the interactions inside the institution are a composition of multiple dialogic activities (message exchanges). These interactions (or *illocutions* [17]) are structured through agent group meetings called *scenes* that follow well-defined protocols. This division of all the possible interaction among agents in scenes allows a modular design of the system, following the idea of other software modular design methodologies such as the Modular Programming or Object Oriented Programming. A second key element of the ISLANDER formalism is the notion of an agent's *role*. Each agent can be associated to one or more roles, and these roles define the scenes the agent can enter and the protocols it should follow. Finally, this formalism defines a graphical notation that not only allows to obtain visual representations of scenes and protocols but is also very helpful while developing the final system, as they can be seen as blueprints.

ISLANDER has been mainly used in *e*Commerce scenarios, and was used to model and implement an electronic Auction house (the *Fishmarket*). Furthermore, the AMELI platform [12] allows the execution of electronic institutions, based on the rules provided by ISLANDER specifications, wherein external agents may participate. The activity of these agents is, however, constrained by *governors* that regulate agent actions, to the precise enactment of the roles specified in the institution model.

ISLANDER provides a sound model for the domain ontology and has a formal semantics [18]. This is an advantage of its dialogical approach to organizations. However, in ISLANDER the normative aspects are reduced to the afore mentioned protocol plus the specification of constraints for scene transition and enactment (the only allowed interactions are those explicitly represented by arcs in scenes), along with the definition of norms that uniquely allow for the firing of obligations. Thus, ISLANDER does not offer expressiveness to specify norms involving prohibitions, permissions, or sanctions. Furthermore, it does not allow the use of temporal operators. And finally, ISLANDER does not allow for the specification of non-dialogical actions.

Our aim is to extend the norms in the ISLANDER formalism with more expressive, abstract norms while providing some mechanisms to implement the enforcement of these norms from the institutional perspective.

3   Norms: Types, Components and Implementation Issues

In order to express complex norms we are going to use a language consisting of deontic concepts (OBLIGED, PERMITTED, FORBIDDEN) which can be conditional (IF) and can include temporal operators (BEFORE, AFTER). It is important to note that, although we do a formal analysis of norms in this section (which could be given a formal semantics as in some of our previous work [8] [10]), in this paper we are focusing on indicating possible implementation guidelines related with the different kinds of norms and the components in each of them.

In order to implement enforcement mechanisms that are well-found, one has to define some kind of operational semantics first. In general, an operational semantics for norms always comes down to either one of the following:

- **Defining constraints on unwanted behaviour.**
- **Detecting violations and reacting to these violations.**

The choice between these two approaches is highly dependent on the amount of control over the addressee of the norms. Prevention of unwanted behaviour can only be achieved if there is full control over the addressee; otherwise, one should define and handle violations (see §4).

Before we look at how differences between the addressees of norms affect the implementation of enforcement mechanisms we will look at the types of norms that exists in human regulations.

3.1   Types of Norms

In the legal domain, norms are descriptions of how a person (or agent) should behave in order to comply with legal standards. If we take a look at human regulations, we can observe three main types of norms:

- **Norms defining (refining) the meaning of abstract terms** (e.g. *"The criminal register administrator can be the Regional Police Force Commander, the Dutch National Police Force commander, the Royal Military Police Commander, the College of the Procurator-General or an official appointed by The Minister of Justice"*).
- **Norms defining (refining) an abstract action by means of sub-actions (a plan), a procedure or a protocol** (e.g. *"A request for examination [of personal data] [...] is sustainable after receipt of the payment of EUR 4,50 on account [...] of the force mentioning 'privacy request'"*)
- **Norms defining obligations/permissions/prohibitions.**

The first and second type of norms are only important in order to define the vocabulary to be used in a given regulation[2]. Work on law formalization focuses on the last kind of norms. We will also focus on the third type of norms in this paper.

---

[2] In an agent-mediated system, these norms would be implemented in the ontology of the system and/or in the refinement process of the actions on the system.

3.2   Addressee of Norms

Although the amount of control over the addressee of a norm influences the operational semantics of the enforcement mechanisms, the detection of unwanted states or behaviour is necessary in both approaches. We distinguish 4 types of norms according to their addressee:

- **Norms concerning entities outside the scope and/or full control of the run-time system.** In this case no real enforcement can be done. This is usually the case of humans and/or outside agencies and systems which interact or affect the institution's behaviour but are outside of the full control. An example is an obligation to the user to provide correct data about a person. The system, having no other sources of information, has to trust the user.
  Implementation Guideline: receive some (external) information about the fulfillment of the norm. This information has to be trusted, because it cannot be directly checked.
- **Norms concerning external agents.** This is the group that has to be highly controlled and on who the majority of the enforcement has to be performed. However, we cannot see their internal mental states or reasoning process, or control it in any way. We can only see their observable behaviour in terms of (public) messages and (visible) actions.
  Implementation Guideline: enforcement depends on the verifiability of the predicates and actions that are present in the norms (see §3.4).
- **Norms concerning internal agents.** This is a group of agents that are internal to the system, performing facilitation tasks needed for the performance of the whole agent society.
  Implementation Guideline: enforcement of this kind of agents is similar to that of external agents, but as they are internal (i.e. built by the designers of the institution) we have some access and control to their internal states.
- **Norms concerning the major enforcers** (root enforcers). In this case enforcement should be done on the enforcers' behaviour. Enforcers are a special case of internal agents, so one possible option is to enforce their norms in a way similar to the internal agents. However, another question might then arise: How to enforce the enforcement on the enforcers? Since this *enforcement chain* can be extended *ad infinitum*, we should stop the enforcement chain somewhere. To achieve this we need to have full trust in our root enforcers, and therefore need full control over their internal architecture's design; their beliefs, goals and intentions.
  Implementation Guideline: 1) introduce the norms a) explicitly as goals and restriction rules interpretable by the enforcers or b) implicitly in the enforcer's code/design. 2) make sure that the environment/platform supports the enforcer on fulfilling the norms by a) providing enough information, and b) providing supporting enforcement mechanisms.

3.3   Norm Expressions and Enforcement

Not only the control over the addressee but also the elements present in the norm expressions (or norm condition) affect the enforcement of norms. Therefore, in this section, we first analyze norms depending on the elements that affect detection and we will discuss methods of enforcing these different kinds of norms. At the end of this section we will introduce a format for expressing the norm conditions. Note that we will use the term norms wherever Obligations (OBLIGED) as well as Permissions (PERMITTED) or Prohibitions (FORBIDDEN) are meant.

For all the norms below, the implementation of enforcement is composed of three related processes a) the detection of when a norm is active, b) the detection of a violation on a norm, and c) the handling of the violations. In this section we are going to focus on the detection mechanisms, as they are central in the enforcement of norms. We talk more about violations, sanctions and repairs in §4. It is also important to note that the precise moment to make the detection checks is highly dependent on the verifiability levels of each check (which we discuss in §3.4).

In the next sections we characterize norms by whether a) they refer to a state or an action, b) they are conditional, c) they include a deadline, or d) they are norms concerning other norms.

Norms Concerning That Agent a Sees to It That Some Condition/ Predicate P Holds. In this case the norm is timeless, that is, the norm on the value of P is active at all times. There are three possible expressions:

$$\text{OBLIGED}(a, P) \quad \text{PERMITTED}(a, P) \quad \text{FORBIDDEN}(a, P)$$

An example of such a timeless norm is the following:

$$\text{FORBIDDEN}(buyer, account(buyer, A) \wedge A < 0)$$

Implementation Guideline: To determine whether the norm results in a violation we need to check whether P holds. Note that this check might be undecidable in general.

Norms Concerning Agent a Performing an Action A. In this case the norm on the execution of A is also timeless, that is, the norm is active at all times.

$$\text{PERMITTED}(a \text{ DO } A) \quad \text{FORBIDDEN}(a \text{ DO } A)$$

There are no unconditional obligations (OBLIGED), since this would express an obligation to execute an action all the time[3]. An example of an unconditional norm would be the following:

$$\text{FORBIDDEN}(seller \text{ DO } bid(product, price))$$

---

[3] In most cases, when such an obligation appears while modelling a human norm, it can be expressed better by means of a timeless obligation on a state. In other cases an implicit condition can be added to the norm for implementability reasons.

Note that action A can be an abstract action, that is, an action that is not present in the repertoire of the agents or defined in the protocol. In such cases A should be translated in more concrete actions to be checked.

Implementation Guideline: In the case of the unconditional PERMITTED, we only have to check whether the agent has the correct role and whether all parametric constraints are met. In the case of the FORBIDDEN operator, we translate the abstract action A into concrete actions α and check on action α. In the case of computational verifiable actions, each one can be checked a) when the action is going to be performed, b) it is being performed, or c) it is done. We will call this process the *detection of occurrence of an action.*

In an agent platform with several agents performing different actions at the same time a question arises on how to implement the detection of the occurrence of actions. Enforcer agents may become overloaded on trying to check any action on any time. We propose to create a) a *black list* of actions to be checked, and b) an *action alarm mechanism* that triggers an alarm when a given action A attempts to start, is running or is done. This trigger mechanism has to do no further checks, only to make the enforcer aware of the occurrence of the action. The action alarm mechanism can only be done with actions defined in the institutions' ontology, which specifies the way each action is to be monitored. For instance, when the performance of the action $bid(product, price)$ should be checked, the action is registered by an enforcer on the black list. Then as soon as $bid(product, price)$ occurs, the trigger mechanism sends an alarm to the enforcer, that will check if the action was legal or illegal given the norms.

When actions are performed by users through a user interface, the action alarm mechanism can be placed in the interface itself. In the case of the following norm:

PERMITTED(*administrator* DO *include(Suspect_Data, Criminal_Register)*)

The inclusion of the personal data of the suspect is done by all users through a special form. Therefore the interface knows when the user is filling in suspect data, and at the moment of submission of such data to the system it can send an alarm to the enforcer.

Norms Concerning a Condition P or an Action A Under Some Circumstance C. The norm is conditional under C. This means that we have to detect the *activation of the norm* (when condition C is true) and *the deactivation of the norm* (when predicate P or action A is fulfilled or C does not hold). An additional issue is to establish the allowed time span between the activation and deactivation of an obligation, i.e. the time that is allowed for the completion of the obligation when it becomes active (e.g. immediately, in some minutes). In theoretical approaches, the semantics are defined in a way that when an obligation becomes active, it has to be fulfilled instantly. But this is impractical for implementation, because agents need some time between detection and reaction. This *reaction time* is ignored in norm theories, but has to be addressed when implementing norms. The length of the reaction time for each norm is highly dependent on the application domain. A violation does not occur when the norm becomes active but when the reaction time has passed[4].

A condition C may be a) a predicate about the state of the system, or b) a state of some action (starting, running, done).

OBLIGED$((a, P)$ IF $C)$ OBLIGED$((a$ DO $A)$ IF $C)$
PERMITTED$((a, P)$ IF $C)$ PERMITTED$((a$ DO $A)$ IF $C)$
FORBIDDEN$((a, P)$ IF $C)$ FORBIDDEN$((a$ DO $A)$ IF $C)$

An example is the following:

OBLIGED$((user$ DO $include(source(Suspect\_data), Criminal\_Register))$
IF $(done(include(Suspect\_data, Criminal\_Register))))$

Implementation Guideline: In the case of OBLIGED, the implementation of the enforcement depends on the verifiability of the condition C (detection of the activation of the obligation) and then the verifiability of P or A (detection of the deactivation of the obligation) In the case of enforcement of a Permission (PERMITTED) or a Prohibition (FORBIDDEN) such as PERMITTED$((a$ DO $A)$ IF $C)$, the order of the checkings should be reversed: first detect the occurrence of the action A or the predicate P, and then check if condition C holds. Detection of occurence of an action A is done again with the *black list* and *action alarm* mecanisms.

Conditional Norms with Deadlines. This is a special type of conditional norm where the start of the norm is not defined by a condition but by a deadline. We distinguish two types of deadlines:

– Absolute deadline (hh:mm:ss dd/mm/yyyy). E.g. 23:59:00 09/05/2004.
– Relative deadline: a deadline relative to an event C' (time(C') +/- lapse) E.g. $time(done(bid)) + 5min$

There are 12 possible expressions with deadlines, by combining the three deontic operators, the temporal operators (BEFORE and AFTER) and applying them to actions or predicates. Examples of such expressions are:

OBLIGED$((a, P)$ BEFORE $D)$ PERMITTED$((a$ DO $A)$ AFTER $D)$
FORBIDDEN$((a, P)$ BEFORE $D)$

Implementation Guideline: In the case of permissions (PERMITTED) and prohibitions (FORBIDDEN), the procedure is as in conditional norms: first detect the occurence of the action or the predicate, and then check the deadline. It is important to note that there is a relationship between permissions and prohibitions:

PERMITTED$((a, P)$ BEFORE $D) \Leftrightarrow$ FORBIDDEN$((a, P)$ AFTER $D)$
FORBIDDEN$((a, P)$ BEFORE $D) \Leftrightarrow$ PERMITTED$((a, P)$ AFTER $D)$

---

[4] Note that this also holds for unconditional norms.

In the case of OBLIGED, the deadline should be checked first, and then the occurence of A or P is verified. But deadlines are not that easy to check. They require a continuous check (second by second) to detect if a deadline is due. If the institution has lots of deadines to track, it will become computationally expensive. We propose to include within the agent platform a *clock trigger* mechanism that sends a signal when a deadline has passed. The idea is to implement the clock mechanism as efficiently as possible (some operating systems include a clock signal mechanism) to avoid the burden on the agents.

Obligations of Enforcement of Norms. In this case the norms concerning agent b generate obligations on agent a.

OBLIGED(a ENFORCE(OBLIGED(b...)))
OBLIGED(a ENFORCE(PERMITTED(b...)))
OBLIGED(a ENFORCE(FORBIDDEN(b...)))

Implementation Guideline: When a is an internal enforcer, as we have full control on internal agents, we implement this norm by placing the enforcement as a goal of the agent (as we discussed in §3.2). When a is not an internal enforcer but an external agent and the system has to enforce that a enforces another agent b's norms, we have two enforcement mechanisms:

- a enforces the norm on b: in this case, depending on b's norm, a has to detect the start and the end of the norm, and the occurrence of a violation, as explained in previous sections. In the case of a violation, a should execute the plan of action defined to solve such a situation.
- *root enforcer* enforces the obligation of a: in this case a root enforcer should detect those situations when b has violated its norm and a has not executed the plan of action to counteract the violation. The safest way would be to have a root enforcer closely checking the behaviour of b just as a should do, detect the start and the end of b's norm and the occurrence of violations, and then verify that a properly executes the plan of action. However, this is computationally expensive (we have two agents doing the same enforcement). If we want to have a safe enforcement we should use an internal agent to do it. Otherwise, if we have delegated some enforcement to agent a, we should not spend lots of resources on verifying a's behaviour. In this case the best option is, depending on the verifiability of the checks, to do some of the checks randomly or when the system has enough resources to detect violations that have not been counteracted.

Norm Condition Expression Language. Using the different kinds of norms that we discussed in the previous sections we can now specify a generic language for expressing norm conditions. This language was already used to express the examples in the previous sections. Although this language can be given a formal semantics, we refrain from doing so for now, but refer to [7] [10].

Definition 1 (Norm Condition).

NORM_CONDITION := $N(a, S \langle$IF $C\rangle) \mid$ OBLIGED(a ENFORCE($N(a, S \langle$IF $C\rangle)$))

$\qquad N :=$ OBLIGED $\mid$ PERMITTED $\mid$ FORBIDDEN

$\qquad S := P \mid$ DO $A \mid P$ TIME $D \mid$ DO TIME D

$\qquad C := proposition^5$

$\qquad P := proposition$

$\qquad A := action\ expression$

$\qquad$ TIME := BEFORE $\mid$ AFTER

Definition 1 shows that norm conditions can either be concerning states, e.g. for a norm such as *"buyers should not have a negative saldo"*, or concerning actions, e.g. for norms like *"administrators are allowed to include personal data concerning suspects in the Criminal Register"*. The definition allows the norm condition to be conditional, allowing the expression of norms like *"one should include the source of the data when including suspect data in the Criminal Register"*, as well as norm conditions including temporal aspects in the form of deadlines, for instance *"personal information in a Criminal Register is to be deleted when no new data has been entered within the last five years proving that the data is necessary for the investigation"*. The other group of norm conditions that can be expressed in the language defined in definition 1 are those concerning enforcement of norms on other agents.

3.4   Verifiability Levels

Now that we know what kinds of norms there are, we have to investigate how to use this information in order to enforce norms. It is easy to see that a protocol or procedure satisfies a norm when no violations occur during the execution of the protocol. The real problem in norm checking lies, however, in determining when that violation occurs. For instance, in criminal investigations, a police officer should not have more (sensitive or private) information than needed for the investigation. So an officer is doing fine as long as no violation occurs, i.e. he does not have too much information. The real problem lies in determining when the officer actually has too much information.

Therefore, the implementation of the enforcement of norms is depending on two properties of the checks to be done: a) the checks being *verifiable* (i.e. a condition or an action that can be machine-verified from the institutional point of view, given the time and resources needed) and b) the checks being *computational* (i.e. a condition or action that can be checked on any moment in a fast, low cost way). We distinguish between the following three levels of verifiability:

---

[5] The conditions (C) and propositions (P) are expressed in some kind of propositional logic. This logic can use deontic (cf. [8] [10]), or temporal (cf. [4] [7]) operators. Note however that this logic should at least include some operational operators like, for instance, DONE and RUNNING.

- **Computationally verifiable**: a condition or action that can be verified at any given moment.
- **Non-computationally verifiable**: a condition or action that can be machine-verified but is computationally hard to verify.
- **Non-verifiable**: a condition or an action that cannot be verified from the system (the institution) point of view, because it is not observable.

Using these levels we can look at their impact on the implementation of norm enforcement:

- **Norms computationally verifiable**: verification of all predicates and actions can be done easily, all the time. For instance:

$$\text{PERMITTED}((user \text{ DO } appoint(regular\_user))$$
$$\text{IF } (access\_level(user, register, 'full\_control')))$$

In this case it is clear that the verification can be easily done, because *authorization* mechanisms should be included on any multiagent platform to ensure security in open MAS.
Implementation Guideline: In this case the verification can be performed each time that it is needed.
- **Norms not computationally verifiable directly, but by introducing extra resources**. In this case the condition or action is not directly (easily) verifiable, but can be so by adding some extra data structures and/or mechanisms to make it easy to verify. The *action alarm* and *clock trigger* mechanisms are examples of extra resources. For instance, in

$$\text{OBLIGED}((buyer \text{ DO } bid(product, price))$$
$$\text{BEFORE } (buyer \text{ DO } exit(auction\_house)))$$

checking that a buyer has done at least one bid in the auction house (i.e., checking all the logs of all the auction rounds) may be computationally expensive if there are no data structures properly indexed in order to check it in an efficient way (e.g. the agent platform keeping, for each buyer, a list of bids uttered, or having a boolean that says whether the buyer has uttered a bid). Another example is the following:

$$\text{OBLIGED}((user \text{ DO } include(source(Suspect\_data), Criminal\_Register))$$
$$\text{IF } (done(include(Suspect\_data, Criminal\_Register))))$$

The detection of the inclusion of data is done by an *action alarm* mechanism placed in the user interface.
Implementation Guideline: include the extra data structures and/or mechanisms, and then do verification through them.
- **Non-computationally verifiable**: the check is too time/resource consuming to be done at any time.
Implementation Guideline: verification is not done all the time, but is delayed, doing a sort of "garbage collection" that detects violations. There are three main families:

- Verification done when the system is not busy and has enough resources.
- Verification scheduled periodically. E.g. each night, once a week.
- Random Verification (of actions/agents), like random security checkings of passengers in airports.

- **Observable from the institutional perspective, but not decidable**: That is, verifiable by other (human) agents that have the resources and/or the information needed. For instance:

  OBLIGED(($register\_admin$ DO $correct(data)$) IF ($incorrect(data)$))

  It is unfeasible for the system to check whether the information provided by users is incorrect without other sources of information. Therefore this check has to be delegated appropriately.
  Implementation Guideline: delegation of only those checks that cannot be performed by the system.

- **Indirectly observable from the institutional perspective**: These can be internal conditions, internal actions (like reasoning) or actions which are outside the ability of the system to be observed or detected (like sending a undetectable message between auctioneers in an auction).
  Implementation Guideline: try to find other conditions or actions that are observable and that may be used to (indirectly) detect a violation.

- **Not verifiable at all**: Should not be checked, because, e.g. it is completely unfeasible to do so (placed here for completeness, but no example found).

4   Violations, Sanctions and Repairs

As described in §3, we cannot assume to have full control over the addressees. Because there may be illegal actions and states which are outside the control of the enforcer, violations should be included in the normative framework. In order to manage violations, each violation should include a plan of action to be executed in the presence of the violation. Such a plan not only includes sanctions but also countermeasures to return the system to an acceptable state (repairs).

In section 3.3 we have introduced a machine-readable format for expressing norm conditions, and have discussed how to detect the activation and violation of norms. In order to link these detections with the violation management, we propose that a norm description includes, at least, the following:

- The norm condition (expressed as seen in §3.3).
- The violation state condition.
- A link to the violation detection mechanism.
- A sanction: the sanction is a plan (a set of actions) to punish the violator.
- Repairs: a plan (set of actions) to recover the system from the violation.

In this format, the *norm condition*-field is denoting when the norm becomes active and when it is achieved. The *violation* is a formula derived from the norm to express when a violation occurs (e.g. for the norm OBLIGED((a, P)

IF C) this is exactly the state when C occurs and P does not, that is, the state where the norm is active, but not acted upon). The *detection mechanism* is a set of actions that can be used to detect the violation (this includes any of the proposed detection mechanisms described in §3.3). The set of actions contained in the *sanction*-field is actually a plan which should be executed when a violation occurs (which can contain imposing fines, expulsing agents from the system, etc.). Finally, the *repairs* contains a plan of action that should be followed in order to 'undo' the violation. Definition 2 show how these elements make up the norm.

Definition 2 (Norms).

$$\text{NORM} := \text{NORM\_CONDITION}$$
$$\text{VIOLATION\_CONDITION}$$
$$\text{DETECTION\_MECHANISM}$$
$$\text{SANCTION}$$
$$\text{REPAIRS}$$
$$\text{VIOLATION\_CONDITION} := proposition$$
$$\text{DETECTION\_MECHANISM} := \{action\ expressions\}$$
$$\text{SANCTION} := \text{PLAN}$$
$$\text{REPAIRS} := \text{PLAN}$$
$$\text{PLAN} := action\ expression \mid action\ expression\ ;\ \text{PLAN}$$

For the formal definition of NORM_CONDITION see definition 1 in section 3.3.

An example (extracted from organ and tissue allocation regulations) is the following:

Norm	FORBIDDEN(*allocator* DO *assign(organ, recipient)*)
condition	IF NOT(*hospital* DONE *ensure_compatibility(organ, recipient)*))
Violation	NOT(*done(ensure_compatibility(organ, recipient))* AND
condition	*done(assign(organ, recipient))*
Detection	{*detect_alarm(assign,' starting')*;
mechanism	*check(done(ensure_compatibility(organ, recipient)))*; }
Sanction	*inform(board, "*NOT*(done(ensure_compatibility(organ, recipient))*
	AND *done(assign(organ, recipient))")*
Repairs	{*stop_assignation(organ)*;
	*record("*NOT*(done(ensure_compatibility(organ, recipient))* AND
	done(assign(organ, recipient))", incident_log);
	detect_alarm(ensure_compatibility,' done');
	check(done(ensure_compatibility(organ, recipient)));
	resume_assignation(organ); }

This example shows how violations and their related plans of action are defined. The violation condition defines when the violation occurs in terms of concrete predicates and actions (in the example, the violation condition uses exactly the predicates and actions in the norm expression as there is no need to refine them). The detection mechanism is defined as a plan (in this case involving an *action alarm* mechanism detecting each time that an assignment is attempted). Sanction plans define *punishment mechanisms*, either direct (fines, expulsion of the system) or indirect (social trust or reputation). In this scenario the punishment mechanism is indirect, by informing the board members of the transplant organization about the incident. Finally, the repairs is a plan to solve the situation (that is, a contingency plan). In action precedence norms (A precedes B), it usually has the same structure: stop action B (*assign*), record the incident in the systems' incident log and then wait (by means of the action alarm mechanism) for action A (*ensure_compatibility*) to be performed.

5   Conclusions

In this paper we have focused on the operational aspects of institutional norms in MAS. We have analized the problem by categorizing norms depending on actors involved, verifiability of states and actions in norm expressions, and temporal aspects. Then we have proposed some implementation guidelines on the enforcement of norms (i.e. detection and management) and the inclusion of some mechanisms (*black lists, action-alarms, clock-triggers, authorization*) to simplify norm enforcement on multiagent platforms.

We have also presented a first draft of a machine-readable format for expressing complex norms, like the ones appearing in domains such as *e*Commerce, *e*Government and *e*Care. Using this format we have proposed a norm description, which includes the norm condition and violation detection and repair techniques, in order make the first steps in implementing norm enforcement in MAS by means of violation handling.

Currently we are taking the first steps towards implementing the enforcement mechanisms presented here by introducing our norm model into ISLANDER, and adding the proposed enforcement mechanism to the E-INSTITUTOR platform.

References

1. A. Artikis. *Executable Specification of Open Norm-Governed Computational Systems*. PhD thesis, Department of Electrical & Electronic Engineering, Imperial College London, November 2003.
2. G. Boella and L. van der Torre. Fulfilling or violating norms in normative multiagent systems. In *Proceedings of IAT 2004*. IEEE, 2004.
3. G. Boella and L. van der Torre. Normative multiagent systems. In *Proceedings of Trust in Agent Societies Workshop at AAMAS'04*, New York, 2004.
4. J. Broersen, F. Dignum, V. Dignum, and J.-J. Ch. Meyer. Designing a Deontic Logic of Deadlines. In *7th Int. Workshop on Deontic Logic in Computer Science (DEON'04)*, Portugal, May 2004.
5. C. Castelfranchi. Formalizing the informal?: Dynamic social order, bottom-up social control, and spontaneous normative relations. *Journal of Applied Logic*, 1(1-2):47–92, February 2003.
6. C. Castelfranchi, F. Dignum, C. Jonker, and J. Treur. Deliberative normative agents: Principles and architectures. In N. Jennings and Y. Lesperance, editors, *ATAL '99*, volume 1757 of *LNAI*, pages 364–378, Berlin Heidelberg, 2000. Springer Verlag.

7. F. Dignum, J. Broersen, V. Dignum, and J.-J. Ch. Meyer. Meeting the Deadline: Why, When and How. In *3rd Goddard Workshop on Formal Approaches to Agent-Based Systems (FAABS)*, Maryland, April 2004.
8. F. Dignum, D. Kinny, and L. Sonenberg. From Desires, Obligations and Norms to Goals. *Cognitive Science Quarterly*, 2(3-4):407–430, 2002.
9. V. Dignum and F. Dignum. Modeling agent societies: Coordination frameworks and institutions. In P. Brazdil and A. Jorge, editors, *Progress in Artificial Intelligence*, LNAI 2258, pages 191–204. Springer-Verlag, 2001.
10. V. Dignum, J.-J.Ch. Meyer, F. Dignum, and H. Weigand. Formal Specification of Interaction in Agent Societies. In *2nd Goddard Workshop on Formal Approaches to Agent-Based Systems (FAABS)*, Maryland, Oct. 2002.
11. M. Esteva, J. Padget, and C. Sierra. Formalizing a language for institutions and norms. In J.-J.CH. Meyer and M. Tambe, editors, *Intelligent Agents VIII*, volume 2333 of *LNAI*, pages 348–366. Springer Verlag, 2001.
12. M. Esteva, J.A. Rodríguez-Aguilar, B. Rosell, and J.L. Arcos. AMELI: An Agent-based Middleware for Electronic Institutions. In *Third International Joint Conference on Autonomous Agents and Multi-agent Systems*, New York, US, July 2004.
13. A Logical Framework for Ethical Behaviour between Infohabitants in the Information Trading Economy of the Universal Information Ecosystem (ALFEBIITE). http://www.iis.ee.ic.ac.uk/~alfebiite/ab-home.htm.
14. A. Lomuscio and D. Nute, editors. *Proc. of the 7th Int. Workshop on Deontic Logic in Computer Science (DEON04)*, volume 3065 of *LNCS*. Springer Verlag, 2004.
15. F. López y López and M. Luck. Towards a Model of the Dynamics of Normative Multi-Agent Systems. In G. Lindemann, D. Moldt, M. Paolucci, and B. Yu, editors, *Proc. of the Int. Workshop on Regulated Agent-Based Social Systems: Theories and Applications (RASTA '02)*, volume 318 of *Mitteilung*, pages 175–194. Universität Hamburg, 2002.
16. F. López y Lopez, M. Luck, and M. d'Inverno. A framework for norm-based inter-agent dependence. In *Proceedings of The Third Mexican International Conference on Computer Science*, pages 31–40. SMCC-INEGI, 2001.
17. P. Noriega. *Agent-Mediated Auctions: The Fishmarket Metaphor*. PhD thesis, Inst. d'Investigació en Intel.ligència Artificial, 1997.
18. J.A. Rodriguez. *On the Design and Construction of Agent-mediated Electronic Institutions*. PhD thesis, Inst. d'Investigació en Intel.ligència Artificial, 2001.

Policies for Cloned Teleo-reactive Robots

Krysia Broda and Christopher John Hogger

Department of Computing, Imperial College London
{kb,cjh}@doc.ic.ac.uk

Abstract. This paper presents a new method for predicting the values of policies for cloned multiple teleo-reactive robots operating in the context of exogenous events. A teleo-reactive robot behaves autonomously under the control of a policy and is pre-disposed by that policy to achieve some goal. Our approach plans for a set of conjoint robots by focusing upon one representative of them. Simulation results reported here indicate that our method affords a good degree of predictive power and scalability.

1 Introduction

This paper examines the problem of designing optimal or near-optimal policies for a group of *teleo-reactive* (TR) robots operating in the context of *exogenous* events. From the viewpoint of any individual robot an exogenous event is any change in the world not caused through its own actions. The characteristics of a TR robot are, typically, that it behaves autonomously under the control of a stored program or policy, that the policy alone instructs it how to react to perceptions of the world, that it possesses very limited computing resources for program storage and interpretation and that it is predisposed by the policy to achieve some goal. The main features of TR robots were introduced in [11] and further developed in [12]. We make two key assumptions about a robot: that it has (i) little or no access to cognitive resources, such as beliefs or reasoning systems, and (ii) only partial observational capability, in that its perceptions may not fully capture the whole environmental state. Such robots could find uses in those applications, for instance nano-medicine or remote exploration, where physical or economic constraints might preclude such access. Informally, a good policy is one which disposes a robot to perform well in pursuit of a defined goal whatever state it is currently in.

A reactive robot responding only to its current perception of the state can be modelled naturally by a Markov Decision Process (MDP). When that perception captures less than the entirety of the state it is often modelled using the framework of Partially Observable MDPs (POMDPs) [7, 5, 10]. Seeking good policies for a given robot within the POMDP framework typically requires, in order to compensate for the lack of full state information, that the actual state be estimated using a history of previous events. When the history is owed *only to actions of known robots*, it is accurately representable. However, it is not accurately representable if arbitrary exogenous events can occur, which is exactly

G. Lindemann et al. (Eds.): MATES 2004, LNAI 3187, pp. 328–340, 2004.

the case in which we, by contrast, are interested. Our approach is somewhat similar in motivation to that of [6], in that we plan for a set of conjoint agents by focusing upon some representative subset of them.

Our position must also be distinguished from that taken by many in the multi-agent community who equip their agents with complex theories about the environment and elaborate communication mechanisms, because of our focus on minimally equipped robots. Nevertheless, the problem remains of dealing with a robot having limited perception.

Choosing a good policy for a given goal is generally difficult. Even simple robots and worlds can offer huge numbers of policies to consider. Most ways of designing TR-(teleo-reactive) policies are learning-based, as in [1] which applies inductive logic programming to determine advantageous associations between actions and consequences. Other learning schemes for TR-planning are [9], [14] and [8].

The core concepts in our approach, first proposed in [2], are as follows. The world in which the robot operates has a total set $\mathcal{O}$ of possible *states*. The robot is presumed to possess perceptors through which it may partially perceive these states; the set of all its possible *perceptions* is denoted by $\mathcal{P}$. The robot is also presumed capable of certain *actions* which form a set $\mathcal{A}$. In any state $o \in \mathcal{O}$, the robot's possible perceptions form some subset $P(o) \subseteq \mathcal{P}$, and in response to any perception $p \in P(o)$ the robot's possible actions form some subset $A(p) \subseteq \mathcal{A}$. A *policy* (or program) for the robot is any total function $f : \mathcal{P} \to \mathcal{A}$ satisfying $\forall p \in \mathcal{P}, f(p) \in A(p)$. The number of possible policies is the product of the cardinalities of the $A(p)$ sets for all $p \in \mathcal{P}$. A *situation* for the robot is any pair (o, p) for which $o \in \mathcal{O}$ and $p \in P(o)$. We denote by $\mathcal{S}$ the set of all possible situations, one or more of which may be designated *goal* situations. Associated with the robot is a unique *unrestricted situation graph* G in which each node is a situation. This graph has an arc labelled by an action a directed from node (o, p) to node (o', p') in every case that $a \in A(p)$ and execution of action a could take the world state from o to o' and the robot's perception from p to p'. The possibilities that $o = o'$ and/or $p = p'$ are not inherently excluded. The policies are evaluated using discounted-reward principles [7] applied to the situation graphs.

A key feature of this approach is that the graph for the robot can represent, besides the effects of its own actions, the effects of exogenous actions, whether enacted by other robots or by other indeterminate agencies. This obviates analysing comprehensively the explicit combinations of all the robots' behaviours. This treatment is one contribution to the control of scalability and is in contrast to that presented in [13], who explicate entirely the joint perceptions of the robots. Scalability can be further controlled by abstraction, by way of replacing sets of concrete situations by abstract generic situations [4]. Situation graphs have also been employed to represent and exploit inter-robot communication [3].

This paper demonstrates the use of situation graphs to predict optimal or near-optimal policies for groups of cloned TR-robots, and assesses their effectiveness on the basis of simulation results. The main contribution is to show that useful designs for robot clones can be obtained by analysing a single robot acting in the context of events instigated by others. Section 2 illustrates how TR-scenarios are formulated and Sect. 3 discusses the evaluation and testing of policies. In Sect. 4 we describe the treatment of multi-robot contexts and some case-studies are presented in Sect. 5. Section 6 uses the results of those studies to discuss some ramifications of the design method, whilst Sect. 7 summarizes our conclusions.

2   An Illustration

The above ideas are now illustrated using *BlocksWorld* for a single robot case. Of course, *BlocksWorld* is just a generic exemplar of a wide range of state transition systems.

In *BlocksWorld* the world comprises a surface and a number of identical blocks. A state is an arrangement of the blocks such that some are stacked in towers on the surface whilst others are each held by some robot, and is representable by a list of the towers' heights. Suppose there are just 2 blocks and one robot which can, at any instant, see just one thing – the surface, a 1-tower or a 2-tower, denoted by $s0$, $s1$ and $s2$ respectively. Further, it can sense whether it is holding a block or not doing so, denoted by h and nh respectively. Its perception set $\mathcal{P}$ then comprises just 5 legal pairings of "seeing" status and "holding" status. At any instant the robot performs whichever action $a \in \mathcal{A}$ corresponds, according to its policy, to its current perception $p \in \mathcal{P}$; this behaviour is assumed to be durative – the action cannot change while perception p persists. The action set $\mathcal{A}$ in *BlocksWorld* is $\{k, l, w\}$. In a k-action ("pick") the robot removes the top block from a tower it is seeing, and afterwards is holding that block and seeing the resulting tower (or the surface, as appropriate). In an l-action ("place") the robot places a block it is holding upon what it is seeing (the surface or some tower), and afterwards is not holding a block and is seeing the resulting tower. In a w-action ("wander") the robot merely updates its perception without altering the state. Figure 1 shows these aspects of the formulation, labelling the states $1 \ldots 3$ and the perceptions $a \ldots e$.

Figure 2a shows the unrestricted graph G, where each node (o, p) is abbreviated to op. There are 16 policies, one being

$$f = \{a \to w, \quad b \to w, \quad c \to w, \quad d \to w, \quad e \to l\}$$

(a) states and perceptions

o	$P(o)$
1	[1, 1]	$\{a, b\}$
2	[1]	$\{d, e\}$
3	[2]	$\{a, c\}$

(b) perceptions and actions

p		$A(p)$
a	$[s0, nh]$	$\{w\}$
b	$[s1, nh]$	$\{k, w\}$
c	$[s2, nh]$	$\{k, w\}$
d	$[s0, h]$	$\{l, w\}$
e	$[s1, h]$	$\{l, w\}$

Fig. 1. Formulation of the 2-block world

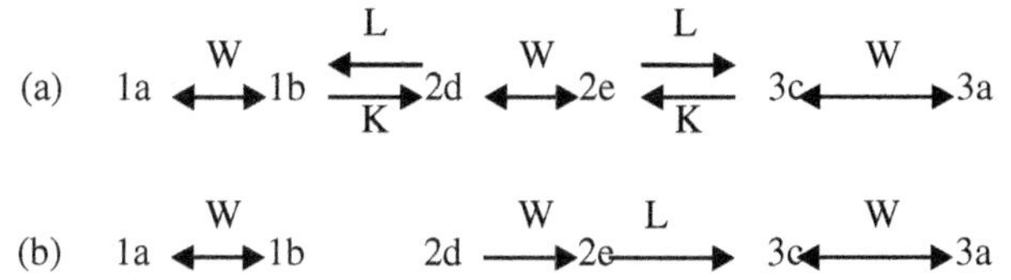

(a)   1a ⟷ 1b ⇄ 2d ⟷ 2e ⇄ 3c ⟷ 3a

(b)   1a ⟷ 1b   2d → 2e → 3c ⟷ 3a

Fig. 2. (a) Unrestricted graph G; (b) f-restricted graph G_f

To adopt this policy is to eliminate certain arcs from G to leave the *f-restricted graph* G_f shown in Fig. 2b. G_f gives the transitions the robot could make under policy f. For a given goal, choosing f partitions the set $\mathcal{S}$ of nodes in G into two disjoint subsets T_f and N_f called the *trough* and *non-trough* respectively. T_f comprises exactly those nodes from which there is no path in G_f to the goal, and N_f comprises all others. Choosing, say, the goal $3c$ in the example yields $T_f = \{1a, 1b\}$ and $N_f = \{2d, 2c, 3c, 3a\}$. Here, no arc in G_f is directed from N_f to T_f. When such an arc does exist, G_f is described as *NT*-bridged. In that case a robot able in principle to reach the goal from some initial node may traverse the bridge and thereafter be unable to reach the goal, since no arc directed from T_f to N_f can exist. Define $\lambda = 100|N_f|/|\mathcal{S}|$. Then for a series of experiments choosing initial situations randomly, the robot's predicted success rate $SR_{\mathrm{pre}}(f)$ (as a percentage) is $< \lambda$ if G_f is *NT*-bridged but is otherwise exactly λ. For the example above $SR_{\mathrm{pre}}(f) = 66.67\%$.

3   Predicting and Testing Policies

This section explains how policies are evaluated in a single-robot context. The extension to the multi-robot context then follows in the next section.

The predicted value $V_{\mathrm{pre}}(f)$ of a policy f is the mean of the values of all situations in G_f, assuming they are equally probable as initial ones. The value of a situation S should reflect the reward accumulated by the robot in proceeding from S, favouring goal-reaching paths over others. If S has immediate successor-set SS then its value $V(S)$ can be measured by the discounted-reward formula

$$V(S) = \Sigma_{s \in SS}(p_s.(rwd(s) + \gamma.V(S_i)))$$

where p_s is the probability that from S the robot proceeds next to s, $rwd(s)$ is the reward it earns by doing so and γ is a discount factor such that $0 \leq \gamma < 1$. In a single-robot context equal probabilities are assigned to those arcs emergent from S. We employ two fixed numbers R and r such that $rwd(s) = R$ if s is a goal and $rwd(s) = r$ otherwise, where $R \gg r$. The situations' values are therefore related by a set of linear equations which, since $\gamma < 1$, have unique finite solutions and so determine a finite value for $V_{\mathrm{pre}}(f)$. In general, choosing $R \gg r$ ranks more highly those policies well-disposed to the reaching of the goal, whilst γ controls the separation (but not, in general, the ranks) of the policies' values. A *Policy*

Predictor program is used to compute policy values by this method, and also to compute (as above) the upper bounds (λ) on their success-rates.

We tested the quality of the *Policy Predictor* by using a *Policy Simulator* program. Each *run* of the simulator takes an initial situation S and subsequently drives the robot according to the given policy f. The simulated robot then implicitly traverses some path in G_f from S. The run terminates when it either reaches the goal or exceeds a prescribed bound B on the number of transitions performed. As the path is traversed, the value $V(S)$ is computed incrementally on the same basis as used by the predictor. Equal numbers of runs are executed for each initial situation S and the mean of all observed $V(S)$ values gives the observed policy value $V_{obs}(f)$. The simulator also reports the observed success rate $SR_{obs}(f)$.

The simulator supports both *positionless* and *positional* simulation modes. The former associates no positional data to the robot or the towers, and so uses the same information about the problem as the predictor. Thus, if the robot picks a block from the 2-tower in the state $[1, 2]$, it is indeterminate as to which tower it will see afterwards in the new state $[1, 1]$. By contrast, the positional mode assigns discrete grid coordinates to the robot and the towers, and exploits these to effect transitions in a manner somewhat closer to physical reality through knowing precisely where the robot is located and what it is seeing. This paper gives results only for positionless simulation, using parameter values $R = 100$, $r = -1$ and $\gamma = 0.9$.

To visualize the correlation of predictions with test outcomes for a set $\mathcal{F}$ of n policies, those policies' observed values are charted against the ranks of their predicted values. Overall predictive quality is reflected by the extent to which the chart exhibits a monotonically decreasing profile. A precise measure of this can be computed as the Kendall rank-correlation coefficient $\tau_{\mathcal{F}}$ for $\mathcal{F}$, as follows. Let (f, g) be any pair of distinct policies in $\mathcal{F}$ satisfying $V_{pre}(f) \leq V_{pre}(g)$. This pair is said to be concordant if $V_{obs}(f) \leq V_{obs}(g)$, but is otherwise discordant. Then $\tau_{\mathcal{F}} = 2(C - D)/n(n - 1)$ where C and D are the numbers of concordant pairs and discordant pairs, respectively, in $\mathcal{F} \times \mathcal{F}$. Its least possible value is -1 and its greatest is +1. It is convenient to map it to a percentage scale by defining $Q_{\mathcal{F}} = 0\%$ when they disagree maximally.

Figure 3 shows the chart for the 2-block example above, choosing the goal as $(3, c)$, i.e. "build and see a 2-tower". Observed policy values are measured along the vertical axis, and predicted ranks (here, from 1 to 16) along the horizontal one. Arcs emergent from $(3, c)$ were suppressed from G to mirror the fact that the simulator terminates any run that reaches a goal. For each policy the simulator executed 1002 runs with $B = 100$. The chart is perfectly monotonic and $Q_{\mathcal{F}} = 100\%$. The optimal policy is $\{a \rightarrow \text{w}, \ b \rightarrow \text{k}, \ c \rightarrow \text{w} \ (or \ \text{k}), \ d \rightarrow \text{w}, \ e \rightarrow \text{l}\}$, which picks a block only from a 1-tower and places a block only upon a 1-tower. Its success rate is 100%.

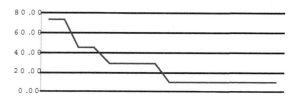

Fig. 3. Policy ranking chart for building a 2-tower

4   Policies for Multiple Robots

Whether or not it is useful to employ multiple robots in the pursuit of a goal depends upon the nature of the world and of the robots' interactions with the world and with each other. With limited perceptions, incognizance of the goal and lack of communication, simple TR-robots of the kind we have considered may cooperate advantageously only by serendipity. Predicting accurately the behaviour of multiple robots presents not only analytical difficulties, in attempting to assess the overall impact of their interactions, but also problems of scale – for just a modest case of a 4-block world with 2 robots there are potentially more than 13,000 policies to consider.

This section explains how a situation graph focusing upon one robot, termed "*self*", can express the effects of other robots acting in concert with it. The key question is whether such a graph enables prediction of good policies for the combined robots without requiring explicit analysis of all the combinations of the situations they occupy.

For this purpose we introduce a special domain-independent action named x that all robots possess in their $\mathcal{A}$ sets. So for *Blocks World* $\mathcal{A}$ is now $\{k, l, w, x\}$. In any situation graph an x-arc directed from (o, p) to (o', p') signifies that, from the viewpoint of *self*, the state transition from o to o' is effected *exogenously* by some other agent(s), here restricted to be other robot(s). So, when *self*'s policy prescribes an x-action for perception p, this is interpreted operationally as requiring *self* to "wait" (that is, to become inactive) until its situation is updated exogenously to (o', p'). On the other hand, when *self*'s policy prescribes some action other than x *self* may alternatively undergo an exogenous transition caused by the action of another robot. We call this *passive updating* of *self*.

Whether or not the robots all have the same policy, it is desirable to reduce the possibility of deadlocks in which they would all be waiting. One way to do this is to arrange that whenever a robot's policy requires it to wait, the transition that it awaits should be achievable in one step by some other robot. In the case that all robots have the same policy f (i.e. are clones) this is called the *clone-consistency principle*, defined as follows. Suppose f contains $p \to x$. If G_f has an x-arc from (o, p) to (o', p') then (i) G_f must also have an arc from (o, q) to (o', q') labeled by an action a other than x and (ii) f must contain $q \to a$. Besides reducing deadlock this principle also reduces very significantly the number of policies requiring to be examined. A weaker one could require that the progression from o to o' be achieved within $k > 1$ steps for some specified k, allowing a more liberal dependence upon exogenous behaviour but at the expense of having more policies to consider.

In the multiple-robot context the predictor assigns probabilities to the arcs of a graph G_f as follows. Each node $S = (o, p)$ has emergent arcs for the action a that *self* performs according to the rule $p \rightarrow$ a in its policy f. If a = x then these x-arcs are the only arcs emergent from S. The predictor counts, for each one, the number of distinct ways its transition could arise, taking account of the number of other robots that could effect it. Their probabilities are then required to be proportional to these counts and to have sum $\Sigma_X = 1$. If a $\neq$ x then S additionally has arcs labeled a and these are assigned equal probabilities having sum Σ_a. In this case Σ_a and Σ_X are made to satisfy $\Sigma_a + \Sigma_X = 1$ and $\Sigma_X = (n - 1)\Sigma_a$ where n is the total number of robots, reflecting the relative likelihood in situation S of *self* being the robot selected to act or one of the others being selected to act.

In the multiple-robot context the simulator effects transitions between *multi-situations*, which generalise situations. A multi-situation is a *physically possible* assignment of the robots to situations that share a common state and differ (if at all) only in perceptions. An example of a multi-situation for the 2 robot example shown in Fig. 4 is $\{(r1, (3, d)), (r2, (3, d))\}$. On the other hand, $\{(r1, (3, d)), (r2, (3, a))\}$ is not a multi-situation as it is physically impossible.

At any given moment in a simulation, some robots may be flagged as *waiting*, because they previously performed x-actions for which they still await the required transitions. Robots not currently so flagged are called *active*. A run begins with an initial multi-situation chosen randomly from the set of all multi-situations distinguishable up to robot identity. Each subsequent transition from a state o is made by randomly choosing some active robot and performing the action a prescribed by its policy, causing the state to become some o'. If a $\in \{$ w, x $\}$ then $o = o'$ and the other active robots' perceptions remain unchanged. If a $\in \{$k, l$\}$ then $o \neq o'$ and the other active robots are passively updated in a manner chosen randomly from all possible ways of updating them to state o', whilst any waiting robots whose required transitions have now been effected become active and acquire the perceptions in state o' that they had awaited.

A transition from the multi-situation $\{(r1, (2, d)), (r2, (2, d))\}$ (again for the example shown in Fig. 4) might be: $r1$ is selected, its policy (say) dictates action k and the new multi-situation would be either $\{(r1, (6, h)), (r2, (6, i))\}$ or $\{(r1, (6, h)), (r2, (6, d))\}$. The situation change for $r2$ in this transition is an example of a passive update corresponding to an x-arc from either $(2, d)$ to $(6, i)$ or $(2, d)$ to $(6, d)$. The simulator chooses randomly from these two possibilities.

A run is terminated when any active robot in the group reaches a goal situation or when the simulation depth bound B is reached. The simulator's successive random choosing of which robot acts next provides an adequate approximation to the more realistic scenario in which they would all be acting concurrently. Owing to the physical constraint that there can be only one state of the world

o		$P(o)$
1	[2,2]	$\{e, i\}$
2	[1,1,1,1]	$\{d, i\}$
3	[1,1,2]	$\{d, e, i\}$
4	[1, 3]	$\{d, f, i\}$
5	[4]	$\{g, i\}$
6	[1,1,1]	$\{a, d, h, i\}$
7	[1, 2]	$\{a, b, d,$ $e, h, i\}$
8	[3]	$\{c, f, h, i\}$
9	[1,1]	$\{a, h\}$
10	[2]	$\{b, h\}$

p		$A(p)$
a	$[s1, h]$	$\{\texttt{1}, \texttt{w}, \texttt{x}\}$
b	$[s2, h]$	$\{\texttt{1}, \texttt{w}, \texttt{x}\}$
c	$[s3, h]$	$\{\texttt{1}, \texttt{w}, \texttt{x}\}$
d	$[s1, nh]$	$\{\texttt{k}, \texttt{w}, \texttt{x}\}$
e	$[s2, nh]$	$\{\texttt{k}, \texttt{w}, \texttt{x}\}$
f	$[s3, nh]$	$\{\texttt{k}, \texttt{w}, \texttt{x}\}$
g	$[s4, nh]$	$\{\texttt{k}, \texttt{w}, \texttt{x}\}$
h	$[s0, h]$	$\{\texttt{1}, \texttt{w}, \texttt{x}\}$
i	$[s0, nh]$	$\{\texttt{w}, \texttt{x}\}$

Fig. 4. Formulation of 4-block world with 2 robots

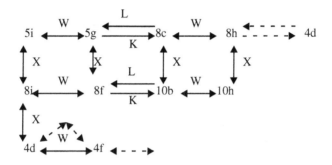

Fig. 5. Graph G for 4-blocks and 2 robots

at any instant, any set of concurrent actions that produced that state can be serialized in one way or another to achieve the same outcome. The simulator's randomness effectively covers all such possible serializations.

An x-arc in the graph thus represents two notions at once. On the one hand it represents the action of deliberate waiting in accordance with *self*'s own policy. On the other hand it indicates how *self* can be impacted by the actions of others.

5   Multiple Clone Examples

All these examples are for a world having 4 blocks, but with various goals and various numbers of cloned robots. The total number of policies is 13,122 but only 480 are clone-consistent. Each of these 480 was given about 1000 simulation runs with $B = 100$, and the reward parameters used were $R = 100$, $r = -1$ and $\gamma = 0.9$.

Example 5.1: [*2 robots building a 4-tower*] The formulation is shown in Fig. 4. The unrestricted graph G has 30 nodes, among which is the goal $(5, g)$. Figure 5 shows a fragment of G ($4d$ appears twice only for drawing convenience). Even this

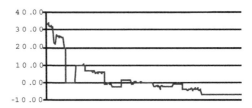

Fig. 6. Policy ranking chart for Example 5.1

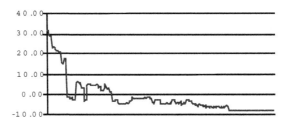

Fig. 7. Policy ranking chart for Example 5.2

fragment has some incident and emergent arcs omitted from the figure. Figure 6 shows the policy ranking chart for the set $\mathcal{F}$ of the best 240 policies. For these, $Q_{\mathcal{F}}$ is 87.90%. The best ones are ranked almost perfectly. The observed optimal one, having predicted rank 2, is

$$\{a \to \text{1}, \ b \to \text{w}, \ c \to \text{w}, \ d \to \text{k}, \ e \to \text{k}, \ f \to \text{w}, \ g \to \text{w}, \ h \to \text{w}, \ i \to \text{w}\}$$

This picks only from a tower of height < 3 and places upon any tower of height < 4 (but not upon the surface).

Example 5.2: [*3 robots building a 4-tower*] The graph G is now a little larger, as there is an extra state. It has 36 nodes. Figure 7 charts the best 240 policies, for which $Q_{\mathcal{F}}$ is 89.94%. For the best 20 it is 85.79%. The observed optimal policy is the same as for 2 robots, and is the predicted optimal one.

Example 5.3: [*4 robots building a 4-tower*] The graph G now has yet one more state (in which every block is being held). It has 39 nodes. Figure 8 charts the best 240 policies, for which $Q_{\mathcal{F}}$ is 90.02%. For the best 20 it is again 85.79%. The observed optimal policy is the predicted optimal one, being

$$\{a \to \text{1}, \ b \to \text{1}, \ c \to \text{1}, \ d \to \text{k}, \ e \to \text{w}, \ f \to \text{w}, \ g \to \text{w}, \ h \to \text{w}, \ i \to \text{w}\}$$

which picks only from a tower of height 1 and places only upon a tower of height < 4.

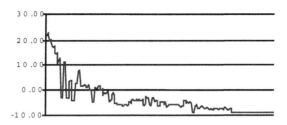

Fig. 8. Policy ranking chart for Example 5.3

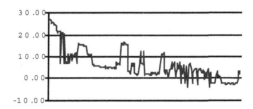

Fig. 9. Policy ranking chart for Example 5.4

Example 5.4: [*2 robots building a 2-tower and two 1-towers*] Here, G is the same graph as in Example 5.1. The goal is now $(3, i)$, i.e. "build one 2-tower, two 1-towers and see the surface". This example is different from the previous three, in that a robot cannot, using a single perception, recognise that the goal has been reached. Figure 9 charts the best 240 policies, for which $Q_{\mathcal{F}}$ is only 78.61%. For the best 20, however, it is 90.53%. The three observed best policies

$$\{a \to \mathrm{w}, \quad b \to \mathrm{w}, \quad c \to \mathrm{w}, \quad d \to \mathrm{w}, \quad e \to \mathrm{w}, \quad f \to \mathrm{k}, \quad g \to \mathrm{k}, \quad h \to \mathrm{l}, \quad i \to \mathrm{w}\}$$

(or $c \to \mathrm{x}$ or $c \to \mathrm{l}$) are the three predicted best ones, sharing the property that they pick only from a tower of height > 2 and can place upon the surface. They differ only in the case that a robot is holding a block and seeing a 3-tower (perception c), and their values are virtually identical. In the case $c \to \mathrm{x}$ the robot waits for another robot to pick from the 3-tower. The case $c \to \mathrm{l}$ is a retrograde choice as there is no merit in building a 4-tower, and it may seem surprising that it occurs in a high-value policy. However, the probability of a 3-tower actually arising is made very low by the other rules in these policies, so that choosing $c \to \mathrm{l}$ has no significant impact upon the policy value. The chart is more volatile in this example. This may be due in part to the looser coupling of state and perception in the goal situation. In the 4-tower examples the perception "seeing a 4-tower" implies that the state contains a 4-tower. In the present example there is no single perception that implies that the goal state has been achieved, so the robots have poorer goal-recognition. However, the volatility in all these examples has other causes as well, as discussed in the next section.

    Though limited in scope, these case studies suggest that, in order to select a good policy, the robot designer is unlikely to go far wrong in choosing from

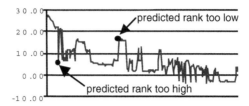

Fig. 10. Prediction anomalies in Example 5.4

the best 10% according to the predictor. The predictor is clearly imperfect, and is inevitably so due to the approximations it makes, but unless the design imperatives are very demanding it is sufficient to seek policies yielding reasonable rather than optimal behaviour.

The option remains open to filter ostensibly high value policies using a more sophisticated predictor, in order to eliminate those that are actually worse than the basic one suggests. Such refinements can employ, for a small selection of policies, analyses that would be impractical in scale if applied to all policies.

6   Factors Affecting Predictive Quality

We dealt with a multi-clone context by optimizing a single clone using only the x-action to represent the effects of other clones. This is our alternative to analysing comprehensively how the clones behave conjointly. The latter analysis would need an unrestricted graph in which each node were a complete multi-situation having emergent arcs for all the real (non-x) actions its members could perform. From this *group-graph* one could then seek the best policy for any one clone. The combinatorial nature of such an analysis makes it generally impractical. Figure 10 repeats the chart for Example 5.4 but highlights two of its many anomalies. The policy indicated with too high a predicted rank is

$$\{a \to \mathtt{w}, \quad b \to \mathtt{l}, \quad c \to \mathtt{w}, \quad d \to \mathtt{w}, \quad e \to \mathtt{w}, \quad f \to \mathtt{k}, \quad g \to \mathtt{k}, \quad h \to \mathtt{l}, \quad i \to \mathtt{w}\}$$

If we examine how its predicted value is calculated, we find that a node $S = (4, f)$ in G_f is assigned a positive value $V(S)$ even though, in reality, the goal is unachievable from S. As noted earlier, the calculation of policy values must take into account passive transitions of *self* (x-updating). Our method sees paths from S to the goal that contain steps in which *self* is assumed to be x-updatable by the other robot, although, in fact, the goal is unachievable from S. In situation S no block is held and *self* is seeing a 3-tower and must pick. From S there is the following ostensible path in G_f that reaches the goal:

(a) *self* is in situation $(4, f)$ and – because of what happens next to it in this path – the other robot must also be in $(4, f)$;
(b) the other robot takes action $\mathtt{k}$ and moves to $(7, b)$, whilst *self* is passively updated to $(7, e)$;

(c) *self* performs two wander actions taking it to $(7, i)$, whilst the other robot remains at $(7, b)$;

(d) the graph shows an x-action from $(7, i)$ to the goal $(3, d)$, which is correct since another robot could be in situation $(7, h)$. However, if this particular path is followed, the other robot would not be in the required $(7, h)$ but in $(7, b)$.

This path is infeasible because to achieve it would require *self* to perform actions and undergo x-updates that the other robot could never fulfil. In the group-graph this joint scenario would not be feasible and any group situations containing $(4, f)$ would be assigned negative node values thereby reducing the policy's rank.

Figure 10 also indicates a policy with too low a predicted rank. Anomalies of this kind arise primarily from inaccuracy in the probabilities on the x-arcs in G_f, again owing to insufficient information about the situations actually occupied by *self*'s partners.

7 Conclusions

We have presented a method using situation graphs for predicting policies for TR-robots in multi-robot contexts. The use of situation graphs enables policies to be evaluated taking account of objective states, yielding greater discrimination than approaches (e.g. [7]) that focus primarily upon perceptions. This discrimination is necessary due to our assumption that exogenous events are not only possible but an inherent fact in a multi-robot context, so that we cannot rely on using histories to estimate current situations. Furthermore, since we wish to find policies to achieve goals not detectable by a single perception, we cannot use the method of back-chaining and the so-called regression property used in [11], since a given perception may not be unique to the goal.

However, inclusion of objective state information poses a greater need for scalable methods, especially in multi-robot contexts. We have demonstrated here that in such contexts good policies are obtainable by analysing how any single robot responds to exogenous effects caused by other robots. This applies whether or not the robots are cloned. It has further been shown in [4] that the approach continues to yield good results in positionally sensitive formulations, even when abstraction is also employed.

Our future work will seek to understand better the relationship between our "self-based prediction graph" and the group graph and to investigate how the use of the former might be refined to give even better predictive power.

References

1. Benson, S. Learning Action Models for Reactive Autonomous Agents, PhD, Dept. of Computer Science, Stanford University, 1996.
2. Broda, K., Hogger, C.J. and Watson, S. Constructing Teleo-Reactive Robot Programs, *Proceedings of the 14th European Conference on Artificial Intelligence*, Berlin, pp 653-657, 2000.

3. Broda, K. and Hogger, C.J. Designing Teleo-Reactive Programs, Technical Report 2003/8, Dept. of Computing, Imperial College London, UK, 2003.

4. Broda, K. and Hogger, C.J. Designing and Simulating Individual Teleo-Reactive Agents, *Poster Proceedings, 27th German Conference on Artificial Intelligence*, Ulm, 2004.

5. Cassandra, A.R., Kaelbling, L.P. and Littman, M. Acting Optimally in Partially Observable Stochastic Domains, *Proceedings 12th National Conference on AI (AAAI-94)*, Seattle, pp 183-188, 1994.

6. Chades, I., Scherrer, B. and Charpillet, F. Planning Cooperative Homogeneous Multiagent Systems using Markov Decision Processes, *Proceedings of the 5th International Conference on Enterprise Information Systems (ICEIS 2003)*, pp 426-429, 2003.

7. Kaelbling, L.P., Littman, M.L. and Cassandra, A.R. Planning and Acting in Partially Observable Stochastic Domains, *Artificial Intelligence* 101, pp 99-134, 1998.

8. Kochenderfer, M. Evolving Hierarchical and Recursive Teleo-reactive Programs through Genetic Programming, *EuroGP 2003*, LNCS 2610, pp 83-92, 2003.

9. Mitchell, T. Reinforcement Learning, Machine Learning, pp 367-390, McGraw Hill, 1997.

10. Nair R., Tambe, M., Yokoo, M., Pynadath, D. and Marsella, M. Taming Decentralised POMDPs: Towards Efficient Policy Computation for Multiagent Settings, *Proceedings of the 18th International Joint Conference on Artificial Intelligence (IJCAI-03)*, pp 705-711, 2003.

11. Nilsson, N.J. Teleo-Reactive Programs for Agent Control, *Artificial Intelligence Research* 1 pp 139-158, 1994.

12. Nilsson, N.J.Teleo-Reactive Programs and the Triple-Tower Architecture, *Electronic Transactions on Artificial Intelligence* 5 pp 99-110, 2001.

13. Rathnasabapathy, B. and Gmytrasiewicz, P., Formalizing Multi-Agent POMDPs in the Context of Network Routing, *Proceedings of 36th Hawaii International Conference on System Sciences (HICSS'03)*, 2003.

14. Ryan, M.R.K. and Pendrith, M.D. An Architecture for Modularity and Re-Use in Reinforcement Learning, *Proceedings of the 15th International Conference on Machine Learning*, Madison, Wisconsin, 1998.

Author Index